THE ROLE OF THE STATE IN
ECONOMIC CHANGE

UNU/WIDER

Studies in Development Economics embody the output of the research programmes of the World Institute for Development Economics Research, which was established by the United Nations University as its first research and training centre in 1984 and started work in Helsinki, Finland, in 1985. The principal purpose of the Institute is policy-oriented research on the main strategic issues of development and international co-operation, as well as on the interaction between domestic and global changes.

THE ROLE OF THE STATE IN ECONOMIC CHANGE

Edited by

HA-JOON CHANG
and
ROBERT ROWTHORN

A study prepared for the World Institute for Development Economics Research of the United Nations University (UNU/WIDER)

CLARENDON PRESS · OXFORD
1995

Oxford University Press, Walton Street, Oxford OX2 6DP

Oxford New York
Athens Auckland Bangkok Bombay
Calcutta Cape Town Dar es Salaam Delhi
Florence Hong Kong Istanbul Karachi
Kuala Lumpur Madras Madrid Melbourne
Mexico City Nairobi Paris Singapore
Taipei Tokyo Toronto
and associated companies in
Berlin Ibadan

Oxford is a trade mark of Oxford University Press

Published in the United States
by Oxford University Press Inc., New York

British Library Cataloguing in Publication Data
Data available

Library of Congress Cataloging-in-Publication Data
The Role of the state in economic change/edited by Ha-Joon Chang and
Robert Rowthorn.
(Studies in development economics)
'A study prepared for the World Institute for Development
Economics Research of the United Nations University.'
Includes bibliographical references.
1. Economic development—Political aspects—Case studies.
2. Economic policy—Case studies.   I. Chang, Ha-Joon.
II. Rowthorn, Bob.   III. World Institute for Development
Economics Research.   IV. Series.
HD87.R653 1995 95-19896
338.9—dc20

ISBN 0-19-828984-7

1 3 5 7 9 10 8 6 4 2

Typeset by Best-set Typesetter Ltd., Hong Kong
Printed in Great Britain
on acid-free paper by
Bookcraft Ltd., Midsomer Norton, Avon

To Lal Jayawardena

PREFACE

The debate about the role of the state (the role of government) in the society emerges or re-emerges from time to time in social sciences, and especially in economics, with a number of ramifications. It oscillates between ideologies; of which one extreme is totalitarian étatism, and the other dogmatic liberalism. By the second half of the 1990s, the debate is not only intense but also broader, enriched by theories, by empirical experiences, by new issues raised in global politics and economics, including the consequences of the systemic changes in the former socialist countries.

In a theoretical framework, the main source of 'enrichment' in the debate is the spread of the ideas of the new institutional economics, sometimes as direct arguments, but more often as indirect outcomes of the debates related to a wide range of issues like allocational efficiency, income redistribution, or technological changes. The new institutional economics, building on, modifying, and extending neo-classical economics, offers a number of propositions. It employs price theory as a key instrument for the analysis of institutions; it models the political process as a critical factor in economic performance, explaining also the diversity among the sources of successes and failures, and the inefficiency of markets. It looks at the role of institutions, as key instruments in reducing uncertainty in human exchange. The new empirical sources of the debate are also widespread. They include the favourable and adverse experiences of the 'market revolution' in the USA and other industrial countries, the increasing interest in the successful economic development experiences in Southeast Asia, the collapse of the étatist regimes in Central and Eastern Europe and in the former Soviet Union, and the rather interesting and controversial fact that the state is building 'from above' the market system in those countries, the African development crisis and the disintegration of a number of states.

The papers in this interesting and worthy volume are the result of a UNU/WIDER research project on the 'Role of the State in Economic Change'. The project was launched by the Institute some years ago, with the intention of showing that governments in all countries play important, and in many fields indispensable, roles in economic and social change and in sustainable and equitable economic growth. Another important goal of the project was to prove that both the achievements of governments in initiating changes—in a way which interacts intelligently with the markets and guides the appropriate response of the economic actors—and the spectacular failures of government interventions, together with excessive regulation, serve as important lessons for the future. The papers on different country experiences and problems not only add new empirical information about the role of the state, but also give some convincing answers to the question, What should be the appropriate role of governments in the complex world of the late twentieth century, both in a national and international context, in promoting the required changes and taking them into account in their policies and actions?

These papers offer an interesting comparative analysis of the diverse conditions in which the government policies develop and interact, as the changes in domestic policies and capacities influence the links between countries and the restructuring of the international system. In this context, the volume is extremely useful not only for those experts who are interested in better understanding the role of the state, but also for the 'practitioners' in national and international policy formation and decision-making.

On behalf of UNU/WIDER, I express my sincere thanks to the contributors of this timely and important volume and particularly to Robert Rowthorn, the Project Director, for his invaluable intellectual and managerial inputs.

Mihály Simai
Director, UNU/WIDER

Helsinki, May 1995

ACKNOWLEDGEMENTS

The papers published in this volume were presented at a seminar held in April 1993 at King's College, Cambridge. They are the outcome of a research project on the role of the state organised under the auspices of UNU/WIDER in Helsinki. We should like to thank the staff of both institutions for their help. We are also most grateful to the former Director of UNU/WIDER, Lal Jayawardena, for his enthusiastic encouragement in the initial stage of this project, and to the present Director, Mihály Simai, for his continuing support.

CONTENTS

PART III   SOCIALIST ECONOMIES IN TRANSITION

CONTRIBUTORS

HA-JOON CHANG, Faculty of Economics and Politics, University of Cambridge, UK.

MICHAEL ELLMAN, Faculty of Economics and Econometrics, University of Amsterdam, Netherlands.

RICHARD KOZUL-WRIGHT, United Nations Conference on Trade and Development, Geneva, Switzerland.

PETER NOLAN, Faculty of Economics and Politics, University of Cambridge, UK.

MIĆA PANIĆ, Selwyn College, Cambridge, UK.

ROBERT ROWTHORN, Faculty of Economics and Politics, University of Cambridge, UK.

AJIT SINGH, Faculty of Economics and Politics, University of Cambridge, UK.

BRIAN VAN ARKADIE, World Food Programme, Dar es Salaam, Tanzania.

JUHANA VARTIAINEN, Labour Institute for Economic Research, Helsinki, Finland.

ROBERT WADE, Institute of Development Studies, Sussex, UK and Institute of Advanced Studies, Princeton, USA.

1

Introduction

Ha-Joon Chang and Robert Rowthorn

As Deane (1989) shows in her masterpiece on the history of economic
thought, the role of the state has occupied the central stage in the development of economics as an independent discipline. As the early names of
the discipline like 'political arithmetic' or 'political economy' suggest, the
very inception of the discipline was prompted by the growing need for
policy advice to the rulers of the emerging nation states whose role was
growing with the development of capitalism in Western Europe. Although
attempts to purge the discipline of those awkward 'political' elements
culminated in the rechristening of the subject as 'economics' around
the turn of the century, the state was brought back into economic theory
and policy-making in a rather dramatic fashion during the interwar
period.

One development which brought the state back into economics was the
birth of welfare economics, pioneered by Arthur Pigou. By explaining why
the free market system purely based on individual maximizing behaviour
may not achieve socially 'optimal' resource allocation predicted by the then
new orthodoxy of neoclassical economics, welfare economics provided
justification for the manipulation of price signals by the state. Although
during the interwar period itself welfare economics remained a rather
esoteric exercise detached from practical policy questions, its use of the
orthodox language of marginalist analysis made it possible for later policy-
makers to break away from *laissez faire* policies without being accused of
unscientific behaviour.

Another, more important, development which produced the come-back
of the state was the birth of Keynesian economics. By showing that the free
market economy may not be able to achieve an optimal resource allocation
at the full employment level of output, the Keynesian 'revolution' justified
the new practice of active budgetary policy to fight unemployment and
business cycles, which was developing simultaneously in the USA (the New
Deal), Germany (Fascist armament programmes), and Sweden (the incipient Corporatist Compromise) (for an excellent account of interwar economic developments in the USA and Germany, see essays in Maier 1987; on
Sweden, see Wright 1991). As we shall see later, the goals of full employment and smoothing business cycles were unchallenged as objectives of
state intervention during the quarter century after World War II, and

consequently Keynesian ideas achieved a pre-eminent status in government policy making.

The consolidation of the socialist central planning system in the USSR was another major interwar development. The rapid industrialization of the USSR, whose achievement was later proven by its success in halting the Nazi advance on the Eastern Front during World War II, provided credentials to certain non-orthodox interventionist measures such as nationalization of industry and investment planning, adopted even by many non-socialist countreis after the war (for the exposition of these theories, see Ellman 1989)—for example, nationalization in the UK and France, medium-term (usually five-year) planning in Japan, France, and many developing countries.

These interwar developments culminated in a dramatic swing of economic theory and practice towards interventionism in the immediate postwar years. With the urgent need for post-war reconstruction in the advanced capitalist countries (henceforth ACCs), the establishment of socialism in parts of Asia and Eastern Europe, and the liberation of many developing nations from colonialism, the states in almost all countries in the world were forced to and willing to assume highly interventionist positions in the immediate postwar years. And during the quarter century after World War II—the period which we are going to call the 'Golden Age', following the first WIDER volume, *The Golden Age of Capitalism*, edited by Stephen Marglin and Juliet Schor—interventionist policies were highly successful across the world, firmly establishing the state as an important and often the leading actor in the functioning of the economy (see also Armstrong *et al.* 1991).

If this rise of the state in theory and practice in the Golden Age was dramatic, its fall after the Golden Age was equally, if not more, dramatic. The collapse of the Golden Age has produced a virulent attack on the state both at the theoretical and at the practical levels, starting from the discrediting of welfare statism in the ACCs, being amplified with the spread of liberalization programmes among developing nations during the 1980s, and culminating in the dismantling of socialist central planning since 1989 and the attempt to establish capitalism in Eastern Europe and what used to be the USSR. Although the 'rolling back' of the state has not proved as easy or straightforward as many anti-interventionists have initially thought, this reversal of trend has had a significant impact on the theory and practice of state intervention.

In this chapter, we survey these developments and provide some critical comments on the major contemporary anti-interventionist theories, which we classify under the general heading of 'neo-liberalism'. The chapter aims to prepare the ground for the later essays in the volume, each of which will look at the issues raised here in more depth. After presenting an account of the rise of the state in the Golden Age in the first section, we move to an account of the fall of the state after the Golden Age. Then we present criticism of some major theoretical underpinnings of neo-liberal theories, using both some new theoretical developments and empirical evidence which question the wisdom of this new orthodoxy.

1. THE GOLDEN AGE AND THE RISE OF THE STATE

In this section, we review the political, intellectual, and economic factors responsible for the widespread extension of state activity during the Golden Age following World War II.

1.1. Advanced Capitalist Countries

World War II produced new political coalitions in the advanced capitalist countries with a strong representation of organized labour—often described as 'corporatist' coalitions. The prominent role of the left in the struggle against Fascism during World War II meant that, in the post-war society of class compromise, full employment and social welfare—the overriding objectives of the working class—were to be on the top of the political agenda. Moreover, given the belief that the rise of Fascism had owed a lot to the Great Depression, active state intervention to smooth the business cycle through the use of new-found Keynesian policy tools was deemed imperative. Although the dominance of cold war politics put strict limits to more radical forms of labour and other political movements, the new regime incorporated the interests of the working class in national policy-making to an unprecedented degree.

As the theoretical possibility of avoiding recession by deliberately injecting purchasing power into the economic system was confirmed by the successes of proto-Keynesian policies during the interwar period (using budget deficits) and of the Marshall Plan in the immediate post-war period (using foreign aid), the state now actively assumed a new role of 'fine-tuning' the economy through budgetary policy (on the Marshall Plan, see Panić 1990). The old dogma of balancing the budget at all costs was abandoned, and budgetary policy was given the role of co-ordinating investment and savings so that the economy could stay at the full employment level. Social welfare systems, which existed in rudimentary form before the war, were vastly extended following the rise of the 'corporatist' political coalitions, and the state was also expected to help stabilize the economy by automatically increasing (reducing) spending in the recessionary (boom) phase of the business cycle.

In many countries, the role of the state expanded much further than the simple maintenance of the level of activity through aggregate demand management. Helped by the success of wartime planning, the old liberal

dogma that centralized co-ordination of economic activities is unworkable
was now rejected, and many states started intervening with a view to
changing the structure of their economies. Japan and France combined
sectoral industrial policy with centralized investment co-ordination through
five-year indicative planning (see Cohen 1977, on France; see Johnson
1982, on Japan). Scandinavian countries operated in a 'social corporatist'
framework, where centralized wage bargaining and active labour market
policy were combined to produce structural change towards high-pro-
ductivity industries with the speed and the orderliness which were beyond
what would have been possible through pure market mechanism (see
Pekkarinen *et al.* (eds.) 1992). Even in the UK and the USA, countries
which were least open to the idea of industrial policy, the state involvement
in industrial development was substantial (see Thompson (ed.) 1989). The
evolution of ECSC and EEC during this period even established some
grounds for an international co-ordination of national industrial policies.

1.2. Less Developed Countries

During the Golden Age, the state took an even more active role in many less
developed countries (henceforth LDCs) than in the advanced capitalist
countries. The desire of the newly independent nations to acquire not only
political but also economic independence from their former colonial mas-
ters put rapid economic development at the top of the political agenda.
And, in this period, it was widely accepted that state-led industrialization
was the fastest and surest way to achieve the aim (see Toye 1987).

The traditional reliance of LDCs on primary commodity exports to
finance the manufactured imports was thought to be a dead end, given (i)
the volatile and apparently falling terms of trade for primary commodity
exports; (ii) the fragility of the international economy, as testified by the
collapse of international trade following the Great Depression; and (iii) the
low income elasticities of primary commodities, which limited the scope for
increase in their exports in the future. Also it was thought that primary
commodity production lacked the self-reinforcing growth mechanism observed in manufacturing, where faster output growth leads to faster productivity growth (the so-called Verdoorn's Law, promoted by Kaldor
1966). Therefore, it was thought, the LDCs should move out of their role
in the traditional international division of labour as the suppliers of primary
products and develop manufacturing industries.

In order for the LDCs to start industrialization, however, it was thought
to be necessary to have an active state intervention. Not only was the
traditional infant industry argument evoked to justify the strategy of state-
led industrialization based on heavy import protection and subsidies, but
also an array of new theories justifying the centralized co-ordination of

industrial investments were developed within the emerging subdiscipline of 'development economics'.

The 'big push' models of Rosenstein-Rodan (1943), Nurkse (1952), and Scitovsky (1954) emphasized the demand complementarity between different industries, which called for an *ex ante* investment co-ordination by the state. Hirschman(1958), while criticizing the 'balanced growth' models, used the same idea of sectoral interdependence in order to develop an 'unbalanced growth' model, where the state-prompted development of the sectors with the most widespread interdependences (what he called linkages) would create imbalances in the economy, which would induce the development of other sectors. Gerschenkron (1966), basing his case on the experiences of earlier European industrializations, provided a further justification of state intervention based on the interaction of technological (the growing minimum efficient scale of production) and institutional factors (the underdevelopment of financial institutions). Gerschenkron suggested that as a country embarks on a developmental process later and later, it needs to raise proportionally bigger and bigger amounts of savings (as the minimum efficient scale of production grows larger), and therefore needs a more and more powerful institution for industrial financing, the state being the most powerful such institution.

These new theories were greeted with enthusiasm by the political leaders and state officials in many post-independence nations of Asia and Africa. In these countries, there existed strong feelings against capitalism, if only for the simple reason that all colonial powers were capitalist. As a result they exhibited preference for more state ownership and central planning, if not outright socialism. On a more practical level, the states in these nations were often compelled to take the role of an entrepreneur, because these nations lacked a well-developed capitalist class which could take over the economic organizations left behind by the colonizers, and whatever little capitalist class there was was often politically discredited as the collaborator with the colonial power (see e.g. Chapter 8 in this volume). Even in the East Asian NICs, where the cold war consolidated the staunchest anti-communist regimes, vigorous state intervention was regarded as legitimate and necessary, and paradoxically functioned much more efficiently than in other LDCs (see Chapter 5 in this volume). Even in Latin American countries, where independence was achieved much earlier and where socialist tendencies were weaker, the political tide was turning for state-led industrialization. The success of state-led import substitution industrialization in Latin America during the interwar period produced new social coalitions that could challenge the landed oligarchy—that is, the alliance between the incipient industrial capitalist class and the urban working class (Peronism being the best example)—and gave them the confidence and power to push further the state-led industrialization programme.

The result was the emergence of a variety of new industrialization strategies in LDCS, in which the state plays the leading role in manufacturing and infrastructure through its control over state-owned enterprises and/or financial resources. As most LDCs experienced rates of growth more vigorous than in the rest of the world during the Golden Age (see Singh 1992a), these strategies—which are usually (and somewhat misleadingly) known as the import substitution industrialization (ISI) strategies—acquired the status of 'the' development strategy.

1.3. Socialist Countries

In addition to the independence of the former colonies, the end of World War II produced another dramatic change in the world political map. The USSR and Mongolia were no longer the only socialist countries in the world. Between the end of the World War II and the early 1950s, socialist regimes had been established in Eastern European and some Asian countries (China, North Korea, and North Vietnam), and this meant, largely thanks to China, that now about one-third of the world's population was under socialist rule. The advance of socialism into other poorer, especially Asian, nations seemed inevitable unless an active policy to 'roll back' Communism was adopted.

In the immediate post-war years, the socialist countries, mostly as the victorious parties either in World War II or in their own anti-imperialist struggle, were full of confidence and hope. The rise of the USSR from one of the most backward nations in Europe to a nation which played a crucial role in saving the world from Fascist takeover convinced many people, except some fierce anti-communists, that central planning was as least as viable as the market mechanism in running the economy. The victory of the USSR over the USA in the early space programme suggested to many that, for large projects requiring concerted efforts on the national scale, central planning was probably superior. The fact that even the most backward socialist countries like North Korea and China made very impressive progress in industrialization in the 1950s seemed to prove that central planning was an effective way to achieve rapid industrialization and massive structural transformation.

To be sure, it was obvious that central planning had its own problems, as revealed in the (largely unsuccessful) attempts by Hungary (1956) and Czechoslovakia (1968) to liberalize their economies. However, many advocates of central planning believed that the relentless development of computers, input-output analysis, mathematical programming techniques, and other tools of planning would eventually ensure that the rational order of socialism would triumph over the irrational anarchy of capitalism. Moreover, the supposed 'classless' nature of their societies made their policy-makers believe that policy-making in socialist societies can be treated as a 'technocratic' rather than a political exercise. With the beliefs in the perfectibility of tools of forecast and computation, on the one hand, and in the absence of fundamental political conflicts, on the other hand, it was not surprising that many saw the seeds of a truly rational and egalitarian society in the existing socialist societies during this period.

2. THE FALL OF THE GOLDEN AGE AND THE NEO-LIBERAL UPSURGE

A series of events which started emerging from the late 1960s began to create growing difficulties for the interventionist models of economic management established during the Golden Age. Especially once the political consensus which buttressed the interventionist regimes started breaking down (see later), policy-makers found it increasingly difficult to mediate the growing conflicts while the theorists could no longer assume political neutrality and ignore the considerations of 'political economy'. To the policy-makers, this meant that more and more policies would have to accommodate demands from specific interest groups, and to economic theorists, it meant that it was increasingly difficult for them to remain technocratic. It is no coincidence that the post-Golden-Age period witnessed the revival of political economy, both from the right and the left.

In this section, we review major contemporary anti-interventionist theories under the broad heading of neo-liberalism, without necessarily implying the existence of a unified political philosophy underlying all the theories we examine. In spelling out these theories, we do not attempt to discuss all the details of individual theories, as our purpose here is to provide a broad overview of the changes in the intellectual climate of the post-Golden-Age era (interested readers can go back to the originals or reviews contained in Cullis and Jones 1987, and Mueller 1979, for the advanced capitalist countries; Toye 1987, and Shapiro and Taylor 1990, for LDCs; Ellman 1989, and Brus and Laski 1989, for the socialist countries).

2.1. Advanced Capitalist Countries

The long post-war boom in Europe and North America was brought to an end by a variety of factors, including a profit squeeze due to the depletion of surplus labour in the rural area and over-accumulation, growing competition from Japan and the Newly Industrializing Countries (henceforth NICs), and the growing globalization of capital which made national macroeconomic management much less effective (see Glyn et al. 1990). With the growing intensity of distributional conflicts in the face of massive structural change and decelerating economic growth, the existing political consensus on the welfare state based on corporatist bargaining and

Keynesian macroeconomic management broke down and, with it, the theoretical consensus on the role of the state.

2.1.1. Monetarism

The best known attack on the theoretical consensus underlying the Golden Age is the monetarist onslaught on Keynesianism. Basing themselves on the assumption of adaptive or rational expectations, and Walrasian market clearing, the monetarists comprehensively rejected the effectiveness of macroeconomic demand management by the state (for a critique, see Kaldor 1985). This exposed a fundamental weakness in the theoretical structure known as the Keynesian compromise. Under this compromise, the role of the state was confined to the regulation of macroeconomic aggregates, leaving the question of resource allocation to the neoclassical doctrine of free markets (Deane 1989). In political terms, the monetarist rendering of its argument—in populist anti-inflationary rhetoric—'inflation erodes the incomes of honest working families and the savings of poor old grannies on pensions'—proved especially effective in making the potentially unpopular recessionary policies widely accepted. (On this topic, see the essays in Lindberg and Maier (eds.) 1985.)

2.1.2. Institutional Sclerosis

This is a line of argument which emphasizes that institutions designed to guarantee politically negotiated economic benefits to certain groups (e.g. welfare provisions, trade protection, labour laws) are bound to create rigidities which are harmful to economic development in the long run. Developed particularly in the European context where the corporatist institutions were strong, the argument is often presented under the heading 'Eurosclerosis' (see Giersch 1986), but it has also seen application in the American context by Olson (1982). The implications of the sclerosis theory for the role of the state were probably more far-reaching than those of monetarism. At a political level, it undermined the credibility of state intervention by identifying the very corporatist institutions, upon which such intervention is based, as the source of sluggish growth and high inflation. At a more fundamental level, the theory challenged belief in collective institution building of any kind by stressing the inevitability of degeneration to which all institutions are subject.

2.1.3. New Contractarianism

Related to the sclerosis argument, with possibly Hayek as the link between the two, is the new contractarianism of libertarian authors like Buchanan and Tullock (1962) and Nozick (1974). The new contractarians argued that any form of state beyond the old liberal minimalist state, which does no more than provide law and order (including, among other things, the protection of property rights) cannot be justified in the eyes of those who believe in the sanctity of individual freedom. A major source of popularity of these writings lay in their emphasis on individual freedom and their articulation of modern discontents with the welfare state and its alleged restrictions on personal choice. The welfare state was no longer to be seen as a benign, if paternalistic, institution, but as a leviathan which must be restrained to preserve our liberties and the vitality of civil society.

2.1.4. Principal–Agent Models of Bureaucracy

Another important development along the anti-interventionist line was the emergence of various types of principal–agent models of bureaucracy developed by authors like Niskanen (1973), Peacock (1979), and Rowley (1983). These models saw the root of many problems of the contemporary capitalist countries—for example, the over-extension of the bureaucracy, the waste of resources in government administration, the inefficiency of the public enterprises—in the inability of the principals (the public) to monitor the self-seeking behaviour of their agents in public affairs (the bureaucrats). These models were usually presented as neutral efficiency arguments, but have had much deeper political impacts. By arguing that the same assumption of self-centred behaviour should be applied both to the private sector agents and the public sector agents, they not only questioned the public's trust in the benign paternalism of the welfare state but also undermined the self-confidence of government officials and their commitment to a public service ethos.

2.2. Less Developed Countries

For the LDCs, the end of the Golden Age arrived slightly later than for the advanced capitalist countries, that is in the 1980s. Although there were growing criticisms of their import substitution strategies, the 1970s was a period of relatively rapid progress for many developing countries, especially for those willing to borrow heavily in the international capital market awash with the so-called petrodollar (see Singh 1992a). However, with the beginning of the monetarist policies in the advanced capitalist countries, industrialization in most LDCs ran into trouble because of the critical shortage of foreign exchange, prompted by high interest rates, falling world demand, and the Debt Crisis (Hughes and Singh 1991). The fragile ruling coalitions in most of these countries could not survive the massive external shocks to systems which were already finding it increasingly difficult to cope with the growing population and the increasing diversification of interests. In the face of severe foreign exchange constraints, most LDCs ended up launching (often unsuccessful) dramatic liberalization programmes along the lines demanded by the Bretton Woods institutions (i.e. the World Bank and the IMF), whose endorsement suddenly became critical in the continuation of foreign exchange inflow (see Chapter 8).

2.2.1. Attack on Import Substitution Industrialization (ISI)

Usually associated with the Bretton Woods institutions, this critique re-asserts the wisdom of the neoclassical doctrines, especially the Heckscher–Ohlin–Samuelson theory of comparative advantage, which were rejected by the proponents of the import substitution industrialization (ISI) strategy (see World Bank 1987 and 1991; for criticisms see Weiss 1990 and Singh 1992b). The argument is that, by producing goods which could be produced more cheaply (in relative terms) in other countries, countries trying to substitute imports forgo the gains from trade. Moreover, given their small market sizes, the protected industries in the LDCs end up being monopolists or oligopolists producing at suboptimal scales and/or under full capacity and having no compulsion to improve their productivity. Finally, it is argued that the artificially cheap price of 'capital' (i.e. artifici-ally low interest rates) created by 'financial repression' associated with ISI leads to lower savings and to the adoption of excessively capital-intensive technologies, which adds to unemployment and income inequality.

2.2.2. Rent-Seeking and the New Political Economy

First developed by Krueger (1974) and Posner (1975), the rent-seeking argument asserts that the creation of entry barriers by the state leads not only to the standard deadweight welfare losses but also to additional 'waste' from expenditures on 'unproductive' political activities intended to influ-ence the state in its capacity as the creator of entry barriers (and the accompanying property rights). In the context of LDCs where the rules of contesting property rights are not as well established as in the advanced capitalist countries, the scope for rent-seeking associated with those state interventions associated with import substitution was seen to be much wider. Associated with this view is the so-called New Political Economy, which shows how a 'predatory' state in LDCs can create a property rights structure which maximizes its revenues rather than social welfare (North 1981; Findlay 1990). An especially influential recent development has been the extension of these theories to what is similar to the eighteenth century liberal attack on mercantilism (see e.g. de Soto 1989).

2.2.3. Attack on Public Enterprises

The late 1970s and the early 1980s saw the proliferation of reassessments of the performance of the public enterprises across the world, especially in the LDCs. While there were many balanced studies (see Baumol (ed.) 1980; Vernon and Aharoni (eds.) 1981; and Jones (ed.) 1982), there were also some damning indictments of public enterprise as the major source of economic inefficiency and stagnation of the LDCs (see e.g. World Bank 1983). Identifying the source of these inefficiencies as emanating from the lack of profit incentives, competition, and financial discipline imposed by the capital market, the neo-liberal arguments for privatization became a centre-piece of their attack on the interventionist economic managements of the Golden Age (for some criticisms of these theories, see Chang and Singh 1993; Rowthorn and Chang 1993). In many LDCs, where the frequent inefficiency of public enterprises was especially damaging given their weight in the manufacturing and infrastructural sectors of the economy, the support for privatization spread like wildfire.

2.3. Socialist Countries

Following a period of impressive achievement after the war, the socialist countries underwent a prolonged economic stagnation associated with lagging technical progress, institutional sclerosis, and growing political disillusionment (see Bleaney 1988; Brus and Laski 1989). Although the sudden collapse of the socialist system in the late 1980s has made the understanding of their experience less important than previously, it is still the case that some of the theories developed in the context of socialist experience have left us with interesting insights into the role of the state.

2.3.1. The Shortage Economy

Based on an economic situation which is almost the polar opposite of what Keynes faced in the interwar period, that is, a situation where the problem of excess demand is institutionalized through a peculiar incentive system, Kornai invented the concept of the 'shortage economy' and developed it into the foundation of his institutionalist critique of socialism (see e.g. Kornai 1979). The fundamental message is that the lack of financial discipline (the so-called 'soft budget constraints') associated with the lack of private property leads to a situation where not only a substantial part of national income is wasted in 'unproductive' activities such as hoarding of material and human inputs but also there is no incentive to improve the productive efficiency. Moreover, when associated with the absolute political commitment to zero unemployment, the need for the stockpiling of labour inputs produces some perverse effects on labour discipline, originally stressed in a capitalist context by Marxist writers but generalized more recently by efficiency wage theorists (Bowles 1985; Akerlof and Yellen (eds.) 1986).

2.3.2. Property Rights Approach

Although it is difficult to suggest that the Property Rights Approach sprang entirely from the research on socialist economies, some critical initial contributions to the development of the approach originated there (for a survey, see Furubotn and Pejovich 1972). The argument basically is that the lack of private property institutions in the socialist societies eliminates the individual incentive to remain efficient and improve productivity. This was a particularly damning indictment for the socialist countries, as they traditionally saw their distinct system of property rights as the source of their supposed economic superiority over the capitalist countries. The recognition that the defining characteristic of their system, namely, state ownership of means of production, might be the root cause of their economic troubles had a profound impact on popular consciousness, as is well proven by the almost irrational obsession with privatization issues in the post-communist reforms in Eastern Europe.

2.3.3. The Austrian Attack on Central Planning

The oldest, but possibly the most fundamental, attack on socialism is the Austrian attack on central planning. Starting from the interwar debate between Mises and Hayek on one side and Lange and Taylor on the other side, the Austrians have constantly asserted the unviability of central planning (for a good survey of the debate, see Lavoie 1985). They argued that, the completely centralized co-ordination of activities in a complex and constantly changing modern economy would require the collection and processing of information on a scale far beyond the capability of any present or future state. More importantly, they argued that only competitive rivalry amongst genuinely independent, profit-seeking agents can generate and utilize the accurate and detailed information required to run a modern economy. Although quite unacceptable in its extreme form—that all forms of state intervention, and not just central planning, are bound to fail or threaten liberty—the power of this argument is now widely accepted even by many who favour an interventionist state.

3. CRITICAL EVALUATION OF THE NEO-LIBERAL THEORIES

As may be seen, different anti-interventionist theories developed in different historical, political, and institutional contexts, on the one hand, and from different theoretical traditions, on the other. Some draw heavily on the neoclassical legacy (e.g. the Bretton Woods critique of import substitution), while others draw on more heterodox traditions like Austrian or institutional economics. However, one thing which is common to most of these theories is that they lay more emphasis on the 'political' rather than 'technocratic' aspects of economic problems. That is, by questioning the very political foundation of interventionist models of economic management, neo-liberal theories have brought issues of morality, justice, and power—although in their own peculiar ways—back into economics. In this section, rather than trying to criticize theories in the neo-liberal tradition individually, we make some general comments on their central theoretical underpinnings.

3.1. Principal–Agent Framework

Common to many neo-liberal theories is the principal–agent framework, where the limited scope for monitoring by the principal creates problems of designing incentives for agents who pursue their own self-interests. Major examples will be the problem of designing optimal welfare or social insurance programmes due to the difficulty of identifying the true 'type' of the potential subscribers (for a survey of related issues, see Barr 1992), and the problem of designing optimal industrial subsidy schemes or optimal public enterprise management rules due to the difficulty of identifying the source of bad performance (e.g. external shock or bad management).

For certain individual problems, the principal–agent framework is a fruitful approach, since it questions the naïvety of traditional welfare economics and its assumption that state officials always have the incentive to correct market failures once these are identified. However, at a more general level, this framework posits an awkward question—who is the principal and who is the agent, especially in a modern mass democracy? For example, in relation to social welfare programmes, we can argue that 'the state' is the principal, but from the points of view of the principal–agent models of bureaucracy or of contractarian political philosophy, the state is an agent of 'the public'. Thus seen, there are inconsistencies in the ways in which different principal–agent models characterize the process of state intervention.

We are *not* arguing that there is only one correct way of deciding who is the principal and who is the agent. Indeed, the very existence of different ways of envisaging principal–agent problems in our society reflects the complexity of modern polity. Our point is that, without an adequate understanding of the complex political process in a modern society, the use of principal–agent models may end up obscuring major issues rather than clarifying them. The political process in a modern society involves collective action and bargaining problems at many different levels (local, industry, or national levels), whose solutions are strongly influenced by social norms (working class solidarity, work ethic, abstinence), political institutions (dictatorial, corporatist, or liberal institutions), and socio-politican 'visions' (socialism, nationalism, welfare statism, free enterprise). The principal–agent model, given its sole emphasis on wealth-maximizing behaviour of selfish individuals, cannot take such complexity of political-economic process into account. Thus seen, there are serious dangers in accepting the radical proposals for rolling back the state derived from such models.

3.2. Mistrust of the State

Another common feature of the neo-liberal theories is their deep mistrust of the state. The new contractarians see the state as a necessary evil with a natural tendency to expand, which has to be put under constant surveillance by sovereign individuals as partners in social contract. The principal–agent model of bureaucracy is another well-known manifestation of this belief. If somewhat less obvious, the monetarist argument for a constitutionally binding money growth target is also symptomatic of the belief that the state cannot be trusted to withstand the demands of 'special interest' groups. Similar to this is the 'regulatory capture' argument propagated by Stigler (1975) that the regulatory agencies may be set up in order to serve public interests but end up serving the interest groups which they are supposed to regulate.

One serious problem with the neo-liberal mistrust of the state is that it uncritically (or intentionally?) assumes that the state (or the bureaucrats as its components) always acts in its (their) own interest. Apart from the obvious observation that individuals and institutions do not always act in their own interest, there are too many facts of life which make this simple self-centredness assumption problematic. Even the most casual observation confirms that different states have different degrees of commitment to the public interest, that the boundaries of the public domain are different in different countries and constantly changing even in the same country, that people operating in different environments (e.g. civil servants and businessmen) have different rules of behaviour, and that even the same individual may apply different rules of behaviour in different circumstances (e.g. a civil servant during and outside his office hours). Policy conclusions drawn from models ignoring these facts are at best misleading and at worst pseudo-scientific renderings of the model-builder's ideological conviction against the state.

More fundamentally, we argue that the more generalized mistrust of collective action, on which the neo-liberal mistrust of the state is based, is problematic. First of all, it is not correct to argue that institutions (e.g. the state, labour unions) are always (or even predominantly) products of social contracts among free-contracting individuals. Human beings have always existed as members of certain collectivities, and the notion of the free-contracting individual is a product of the capitalist order (Polanyi 1957). Individuals are perhaps more a product of institutions than the latter are the products of contracts among individuals. Secondly, the neo-liberal preference for individual actions over group actions has some awkward political implications. Neo-liberals often attack 'interest groups', but after all, those interest groups are aasociations of individuals who the neo-liberals regard as absolutely sacred. How can a consistent liberal deprive the individuals of the freedom to join a collectivity he/she likes? And, indeed, the neo-liberals *do* endorse certain interest groups such as, for example, private firms. If some interest groups are legitimate and others are not, what is the criterion to decide which groups belong to which category? The anti-collectivist rhetoric of the neo-liberals merely obscures the existence of a hidden political agenda against certain particular groups.

3.3. Trust in Individual Entrepreneurship

The other side of the coin of the neo-liberal mistrust of the state is the trust in individual entrepreneurship. While all pro-market theories believe that 'wrong' institutions and state policies lead to allocative inefficiency, many neo-liberals would go even further and argue that state intervention impairs the ability of individuals to improve the productive capacity of the economy by generating new knowledge (i.e. innovation) in their attempts to capture profit.

One problem with this position is that it sees entrepreneurship as essentially an individual activity. This view stems from the belief that knowledge is always deposited in individuals, but it ignores the fact that, at least in modern economies, institutions and organizations are also depositories of knowledge. Contrary to what Schumpeter (1987) predicted, insitutionalization of R&D did *not* decelerate innovation in modern economies, and if anything, accelerated it. This is because, as the recent literature on technical change shows (see e.g. Dosi *et al.* (eds.) 1988), innovative activities often are facilitated by collective effort, including, among other things, state support. This means that the old concept of entrepreneurship based entirely on individuals is no longer valid (Chang and Kozul-Wright 1994). That is, entrepreneurship has increasingly become a collective effort.

Equally problematic is the argument that state intervention creates an incentive to divert entrepreneurship into 'wasteful' activities of securing property rights through political means (e.g. Krueger 1974; Bhagwati 1982; de Soto 1989). Although this position is not necessarily wrong, this brings back something the mainstream economists tried so hard to eliminate from the discipline, that is, value judgements. As the definition of productive and unproductive activities needs some criteria to tell whether a certain activity is 'necessary' for the functioning of the economy, it is impossible come up with a viable concept of unproductive labour without calling in some political and moral value judgements (Driver 1980; Boss 1990). Many of those who condemn political competition (e.g. rent-seeking) as wasteful do not recognize this dilemma, but implicitly assume that a simple deregulation of the present economy will eliminate all 'unproductive' activities, which is not necessarily the case (see Chang 1994: ch. 2).

3.4. Anti-Utilitarianism

Strong anti-utilitarianism, or more broadly anti-consequentialism, runs through most neo-liberal theories (for some philosophical debates on consequentialism, see essays in Scheffler (ed.) 1988). Of course, there exists a well-known tension between utilitarianism and political liberalism (on this, see Berlin 1969), and those neo-liberal theorists who have been brought up in a strongly utilitarian tradition of neoclassical economics would find it difficult to totally abandon the utilitarian legacy in their thinking. However, many neo-liberal positions—such as the new contractarian defence of the rule of law, the Austrian adherence to free competition, and the monetarist insistence on constitutional limits on the formulation of monetary policy—are all based on the idea that there are certain fundamental rules that have to be abided by regardless of their consequences (i.e. individual freedom, freedom of entry, zero inflation). Indeed, many neo-liberals claim to be willing to 'trade off economic efficiency for individual freedom where such a policy conflict becomes apparent' (Peacock and Rowley 1979: 26).

However, is this really a tenable position? We think not, because any defence of a certain rule (or procedure) assumes a preference for a certain consequence. Otherwise, we would have to assume that the rule is God-given or totally randomly chosen, which would not be acceptable even to most neo-liberal theorists. For example, we may say that we value the principle of majority rule and therefore are willing to accept certain 'suboptimal' outcomes if they are the results of that rule, but why did we decide to value majority rule in the first place? Wasn't it essentially because we thought that it, on average, would produce the 'best' outcome in some sense? If this is the case, the neo-liberals are calling for no more than a higher order utilitarianism, so to speak, based on the recognition of human fallibility (e.g. imperfect foresight, imperfectly transferable knowledge, weakness of will, whim, etc.), which makes it impossible to custom-design rules for every contingency in order to produce the optimal outcome. Of course, it is possible to get out of this dilemma by arguing that the neo-liberal rules are beyond dispute and therefore cannot be interpreted as a product of a higher order utilitarianism. However, for those who do not dogmatically accept these rules, it is not clear how any man-made rule can be totally devoid of consequentialist thinking.

CONCLUSION

The neo-liberal revival represents a partial return to the nineteenth-century *laissez faire* tradition, supplemented by an Austrian emphasis on the limited transferability of knowledge and the role of entrepreneurship. The neo-liberal approach stresses the efficacy of the free market, and insists on the inefficiency and/or counterproductiveness of state intervention. It blames the past and present state interventions for most recent economic ills, and its prescriptions for most economic problems consist largely of deregulation and reducing the economic role of the state to that of a 'night-watchman'. The failings of state intervention are ascribed either to an inherent shortage of information (the Austrians) or to the self-seeking behaviours of the bureaucrats (Niskanen, Peacock, and Rowley) and/or organized interest groups (rent-seeking, institutional sclerosis).

From the mid-1970s onwards, neo-liberal doctrines gained a wide following throughout the world. They inspired liberalization and privatization in many developed and developing countries, and even political revolution in many socialist countries. Amongst the advanced capitalist countries, neo-liberal programmes were implemented vigorously in the UK and the USA, and somewhat less vigorously in most of the rest. Many developing countries have also implemented neo-liberal programmes in the areas of trade, industry, and labour market policy—sometimes by choice and sometimes under pressure from external creditors. As a rule, the promise of these programmes has been that the freeing up of markets and the reduction in direct state intervention would make economies more flexible and creative, helping to solve their immediate economic problems and contribute to their long-run economic dynamism.

It is now frequently, though by no means universally, accepted that the neo-liberal programmes have mostly failed to live up to their promise. The problems of the world economy remain formidable; many developing countries which have followed this programme are still in great difficulty; in the advanced capitalist world, the Thatcherite experiment in the UK was conspicuously unsuccessful in making the economy more competitive, and recently the Clinton administration in the USA has overtly refuted the ideas associated with Reaganomics. As a result of this experience, there is growing disenchantment with the neo-liberal programme. One partial exception to this new trend is perhaps Eastern Europe and the Soviet Union, but even there the initial optimism in the efficacy of the free market is fading fast.

In this introductory chapter, we have provided some criticism of the neo-liberal theories. We have pointed out that most neo-liberal theories do not take into account the complexity of human motivation (which differs across agents, societies, and time), the complexity of modern polity (who is the principal and who is the agent?), the importance of the legitimatization process in policy-making and implementation, the inevitability of collective managements, in one form or another, of complex modern economy, and so on. Their simplistic notion of politics makes the neo-liberal arguments at best misleading and at worst deceitful. To be consistent, neo-liberals must either be so naïve as to believe that a rewriting of the constitution to ban virtually all collective action (except the minimal state) is possible, or else have a hidden agenda behind their populist rhetoric, whose aim is simply to roll back the gains made by working class and other 'progressive' movements during this century.

Neo-liberals, especially those with Austrian influence, are correct in saying that central planning is not the most rational way to run a complex and constantly changing modern economy that its advocates thought it to be. However, it is erroneous to jump from this to the conclusion that all forms of state intervention are doomed to failure. For one thing, even central planning works better than the market for situations where there is one overriding objective, as in wartime or in a space programme. Moreover, there are other types of state intervention which are not as informationally demanding as central planning and at least equally effective, for example, East Asian style industrial policy (see Chang 1994: ch. 3). Contrary to what Hayek says, there is a third way, or rather, there are many third ways.

More broadly, the neo-liberal belief that no collective organization, other than the minimalist state, has any positive economic role to play is not acceptable. For one thing, the firm is after all not a purely individualistic organization made up only of arms-length contracts, but has a lot of 'hierarchical' and 'relational' elements (Williamson 1975; Pagano 1985). Moreover, there exist extensive 'networks' in the modern economy, which are not pure contractual relationships but are based on trust and solidarity (see Thompson et al. (eds.) 1991). In other words, the world as envisaged by the neo-liberals, which is populated by lone individuals whose interactions with each other are only ephemeral, has never existed and probably will never exist (among others, see Polanyi 1957).

Having made the above criticisms, we should point out that even the most ardent critics of neo-liberalism would now recognize that it contains some important insights about the economic role of information, the importance of competition, and the like. There is now a widespread agreement that the management of a complex modern economy requires a market which is independent from the state to a considerable degree, although there is still a considerable amount of disagreement regarding to what extent a well-functioning market needs private property (see essays in Rowthorn (ed.) forthcoming). The more important point is that the nature and extent of intervention will vary with circumstances. This means that, although one can talk of certain general principles, there is no hard and fast rule to determine the optimal degree and the desirable areas of state intervention, and that it can only be determined in the concrete historical, institutional, and geographical context (see Chapter 2 in this volume).

The Neo-Liberals have served the useful historical function of questioning the viability of the existing forms of state intervention, some of which clearly had serious problems, and of opening lines of inquiry leading to the basis for new forms of intervention. Nevertheless, they have failed to provide a intellectually successful and politically workable programme for comprehensively rolling back the state and achieving their vision of the 'brave new world'. Few now believe that it is either possible or desirable to turn the intellectual clock back twenty years to the time before the neo-liberal upsurge. Not only has the world economy changed considerably, but both practical experience and the neo-liberal critique have revealed some of the flaws in old ways of thinking. The challenge, therefore, is not simply to return to some previous intellectual golden age, but to form a new synthesis in which the valid insights of neo-liberalism are stripped of their ideological baggage and integrated into a wider and more objective intellectual framework. This is the aim which informs the present volume of essays, which explore the economic role of the state in a wide variety of contexts.

THE CHAPTERS IN THIS VOLUME

The chapter by Chang and Rowthorn attempts to go beyond the old welfare economics perspective on the state, by incorporating insights from the New Political Economy, institutional economics and Austrian economics. They argue that the state has to play two important roles in times of major change, namely, that of entrepreneur and that of conflict manager. The pervasive uncertainties associated with a complex modern economy impart an important entrepreneurial role to the state. Such a role has various dimensions. Thanks to its strategic position as the central agent in the society, the state can provide a vision of the future development of the economy, around which other agents can co-ordinate their actions. Moreover, as the ultimate institution-builder, it can give an institutional reality to its own vision as well as institutionalize any emerging co-ordination structure. Moving to the issue of conflict management, Chang and Rowthom argue that because of its role as the guarantor of property rights and as the most important designer and executioner of the public agenda, the state is the ultimate manager of conflict. They emphasize that conflict management by the state goes beyond merely 'taking care of the social dimension' and has the important 'productive' aspect of providing a governance structure through which risk can be socialized. They conclude that the creation of a state able to provide these different functions is required in many 'reforming' countries in the developing and former socialist worlds, which are currently in the grip of massive economic and social dislocation.

Most of the chapters in this book focus primarily on the internal factors which shape the role of the state and determine its effectiveness in promoting economic change. Whilst some of them do consider external economic relations, these are not their main concern. This gap is filled by Mića Panić in his chapter, 'International Economic Integration and the Changing Role of National Governments'. In this chapter, he argues that international political and economic relations are of central importance in determining the effectiveness of government economic policies. Of particular importance are the degree of economic sovereignty of the country concerned and the nature of international economic co-operation. He then examines how these have affected the post-war experience. Following rapid economic growth in the 1950s and 1960s, there has been a marked slow-down since 1973 in most of the world economy. Panić ascribes this to a combination of two factors: (1) much closer economic integration which has reduced the scope for independent national policies, and (2) a decline in international economic co-operation with the demise of US hegemony. The result is an impasse whereby much of the world is locked into a deflationary circle, from which individual countries can no longer escape, but the collective action to escape is not forthcoming. Panić concludes his chapter with a sobering assessment of future prospects.

Richard Kozul-Wright starts his chapter on the role of the state in American history by repudiating the very existence of the so-called 'Anglo-Saxon' pattern of development based on the doctrine of *laissez faire*. He argues that, in fact, the American state has always played an active role in economic development, although it was constrained by limits arising from the tradition of an anti-state ideology and the consequent absence of a clear institutional basis for state activism. He also criticizes the popular American political and academic tradition, which regards the country's history as a fall from some 'golden age' of a minimal state into a 'dark age' of creeping bureaucratization and waste generated by a predatory state and redistributive coalitions. He argues that the American state played an especially active entrepreneurial role during the period of catching up in the late nineteenth century—assigning property rights in natural resources, supporting public research, organizing a transport network, and protecting infant industries through tariff and procurement policies. State support of industry continued afterwards, in a more subdued manner, through the imposition of industry standards, public research, procurement policy, and later targetted support for defence-related industries such as electronics and aircraft. Kozul-Wright concludes that the ability of the American state to meet the current challenge of industrial restructuring will depend on whether it can overcome the institutional and ideological legacies which now cripple its ability to act as an entrepreneurial agent.

Robert Wade takes up a controversial issue, namely, the role of the state in East Asia. He criticizes the neo-liberal view, which attributes the East Asian success to state policies which supposedly mimic the market, as not firmly grounded on hard evidence. He argues that East Asian state intervention is better characterized as 'governing the market'. He discusses the education policy and trade policy in Korea and Taiwan, showing how individual preferences for career and consumption—which in the neo-liberal view should ultimately rule the economy—have been constrained and shaped by a powerful state in these countries. This naturally brings him to the question as to how such powerful states did not generate the perverse 'government failures' predicted by the neo-liberals. After showing how this was done in East Asia, he takes up the issue of the replicability of East Asian experience. While being sceptical about the possibility of a wholesale replication of the East Asian experience on the ground of current world economic conditions and political constraints, he draws a cautiously optimistic conclusion that other countries can benefit from the introduction of some East Asian-style policy measures and institutions, which are themselves of recent origin and by conscious design. He concludes his chapter by making some important observations on the interaction between economic policy and the broader political economy.

Juhana Vartiainen's paper is concerned with successful state-led industrialization in Europe. He focuses primarily on the instructive, but neglected examples of Austria and Finland, where the role of the state has been remarkably similar to that in East Asian countries such as Korea and Taiwan. He argues that this similarity is no accident, but reflects common political and institutional features, which have both encouraged and made possible effective state intervention in these various countries. Vartiainen's basic contention is that effective state intervention requires the existence of a state which is politically autonomous and able to discipline the various private agents of the economy. However, there should be a delicate balance, so that the fate of the state bureaucracy itself depends on the success of the economy. Vartiainen argues that these conditions were satisfied in both Austria and Finland and also in East Asia. Whilst stressing that he has no grand theory to explain why successful state intervention occurs, he emphasizes the importance of factors such as strong bureaucratic and administrative traditions, together with the role of an external challenge in forcing crucial elites to support a vigorous interventionist strategy. He also underlines the role of expectations about future property rights. Economic planning or extensive state interventon has occurred in countries as diverse as Korea, Taiwan, Austria, Finland, Norway, Chile, and France. He argues that the success or failure of such activity by the state has had much to do with basic ideological commitments and expectations about future political norms. Capital owners may be willing to swallow a lot of planning or state intervention provided that there is a basic commitment to respect property rights, both now and in the future.

Ajit Singh examines the role of the state in fostering industrialization in India. He shows how industrial growth has been significantly slower than in East Asian countries such as South Korea, Taiwan, and China, but faster than in many other less developed countries. It has also been subject to fluctuations, slowing down somewhat in the mid-1960s and then recovering strongly in the 1980s. Many economists, especially in Western countries, blame the slow-down on bureaucracy and excessive interference by the Indian government, whilst ascribing the later recovery to the gradual liberalization of the economy and growing reliance on market forces. Singh criticizes this interpretation. He argues that the fluctuations in growth were due to government macroeconomic policy in response to external shocks. The slow-down from the mid-1960s onwards was the result of deflationary policies following the Indo-Pakistan war and the first Oil Shock, whilst the strength of the later recovery reflected the expansionary macroeconomic policies pursued in the 1980s. Although Singh defends the interventionist approach of the state in India, he also identifies certain weaknesses. Whilst rejecting a free trade regime of the kind advocated by the neo-liberals, he argues that India could have done much more to promote exports. He thinks that India should have pursued an East Asian style policy of promoting exports whilst continuing to protect the home market. Such a policy of export promotion through import protection would have been perfectly feasible from a political point of view, but was rejected by the Indian elite, whose intellectual and ideological formation made them prefer autarky.

Brian Van Arkadie, in his chapter on Africa, draws a very different picture from that of Wade. As he points out at the beginning, in a continent where almost all states have become financially dependent on international donors, many have lost control over a large part of their national territory, and some have practically ceased to exist, discussing the role of the state is a very difficult matter. From his review of post-independence African experience, Van Arkadie identifies three major factors leading to weak states, which in his view constitute the main causes of the crisis: the absence of national projects based on domestic economic interests; the absence of a strong bureaucratic tradition; and the limited historical roots of the nation states. Moving to an assessment of the current experience of structural adjustment programmes, he acknowledges that these programmes had some modest success in reviving private sector economic activity. However, in his view, they have been singularly unsuccessful in restoring the administrative capacity of the state, which makes him sceptical about the prospects for long-term sustained growth. He argues that, however difficult it may be, the reconstruction of public institutions is the only way forward for Africa, even in the context of a much more private-sector-oriented economy than was previously the norm in the continent. Finally, he discusses the role of international donors, which are currently acting as quasi-governments in many African countries. He argues that reform of the state ultimately has to come 'by a process owned by and embedded in the national government structure', and that the international donors, rather than continuing their current policies which have been one major factor eroding the capacity of governments, should help African countries to reconstruct their badly damaged public institutions.

Peter Nolan's chapter on the reform experience of China confronts head on the orthodox view that the combination of rapid economic liberalization and thorough political democratization is the only way forward for reforming the socialist economies. He carefully documents how an incrementalist reform strategy in China, which led to the emergence and coexistence of a multiplicity of economic institutions, produced a most remarkable economic performance. In the light of such experience, he argues that the simple market–state divide implicit in the orthodox view (and in the old Stalinist view) and its simplistic conception of political economy may be too limiting for the design of a successful reform package. While arguing that other countries have a lot to learn from the Chinese experience, Nolan acknowledges that the Chinese strategy may not be directly applicable to other former socialist countries, if only because their state apparatuses have been seriously damaged and their social fabrics are unravelling. However, in his view, such conditions were partly created by the very failure of their radical reform packages. This leads him to conclude that the emergence of 'a new authoritarian political leadership based upon cultural and economic nationalism becomes increasingly probable' in these countries.

Michael Ellman's chapter explores the role of the state under socialism and post-socialism. He explains how the socialist states, which were supposed to 'tower above society and reshape it', failed to deliver the promises of high productivity, political democracy, and social justice, resulting in what he calles 'liberal revolutions'. While agreeing that the liberal revolution brought about an expansion of freedom in various areas, Ellman argues that it is proving to be a costly process. According to him, there are extremely high 'costs of revolution' in the form of a weakened state apparatus which cannot provide even the most basic services like stable money or law and order, and also in the form of overt and covert conflicts arising from the breakup of the old states, as in Yugoslavia and the Central Asian Republics of the former USSR. He also argues that there are 'costs of liberalism' such as unemployment, crime, poverty, inequality, and the atrophy of 'high culture'. Then he points out that these costs have recently prompted a re-evaluation of the role of the state even amongst the leaders of the liberal revolution. He argues that, although there is growing recognition of the need for efficient state intervention, most post-socialist countries suffer from deficiencies which inhibit such intervention—lack of sovereign integrity, financial constraints, lack of a suitable bureaucratic apparatus, pressure from creditors, and so on. He emphasizes that conditions vary widely across post-socialist societies and he foresees the emergence of a 'spectrum of roles for the state, differing between countries, depending on structural and conjunctural factors'.

In a similar vein, in his chapter on the experience of Vietnam and Laos, Brian Van Arkadie explores how the reform process has been successfully managed by these two former socialist countries, in the face of exceptionally harsh external conditions (especially in the case of Vietnam). He argues that the relative success of these countries was possible largely (but not solely) because they never made an ideological break with the past and therefore could take a more patient and pragmatic view of the reform. He shows how the reforms in these countries had to involve institution building which is complicated and time-consuming, especially given the insufficient managerial capability and stringent political constraints facing the transitional economies. The chapter shows that maintaining a balance between the need for fundamental institutional reform and the need for maintaining a high level of economic activity and political stability, which can easily be thwarted by too rapid institutional reform, is a central question for transforming socialist economies. By showing that the states in Vietnam and Laos struck this difficult balance through the kind of pragmatic and gradualist approach adopted also in China, his chapter effectively challenges the orthodox belief that there can be no 'half-way house' in reforming socialist economies.

REFERENCES

AKERLOF, G. and YELLEN, J. (eds.) (1986). *Efficiency Wage Models of the Labour Market*. Cambridge: Cambridge University Press.

ARMSTRONG, P., GLYN, A., and HARRISON, J. (1991). *Capitalism since 1945*. Oxford: Blackwell.

BARR, N. (1992). 'Economic Theory and the Welfare State: A Survey and Interpretation', *Journal of Economic Literature*, 30/2.

BAUMOL, W. (ed.) (1980). *Public Enterprise in a Mixed Economy*. London and Basingstoke: Macmillan.

BERLIN, I. (1969). 'Two Concepts of Liberty' in *Four Essays on Liberty*. Oxford: Oxford University Press.

BHAGWATI, J. (1982). 'Directly Unproductive Profit-Seeking (DUP) Activities', *Journal of Political Economy*, 90/5.

BLEANEY, M. (1988). *Do Socialist Economies Work?* Oxford: Blackwell.

BOSS, H. (1990). *Theories of Surplus and Transfer*. Boston: Unwin Hyman.

BOWLES, S. (1985). 'The Production Process in a Competitive Equilibrium: Walrasian, Neo-Hobbesian, and Marxian Models', *American Economic Review*, 75/1.

BRUS, W. and LASKI, K. (1989). *From Marx to the Market*. Oxford: Clarendon Press.

BUCHANAN, J. and TULLOCK, G. (1962). *The Calculus of Consent: Logical Foundations of Constitutional Democracy*. Ann Arbor: University of Michigan Press.

CHANG, H.-J. (1994). *The Political Economy of Industrial Policy*. London and Basingstoke: Macmillan.

—— and KOZUL-WRIGHT, R. (1994). 'Organising Development: Comparing the National Systems of Entrepreneurship in Sweden and South Korea', *Journal of Development Studies*, 30/4.

—— and SINGH, A. (1993). 'Public Enterprises in Developing Countries and Economic Efficiency', *UNCTAD Review*, no. 4.

COHEN, S. (1977). *Modern Capitalist Planning: The French Model*, 2nd edn. Berkeley: University of California Press.

CULLIS, J. and JONES, P. (1987). *Microeconomies and the Public Economy: A Defence of Leviathan*. Oxford: Blackwell.

DEANE, P. (1989). *The State and the Economic System*. Oxford: Oxford University Press.

de SOTO, H. (1989). *The Other Path*. New York: Harper & Row.

DOSI, G., FREEMAN, C., NELSON, R., SILVERBERG, G., and SOETE, L. (eds.) (1988). *Technical Change and Economic Theory*. London: Pinter Publishers.

DRIVER, C. (1980). 'Productive and Unproductive Labour: Uses and Limitations of the Concepts', Thames Papers in Political Economy, spring 1980.

ELLMAN, M. (1989). *Socialist Planning*, 2nd edn. Cambridge: Cambridge University Press.

FINDLAY, R. (1990). 'New Political Economy', *Economics and Politics*, 2/2.

FURUBOTN, E. and PEJOVICH, S. (1972). 'Property Rights and Economic Literature: A Survey of Recent Literature', *Journal of Economic Literature*, 10/4.

GERSCHENKRON, A. (1966). 'Economic Backwardness in Historical Perspective' in *Economic Backwardness in Historical Perspective*. Cambridge, Mass.: Belknap Press.

GIERSCH, H. (1986). 'Liberalisation for Faster Economic Growth', IEA Occasional Paper, no. 74. London: Institute of Economic Affairs.

GLYN, A., HUGHES, A., LIPIETZ, A., and SINGH, A. (1990). 'The Rise and Fall of the Golden Age' in Marglin and Schor (eds.).

HIRSCHMAN, A. (1958). *The Strategy of Economic Development*. New Haven: Yale University Press.

HUGHES, A. and SINGH, A. (1991). 'The World Economic Slowdown and the Asian and Latin American Economies: A Comparative Analysis of Economic Structure, Policy, and Performance' in T. Banuri (ed.), *Economic Liberalisation: No Panacea*. Oxford: Clarendon Press.

JOHNSON, C. (1982). *MITI and the Japanese Miracle*. Stanford, Calif.: Stanford University Press.

JONES, L. (ed.) (1982). *Public Enterprise in Less-developed Countries*. Cambridge: Cambridge University Press.

KALDOR, N. (1966). *Strategic Factors in Economic Development*. Ithaca, NY: Cornell University Press.

—— (1985). *The Scourge of Monetarism*, 2nd edn. Oxford: Oxford University Press.

KEYNES, J. M. (1926). 'The End of Laissez Faire' in *Essays in Persuasion*. London and Basingstoke: Macmillan.

KORNAI, J. (1979). 'Resource-Constrained versus Demand-Constrained Systems', *Econometrica*, 47/4.

KRUEGER, A. (1974). 'The Political Economy of the Rent-Seeking Society', *American Economic Review*, 64/3.

LAVOIE, D. (1985). *Rivalry and Central Planning*. Cambridge: Cambridge University Press.

LINDBERG, L. and MAIER, C. (eds.) (1985). *The Politics of Inflation and Economic Stagnation*. Washington, D.C.: The Brookings Institution.

MAIER, C. (1987). *In Search of Stability*. Cambridge: Cambridge University Press.

MARGLIN, S. and SCHOR, J. (eds.) (1990). *The Golden Age of Capitalism*. Oxford: Clarendon Press.

MUELLER, D. (1979). *Public Choice*. Cambridge: Cambridge University Press.

NISKANEN, W. (1973). *Bureaucracy: Servant or Master?* London: Institute of Economic Affairs.

NORTH, D. (1981). 'Neoclassical Theory of the State' in *Structure and Change in Economic History*. New York: W. W. Norton & Co.

NOZICK, R. (1974). *Anarchy, Utopia and the State*. Oxford: Blackwell.

NURKSE, R. (1952). 'Some International Aspects of the Problem of Economic Development', *American Economic Review*, 42/2.

OLSON, M. (1982). *The Rise and Decline of Nations*. New Haven: Yale University Press.

PAGANO, U. (1985). *Work and Welfare in Economic Theory*. Oxford: Blackwell.

PANIĆ, M. (1990). 'Managing Reform in the East European Economies: Lessons from the Postwar Experience of Western Europe', paper presented for the United Nations Economic Commission for Europe.

PEACOCK, A. (1979). 'Appraising Government Expenditure: A Simple Economic Analysis' in A. Peacock, *The Economic Analysis of Government*. Oxford: Martin Robertson.

—— and ROWLEY, C. (1979). 'Pareto Optimality and the Political Economy of Liberalism' in Peacock, *The Economic Analysis of Government*.

PEKKARINEN, J., POHJOLA, M., and ROWTHORN, R. (eds.) (1992). *Learning from Corporatist Experiences*. Oxford: Clarendon Press.

POLANYI, K. (1957). *The Great Transformation*. Boston: Beacon Press.

POSNER, R. (1975). 'The Social Costs of Monopoly and Regulation', *Journal of Political Economy*, 83/4.

ROSENSTEIN-RODAN, P. (1943). 'Problems of Industrialisation of Eastern and South-Eastern Europe', *Economic Journal*, 53/3.

ROWLEY, C. (1983). 'The Political Economy of the Public Sector' in B. Jones (ed.), *Perspectives on Political Economy*. London: Frances Pinter.

ROWTHORN, B. (ed.) (forthcoming). *Enterprise Democracy*. London: Routledge.

—— and CHANG, H-J. (1993). 'Public Ownership and the Theory of the State' in T. Clarke and C. Pitelis (eds.), *The Political Economy of Privatisation*. London: Routledge.

SCHEFFLER, S. (1988). *Consequentialism and its Critics*. Oxford: Oxford University Press.

SCHUMPETER, J. (1987). *Capitalism, Socialism and Democracy*, 6th edn. London: Unwin Paperbacks.

SCITOVSKY, T. (1954). 'Two Concepts of External Economies', *Journal of Political Economy*, 62/2.

SHAPIRO, H. and TAYLOR, L. (1990). 'The State and Industrial Strategy', *World Development*, 18/6.

SINGH, A. (1992a). 'The Actual Crisis of Economic Development in the 1980s: An Alternative Policy Perspective for the Future' in A. K. Dutt and F. Jameson (eds.), *New Directions in Development Economics*. Aldershot: Edward Elgar.

—— (1992b). ' "Close" vs. "Strategic" Integration with the World Economy and the "Market-Friendly Approach to Development" vs. an "Industrial Policy": A Critique of the *World Development Report 1991* and an Alternative Policy Perspective', mimeo. Faculty of Economics & Politics: University of Cambridge.

STIGLER, G. (1975). *The Citizen and the State*. Chicago: University of Chicago Press.

THOMPSON, G. (ed.) (1989). *Industrial Policy: USA and UK Debates*. London: Routledge.

—— FRANCES, J., LEVACIC, R., and MITCHELL, J. (eds.), (1991). *Markets, Hierarchies, and Networks*. London: Sage.

TOYE, J. (1987). *Dilemmas of Development*. Oxford: Blackwell.

VERNON, R. and AHARONI, Y. (eds.) (1981). *State-Owned Enterprises in the Western Economies*. London: Croom Helm.

WEISS, J. (1990). *Industry in Developing Countries*. London: Routledge.

WILLIAMSON, O. (1975). *Markets and Hierarchies*. New York: The Free Press.

WORLD BANK (1983). *World Development Report 1983*. New York: Oxford University Press.

—— (1987). *World Development Report 1987*. New York: Oxford University Press.

—— (1991). *World Development Report 1991*. New York: Oxford University Press.

WRIGHT, R. (1991). 'Three Essays in Comparative Institutional Economics', unpublished Ph.D. dissertation. Faculty of Economics & Politics: University of Cambridge.

PART I

THEORETICAL OVERVIEWS

2

Role of the State in Economic Change: Entrepreneurship and Conflict Management

Ha-Joon Chang & Robert Rowthorn

1. BEYOND MARKET FAILURE: NEW POLITICAL ECONOMY, INSTITUTIONAL ECONOMICS, AUSTRIAN ECONOMICS, AND BEYOND

Conventional discussions of the role of the state have been conducted in terms set by welfare economics and consequently centred around the concept of market failure, which may be defined as the failure of decentralized agents to produce decisions to fulfil the conditions of competitive equilibrium. Such failure arises because conditions like indivisibility, lack of exclusive property rights, and strategic behaviour lead to discrepancies between private and social costs and benefits, manifested in problems like public goods, externalities, and monopolies. In the market failure framework, the state is seen as the social guardian (or the modern equivalent of Plato's Philosopher King) and is therefore expected to correct for the failures of the market, using means like public production, regulation of pricing, franchise bidding, tax, subsidies, and reallocation of property rights.[1] Criticisms of this framework are many, but we identify three types of argument as most important.

The first type of criticism is closely associated with the neo-liberal argument which we examined in detail in the introductory chapter. Under various headings like New Political Economy, public choice, government failure, and neoclassical political economy, numerous authors have argued that the state is not the benevolent, omniscient, and omnipotent agent as depicted in welfare economics. State intervention may not improve social welfare or even may make things worse, it is argued, either because there are certain 'transaction costs' involved in such operations (e.g. informational costs, rent-seeking wastes) or because the state apparatus may

We wish to thank Rathin Roy for his extensive comments on this chapter.

[1] The Keynesian idea of aggregate demand management can also be interpreted as an attempt to centrally co-ordinate savings and investments which are carried out by different agents or at least with different motives even when carried out by the same set of agents (Leijonhufvud 1981).

be controlled by political rulers, bureaucrats, or interest groups, whose interests do not coincide with that of society in general.[2] Hence the notion of government failure. The proponents of New Political Economy believe that government failures are, on the whole, more serious than market failures, and that the role of the state should therefore be no more than that of a night-watchman.

The second type of criticism against the market failure framework is provided by those who can be broadly called institutional economists. The market failure framework implicitly grants institutional primacy to the market, by seeing the state as reacting to, and not leading, the market. Note that giving institutional primacy to the market is not equivalent to believing in less state intervention, as the extent of intervention may turn out to be absolutely gigantic due to the pervasiveness of market failure. Institutional economists, however, have emphasized that the market is only one of many economic institutions and not necessarily the 'primary' one (see Simon 1991). In particular, they point out that historically many states have actively created the market mechanism itself, not to speak of individual markets, rather than merely reacting to the failures of some existing markets (see Polanyi 1957; Coase 1988). This is a very different approach from that of the market failure framework, in which state intervention (and other forms of centralized co-ordination like organizations) is seen as only a second best 'man-made' substitute, which arises when the 'natural' order of the market fails to produce the promised outcome (Arrow 1974 is representative of this view).[3]

The third criticism of the market failure framework is provided by Austrian economists like Hayek (1949, 1988) and Mises (1929, 1979). They have argued that the whole exercise in welfare economics is misplaced, as the idealized condition of competitive equilibrium, against which the existence of market failures can be identified, is a meaningless fantasy. According to the Austrians, our economic life is permeated with fundamental uncertainties, and consequently has to be understood as a process of continuous discovery and creative destruction through rivalry amongst entrepreneurs. In this situation, the 'data' which are necessary to determine the competitive equilibrium (e.g. technologies, institutions) are in constant

[2] The view that the state is controlled by sectional interests is, of course, a fundamental proposition of Marxist thought. However, we do not deal explicitly with Marxist theories of the state for the following reasons. These theories are primarily concerned with strategic political issues such as the preservation of class power, where their insights have been many and powerful. To the extent that they deal with economic questions, Marxist theories overlap to a considerable degree with other theories of the state, including welfare economics and the New Political Economy. Moreover, although Marxist theories of the state still have a number of adherents in academic circles, their influence has declined and their impact on the recent policy debate has been limited.

[3] According to Arrow, non-market institutions, which he calls 'organisations' as a shorthand, are simply 'means of achieving the benefits of collective action in situations in which the price system fails' (Arrow 1974: 33).

flux, and therefore it becomes meaningless to say whether the market 'fails' or not, because the 'market process' does not allow us to identify the ideal against which such failures are to be identified.[4]

All these three criticisms have important implications for the theory of the state. New Political Economy has launched an effective attack on the naïve political assumptions of state neutrality and omnipotence held by welfare economics, whose demolition makes it necessary to bring politics explicitly back into our discussion of state intervention. Of course, this does not mean that we should follow the proponents of the New Political Economy and believe that politics necessarily 'corrupts' the economy, and therefore that it should be kept at bay by limiting the extent of state intervention to the minimum. As we argued in the introductory chapter and as we shall argue in the rest of this chapter, New Political Economy suffers from some severe limitations resulting from its rather simplistic view of the political process. To overcome such limitations, we need to explore more carefully such issues as the role of ideologies and institutions in the determination of the agenda for state intervention, the (relative) autonomy of the state vis-à-vis interest groups in setting and executing such agendas, and different forms of interest group representation and their differential implications for the process and outcome of state intervention. Although this chapter does not attempt to fully deal with these issues, it will sketch how they may be tackled in future research (for some seminal works from political science along these lines, see essays in Evans et al. (eds.) 1985 and Hall (ed.) 1989).

The institutionalist critique of the market failure framework makes our task more complex. If we stop believing in the institutional primacy of the (competitive) market, we face a more complex problem of institutional design. Obviously drawing the boundary between the state and the market will be one part of such design, but the task is more complicated than that, as now we leave the world of market–state dichotomy and enter a world a with a multiplicity of institutions. What does this mean for the theory of the state? In our opinion, this means that we need to give our attention to the ability of the state to set, excute, and change laws regarding property rights and other entitlements as well as its ability to manipulate people's value systems through its influence on education, mass media, and other cultural institutions—obviously with the recognition that such abilities will differ across countries and across

---

[4] The Austrian theory, or any other theory which emphasizes uncertainties of the future (as opposed to quantifiable risk), has often been reinterpreted as another type of market failure argument, namely, that of 'missing markets' in futures. According to this interpretation, it may be argued that, although the ideal of competitive equilibrium may not be *achievable* due to the absence of futures markets, it is at least *identifiable* through an inter-temporal optimization exercise. However, this is beside the point, as the very essence of the economic process as identified by the Austrians is the existence of pervasive uncertainties, which defy the very idea of inter-temporal optimization.

time.[5] In other words, we need to develop a theory which takes into account the role of the state as the designer, defender, and reformer of many formal and informal institutions.

The task takes on a new dimension, once we accept certain points raised by the Austrian critique of welfare economics (and neoclassical economics in general). If we are living in a world with pervasive uncertainties where everyone, including the state, is 'groping in the dark', there seems to be no reason to expect that state intervention will necessarily make things better, *even if* we do not define 'improvement' in terms of static allocative efficiency used in the market failure framework. Does this mean that we also have to accept the conclusion of the Austrian economists that state intervention should be minimized? We do not think so. Accepting the Austrian critique *does* mean accepting that state intervention can no longer be based on static (or even dynamic) equilibrium analysis and that sometimes state intervention can go drastically wrong. But this does not mean that there is no role for the state or that state intervention is always, even usually, harmful. Contrary to the Austrian claim, 'spontaneous' order of the market is only a part of our economic order. 'Constructed' order associated with consciously designed or deliberately modified organizations, networks, and state interventions plays an equally important role (see the next section for the argument; also see Simon 1991). As we shall argue later, the recognition of this opens up a whole new field of inquiry, namely, the role of the state as an entrepreneur whose task is to provide a 'vision' for the society and create new institutions required to achieve the vision.

So what comes out of our discussion of the implications of three main criticisms of the market failure approach? We have suggested three critical elements which a satisfactory theory of state intervention should incorporate. The first is the need to bring politics back into the theory. The second is the role of the state as the creator and manipulator (both in good and bad senses) of institutions. The third is the role of the state as an entrepreneur, a notion which has been talked about a lot but with little theoretical treatment (possible exceptions are Hirschman 1958, and Gerschenkron 1966). In the following, we attempt to take a first step towards a new synthetic theory of *the state as an agent of economic change* which takes all these elements on board, drawing both on some recent developments in economic theory (such as institutional economics, theories of technical progress, and political economy) and on case studies of the role of the state in past and present economic developments.[6]

---

[5] In this sense, we are sympathetic to a Marxist tradition which sees the state apparatus as composed not only of the 'government' but also educational, cultural, and religious institutions (see Althusser and Balibar 1970, and Gramsci 1988; also see Kitching 1989).

[6] See Polanyi (1957), Gerschenkron (1966), and Maier (1975 and 1987) on pre-war Europe. See Armstrong *et al.* (1991), Zysman (1983), Graham and Seldon (eds.) (1990) on post-war experience of OECD countries. See Johnson (1982), Dore (1986), and Okimoto (1989) on Japan. See Bates (1981), Sandbrook (1985), and Sender and Smith (1986) on

2. ENTREPRENEURSHIP: PROVISION OF VISION AND INSTITUTION BUILDING

In a modern economy with a complex industrial structure, 'it is difficult to replace one part of the complex with modern and efficient elements without a costly rebuilding of other components' (Abramovitz 1986: 401–2). However, the factors of production in a non-socialist economy are, to borrow from Abramovitz again, 'interdependent in use but dispersed in ownership' (ibid. 402). This means that a major transformation in the economic structure requires simultaneous changes in many components of the economy, but that those who control individual components may be unable to initiate and achieve the transformation, because they suffer from the lack of 'systemic' vision (as their own sectional interests dominate over concerns for the whole economy) and/or from strategic uncertainty as to the behaviour of the other relevant agents. Indeed, this reasoning formed the basis of some earlier theories of industrialization. The so-called 'balanced growth' or 'big push' model of industrialization, advocated by Rosenstein-Rodan (1943) and Scitovsky (1954), argued that, if underdeveloped economies are to industrialize, the state needs to co-ordinate investments in industries with demand complementaries.

However, such 'co-ordination' of the major economic transformation should not simply be interpreted as co-ordinating a shift from one equilibrium position to a higher level equilibrium (for example, as Stiglitz 1992 does), although such a formulation may be useful for certain puroses.[7] In this view, it is assumed that all agents are aware of all the possible equilibria and know, or at least can calculate, which of them is the best outcome. In such a world, the only obstacle to change would be the difficulty of simultaneous movement. However, as the Austrians have persuasively argued, one central problem of our economic life is exactly that we are not aware of the full range of possibilities, not to speak of being able to tell which of them is the best. And therefore, as Hirschman (1958) pointed out in his celebrated critique of the balanced growth approach, major economic transformation, or economic development, 'depends not so much on finding optimal combinations for given resources and factors of production as on calling forth and enlisting for development purposes resources and abilities that are hidden, scattered, or badly utilised' (p. 5).

Thus seen, a major economic transformation requires much more than simple co-ordination, which implies choosing from a pre-existing choice

---

Africa. See Bardhan (1984), Rudolph and Rudolph (1987), and Khan (forthcoming) on South Asia. See Deyo (ed.) (1987), Amsden (1989), Wade (1990), and Chang (1993) on East Asia. See Fishlow (1990), Dornbusch and Edwards (ed.) (1991), Ffrench-Davis *et al.* (forthcoming) on Latin America.

[7] Some arguments in the so-called 'social-corporatism' literature share a similar view. See e.g. Schmitter (1979).

set. It requires formulating the choice set itself and setting an agenda for economic change and for the evolution of private tastes and perceptions— namely, the provision of a 'vision' for the future. And the state, given its ability to affect (if not determine) the way in which such an agenda is set, can perform an important role in the process of economic change, if it can provide a coherent (but not necessarily the best) vision of the future. By providing a coherent vision of the future economy at an early stage of the transformation, the state can drive private sector agents into a *concerted action* without making them spend excessive resources in information gathering and processing, political bargaining, and so on.[8] The fact that the state engineering a major economic transformation is providing a 'vision' rather than merely co-ordinating a move to a higher 'equilibrium' means that there is an important *entrepreneurial* element in the exercise.[9]

Note that we are here not asserting that the state necessarily has a superior ability to identify a better future course for the national economy (although this may well be the case, as in the case of some Japanese high-tech industries, see Okimoto 1989), but only that the provision of a 'focal point' around which economic activities may be organized in times of major economic change can be extremely useful.[10] Our case for state entrepreneurship, then, is mainly based on its *strategic position*—that the state, by definition, is the only agent which may (although it may not) represent the

---

[8] The enormous potential of the 'vision' provided by the state in facilitating a major economic transformation can be vividly seen in the success stories of 19th century Germany and late 20th century Japan in 'leapfrogging' the then most advanced nations, namely, Britain and the USA, respectively. The Bismarckian vision of a unified Germany as a military power provided a strong focal point for a concerted effort to construct heavy and chemical industries, whereas the MITI-led vision of a future Japan as a highly skilled, software-based society provided an important rallying point for the development of information technology in the country. Thus Renshaw (1986), writing on Japan, points out that 'a sense of overall direction to the overall evolution of the economy has been provided by the annual economic white papers of the Economic Planning Agency with their thematic titles and by the forward looks or "visions" published every two or three years by the MITI, via the Structure Council. . . . In practical terms, these documents provide criteria or orientation against which countless individual decisions by private and public officials can be tested and hence given *order and coherence which could otherwise only be achieved by a much higher degree of centralisation*' [italics added] (p. 144).

[9] Be it private or public (state), entrepreneurship requires the ability to provide a new vision, however grand (as in the case of Henry Ford's vision on mass production or the Japanese state's vision of a highly skilled, software-based economy) or limited (as in numerous cases of incremental innovation) its scope may be. Another critical element of entrepreneurship is the ability to mobilize resources to implement the vision. In the existing literature, the role of the state in resource mobilization is widely discussed, but it has rarely been combined with the analysis of its role as a provider of 'vision'.

[10] In this connection, note the observation that the economic bureaucracy in certain East Asian countries with successful interventionist records has been manned by lawyers and engineers rather than economists. This suggests that what makes successful intervention may not be 'specialist' knowledge about economics but the ability to co-ordinate decisions. See Johnson (1982) and Sheridan (1993) on Japan. See Wade (1990) on Taiwan and Korea. See Chang (1994) on Korea and Japan.

interest of the whole society[11]—although it will be naïve to assume that all existing states have the organizational coherence, the political desire, or the power to exploit such a strategic position to national advantage.

We want to emphasize that the vision provided by the state as an entrepreneur can be 'wrong' from the start, or become so due to a failure to modify it according to changes in the environment. In other words, the provision of a vision may be a necessary condition for an effective achievement of a major economic transformation but it is by no means a sufficient one. However, the possibility that the state can hold a wrong vision does not, in itself, provide a definitive case against state entrepreneurship, as all entrepreneurial visions, private or public, run the risk of being wrong—in a world where this is not the case, entrepreneurship would have no place to begin with. We argue that such a possibility should be minimized not by abandoning the attempts at state entrepreneurship altogether (as many neo-liberals would want), but by building a mechanism to put together and compare different 'visions' extant in the society, including the one held by the state, and to create a 'consensus' out of them.[12] This is because there are kinds of 'entrepreneurial' decisions which can only be sensibly made and co-ordinated at the national level, and only the state is (potentially) positioned to make and implement such decisions.[13]

State entrepreneurship does not stop at the provision of the vision of the future. If its vision is to be implemented, the state has to provide an institutional reality to it. And this means that we need to look at the role of the state as an *institution builder*. This, of course, may be criticized by the Austrians as an exercise in 'rational constructivism' (Hayek 1988), which does not realise that order in a complex system can emerge only 'spontaneously' and mistakenly believes that human agents (especially the state) can construct a viable order. While it is true that some early believers in state intervention had too much confidence in the feasibility of rationalist institutional design, this does not mean that all attempts at institution building

[11] This point is essentially what many Maxists had in mind when they argued that the growing socialization of production leads to more centralized forms of co-ordination, starting from the rise of the factory system, leading to growth of monopoly and expansion of state intervention, culminating in central planning under socialism. A similar reasoning lies behind the theory of 'enocompassing' organizations (Olson 1982) and theories of centralized wage bargaining and social corporatism (Schott 1984; Bruno and Sachs 1985; Pekkarinen *et al.* (eds.) 1992). The common theme here is how the centralization of the decisions by sub-societal groups which can potentially have economy-wide impacts may be beneficial for the society.

[12] When we say 'consensus', we do not necessarily imply that it emerges out of a harmonious process, but only that it is something that is eventually accepted by the relevant actors, even if it may emerge out of an ugly process of power struggle and bargaining.

[13] To emphasize again, this does not imply that no existing states are liable to make 'wrong' decisions or fail to implement a 'good' decision, due to reasons like its organizational incoherence, interest group pressures, and the self-interests of those who make up the state apparatus.

are likely to fail. In fact, the most important part of (successful) private entrepreneurship, which the Austrians praise so much, has been the creation of 'constructive' order through the building of new institutions—as seen in the cases of British railway companies, German 'Finanz Kapital', Carnegie's US steel, Toyota's new shop-floor organization (also see Chandler 1990, and Lazonick 1991).

When a process of major economic transformation is under way, new interdependences will appear and old ones disappear. The new pattern of interdependences will undermine the assumptions underlying the currently employed 'decomposition' of the complex and large system into relatively simple subsystems, assumptions which ease informational constraints by allowing agents to ignore certain (extant but relatively unimportant) interdependences in working out the co-ordinated outcome (on the 'decomposability' argument, see Simon 1983, and Loasby 1991: ch. 6). Under the circumstances, there is a need to quickly establish a new co-ordination structure (or new 'principles of efficient co-ordination', as Loasby 1991: 11 puts it) which reasonably (but not necessarily perfectly) corresponds to the new pattern of interdependences, as the informational costs for all agents, private and public, of operating in an 'age of uncertainty' will be significant.[14] Here note that what is required is a set of co-ordination *principles or rules* rather than individually 'optimal' decisions, as the co-ordination of the growth of knowledge (which is essential for economic development) 'depends on rational structures and rational procedures rather than rational choice' (Loasby 1991: 101).[15]

The establishment of a new co-ordination structure *necessarily* requires state involvement. Except in societies where the state apparatus is totally disintegrating, the state has the sole ability to legalize, and the greatest ability to give implicit but effective backing to, the new property rights and the new relations of power (both at the societal level and at the enterprise level), which provide an *institutional reality* to the new co-ordination struc-

---

[14] Loasby (1991) sums up the point in a succinct way: 'We try to make sense of the world by imposing patterns on it, and sticking to them as long as they are tolerably successful in allowing us to feel that we understand what we observe and what we experience [p. 6]. . . . People prefer not to have to think; but what they like even less is the feeling that they do not understand, and in such a situation they are driven to seek an explanation. A satisfactory explanation is one that will somehow associate the disturbing phenomenon with what is already familiar, and thus restore a pattern of coherence [p. 7].'

[15] In other words, there is a tremendous difference between the principles of efficient co-ordination applied to 'a rational choice of specialisation in order to gain access to the well-specified benefits of a superior production function' and the ones applied to 'the attempt to create a superior system for generating new knowledge, the content of which, and therefore the benefit of which, cannot be known before it has been discovered' (Loasby 1991: 11). Of course, 'even though future knowledge cannot be predicted if it is to remain *future* knowledge, it may often be possible to set limits on it—to say what cannot be done. Even that kind of prediction may be wrong, because . . . there is no way of proving any general proposition to be true' (p. 103). Nevertheless, this is the kind of world we are living in, and we have to make the best out of it.

ture. In other words, by giving the emergent co-ordination structure an institutional reality, the state will help agents with bounded rationality to establish new organizations, new routines, and new contracts to deal with the 'new world'. In this process, the state is not merely responding to changes, even when it is trying to ratify *ex post* what has been initiated by the privated sector, as it cannot grant property (and other) rights in a coherent way unless it has a certain 'vision' of what it *thinks* is a desirable future. And holding a vision means that the state is also leading the changes. In this sense, the state is both responding to *and* shaping the course of changes, as any entrepreneur would do.

Of course, establishing a new co-ordination structure is easier said than done, for several reasons.

First of all, it is not simple to identify the optimal *timing* of such institutionalization. For example, sometimes early institutionalization of new practices (e.g. standardization of technology) boosts change, while at other times preventing a premature institutionalization of new practices by the private sector—which, if allowed, the state will eventually be compelled to ratify—may be more desirable (for examples, see Chang 1994: ch. 3). However, the recognition of the fundamental difficulty in predicting the future course of the economy should not deflect our attention away from the enormous potential benefits from a timely institutionalization by the state of emergent co-ordination structures.

Another problem facing the attempt to institutionalize the emergent co-ordination structure is that it may not be altogether feasible because of the incongruence between the boundaries of economic interdependences and the boundaries of the legal framework. One obvious, if not common, case is the inability of certain states to exercise effective control over all of their territory—as in the cases of Russia and the USA in the nineteenth century or some African countries today. More commonly, given that most laws are enforced only within the borders of nation states, internationalization of economic activities poses severe problems for the establishment of a co-ordination structure. The examples include the well-known difficulty of regulating trade flows due to the constant emergence of new products and new sources of supply from abroad, the difficulty of macroeconomic management in the world of internationalized financial markets, and the difficulty of affecting the pattern of production and employment through policy variables in a country dominated by large MNCs (see Rowthorn 1971; Banuri and Schor (eds.) 1991).[16]

---

[16] This reasoning also gives us some clues towards a better understanding of issues like the close relationship between industrialization and the rise of the nation state as an agent to establish the 'national' market (through abolishing 'internal' tariffs and providing certain legal frameworks) or the stability or otherwise of economic 'blocs' depending on the correspondence between politico-legal boundaries and boundaries of economic interdependences (ranging from those old-fashioned 'empires', large 'nations' like the USA and the former USSR, EC, and other international 'communities').

The question of feasibility also arises because of the resistance of certain groups which may lose out under the new co-ordination structure. A new co-ordination structure requires a new property rights structure, which may result in an unacceptable reduction in the economic benefits enjoyed under the old structure by some groups. And if this is the case, those who are to lose out will try to mobilize against the new institutional arrangements and sometimes succeed in doing so. Indeed, the resistance from such 'vested interests' has traditionally been identified as an important reason for 'sclerosis' of certain mature economies (Olson 1982; Giersch 1986; Hodgson 1989). However, the role of the state in speeding up economic transformation by reducing the resistance to the implementation of its vision has rarely been discussed, and this is what we intend to discuss in the next section of the chapter.

Let us sum up the discussion in this section. The coexistence of widespread interdependences and private control of the means of production means that success in a major economic transformation requires concerted efforts co-ordinated by the state. However, this exercise is something much more than choosing between multiple equilibria (a simple co-ordination), because of the fundamental uncertainties pervading our economic life which impart an important entrepreneurial function to the state. The role of the state as an entrepreneur, however, does not stop at providing a 'vision' around which concerted efforts can be organized. As in many cases of private entrepreneurship, it requires social engineering (or institution building) which gives an institutional reality to the vision by shaping the emergent co-ordination structure. This task of institution building is made complicated by the difficulty of identifying the adequate timing of implementing new institutions, the existence of international interdependences, and the resistance from vested interests, but this does not make the task any less important.

3. CONFLICT MANAGEMENT: POLITICAL PRICES AND SOCIALIZATION OF RISK

Economic development is a creative *and* destructive process at the same time. Technological and institutional innovations occurring during the process of development inevitably involve changes in the ways in which different (old and new) productive assets are combined with each other, and this often gives rise to the need for a large-scale movement of certain productive assets into new employment. With perfectly mobile factors of production, this movement should not cause a problem, as the owners of those productive assets which need to find alternative employment will easily be able to switch to the next best option, whose return will be only 'marginally' lower (in a perfectly competitive economy).

However, when the mobility of certain assets is limited for reasons such as limited malleability of physical or human capital, the owners may suffer substantial cuts in their incomes if they accept the 'imperatives of the market' and move to the 'next best' option. When this reduction brings incomes (and other economic benefits) below a certain level considered 'fair', the owners of these assets may not accept the imperatives of the market and may take 'political' action to redress the situation (e.g. petition, strikes, bribing, horse-trading), thereby provoking counteraction from others in the society. This makes the process of economic development inherently conflictual.

What is the role of the state in resolving such conflicts? Certain governments, especially the ones with an ideological commitment to the free market, may not wish to be involved in the conflict resolution processes, but they cannot avoid some involvement. This is because the government is, again except in societies where the state apparatus is disintegrating, the ultimate guarantor of property (and other) rights, *de jure* and/or *de facto*, and is also usually the main actor in setting and executing the public agenda for changes in rights. Needless to say, the way a state manages such conflicts varies according to the place, the time, and the issue. Moreover, different methods of conflict management will have different implications for efficiency, productivity, equality, to name just a few. Now, what are the major types of conflict management and what difference do they make?

First of all, there is the classic method of conflict management in the capitalist economy, that is, leaving things to the market, thus compelling the losers to accept the market outcome. This does not mean that the state is not 'taking sides' in the conflict, because, as we shall argue in more detail later, there is nothing natural or inevitable about a certain market outcome. Moreover, when the adjustments that need to be made by the losers are large, this method creates a lot of tension, and therefore may be used only when the state can prevent the losers from organizing a countervailing political action. Hence the paradox that a free market requires a strong state (Gamble 1987). This solution may, in addition, result in the unnecessary writing off of many specific assets, a point powerfully conveyed by the image of a middle-aged redundant steel worker flipping hamburgers in McDonald's (more on this later).

Secondly, the state can employ more 'clandestine' (but not necessarily deliberate) measures like monetary, and to a lesser extent fiscal, policy. These are 'clandestine' because they appear to be neutral while in fact favouring certain groups over others. In the case of fiscal policy, this point may be more obvious, as most fiscal spending has easily identifiable recipients (if not necessarily contributors). In the case of monetary policy, this point may be less obvious. However, as the conflict theories of inflation tell us, monetary policy affects the outcome of distributional conflicts manifested in inflation (Rowthorn 1977, and essays in Lindberg and Maier (eds.) 1985). Also in countries where the state has control over credit rationing, aggregate monetary figures may conceal the highly selective extension of credit to certain groups. Monetary and fiscal policies allow the state to compensate the losers to an extent without necessarily giving the impression that it is defying the logic of the market, but the room for manoevre for the state using them is inevitably limited, as the precise 'targeting' of the beneficiaries is difficult with these policies.

Thirdly, the state can endorse the interest of a certain group in a more explicit way by openly defying the 'imperatives of the market' to various degrees. The form and degree with which the state defies the market logic can vary, and examples include the protection and restructuring of the losers through an outright state takeover of technically bankrupt private enterprises (as seen in the nationalization of Swedish shipbuilding industry or of Volkswagen in West Germany in the late 1970s) and the political renegotiation of prices (as was the case in the recent coal crisis in UK).[17] Openly defying the market logic may allow the state to resolve the conflicts in a less adversarial manner, but it can open the door for what is often termed as an 'unmanageable politicization of the economy' (more on this later).

Finally, the state may try to resolve conflict by resetting the public agenda and thereby changing the 'accepted' boundary (which, of course, may still remain 'fuzzy') between the economic and the political (for the importance of agenda setting in politics in general, see Skocpol 1985).[18] The resetting of the public agenda, of course, may involve making more or fewer issues 'politically negotiable', depending on the objective of such action. And the same issue may be put on and taken away from the public agenda under different conditions. The best example of this is provided by the fate of employment as a public issue in OECD economies. Employment in the early days of capitalism was a vital issue on the public agenda (as seen by the importance of the Poor Law), until it was struck off the agenda with the establishment of a working labour market and the rise of free market ideology (Polanyi 1957). It came back on the public agenda as the top priority item after World War II, but has almost disappeared again with the emphasis placed on the importance of labour market flexibility by right-wing governments in the 1980s (see also the introduction to this volume).

Our preceding discussion immediately reveals to us the problem with many neo-liberal arguments that the 'political' determination of prices is

[17] The fact that many of our examples of the state's defiance of the market logic involves avowed 'free-marketeer' governments—the right-wing coalition in Sweden and the Conservative government in the UK—shows the inevitability of state involvement in conflict management.

[18] Needless to say, no state is completely free to reset the boundary. The scope for such action will be limited by things like the dominant economic ideology, interest group pressures, or international economic situations.

undesirable, as it goes against the 'objective' prices set by the market, and their consequent call for 'depoliticization' of the economy. This position has a long intellectual history, as documented by Polanyi (1957), and indeed has some justification. Politicization of everything, as in the former socialist countries, may indeed create all sorts of problems—for example, the 'waste' of time and resource in bargaining, the difficulty of setting 'objective' performance standards, difficulty of containing certain redistributive demands, and so on. And one may argue that a well-functioning economy needs a substantial degree of depoliticization of decisions regarding production and distribution of goods and services through the use of market mechanism.

However, the boundary between the 'economic' and the 'political' is *not* something 'naturally' given, as we can see from our discussion, and therefore there is nothing sacred about the existing boundary, or, more to the point, the boundary drawn along the conventional market failure–government failure axis.[19] All prices are *potentially* 'political' (as Oskar Lange long ago pointed out), and there is no 'scientific' rule that will tell us which prices are (or should be) 'political' or not.[20] While there may be a quantitative limit to the expansion of the state (as seen in the former socialist countries), it is difficult to lay down in abstract exactly which areas of the economy the state should or should not be involved with. This point becomes more obvious when considering the fact that a few critical 'prices' which affect almost every sector, namely, wages (especially when considering immigration control) and interest rates, are politically set to a very large degree. If this is the case, there is no reason to assume any inherent primacy of the resolution of conflicts through the market logic (analogous to the institutional primacy accorded to the market by the market failure approach).

Another important point relating to the issue of conflict management by the state is that it should *not* be seen merely as taking care of the 'social' or 'human' dimension of adjustment—as the talks of 'safety net' in Eastern European reform or of 'adjustment with human face' in IMF stabilization

[19] For example, in many developing countries, strikes are banned, and therefore striking, and activity which would be regarded as 'economic' in most OECD economies, becomes a political act.

[20] Of course, at a point of time, for the purpose of policy prescription, some prices may be approximately treated as largely 'economic' ('political'), and therefore more 'market-oriented' ('political') means may be applied in resolving conflicts relating to them. In the longer run, however, the boundary between the economic and political does not stay the same even in the same society. For instance, take the case of the unemployment issue in OECD economies. In more corporatist economies, the dominant ideology (or value system) will regard unemployment as something that can be negotiated in the domain of politics, and there will be institutional mechanisms to sanction such negotiations. In contrast, in less corporatist economies, unemployment may be regarded as being beyond such negotiation and may be accepted as the outcome of 'imperatives of the market', and there often will be few institutional mechanisms to sanction such negotiations, even if unemployment can be somehow made a subject of 'political' negotiation.

programmes in LDCs imply. We argue that conflict management also has an extremely important 'economic' role, which seems to go a long way in explaining the differential performances between economies with different methods of conflict management.

By providing 'governance' which allows people to receive 'fair treatment' in unforeseen circumstances, the state in its role as the conflict manager, is providing 'insurance' to the members of the society. This 'insurance' function of the state is related to, but by no means the same as, the notion of the welfare state as improving allocative efficiency through the pooling of risk (see e.g. Barr 1992). Our insurance function of the state goes beyond that, and involves improving the productivity of the economy in the medium to long run by encouraging risk-taking behaviour in general (the good old 'socialization of risk' for investment activities) and investments in *specific* assets (a point that has hardly been discussed before)—although it is possible that it harms the economy when it creates too much room for 'moral hazard'.

In societies where the state fails to manage conflict in an appropriate way, people will be reluctant to take risk or commit their resources in specific investments, and therefore the dynamism of the economy may suffer. The examples of many developing countries where the lack of a reliable mechanism for conflict resolution discourages industrial investments (which would usually involve specific investments) and encourages the holding of liquid assets like gold and (if the government is expected to last at least in the foreseeable future) money. Another example of the adverse effect of a deficient conflict resolution mechanism on the dynamic efficiency of the economy is given by the British economy in this century. There is a popular argument that British capitalists are slow in introducing new technology (and hence new work practices) as they have to worry about the possible resistance of the workers, while their workers are unwilling to accept new technology and adopt new work practices because it usually means unemployment and/or substantial reductions in the value of their existing 'human capital' stock. That is, in the absence of a more comprehensive industrial policy with a functioning conflict management regime, the traditional craft divisions have survived as a means to defend the specific investments made by workers in their skills, discouraging the capitalists from introducing new technology and/or making it inevitable for them to write off a whole lot of human capital if they want to introduce a major technical change.

Conflict management by the state becomes much more difficult when it involves agents who do not fall within the jurisdiction of a particular state, that is, the MNCs. As the consequences of state actions to restrict their gains (when they are the winners in a conflict) or to compensate for their losses (when they are the losers) will easily spill over the national boundary, the involvement of the MNCs in a conflict during a process of structural change gives rise to certain fundamental 'property right' questions.

Especially in the case of small countries where individual MNCs may account for a significant portion of industrial output, the state may be reluctant to 'aid business' or 'help an industry', as the positive effects of such actions may not be contained within its own national boundary. This may require at least one of the following two outcomes, both of which do not seem politically feasible in many countries in the near future. One is that the attitude of the state towards MNCs may have to become more explicitly 'contractual' ('We will give you this. You do that in return.'). Such explicitness, however, may not be acceptable especially for a state which wants to preserve the impression that conflict resolution is not its business. Alternatively, we may want an international body (or even a world state) to deal with such multinational externality problems. This, however, does not seem politically feasible outside the EC in the foreseeable future.

Let us sum up our argument in this section. Economic change involves creative destruction of existing productive assets. In the presence of asset specificity and other sources of factor immobility, this may lead to a substantial reduction in the economic benefits enjoyed by certain groups. These groups, in turn, may try to resist such a reduction and in that process may provoke counteractions from others, making the process of economic development extremely conflictual. The state, for reasons we explained, is bound to be involved in resolving at least some of the conflicts. And it can manage the conflicts in many different ways, many of which will be defying the market logic and thus 'political'. Although an excessive politicization of the economy may be undesirable, there is no reason to assume that a more or less politicized variety of conflict management is more desirable in a particular situation. We also argued that the establishment of a well-functioning conflict management regime has an important implication for the dynamism of the economy, as it provides a governance structure which will allow people to invest more readily in long-term specific assets. Without a well-functioning regime of conflict management by the state, which obviously is not easy to construct, the economic dynamism of the economy may suffer. As in the case of state entrepreneurship, multinationalization of economic activities remains a barrier to the effective functioning of such a regime.

CONCLUSION: TOWARDS A NEW SYNTHESIS

In this chapter, we have sketched a synthesis of four important views of state intervention, namely, welfare economics, New Political Economy, institutional economics, and Austrian economics. The co-ordinating role of the state emphasized by welfare economics was expanded to deal with the existence of conflicting interests emphasized by New Political Economy,

the institutional diversity of capitalism emphasized by institutional economics, and the prevalence of uncertainties emphasized by the Austrians.
The resulting construction may seem too eclectic for some, but we believe
that the role of the state in economic change can only be adequately dealt
with by a theory which takes full account of uncertainty and innovation,
institutions, and political economy.

Our conclusion is that a major economic transformation in (or towards)
a modern economy requires a state which can effectively perform the roles
of the ultimate entrepreneur and the conflict manager. Of course, whether
a particular country can have a state which wants, can, and does perform
such roles will be dependent on a host of factors. A thorough discussion of
such factors are beyond the scope of this chapter, but we may suggest a few
obvious examples.

To begin with, history and current experience show that states can
practically 'disappear' or lose the capability for anything beyond the provision of minimum current services. Some states may not want to take up
the kind of active role we suggested because the prevailing ideology or
current political agenda does not provide any legitimacy for such a role (as
in current Eastern European countries; see the Chapter 9 in this volume).
Some other states may not be interested in playing such a role and may
actually obstruct structural change because of the nature of the groups
occupying and influencing the state apparatus. There may be still other
cases where a state which wants to play an active role in economic change
cannot, because there are so many opposing interests or because they face
severe financial constraints (as in some Latin American and African countries now).

Currently, so many states are seen as too weak, too corrupt, or too
unwilling to play such a role. However, this does not mean that therefore
the role of the state should be minimized. The recent experiences of neo-
liberal reform programmes in many Eastern European countries and in
many LDCs, which aimed for a minimization of the role of the state, starkly
illustrates this point. Such programmes undermined, partly intentionally
but partly unintentionally, the state apparatus, which had already been
weakened under various economic and political pressures. This meant that,
although the neo-liberal programmes revived the private sector, such a
revival was often restricted to small-scale, low-tech, non-tradable areas
(except primary exports), which do not need any extensive state support.
There is no sign as yet that these programmes will be able to bring about a
positive structural change in these countries towards more productive,
internationally competitive industries (see Chapter 8).

Without an effective state, a major economic change (except, perhaps, a
total collapse of the economy) is unlikely to come about, and therefore what
is required in these countries is reform of the state apparatus and rebuilding
of destroyed public institutions. Such reform will certainly involve state

withdrawal in some areas but will require strengthening of the state functions in other areas.

Needless to say, reforming the state is not an easy task, especially for countries in a downward spiral where faltering economic performance is destroying even the minimal social fabric, the existence of which is necessary for an effective reform of public institutions, including the state. Moreover, the scope for such reform is different in different societies, and the type and extent of such reform need not, and cannot be, uniform across countries (see Chapter 9 in this volume). However, the failure to reform the state apparatus (and other public institutions) will only delay the emergence of a coherent co-ordination structure and a functioning regime of conflict management, and consequently make the country unable to achieve a major economic transformation, if ever, except with considerable waste and/or social division.

REFERENCES

ABRAMOVITZ, M. (1986). 'Catching Up, Forging Ahead, and Falling Behind', *Journal of Economic History*, 46/2.

ALTHUSSER, L. and BALIBAR, E. (1970). *Reading Capital*. London: Verso.

AMSDEN, A. (1989). *Asia's Next Giant*. New York: Oxford University Press.

ARMSTRONG, P., GLYN, A., and HARRISON, J. (1991). *Capitalism since 1945*. Oxford: Blackwell.

ARROW, K. (1974). *The Limits of Organisation*. New York and London: W. W. Norton and Company.

BANURI, T. and SCHOR, J. (eds.) (1991). *Financial Openness and National Autonomy*. Oxford: Clarendon Press.

BARDHAN, P. (1984). *The Political Economy of Development in India*. Oxford: Blackwell.

BARR, N. (1992). 'Economic Theory and the Welfare State: A Survey and Interpretation', *Journal of Economic Literature*, 30/2.

BATES, R. (1981). *Markets and States in Tropical Africa*. Berkeley: University of California Press.

BRUNO, M. and SACHS, J. (1985). *Economics of Worldwide Stagflation*. Cambridge, Mass.: Harvard University Press.

CHANDLER, A. (1990). *Scale and Scope*. Cambridge, Mass.: Belknap Press.

CHANG, H.-J. (1993). 'The Political Economy of Industrial Policy in Korea', *Cambridge Journal of Economics*, 17/2.

—— (1994). *The Political Economy of Industrial Policy*. London and Basingstoke: Macmillan.

COASE, R. (1988). 'The Firm, the Market, and the Law' in *The Firm, the Market, and the Law*. Chicago: University of Chicago Press.

DEYO, F. (ed.) (1987). *The Political Economy of the New Asian Industrialism*. Ithaca and London: Cornell University Press.

DORE, R. (1986). *Flexible Rigidities: Industrial Policy and Structural Adjustment in the Japanese Economy 1970–80.* London: Athlone Press.

DORNBUSCH, R. and EDWARDS, S. (eds.) (1991). *The Macroeconomics of Populism in Latin America.* Chicago: University of Chicago Press.

EVANS, P., RUESCHEMEYER , D., and SKOCPOL, T. (eds.) (1985). *Bringing the State Back In.* Cambridge: Cambridge University Press.

FFRENCH-DAVIS, R., MUNOZ, O., and PALMA, G. (forthcoming). 'The Latin American Economies from the 1950s to the 1980s: Achievements and Limitations of Peripheral Capitalism' in L. Bethell (ed.), *Cambridge History of Latin America*, viii. Cambridge: Cambridge University Press.

FISHLOW, A. (1990). 'The Latin American State', *Journal of Economic Perspectives*, 4/3.

GAMBLE, A. (1987). *The Free Market and the Strong State.* London and Basingstoke: Macmillan.

GERSCHENKRON, A. (1966). 'Economic Backwardness in Historical Perspective' in *Economic Backwardness in Historical Perspective.* Cambridge, Mass.: Belknap Press.

GIERSCH, H. (1986). 'Liberalisation for Faster Economic Growth', IEA Occasional Paper, no. 74. London: Institute of Economic Affairs.

GRAHAM, A. and SELDON, A. (eds.) (1990). *Government and Economies in the Postwar World: Economic Policies and Comparative Performance 1945–85.* London: Routledge.

GRAMSCI, A. (1988). *A Gramsci Reader*, ed. D. Forgacs. London: Lawrence & Wishart.

HALL, P. (ed.) (1989). *The Political Power of Economic Ideas.* Princeton: Princeton University Press.

HAYEK, F. (1949). *Individualism and Economic Order.* London: Routledge & Kegan Paul.

—— (1988). *The Fatal Conceit.* London: Routledge.

HIRSCHMAN, A. (1958). *The Strategy of Economic Development.* New Haven: Yale University Press.

HODGSON, G. (1989). 'Institutional Rigidities and Economic Growth', *Cambridge Journal of Economics*, 13/1.

JOHNSON, C. (1982). *MITI and the Japanese Miracle.* Stanford, Calif.: Stanford University Press.

KHAN, M. H. (forthcoming). *Clientelism, Corruption, and Capitalist Development: An Analysis of State Intervention with Special Reference to Bangladesh.* Oxford: Oxford University Press.

KITCHING, G. (1989). *Karl Marx and the Philosophy of Praxis.* London: Routledge.

LAVOIE, D. (1985). *Rivalry and Central Planning.* Cambridge: Cambridge University Press.

LAZONICK, W. (1991). *Business Organisation and the Myth of the Market Economy.* Cambridge: Cambridge University Press.

LEIJONHUFVUD, A. (1981). *Information and Coordination.* New York: Oxford University Press.

LINDBERG, L. and MAIER, C. (eds.) (1985). *The Politics of Inflation and Economic Stagnation.* Washington, DC: The Brookings Institution.

LOASBY, B. (1991). *Equilibrium and Evolution*. Manchester: Manchester University Press.

MAIER, C. (1975). *Recasting Bourgeois Europe*. Princeton: Princeton University Press.

—— (1987). *In Search of Stability*. Cambridge: Cambridge University Press.

MISES, L. (1929). *A Critique of Interventionism*, tr. H. Sennholz (1977). New Rochelle, New York: Arlington House.

—— (1979). *Economic Policy*, Chicago: Regnery Gateway.

OKIMOTO, D. (1989). *Between MITI and the Market: Japanese Industrial Policy for High Technology*. Stanford, Calif.: Standford University Press.

OLSON, M. (1982). *The Rise and Decline of Nations*. New Haven: Yale University Press.

PEKKARINEN, J., POHJOLA, M., and ROWTHORN, B. (eds.) (1992). *Social Corporatism*. Oxford: Clarendon Press.

POLANYI, K. (1957). *The Great Transformation*. Boston: Beacon Press.

RENSHAW, J. (1986). *Adjustment and Economic Performance in Industrialised Countries*. Geneva: ILO.

ROSENSTEIN-RODAN, P. (1943). 'Problems of Industrialisation of Eastern and South-Eastern Europe', *Economic Journal*, 53/3.

ROWTHORN, B. (1971). 'Imperialism in the Seventies—Unity or Rivalry?', *New Left Review* (Sep.–Oct.).

—— (1977). 'Inflation and Crisis', *Marxism Today* (Nov.).

—— (ed.) (forthcoming). *Enterprise Democracy*. London: Routledge.

RUDOLPH, L. and RUDOLPH, S. (1987). *In Pursiut of Lakshimi*. Chicago and London: Chicago University Press.

SANDBROOK, R. (1985). *The Politics of Africa's Economic Stagnation*. Cambridge: Cambridge University Press.

SCHELLING, T. (1960). *The Strategy of Conflict*. Cambridge, Mass.: Harvard University Press.

SCHMITTER, P. (1979). 'Still the Century of Corporatism?' in P. Schmitter and G. Lehmbruch (eds.), *Still the Century of Corporatism?* London: Sage Publications Ltd.

SCHOTT, K. (1984). *Policy, Power and Order*. New Haven and London: Yale University Press.

SCITOVSKY, T. (1954). 'Two Concepts of External Economies', *Journal of Political Economy*, 62/2.

SENDER, J. and SMITH, S. (1986). *The Development of Capitalism in Africa*. London: Methuen & Co. Ltd.

SHAPIRO, H. and TAYLOR, L. (1990). 'The State and Industrial Strategy', *World Development*, 18/6.

SHERIDAN, K. (1993). *Governing the Japanese Economy*. Cambridge: Polity Press.

SIMON, H. (1983). *Reasons in Human Affairs*. Oxford: Blackwell.

SIMON, H. (1991). 'Organisations and Markets', *Journal of Economic Perspectives*, 5/2.

SKOCPOL, T. (1985). 'Bringing the State Back In' in Evans, Rueschemeyer, and Skocpol (1985).

STIGLITZ, J. (1992). 'Alternative Tactics and Strategies in Economic Development' in A. K. Dutt and K. Jameson (eds.), *New Directions in Development Economics*. Aldershot: Edward Elgar.

TAYLOR, L. (1987). *Varieties of Stabilization Experience: Towards Sensible Macroeconomics in the Third World*. Oxford: Clarendon Press.

TOYE, J. (1987). *Dilemmas of Development*. Oxford: Blackwell.

WADE, R. (1990). *Governing the Market*. Princeton: Princeton University Press.

WILLIAMSON, O. (1975). *Markets and Hierarchies*. New York: The Free Press.

ZYSMAN, J. (1983). *Governments, Markets, and Growth*. Oxford: Martin Robertson.

3

International Economic Integration and the Changing Role of National Governments

Mića Panić

Arguments concerning the role of government in economic change—the theme of this book—have been at the centre of economic debate since the eighteenth century. Yet, if anything, they are probably even further from producing a consensus now than they were more than two hundred years ago when two eminent Scots championed the familiar, diametrically opposed views: Sir James Steuart ([1767] 1966) that the state had a critical role to play in economic development and Adam Smith ([1776] 1976) that the role would be performed much more effectively by markets guided by the invisible hand of self-interest.

As far as the history of economic thought is concerned, Smith appears to have won the argument convincingly. Every economist is aware of his work, though few have actually read it. Most economists have never even heard of Steuart. However, when it comes to the policies actually pursued by individual countries since the beginning of the Industrial Revolution, it is arguable that the approach advocated by Steuart has been at least as influential.

Britain adopted some of Smith's key policy prescriptions, such as free trade, in the middle of the nineteenth century, long after his death and not before it had achieved global pre-eminence of a kind emulated only by the United States for a short period after the World War II. But even this qualified adherence to the doctrine of *laissez faire* did not last long. Many of the policies were abandoned early in the twentieth century, as problems associated with the two world wars and the country's relative economic decline mounted. Elsewhere in the industrial world, the state played an even more active role in promoting and sustaining economic development (Brebner 1962; Lockwood 1965; Gerschenkron 1966; Supple 1973; Milward and Saul 1977; Cain and Hopkins 1980; Sen 1984; Mathias and Pollard 1989).

The extent of state involvement in national economic management has tended to fluctuate over time, depending on whether the governments or the markets were held to be responsible for a major and prolonged loss in economic welfare (Hirschman 1982; Panić 1993). Nevertheless, there is no industrial country in which government has failed to play an influential role in promoting and supporting economic change.

This is hardly surprising. Even Adam Smith agreed that the state should bear full responsibility for the external security and internal order of a country; and, since the beginning of the Industrial Revolution, both of these have become increasingly dependent on the level of development and economic performance. Consequently, whatever their ideological preferences, governments have been forced to act as the allocator of last resort (underwriting or financing directly large or risky investment projects that the private sector is unwilling to undertake); the distributor or reconciler of last resort (reducing disparities in income and wealth, and with them the risk of social conflicts and political instability); the stabilizer of last resort (smoothing out the instabilities inherent in a market economy, a phenomenon analysed by a number of influential economists from Malthus to Keynes); and, finally, the co-ordinator of last resort (influencing through its own actions the expectations and behaviour in the rest of the economy—see Panić 1988: ch. 14).

The extent to which governments have done this has varied from country to country and, in the long run, within the same country—depending on its level and structure of economic development, economic performance, and socio-political conditions. Nevertheless, the question whether governments have an important role to play in macroeconomic management is superfluous. As Dr Erhard, who presided over the creation of the German social *market* economy, pointed out: 'In modern times a responsible government cannot resign itself merely to being a night-watchman. Such a perverted form of liberty would contain the seeds of disaster' (quoted in Oules 1966: 320–1). The important issue, therefore, is not whether governments should have overall responsibility for the economic performance of their countries but under what conditions they are likely to discharge it most effectively.

This chapter analyses a number of key conditions that have to be met, and the way that changes in some of them have been responsible for the apparent success of government policies at the *national* level in the twenty-five years before 1973, especially in the post-war reconstruction period, and for their equally apparent failure since then.

WHY SOME GOVERNMENTS ARE MORE SUCCESSFUL THAN OTHERS

It is customary, both in economic analysis and in public debate, to attribute the success or failure of a government's economic strategy to its competence and, occasionally, its integrity. The judgement may refer either to the government's choice of priorities or to its choice and/or implementation of particular policies.

There is a serious problem with such a simplistic approach to the analysis of the economic performance of governments. In the very short run, it is not inconceivable for a government, like anyone else, to make a mistake, even a serious mistake, especially when confronted with an unfamiliar problem. However, if a government continues to act 'incompetently' over a longer period despite changes in its membership and advisers, or, even more puzzling, if a succession of different, democratically elected governments continue to do so—as in the interwar period and since the early 1970s—it is surely time to ask a rather obvious question: why do so many governments, not all of the same political persuasion or economic philosophy, have one characteristic in common—incompetence? Equally relevant, why do electorates keep electing apparently incompetent politicians? Or, if they have no other choice, why do competent people keep out of politics?

The problem is that questions such as these take us into the realm of the non-economic determinants of economic performance, a field of exploration in which we, modern economists, rarely feel at ease. Yet they cannot be avoided if we wish to examine seriously the reasons responsible for the success or failure of government economic policies. Once we do this, however, the whole issue assumes a different, much more intricate complexion.

Table 3.1 lists a number of factors that normally determine whether or

Table 3.1 Factors which determine the effectiveness of government economic policies

---

1. Economic sovereignty
    (a) political independence
    (b) size of country (national self-sufficiency)
    (c) degree of openness (international specialization)
        tariffs
        quotas
        exchange controls

2. Institutional framework
    (a) constitutional responsibilities/limitations
    (b) institutional arrangements at the national level

3. Degree of economic consensus
    (a) national
    (b) international

4. A feasible economic strategy
    (a) realistic priorities
    (b) applicable, effective policies

5. Competence in implementing the strategy
    (a) constrained by (1)–(3) above
    (b) dependent on the ability and political skill of those in power

---

not economic policies pursued by a government are likely to have the desired effect.

Political independence (1a) is clearly one of the key factors. No government can have an effective economic policy, still less a mix of such policies, if its decisions are either imposed by some outside authority or can be changed by it with little or no regard for the country's problems and needs.

For obvious reasons, governments of large countries (1b) are less likely to find themselves in such a position than are those of small ones. Their capacity to pursue much more independent economic policies stems from the fact that the degree of self-sufficiency is far greater in large than in small economies—especially at higher levels of industrialization (Panić 1988: ch. 2). Consequently, they are less affected by external developments.

However, whatever the size, level of development, or nature of the economic system, governments of countries with lower barriers to trade and financial flows (1c) will have less control over their economies than those whose economies are well protected. *Ceteris paribus*, the more open an economy is the higher will be the level of its international specialization and, therefore, its dependence on developments in other countries. As a result, the short-term stability and long-term progress of such an economy will be affected not only by the policies of its own government but also by the actions of governments in the countries with which it has close economic ties.

Over time, the economic sovereignty of a country and the effectiveness of its government's policies will diminish if it becomes party to international economic treaties and agreements which reduce its political independence. The same will also be true if its barriers to trade are lowered, increasing its economic links with other countries. The effectiveness of the policies pursued by national governments will obviously increase if these trends are reversed.

Whatever the degree of a country's economic sovereignty, the ability of its government to influence economic performance significantly in either short or long run will depend also on its institutional framework. For instance, the parliament (2a) may empower government to discharge specific economic responsibilities—such as the objective of full employment which was incorporated into the US Employment Act of 1946. Alternatively, parliaments may limit the ability of national governments to use a particular policy instrument. West German and Japanese governments were prevented from pursuing an active fiscal policy for twenty years after World War II because the victorious allies insisted that each country should make it obligatory by law for the government to balance its budget (Kaspar 1972; Nakamura 1981).

A highly decentralized form of government, as in Germany and Switzerland, will also limit the ability of *national* authorities to employ an active fiscal policy, forcing them instead to make much greater use of monetary policy. However, even this option may be limited if, as in Germany and the United States, the constitution gives a good deal of autonomy to the central bank, making it largely responsible for the country's monetary policy.

The way that economic institutions are traditionally organized in a country (2b) may make it possible for the government to increase the range of policy instruments at its disposal. Highly centralized forms of wage bargaining, as in Sweden and Austria, enabled the governments to employ incomes policies as an additional, and for a long time very effective, anti-inflationary weapon (Romanis Brown 1975; OECD 1979; Faxen 1982). They were able to do this by participating in the income determination process either directly (Austria) or indirectly (Sweden). A long tradition of co-operation between industry, banks, and government (as in Japan) will enable the government to play an important role in promoting rapid modernization and restructuring of industry (Magaziner and Hout 1980; Dore 1986). The result is a rate of transformation that countries which are in no position to replicate that kind of co-operation find impossible to match.

However, both these instruments (incomes and industrial policies) require more than an appropriate institutional framework to produce the desired results: they need to be supported by a strong national consensus (3a), which is impossible without a high degree of social harmony. In a democracy this is also true of other economic policies and objectives, though not to the same degree. No matter how imaginative or theoretically sound a particular course of action may seem, it is bound to fail unless there is widespread national support for it. In other words, whatever a country's economic potential, serious social division and the political instability that normally accompanies it will ensure that its rate of economc progress lags markedly behind that of the nations with a more favourable socio-political environment, even though the latter may be at a considerable disadvantage in terms of natural resources. The remarkable success of Japan, and the equally remarkable failure of countries such as Argentina and Brazil to realize their potential provide classic examples of this kind.

Achieving a national consensus is never an easy task, especially in the absence of obvious external threats. The more remote or unlikely the threats are the less urgent it becomes to resolve internal conflicts between sectional interests and, consequently, the more difficult it is to mobilize the consensus for a course of action which is for the benefit of the country as a whole.

The problem becomes even more acute at the international level (3b). Yet a 'harmony of interests' between countries is essential when their economies become integrated and interdependent. The higher the degree of interdependence the more difficult it is for the government of one country to achieve its national objectives unless the governments of the other countries are prepared to co-operate. They are more likely to do so if their national problems and priorities are the same than if they differ.

However, even in the latter case, there are bound to remain serious limits to such co-operation—set by differences in national constitutions, institutional frameworks, history and culture.

As a result, it will not be always easy for governments representing different national interests to agree on the same or similar priorities; and even if they manage to do so, it may not be possible—for reasons mentioned earlier—for them to pursue similar, let alone identical, policies. Realistically, therefore, the co-operation may not extend in practice beyond the pursuit of *compatible* policies.

In the same way that individual economic policies are not applicable to the same extent in all countries—no economic policy or policy mix can be expected to be equally effective in both the short and the long run within the same country. The economic and social characteristics of countries change over time; and, as a result, priorities and policy mixes have to be altered to reflect these new conditions and needs (4a and 4b). In most cases, it is the very success of a particular economic strategy that will make it essential to adopt new objectives and policies. That, in turn, may require new institutions. The success or failure of individual economies is largely determined by the ease with which their institutions and policies can be adapted to the new realities and problems.

In other words, economic and institutional dynamics are closely related and will, therefore, progress and stagnate together. As the peaceful transformation of increasingly outdated outlooks and institutions is more difficult the more entrenched they become (Olson 1982), it is not surprising that countries often rediscover their economic dynamics after losing a major war which discredits the old institutions and practices.

Finally, the scope and ultimate success of an economic strategy will depend on the conditions described earlier (5a) and on the ability, inventiveness, and political skills of those in power (5b)—with the former usually as the dominant factor. A government whose involvement in economic management of the country is strictly limited by law or external factors is unlikely to achieve much, no matter how skilful and able its members may be.

Consequently, what a government can do and the ability of those doing it will tend to be closely related. The more important and effective is the role that national government can play in the economic life of the country, the more likely is it to attract people of high calibre, both at the political and the administrative level. This will be particularly true when economic policy is accorded a key role—exercising a major influence on virtually all aspects of government. In contrast, decline in the ability of governments to achieve economic and, through them, other important objectives will lead to frustration, a fall in the prestige with which government employment is held, and an exodus of able politicians and civil servants. Their successors are then increasingly regarded as second- and third-rate opportunists of limited ability, even less understanding of the complex issues confronting them, and little or no feeling of social responsibility.

This explains the often observed paradox that a country is least likely to have a government of high calibre precisely at the time when it needs it most, for the simple reason that its ablest people will prefer other occupations which provide them with a much greater opportunity to use fully their professional, organizational, and executive talents. Only an exceptional crisis, such as war, makes it possible to alter this imbalance by giving government the power to mobilize these people to work in the national interest.

In conclusion, some governments are more successful than others mainly because they operate in conditions that make it easier for them to discharge their responsibilities effectively and to general satisfaction—assisted by the fact that it is these very conditions that will attract people of high calibre who will then use them to full effect. Virtuous and vicious circles are as common here as in most areas of human activity.

THE SUCCESS OF GOVERNMENT ECONOMIC POLICIES BEFORE 1973

Whatever else we may disagree about, no serious economist or economic historian would dispute the fact that, as Table 3.2 shows, economic performance of the most advanced industrial economies was between 1950 and 1973 quite unique historically. (See also Rostow 1978, Maddison 1989 and 1991.) Rates of growth of output, productivity, investment, and trade were markedly higher and more stable than during any comparable period since the beginning of the Industrial Revolution. At the same time, unemployment levels were considerably lower than either before World War II or since 1973. The average rate of inflation, at 4.2 per cent, though higher than in the interwar period, was low compared with that recorded subsequently—with many countries achieving remarkable price stability. In addition, although some of them experienced crises, no country had persistent difficulty in balancing its current external accounts. Finally, available evidence indicates a clear reduction in income and wealth inequalities during the period, both within and between the countries (Atkinson 1973 and 1975; Sawyer 1976 and 1982; Panić 1988)—a trend that has been reversed significantly since the early 1980s (Atkinson 1991; Taylor 1992).

Unlike the statistical record, which is unambiguous, the underlying causes are difficult to disentangle, let alone quantify, so that the economic performance of the industrial countries between 1950 and 1973 is subject to different interpretations. However, most experts would probably agree on a list containing the following: post-war recovery; the movement of labour from agriculture and other sectors of the economy where

Table 3.2 Long-term economic performance of sixteen leading industrial countries

Annual averages, per cent

	Growth of GDP	Amplitude of recessions in total output[a]	Growth of GDP per man-hour	Average rate of unemployment	Average rate of inflation (consumer prices)	Growth of non-residential fixed capital	Growth of exports (volume)	Current account balance as % of GDP at current prices
1870–1913	2.5	−5.6	1.7	n.a.	n.a.	3.4	3.9	n.a.
1920–38	2.2	−12.4	1.9[b]	7.5	−0.6	2.0[b]	1.0	n.a.
1950–73	4.9	0.2	4.5	2.6	4.2	5.8	8.6	−0.2[c]
1973–89	2.6	−1.8	2.3	5.7	7.5	4.2	4.7	−1.1
1974–81	2.4	—	1.9	4.6	10.0	—	—	−2.0
1982–89	3.2	—	2.4	6.8	5.0	—	—	−0.1

[a] Maximum peak—through fall in GDP or lowest rise (annual data).
[b] 1913–50.
[c] 1961–73.

Source: Maddison (1989: 50, 51, 75, 87, 113, 118, 170, 171, and 186).

productivity was low to those where it was high; liberalization of trade which stimulated international specialization and, in doing so, accelerated growth by increasing opportunities to exploit economies of scale; a backlog of technical inventions and innovations accumulated during the interwar and war years; low commodity prices, including those of petroleum, which encouraged worldwide substitution of oil for other primary sources of energy; and the international financial stability provided by the Bretton Woods System which, through the regime of fixed exchange rates, acted as an important external constraint on domestic inflationary pressures.

There is little doubt that all these factors made an important contribution to the extraordinary economic performance of the advanced industrial economies between 1950 and 1973. But can they really account for all of it?

The problem is that most of them were also present in the other three periods shown in Table 3.2 (1870–1913, 1920–38, and 1973–89). For instance, there have been important opportunities in each of the three periods to 'embody' technical change in new investment, to catch up with the leading industrial country of the time, and to provide employment for a sizeable proportion of the labour force made redundant by structural changes. Moreover, before 1914 the classical Gold Standard made even less allowance for inflationary indiscipline than did the Bretton Woods system half a century later. The period of floating exchange rates since 1973 has been much less demanding in this respect. Nevertheless, many of the countries in Maddison's sample have been members of the European Exchange Rate Mechanism since 1979, fixing their exchange rates to each other's currencies either officially or by 'shadowing' the Deutschmark. As for barriers to trade and capital flows, the 1930s are the only decade during the three periods when such polices became a serious obstacle to international specialization and exchange. Finally, although sharp increases in primary commodity prices in the 1970s, above all the two oil crises, gave a major structural shock to the international economic system, commodity prices presented no greater problem before World War II or after the early 1980s than they did between 1950 and 1973.

The one factor that is missing from the list given so far, and one which also happens to be unique to the 1950s and 1960s, is that of deliberate peacetime control and macroeconomic management of the highly industrialized economies by their governments—designed specifically to achieve certain clearly defined national objectives. The success with which this was done varied from economy to economy. Moreover, whatever the degree of success, it would obviously be wrong to attribute it entirely to government action. Modern economies are too complex for their performance to be explained in terms of one factor, or by the actions of one economic agent.

Nevertheless, the importance of the role played by national governments during the period 1950–73 cannot be denied. For instance, Samuelson (1967: 581) captured the general feeling of confidence in the ability of governments to deal with major economic problems which existed in the 1960s when he reassured would-be economists that: 'By proper use of monetary and fiscal policies, nations to-day can successfully fight off the plague of mass unemployment and the plague of inflation.' Almost a quarter of a century later, Maddison (1991: 173) was even more explicit in attributing the exceptionally rapid, widely diffused improvements in economic welfare between 1950 and 1973 to government action based on a 'clear bias in favour of growth and employment, the lowered attention to risks of price increases or payments difficulties, and the absence of crassly perverse deflationary policies', as his historical analysis led him to single out these aspects of national economic management as 'the most important features differentiating post-war from prewar domestic policy'.

In contrast, there has been growing discontent with government economic performance since the early 1970s, reflected in an increase in political instability in most industrial countries. Can this be explained by changes that have taken place since the 1960s in the conditions listed in Table 3.1?

One conclusion which emerges clearly from even the most cursory reading of post-war economic history is that national governments enjoyed considerable control over their economies in 1945 (cf. Chester 1951; Maddison 1964; Cairncross 1985; Milward 1987a). Many of the controls were not dissimilar to those introduced during World War I. The difference was that on this occasion they and the administrative apparatus that enforced them were dismantled only gradually—a completely different approach to that adopted after 1918 (see, for instance, Lowe 1978).

An important consequence of this was that after 1945 the industrialized countries enjoyed a considerable degree of economic sovereignty—mainly thanks to the strict restrictions on trade and capital flows. With the exception of a few countries (West Germany, Japan, and Austria) in the early post-war period, there was no significant change in the ability of national governments in the industrial countries to act independently, despite some limitations on their actions imposed by membership of various international organizations. West Germany apart, there was also little change in size of the countries. Hence, it was their greater control over economic links with the outside world that was largely responsible for the ability of national governments to manage their economies without foreign interference. For although committed to a more liberal trading system, few governments were in a hurry to implement it until they were confident that lower trade barriers would not prevent them from achieving their major economic objectives. Quotas were phased out during the 1950s and tariffs reduced significantly only in the second half of the 1960s. But exchange and other controls on capital flows in many cases remained in force until the 1980s (cf. Maizels 1963; OECD 1985; Swoboda 1976; Germany and Morton 1985; Walter 1993).

The ability of West European countries and Japan to act independently was not diminished by their heavy reliance on the United States for post-war reconstruction (Milward 1987a; Panić 1991). The reason for this was that the aid generously provided by the Americans determined the speed of the post-war reconstruction and minimized its social cost. But the United States did not interfere with the character of the economic policies pursued by these countries, or insist on imposing a rigid timetable on them (Panić 1991). Hence, it was the actions of national governments that determined the pace of the reintegration of these countries into the world economy as well as the policy mixes that they adopted domestically.

Moreover, where necessary, institutional frameworks were changed to enable the governments to acquire greater control over the stability and growth of their economies. In the United Kingdom and France a number of sectors and firms were nationalized, giving their governments direct control over decisions concerning output, investment, employment, prices, and wages; and in Italy the size of the public sector, already large, was increased further (Robson 1960; Einaudi et al. 1955). France, the Netherlands, and Norway, all with highly centralized policy-making institutions, were able to resort to indicative planning of a kind unique in market economies (cf. Cohen 1969; UN 1965). Sweden, Austria, and the Netherlands, as already mentioned, developed highly centralized systems of wage bargaining which enabled them to pursue incomes policies that were the envy of other countries. In the mid-1960s, West Germany and Japan changed their 'stabilization laws', enabling their governments to engage in more active fiscal policies (Kaspar 1972; Nakamura 1981). All these governments were also empowered to reintroduce or tighten certain measures if these were required to deal with a particular problem. Thus in the 1960s most industrial countries brought back exchange controls on short-term capital movements, or tightened those already in existence, in order to reduce the pressure of speculative flows on their exchange rates (Swoboda 1976).

The main reason that governments were able to retain such wide-ranging powers in peacetime was the consensus in favour of active government involvement in national economic management that developed during World War II. The collapse of largely unregulated market economies in the 1930s—causing massive unemployment, social unrest, the rise of political extremism, and, ultimately, the most destructive global war in history—produced a widely based consensus that economic failure on such a scale could not be allowed to happen again (cf. Polanyi 1944; Horsefield 1969; Milward 1987b; Van Dormael 1978). To avoid it, general economic welfare had to be maintained and, if possible, improved; and the only economic entity with command over sufficiently large resources to help achieve such an objective was the state.

Hence, throughout the industrialized world, governments of different political complexions accepted the responsibility of managing their economies in order to achieve a number of important objectives. Among these, five were given particular prominence: full employment; a satisfactory rate of growth (i.e. the rate needed to sustain a high level of employment in the long run); price stability; external—current account—balance (partly to allow each country the freedom to pursue its domestic objectives without foreign interference and partly to avoid the adverse effects of external imbalances on growth, employment, and price stability); and an equitable distribution of income (to ensure the consensus without which the other objectives could not be reconciled in a democracy). (Cf. Kirschen 1974; Maddison 1964; Boltho 1982.)

The fact that all these countries were committed to the same objectives meant that the consensus was not only national but also international. The desire to work towards the same goal was reinforced by two important factors: the cold war which compelled powerful vested interests in the industrialized world to co-operate in order to protect the existing economic and political systems on which their wealth, influence, and power depended; and the clear division between countries such as those in Western Europe and Japan, that needed urgently to rebuild their economies and societies, and the few countries in North America and Oceania—dominated by the United States—that were in a position to help them. Consequently, so long as the Americans were willing to provide the necessary assistance, there was no danger that the key economies would follow different objectives, thus making it impossible for any one of them, and economies dependent on them, to achieve their economic and social goals.

However, although the objectives were the same, the emphasis given to any one of them varied from country to country, determined by the nature of the problems confronting them. An important characteristic of economic policy in the industrialized countries in the early post-war period was the extent to which, as Myrdal (1960) observed at the time, it was guided by their needs rather than by the ideological preferences of those in power. Thus, exceptionally rapid growth and the threat of overheating made it necessary for West Germany to give high priority to price stability (Hardach 1976; Hennings 1982). In contrast, the experience of social divisions and political instability—held responsible for the country's rapid collapse in 1914 and 1939—led French governments to pay less attention to inflation and given high priority to economic growth in the hope that it would produce greater social harmony (Sautter 1982). The United Kingdom was unique among the industrial countries in experiencing frequent balance of payments problems and currency crises (Dow 1964; Blackaby 1978), both in effect self-imposed, as the country desperately insisted on continuing to play a major military and financial role on the world scene despite its apparent lack of the required resources. Nevertheless, although the emphasis varied, the basic objectives remained the same in all these countries.

At the same time, economic policies differed, often appreciably, reflecting differences in the countries' institutions and the degree of social harmony and political consensus. The United Kingdom, Sweden, and Austria—all with strong central relative to regional authorities—made active use of demand management, with monetary policy playing a subordinate role to fiscal measures. West Germany and Switzerland, both with strong regional authorities, relied much more on monetary policy. In all these, as in the other cases, the exact policy instruments varied from country to country (Maddison 1964; Boltho 1982). As already mentioned, Japan pursued a uniquely active and successful industrial policy. West Germany lacked the institutional set-up, or indeed the need, to replicate the Japanese model. But its government had sufficient authority and enough policy instruments to play an important role in influencing the volume and pattern of private investment, helping to remove bottlenecks in a number of key sectors with remarkable speed (Roskamp 1965). Direct government involvement in investment allocation was even greater in France where the state owned large financial intermediaries, enabling it to channel their investment funds into the sectors given high priority by the planners (Sheahan 1963; Cohen 1969; Adams and Stoffaes 1986). Finally, although all the countries greatly improved their welfare provisions, they were much more extensive and generous in Western Europe than elsewhere (Wilensky 1975; Sawyer 1982). This was especially true of the countries that had to rebuild their social harmony and political consensus, both shattered by the war. Many of them were also vulnerable to the threat posed by the cold war because of their geographic proximity to the Soviet bloc.

Lastly, the war and the apparent success of these policies enabled the state in all these countries to attract politicians and technocrats of high calibre. Many of them had lived through the horrors of the two world wars and the Great Depression. As a result, they were determined—irrespective of their ideological preferences—not to allow something similar to happen again; and the best way to ensure this was to create economic and social conditions that would make a repetition of such events virtually impossible. Equally important, the close links between government, industry, the financial sector, and labour unions developed during the war provided those in positions of responsibility in all these sectors with experience of working together towards a common objective (Milward 1987b). The need for co-operation diminished once the war was over. But the cold war ensured that the ties would continue to be cultivated and the government allowed to co-ordinate national economic activity through macroeconomic policies.

As usual, it was the extraordinary success of all these institutional adaptations and policies, as well as the passage of time, that altered the basic conditions under which the governments of industrial countries operate. In the process, the changes have made it much more difficult for governments

to cope at the *national* level with the shocks that have altered the character
and performance of the world economy since the early 1970s.

WHAT HAS GONE WRONG SINCE 1973?

It is clear from Table 3.2 that the economic performance of the most
advanced industrial countries has been far less impressive since 1973 than
during the preceding twenty-five years. The difference would be even more
pronounced if the latter period included the early 1990s. Contrary to what
one might expect from countries at this level of development (Panić 1988),
all of them have been struggling continuously, and in most cases unsuccess-
fully, to reconcile their internal and external balances—in other words, to
achieve all the major policy objectives simultaneously. Following the preceding analysis, the question which immediately poses itself is: what has
prevented governments of these countries from promoting economic stability and progress since the early 1970s as successfully as they managed to
do in the early post-war period?

The best way to answer this question is again to analyse changes in the
factors (listed in Table 3.1) that determine the effectiveness of government
policies.

The first important change to note is the extent to which *national* economic sovereignty has weakened over the period. This has had nothing to do
with the political status (1*a*) or size of the countries (1*b*), as both were the
same in 1989 as in 1950. The changes—caused partly by deliberate government decisions and partly by developments at industry and firm level
which were frequently contrary to government wishes and policies—have
thus come entirely from the opening up of national economies and,
consequently, from the growing dependence of individual economies on
the actions of governments and economic agents operating outside their
borders (1*c*).

The need for greater international economic co-operation in order to
avoid a repetition of the interwar experience, to which those participating at
the Bretton Woods conference committed themselves in 1944, and the
success in achieving full employment and the other objectives after the
war—encouraged the governments of industrial countries to liberalize first
international trade and then capital flows, with the most successful economies, as one would expect, in the forefront of initiating these changes.

Thus, in the late 1940s, when it dominated the world economy, the
United States, normally one of the most protectionist countries (see Panić
1990), unilaterally reduced its duties on imports (Anderson 1972). Moreover, the dollar was the only major currency to be fully convertible. Other
industrial countries abolished most quantitative controls and reduced
some tariffs in the 1950s—with the successful economies, such as those of

West Germany and Switzerland, leading the way (Patterson 1966; Morgan 1971). By the end of 1958, West European countries were confident enough to allow convertibility of their currencies for current account transactions—a step for which Japan did not feel ready until the mid-1960s.

The process accelerated in the 1960s and early 1970s with worldwide reductions in tariffs under the Dillon, Kennedy, and Tokyo Rounds. In addition, there was regional liberalization of trade in Western Europe, following the formation of the European Economic Community and the European Free Trade Association. Consequently, although there was some increase in non-tariff barriers to trade in the 1970s, levels of protection in international trade are probably lower now than at any time since the middle of the nineteenth century (cf. Bairoch 1989; Panić 1990; OECD 1985). The same is not true of controls on capital flows—though most of these were either reduced or abolished in industrial countries in the 1970s and 1980s (see Germany and Morton 1985; Bryant 1987). The two oil shocks made this necessary, in order to finance the large current account deficits, a process that intensified with the election of governments committed to economic deregulation, both national and international.

This liberalization also produced important innovations in international finance (Bank for International Settlements 1986, Eiteman and Stonehill 1989) which expanded the volume of transactions even further. For instance, the combined share of exports and imports in GDP was significantly higher in the 1980s than in the 1960s even in the three largest industrial economies, as the following figures show (average percentage shares per decade, with the 1960s figures in brackets): United States 19 (10), Japan 24 (19), West Germany 56 (36) (EC, *European Economy*, December 1990). With the exception of Japan, the extent of international specialization and exchange has become particularly large in manufacturing. This can be seen by comparing import penetration (imports as a percentage of manufacturing value added at current prices) in the largest industrial economies in 1960 and 1987 (with the former figures in brackets): United Kingdom 72 (16), West Germany 43 (25), United States 35 (5), and Japan 10 (8) (Walter 1993: 232). As all these shares are normally higher in smaller economies, it is not surprising that by 1990 the annual value of world trade had risen to over $5 trillion, roughly comparable to the size of US GDP in that year (ibid. 196).

The growth of international financial markets has been even more remarkable. For example, in 1964 the value of gross deposits (i.e. including inter-bank deposits) on Eurocurrency markets was $19 billion, rising to $86 billion in 1970. Ten years later, in 1980, it stood at $1,574 billion, with a further, almost three-fold increase over the next seven years to $4,509 billion in 1987 (Pilbeam 1992: 312). Daily turnover on world foreign exchange markets was estimated at $1 trillion at the end of the 1980s—

considerably greater than the combined foreign exchange reserves of central banks which amounted to $800 billion (Walter 1993: 197 and 198).

Moreover, a high proportion of international transactions is controlled by a relatively small number of transnational corporations and financial institutions (United Nations 1981 and 1988)—with a good deal of it taking place, in fact, *within* the transnationals (TNEs). Thus, it has been estimated that intra-firm trade of the world's 350 largest TNEs accounts for no less than 40 per cent of world trade (World Bank 1992: 33). This, plus the growing importance of joint ventures even among the giant TNEs, makes it increasingly difficult to disentangle who exactly is producing a particular product and how much of it originates in any one country.

All these changes have invariably reduced the scope for unilateral government measures by increasing the degree of uncertainty associated with any particular course of action. Unlike in the early post-war period, the outcome now depends on the reactions of a large number of powerful decision-making entities, governments, and TNEs, many of them with different problems and objectives. As a result, uncertainty, never absent from economic activity, has grown to the point where it stifles investment and growth, giving rise to permanently underutilized productive capacity and high levels of unemployment. Events since the early 1970s have shown the extent to which even the economic sovereignty of the United States has been eroded by the opening up of national economies.

At the root of all these difficulties is the fact that the rapid increase in international economic integration and interdependence has made the existing institutional framework inadequate for dealing satisfactorily with problems most of which are now international in character. Under these conditions, no government is in a position to react effectively to unfavourable developments, irrespective of the range of policy instruments at its disposal, for the simple reason that in many cases they originate outside the area of its jurisdiction.

That leaves four options for adjusting the existing institutional framework to the new economic environment. They have all been tried since the early 1970s—hesitantly, cautiously, and therefore not very successfully.

The first option consists of reversing the process of international integration by insulating individual economies—a precondition for enabling national governments to engage actively in economic management, as they did after the World War II. Selective attempts were made in this direction in the 1970s and 1980s, with the governments of industrial countries employing for the purpose non-tariff barriers to trade (Page 1979, OECD 1985) and competitive devaluations. However, international production, distribution, and financial networks are too interwoven and complex now for industrial countries to risk economic warfare of the kind that became common in the 1930s. As for devaluations, Table 3.3 shows that the economic performance of those countries which resorted to them

Table 3.3 Exchange rate changes and overall economic performance of selected industrial countries, 1976–1989

	Effective exchange rate changes (%)[a]		Annual averages (%)				Growth of the volume of trade in goods and services	
	Nominal	Real[b]	Growth of GDP	Unemployment rates	Inflation rates	Current balance balance of payments as % of GDP	Exports	Imports
Japan	130.1	0.3	4.2	2.4	3.5	1.7	7.1	5.2
West Germany	52.4	−6.5	2.3	4.9	3.2	1.7	5.2	4.5
Switzerland	50.4	6.5	2.0	0.5	3.0	4.2	4.3	3.0
Austria	31.6	−19.1	2.4	2.7	4.3	−0.9	5.9	4.3
UK	−7.7	25.7	2.5	8.3	8.9	−0.1	3.6	8.9
France	−11.2	−0.8	2.6	8.0	8.0	−0.4	4.7	8.0
USA	−12.3	12.1	3.0	7.1	6.0	−1.4	5.4	6.0
Sweden	−31.4	−8.8	1.8	2.0	9.1	−1.4	4.2	9.1

[a] Appreciation = +; Depreciation = −.
[b] Nominal exchange rates adjusted for changes in relative export prices.
Sources: IMF, *International Financial Statistics* and OECD, *Economic Outlook*.

was not superior in the long term to that of countries whose currencies appreciated.

Secondly, governments can co-operate in such a way that the overall effect of their policies is similar to the one that could be achieved by a supranational economic authority (Panić 1988). However, in practice, this is possible only if their problems, objectives, and institutions are so similar that the chosen policy options can be confidently expected to work with more or less equal effectiveness in all of them. As already emphasized, although they share many characteristics, industrial countries are far from being identical—which explains why their attempts at international co-operation have tended to be short-lived. The existing national differences and the diffusion of economic power have made it very difficult to sustain such initiatives even when national governments are willing to co-ordinate their policies.

Thirdly, economic integration can be accompanied by political integration, with nation states transferring sovereignty to a supranational authority. Although perfectly feasible in theory, no attempt of this kind has produced an outcome in which supranational institutions have been able to discharge their responsibilities as successfully as their national counterparts. The IMF and the World Bank have been of marginal importance in the post-war international system; and it is increasingly unlikely that the even more ambitious attempt to centralize EC institutions, proposed in the Treaty of Maastricht in 1991 (EC Council 1992), will be able in the foreseeable future to overcome the mounting opposition in member countries.

The final option is to deregulate, privatize, and thus let the markets reconcile internal and external balances—in other words, achieve the five major objectives. The problem is that, as already pointed out, it was precisely the failure of unregulated markets to achieve this in the interwar period that produced in the 1940s the international consensus in favour of greater state involvement in economic management. There is little doubt that Keynes was speaking for most of his contemporaries when he expressed the view that: 'To suppose that there exists some smoothly functioning automatic mechanism of adjustment which preserves equilibrium if only we trust to methods of *laissez faire* is a doctrinaire delusion which disregards the lessons of historical experience without having behind it the support of sound theory' (quoted in Van Dormael 1978: 32). It is no accident that the economies of the United States and the United Kingdom which have gone furthest along this road since the 1970s have also experienced serious economic decline relative to the rest of the industrialized world.

The main reason that it has proved so difficult to create the right kind of institutional framework is the breakdown of both national and international consensuses since 1973.

The early post-war period achieved conditions which were, basically, conducive to greater social harmony: as a result of rapid economic growth and full employment, the standard of living of the less well off sections of the population in the industrialized countries could be improved significantly without making the rest worse off. This factor, the fear of a repetition of what had happened in the 1930s and 1940s, and the cold war enabled the newly created welfare state to undertake a major redistribution of income which, in turn, ensured widespread support for the economic system and the policies that made it function so successfully.

In contrast, the slowing down in economic growth after the first oil shock in 1973, the sharp increases in unemployment, and the historically unprecedented peacetime inflation rates brought with them a return of 'zero-sum' economic preoccupations and behaviour, and the inevitable weakening of social cohesion that such behaviour brings about. The second oil shock simply accentuated these tendencies.

Unemployment affects different occupational groups, sectors, and regions unequally, as does an accelerating inflation rate. The internal disequilibrium caused by the first oil shock, and its persistence, were bound, therefore, to lead sooner or later to a breakdown in the national consensus built up after the war. Some groups began to favour deflationary policies because they were in their interest and others continued to support expansionary policies either for the same reason (see Frieden 1991) or because they were concerned about the social and political effects of economic stagnation. This division was exacerbated by internal deregulation and external liberalization, as they intensified the conflict of interest between capital (which became highly mobile internationally and, consequently, less concerned with the long-term effects of its actions on any one country) and labour (which remained largely immobile internationally, with its well-being, therefore, closely tied to economic, social, and political developments in its country of residence). As a result, there has tended to be a sharp division of opinion since the early 1970s in many countries between the priorities and policies advocated by employers' associations and those favoured by the labour unions.

The apparent dependence of their economies on TNEs, and the realization that these corporate entities feel no particular allegiance to any one country, has forced governments to give their owners and managers tax concessions and subsidies in order to make it less attractive for them to move elsewhere (Reich 1991). Those aspiring to political power have also increasingly had to buy support by promising to ease the tax burden of those in employment. This has opened up further divisions in society by making it difficult for the state to provide adequate welfare for the growing number of elderly, unemployed, and poor, or to cope with the rapidly growing demand on the social services and the law-enforcing agencies created by the adverse effect of greater economic and social inequalities on health and crime (Patrick and Scambler 1986; Burchell 1992; Field 1990).

Not all industrial countries have experienced these problems to anything like the same extent. This explains why Japan and a number of small states in Western Europe have managed to cope remarkably well since the early 1970s with the energy and other crises by using a combination of industrial, incomes, and social policies made possible by their strong social and political consensuses (cf. Pekkarinen et al. 1992; McCallum 1983 and 1986). Elsewhere, governments have had little success in mobilizing a broadly based national support in favour of the institutions, objectives, and policies required to solve their countries' economic and social problems— especially as the easing of cold war tensions in the 1970s and 1980s removed the only serious external threat to the prevailing socio-economic order.

This last factor has also made it very difficult to recreate the international consensus which contributed so much to post-war economic recovery. However, although important, this was by no means the only development that weakened the readiness of industrial countries to work towards the same objectives.

The demise of the Bretton Woods system encouraged governments to ignore the interdependence of their economies and pursue 'independent' macroeconomic policies in the belief that the floating exchange rates would enable them to reconcile their internal and external balances. It did not take long for at least one of the advocates of this policy approach to describe the whole idea as 'a chimera' (Kaldor 1978). Nevertheless, so long as they are confronted with serious economic problems and there are no international mechanisms for solving them collectively, governments under pressure will tend to resort to policy instruments which, although incapable of producing permanent solutions, will at least make the problems manageable in the short run.

The tendency to do this has not been helped by the fact that there have been important differences in the kinds of difficulty experienced by both large and small countries, with no country in the position which enabled the United States after World War II to secure international consensus and manage the system (Panić 1988; Walter 1993).

For instance, some countries have been earning persistent and fairly large surpluses on their current balances of payments since the early 1970s (Japan, West Germany, Switzerland, and the Netherlands), making it less necessary for them to frame their policies in accordance with the require-ments of foreign and domestic capital. Others (the United States, the United Kingdom, France, and Sweden) have had to do precisely that for most of the period because of their persistent current account deficits. There has also been a similar divergence of experience concerning countries' internal disequilibria—with some of them maintaining low unemployment thanks to the flexibility of their institutions and policies (Japan, Norway, and Sweden) and others because they were able to pass the problem on to other nations by sending back immigrant workers (West Germany, Switzerland, and Austria). At the same time, many industrial countries have had to cope with high and rising unemployment (Italy, the United Kingdom, Canada, and Belgium).

With no country in a dominant position, it is virtually impossible to agree on a common course of action, or to be confident that, if agreed, it will be followed for long by all those who approved it.

It is clearly difficult to avoid such an outcome when industrial countries—including the key members of the international economic community—are experiencing different problems, as this will influence their priorities which, in turn, will determine their choice of policies.

After the war, when, with a few exceptions, most industrial countries were confronted with similar difficulties, it was relatively easy for them to agree on a common course of action. With time, the unequal success in achieving the objectives that they set themselves made it necessary for individual countries to alter their priorities in a way that was consistent with the new problems. The two oil crises sharpened these divisions as, suddenly, it became much more difficult for every single industrial country to achieve any one of its major aims of economic policy.

Thus, the governments of the United Kingdom, Sweden, and Italy, alarmed by the levels of unemployment that could result from the first oil crisis, reacted to it by attempting to avoid deflation, arguing, not unreasonably, that short-term stabilization measures were inappropriate to deal with a problem that was clearly of a long-term structural nature. The United States, in the grip of the monetarist counter-revolution, and West Germany and Japan, with low unemployment levels for reasons described above, took exactly the opposite view and introduced deflationary policies. The response to the second oil crisis was no more harmonious. For instance, the newly elected socialist government in France gave high priority to faster growth and lower unemployment, while the new conservative governments in the United Kingdom and the United States were determined to ignore all other objectives in order to achieve the single goal of a low and stable rate of inflation (cf. Ross et al. 1987; Michie 1992; Stockman 1985).

Unfortunately for the industrialized countries and the world economy, these differences have become pronounced precisely at a time when they are likely to inflict maximum damage on all concerned.

The extraordinary international harmony of interests in the early post-war period occurred at a time when, because of their relatively high degree of insularity, most industrial countries could have set themselves economic objectives that were radically different from those pursued by the rest of the world. It would, no doubt, have taken longer to get there and the outcome would have been less impressive than the one they actually achieved.

Nevertheless, there was a reasonable chance that they would have improved their standard of living by pursuing an independent course of action. That, after all, is what happened in centrally planned economies. In contrast, with their economies open and closely linked to those of other countries, it is now virtually impossible for an industrial country to adopt a radically different, independent macroeconomic policy stance for long without experiencing serious welfare losses. As a result, even governments of medium and large economies have been forced to reverse their policies for reasons such as: a socially and politically dangerous level of unemployment (the United Kingdom), sharply rising inflation rates (Italy and France), and an unsustainable increase in external indebtedness incurred in order to finance current account deficits (the United States).

At the same time, it is both too easy and misleading to exaggerate the impotence of governments by focusing exclusively on macroeconomic policies and *national* governments. After all, regions within individual countries differ, often significantly, in the nature of their economic problems and priorities and have even less scope for independent macroeconomic policies than do the national governments of countries with open economies. Nevertheless, a combination of industrial and regional policies, pursued jointly by national and regional governments, played a major role in enabling industrial countries to achieve their remarkable successes after World War II (Nicol and Yuill 1982; Armstrong and Taylor 1985). International integration does not diminish the ability of regional governments to pursue polices which are normally within their domain. In fact, as Japan, Austria, and Sweden have shown, it need not necessarily reduce the capacity of national governments to promote highly successful industrial and incomes policies.

However, economic and political developments since the early 1970s have combined in most countries to create a serious obstacle to the successful application of such policies in the absence of closer international collaboration.

There are, basically, three reasons for this. First, as already mentioned, the breakdown of national consensuses has made it extremely difficult for political parties to be elected to power unless they commit themselves to a policy of low taxation. Consequently, once elected, national governments have tended to find that they have inadequate resources to promote major industrial and regional adjustments without foreign borrowing. The greater the need for external funds the higher will be the cost of raising them (as the risk premiums will go up). That is bound to set a limit to the adjustment process, unless the country or region in question can attract official transfers from either foreign governments or, more likely, supranational institutions. As experience within the European Community shows, the need for external assistance is likely to be particularly serious in the countries and regions where the need for adjustment is greatest.

Secondly, given the extent to which they dominate international production and trade, a successful application of industrial and regional policies increasingly requires the active co-operation of TNEs. The problem is that the objective of these corporations is to maximize their shareholders' income, and not to assist any one country to achieve its objectives. Indeed, if they are to operate internationally without interference from national governments they cannot afford to appear to make their decisions on the basis of anything other than purely commercial criteria. The result has been an increase in competitive bidding for their investment, involving national and regional authorities, which has raised the cost of attracting TNEs—working, again, to the advantage of wealthier regions and countries (Reich 1991).

Finally, international agreements, such as the Single Europe Act, are making it increasingly difficult for national governments within the European Community to assist their industries and regions (EC Commission 1991). The intention is that industrial and regional policies should be administered by regional and supranational authorities, with the EC Commission in the latter role. There is much to be said in favour of this idea, as the preceding analysis shows, except that member governments have never given the Commission sufficient resources to play such a role effectively (EC Commission 1977; Kowalski 1989; Jacquemin 1984).

Hence, as in the case of macroeconomic policies, the national governments of industrial countries have introduced institutional changes which deprive them increasingly of adequate policy instruments at the microeconomic level. Not surprisingly, in the absence of an alternative authority to take over the task of allocator and co-ordinator of last resort, economic failure, social problems, and political instability are on the increase in most of these countries, with the esteem in which governments and politicians in general are held at unusually low levels.

This is not difficult to understand. The objective of improving national well-being was adopted slowly by governments from the middle of the nineteenth century as a result of the growth of democratic ideas and institutions. The inability of governments to ensure this objective becomes, therefore, a direct threat to these institutions which is why—with their experience of the rise of political extremism in the interwar period—politicians of different ideological persuasion attached so much importance after 1945 to achieving the five economic objectives listed above. In other words, governments of both the left and the right realized that if their countries were to avoid the horrors of the 1930s and 1940s they had to pursue policies that were in the national rather than in any purely sectional interest. Given the inherent inequalities of wealth, influence, and power in modern industrial societies, the state had to step in to achieve these objectives, since, given their past performance, sectional interests could not be trusted to act for the good of all.

The problem is even more acute now with the opening up of national economies and the growth of TNEs in every tradable sector. For instance, a policy of lower taxes may, as intended, increase the volume of savings. However, there is no guarantee that these savings will be invested in the country, raising its rate of growth and employment. Hence, contrary to government expectations, the result may be a deterioration in the country's economic performance, government revenues, and the quality of essential social services, thus increasing political dissatisfaction and instability. Emasculating labour unions in order to reduce wage levels and thus attract TNEs by promising to raise their profits is likely to have a similar effect in the long run. TNEs tend to operate predominantly in prosperous countries with a record of social and political stability.

As these are precisely the policies that governments in many industrial countries have been adopting since the early 1980s, it is hardly surprising that the voters have been turning away from the established parties (cf. Mackee and Rose 1991; Taylor 1992). This may not pose a serious threat at the moment to existing institutions and social order. But German experience in the early 1930s shows how quickly economic failure can be translated into a massive support for an extremist national party. (See Mackee and Rose 1991; and, also, Moore 1967.)

CONCLUSION

The institutional framework that defines the nature of an economic system, its *modus operandi*, is determined by the state. This is as true of *laissez faire* as of the most rigid form of central planning. To the extent that economic performance is influenced by the institutional framework (i.e. the way that economic relationships and processes are defined and organized), other things being equal, changes for the better or for the worse will be the outcome of state action.

The reforms introduced after 1945 were obviously a major improvement, as they led to the most remarkable period of economic growth and prosperity achieved by the industrial countries since the beginning of the Industrial Revolution. Their strength is that, unlike the changes brought in since 1973, they were designed to deal with the realities and aspirations of the time. National governments can play an active and effective role in relatively closed economies. Open economies, as I have argued elsewhere (Panić 1988), require a different, supranational form of political organization and economic management to satisfy the same aspirations—unless nation states are prepared to risk a return to the economic warfare of the 1930s. The failure of national governments and parliaments to agree on one of these two courses of action has been a major reason why since the early 1970s industrial countries have found it much more difficult than before to achieve their economic objectives.

REFERENCES

ADAMS, W. J., and STOFFAES, C. (eds.) (1986). *French Industrial Policy*. Washington, DC: The Brookings Institution.

ANDERSON, J. E. (1972). 'Effective Protection in the US: A Historical Comparison', *Journal of International Economics* (Feb.).

ARMSTRONG, H. and TAYLOR, J. (1985). *Regional Economics and Policy*. London: Philip Alan.

ATKINSON, A. B. (ed.) (1973). *Wealth, Income and Inequality*. Harmondsworth: Penguin Books.

—— (1975). *The Economics of Inequality*. Oxford: Clarendon Press.

—— (1991). 'What is Happening to the Distribution of Income in the UK?', Keynes lecture presented at the British Academy, mimeo.

BAIROCH, P. (1989). 'European Trade Policy, 1815–1914' in Mathias and Pollard (eds.).

Bank for International Settlements (1986). *Recent Innovations in International Banking*. Basle.

BLACKABY, F. (ed.) (1978). *British Economic Policy 1960–74*. Cambridge: Cambridge University Press.

BOLTHO, A. (ed.) (1982). *The European Economy*. Oxford: Oxford University Press.

BREBNER, J. B. (1962). 'Laissez-Faire and State Intervention in Nineteenth Century Britain' in E. M. Carus-Wilson (ed.), *Essays in Economic History*, iii. London: Edward Arnold.

BRYANT, R. C. (1987). *International Financial Intermediation*. Washington, DC: The Brookings Institution.

BURCHELL, B. (1992). 'Changes in the Labour Market and the Psychological Health of the Nation' in Michie (ed.).

CAIN, P. J. and HOPKINS, A. G. (1980). 'The Political Economy of British Expansion Overseas, 1750–1914', *Economic History Review* (Nov.).

CAIRNCROSS, A. (1985) *Years of Recovery—British Economic Policy 1945–51*. London: Methuen.

CHESTER, D. N. (1951). 'The Central Machinery for Economic Policy' in D. N. Chester (ed.), *Lessons of the British War Economy*. Cambridge: Cambridge University Press.

COHEN, S. S. (1969). *Modern Capitalist Planning—the French Model*. Cambridge, Mass.: Harvard University Press.

DORE, R. (1986). *Structural Adjustment in Japan 1970–82*. Geneva: International Labour Office.

DOW, J. C. R. (1964). *The Management of the British Economy 1945–60*. Cambridge: Cambridge University Press.

EC COMMISSION (1977). *Report of the Study Group on the Role of the Public Finance in European Integration*, 2 vols. Brussels.

—— (1991). 'Fair Competition in the Internal Market: Community State Aid Policy', *European Economy*, Sept.

EC COUNCIL (1992). *Treaty on European Union* ('The Maastricht Treaty'). Luxemburg: Office for Official Publications.

EINAUDI, M., BYE, M., and ROSSI, E. (1955). *Nationalisation in France and Italy*. Ithaca, NY: Cornell University Press.

EITMAN, D. K. and STONEHILL, A. I. (1989). *Multinational Business Finance*, 5th edn. Reading, Mass.: Addison Wesley.

FAXEN K. O. (1982). 'Incomes Policy and Centralised Wage Formation', in Boltho (ed.).

FIELD, S. (1990). *Trends in Crime and their Interpretation*. London: HMSO.

FRIEDEN, J. A. (1991). 'Invested Interests: The Politics of National Economic Policies in a World of Global Finance', *International Organisation* (autumn).

GERMANY, J. D. and MORTON, J. E. (1985). 'Financial Innovation and Deregulation in Foreign Industrial Countries', *Federal Reserve Bulletin* (Oct.).

GERSCHENKRON, A. (1966). *Economic Backwardness in Historical Perspective*. Cambridge, Mass.: Belknap Press of Harvard University Press.

HARDACH, K. (1976). 'Germany 1914–1970' in C. M. Cipolla (ed.), *The Fontana Economic History of Europe*, vi, *Contemporary Economies, Part One*. Glasgow: Collins Fontana Books.

HENNINGS, K. H. (1982). 'West Germany' in Boltho (ed.).

HIRSCHMAN, A. O. (1982). *Shifting Involvements—Private Interest and Public Action*. Princeton: Princeton University Press.

HORSEFIELD, J. K. (1969). *The International Monetary Fund 1945–1965*, iii. Washington, DC: IMF.

JACQUEMIN, A. (ed.) (1984). *European Industry: Public Policy and Corporate Strategy*. Oxford: Clarendon Press.

KALDOR, N. (1978). *Further Essays in Applied Economics*. London: Duckworth.

KASPAR, W. (1972). 'Stabilisation Policies in a Dependent Economy—Lessons from the West German Experience of the 1960s' in E. Claasen and P. Salin (eds.), *Stabilisation Policies in Interdependent Economies*. Amsterdam: North-Holland.

KIRSCHEN, E. S. (ed.) (1974). *Economic Policies Compared*, i, *General Theory*. Amsterdam: North-Holland.

Kowalski, L. (1989). 'Major Current and Future Regional Issues in the Enlarged Community' in L. Albrechts, F. Moulaert, P. Roberts, and E. Swyngedouw (eds.), *Regional Policy at the Crossroads—European Perspectives*. London: Jessica Kingsley.

LOCKWOOD, W. W. (ed.) (1965). *The State and Economic Enterprise in Japan*. Princeton: Princeton University Press.

LOWE, R. (1978). 'The Erosion of State Intervention in Britain, 1917–1924', *Economic History Review* (May).

MACKEE, T. and ROSE, R. (1991). *International Almanac of Electoral History*. London: Macmillan.

MCCALLUM, J. (1983). 'Inflation and Social Consensus in the Seventies', *Economic Journal* (Dec.).

—— (1986). 'Unemployment in OECD Countries in the 1980s', *Economic Journal* (Dec.).

MADDISON, A. (1964). *Economic Growth in the West*. London: Allen and Unwin.

—— (1989). *The World Economy in the 20th Century*. Paris: OECD.

—— (1991). *Dynamic Forces in Capitalist Development*. Oxford: Oxford University Press.

MAGAZINER, I. C. and HOUT, H. M. (1980). *Japanese Industrial Policy*. London: Policy Studies Institute.

MATHIAS, P. and POLLARD, S. (eds.) (1989). *The Cambridge Economic History of*

Europe, viii, *The Industrial Economies: The Development of Economic and Social Policies*. Cambridge: Cambridge University Press.

MAIZELS, A. (1963). *Industrial Growth and World Trade*. Cambridge: Cambridge University Press.

MICHIE, J. (ed.) (1992). *The Economic Legacy 1979–1992*. London: Academic Press.

MILWARD, A. S. (1987*a*). *The Reconstruction of Western Europe 1945–51*. London: Methuen.

—— (1987*b*). *War, Economy and Society 1939–1945*. Harmondsworth, Middlesex: Penguin Books.

—— and SAUL, S. B. (1977). *The Development of the Economies of Continental Europe, 1850–1914*. London: Allen and Unwin.

MOORE, B. (1967). *Social Origins of Dictatorship and Democracy*. Harmondsworth, Middlesex: Penguin Books.

MORGAN, A. D. (1971). 'Imports of Manufactures into the United Kingdom and Other Industrial Countries', *NIESR Economic Review* (May).

MYRDAL, G. (1960). *Beyond the Welfare State*. New Haven: Yale University Press.

NAKAMURA, T. (1981). *The Postwar Japanese Economy—Its Development and Structure*. Tokyo: Tokyo University Press.

NICOL, W. and YUILL, D. (1982). 'Regional Problems and Policy' in Boltho (ed.).

OECD (1979). *Collective Bargaining and Government Policies in Ten OECD Countries*. Paris.

—— (1985). *Costs and Benefits of Protection*. Paris.

OLSON, M. (1982). *The Rise and Decline of Nations*. New Haven: Yale University Press.

OULES, F. (1966). *Economic Planning and Democracy*. Harmondsworth, Middlesex: Penguin Books.

PAGE, S. A. B. (1979). 'The Management of International Trade' in R. Major (ed.), *Britain's Trade and Exchange Rate Policy*. London: Heinemann Educational Books.

PANIĆ, M. (1988). *National Management of the International Economy*. London: Macmillan, and New York: St Martin's Press.

—— (1990). 'Economic Development and Trade Policy', *Department of Applied Economics Working Paper 9006*. University of Cambridge.

—— (1991). 'Managing Reforms in the East European Countries: Lessons from the Postwar Experience of Western Europe', *ECE Discussion Paper no. 3*. New York: United Nations.

—— (1993). 'The Future Role of the State in Eastern Europe' in D. Crabtree and A. P. Thirlwall (eds.), *Keynes and the Role of the State*. London: Macmillan.

PATRICK, D. L. and SCAMBLER, G. (1986). *Sociology as Applied to Medicine*, 2nd edn. London: Baillière, Tindall.

PATTERSON, G. (1966). *Discrimination in International Trade—the Policy Issues 1945–66*. Princeton: Princeton University Press.

PEKKARINEN, J., POHJOLA, M., and ROWTHORN, B. (eds.) (1992). *Social Corporatism— A Superior Economic System?* Oxford: Clarendon Press.

PILBEAM, K. (1992). *International Finance*. London: Macmillan.

POLANYI, K. (1944). *The Great Transformation*. New York: Rinehart.

REICH, R. B. (1991). *The Work of Nations*. London: Simon and Schuster.

ROBSON, W. A. (1960). *National Ownership and Public Industry*. London: Allen and Unwin.

ROMANIS BROWN, A. (1975). 'The Role of Incomes Policy in Industrialised Countries since World War II', *IMF Staff Papers* (Mar.).

ROSKAMP, K. W. (1965). *Capital Formation in West Germany*. Detroit: Wayne State University.

ROSS, G., HOFFMAN, S., and MALZACHER, S. (1987). *The Mitterand Experiment*. Cambridge: Polity Press.

ROSTOW, W. W. (1978). *The World Economy—History and Prospects*. London: Macmillan.

SAMUELSON, P. A. (1967). *Economics—An Introductory Analysis*, 7th edn. New York: McGraw-Hill.

SAUTTER, C. (1982). 'France' in Boltho (ed.).

SAWYER, M. (1976). 'Income Distribution in OECD Countries', *OECD Occasional Studies*, July.

—— (1982). 'Income Distribution and the Welfare State' in Boltho (ed.).

SEN, G. (1984). *The Military Origins of Indurstrialisation and International Trade Rivalry*. London: Frances Pinter.

SHEAHAN, J. (1963). *Promotion and Control of Industry in Postwar France*. Cambridge, Mass.: Harvard University Press.

SMITH, A. ([1776] 1976). *An Inquiry into the Nature and Causes of the Wealth of Nations*. Oxford: Clarendon Press.

STEUART, J. ([1767] 1966). *An Inquiry into the Principles of Political Oekonomy*, 2 vols. Edinburgh: Scottish Economic Society.

STOCKMAN, D. A. (1985). *The Triumph of Politics*. New York: Harper and Row.

SUPPLE, B. (1973). 'The State and the Industrial Revolution, 1700–1914' in C. M. Cipolla (ed.), *The Fontana Economic History of Europe*, iii, *The Industrial Revolution*. Glasgow: Fontana Collins.

SWOBODA, A. (1976). *Capital Movements and their Control*. Leiden: Sijthoff.

TAYLOR, C. R. (1992). *Growth, Inequality and the Politics of Discontent in the Industrial Countries*. New York: Group of Thirty.

UNITED NATIONS (1965). *Economic Planning in Europe*. Geneva.

—— (1981). *Transnational Banks: Operations, Strategies and their Effects on Developing Countries*. New York.

—— (1988). *Transnational Corporations in World Development—Trends and Prospects*. New York.

VAN DORMAEL, A. (1978). *Bretton Woods—Birth of a Monetary System*. London: Macmillan.

WALTER, A. (1993). *World Power and World Money*. London: Harvester Wheatsheaf.

WILENSKY, H. (1975). *The Welfare State and Equality*. Berkeley: University of California Press.

WORLD BANK (1992). *Global Economic Prospects and the Developing Countries*. Washington, DC.

PART II

MARKET ECONOMIES

4

The Myth of Anglo-Saxon Capitalism: Reconstructing the History of the American State

Richard Kozul-Wright

INTRODUCTION

According to Nobel laureate Douglas North, 'The central puzzle of human history is to account for the widely divergent paths of historical change' (North 1990: 6). To begin to answer this puzzle it is essential to take the processes of economic change out from the familiar terrain of a neoclassical world.[1] Although it would be unrealistic in a largely descriptive paper to engage the reader in a lengthy analytical dialogue, two basic criticisms can be offered by way of justifying this starting-point. First, where increasing returns, uncertainty, asymmetries of information, and learning economies are pervasive, prices alone cannot provide the necessary signposts to undertake longer-term productive activity. In this world, markets—whether 'working' or 'failing'—are not assumed to hold institutional primacy and a richer institutional framework is called for than permitted by neoclassical theory. Secondly, because economic change is a continuous and irreversible process marked both by incremental additions to the components of wealth creation and structural shifts in the pattern of economic activity but always constrained by decisions made in the past, it is inconsistent with the idea of market forces returning the economy to an equilibrium point fixed outside history (Kaldor 1985).[2]

Economic historians have long been persuaded of the validity of these criticisms. A rich comparative literature on 'late development' has, in this

The views expressed in this paper are the author's and in no way reflect those of the United Nations Secretariat. The author would like to thank Shahen Abrahamian for helpful comments on an earlier draft.

[1] In his Nobel lecture North himself recognizes this explicitly, 'Neoclassical theory is simply an inappropriate tool to analyse and prescribe policies that will induce development' (North 1994: 359).

[2] Conventional economic theory has recently begun to discuss these elements of a more dynamic approach. Other than Douglas North's own work on transaction costs and property rights, (endogenous) growth theorists and (strategic) trade theorists have recently indicated their willingness to move in this direction. For a review of the links between these and the older tradition of development economics, see Bardhan 1993.

vein, explored distinct patterns of national economic development established around the processes of catching up, forging ahead, and falling
behind, including the role of the state as essential to the institutional
conditions for growth and development.[3] However, the approach has only
occasionally been applied to one of the most successful episodes of modern
economic development, that of the United States.[4] This chapter takes a
tentative step towards filling this gap. Its opening sections challenge some
entrenched conceptions of American development that have closed off
analysis to a more constructive role for the state. It begins by considering
the anti-state bias in many interpretations of American economic history,
particularly the idea of the state as predatory, and outlines an alternative
developmental role for the state—also with American roots—within a
national system of entrepreneurship. Next it questions the idea of a development path transplanted from Britain—an Anglo-Saxon model of capitalist development—and considers some distinct aspects of the American
process of catching up and forging ahead. Finally, it sketches some of the
actions by and through which the Federal state supported the process of
catching up and then of forging ahead of rival economies.

1. NOT ABSENT, TECHNOCRATIC OR PREDATORY: AN ALTERNATIVE FRAMEWORK FOR EXPLORING THE ACTIONS OF THE AMERICAN STATE

Economic historians have tended to view the process of industrialization
through Eurocentric-tinted spectacles. Much of their attention has concentrated on distinguishing continental models from the early experience of
Britain, with occasional reflections on the links to socialist economic development and the Asian industrialization experience (Cameron 1985;
Ashworth 1985; Amsden 1989). The industrial progress of the United
States has sat unconfortably in this company and, almost by default, an
'Anglo-Saxon' pattern of development has emerged from the idea of a
common cultural heritage. In particular, the 'extraordinary privileged position' of exit over voice in the American tradition (Hirschman 1970: 106)
has appeared to confirm a shared adherence to *laissez-faire* ideas, whereby
an economic realm of freely entered (and exited) individual market exchange would be allowed to function independently of a political realm of
collective force and constraint where 'the intervention of the state, however

[3] Gershenkron 1966; Berend and Ranki 1974; Abramovitz 1989. Recently, this perspective
has helped to salvage the experience of rapid growth in East Asia from a simplistic 'market-
friendly' description and embody it in a rich institutional context, including a significant role
for the state; see Wade 1990; Amsden 1989; Lall 1991; Chang 1993. For an attempt to link
historical episodes of late development, see Chang and Kozul-Wright 1994.

[4] Such efforts have usually focused on the role of technological change in the development
of the US economy. For an excellent survey, see Nelson and Wright 1992.

Table 4.1 Government expenditure as a share of GDP, 1880–1980

	1880	1913	1929	1938	1950	1980
United Kingdom	9.9	13.3	23.8	28.8	34.2	44.7
United States	—	8.0	10.1	18.5	22.5	33.7
France	11.2	9.9	12.0	21.8	27.6	46.1
Germany	10.0	17.7	30.6	42.4	30.4	48.3
Netherlands	—	8.2	11.2	21.7	26.8	57.5
Japan	9.0	14.2	18.8	30.3	19.8	32.6

Source: Maddison 1985; OECD *Historical Statistics, 1906–1990* (Paris, OECD).

well meant, worked to hobble initiatives, distort the market and cripple the invisible hand' (Landes 1990: 2). As the United States assumed Britain's place as industrial hegemon around the turn of the century, and the mantle of free trade, following the difficult interlude of the interwar years, the triumph of the market over the state in accounting for the growth of the American economy appeared to confirm the separateness of these experiences from that of other industrial nations. This, however, would be a hasty conclusion.

Even the most cursory comparative assessment of the development of modern capitalist economies does not readily confirm a common Anglo-Saxon model of market–state relations (Table 4.1). All these economies have witnessed a significant expansion of state activity since the late nineteenth century, and, whilst industrial transformation did not create an American state comparable in size to that of Germany or Japan, it is equally apparent that the United States did not follow a pattern of state building inherited from Britain. For much of the period during which the United States was catching up and forging ahead of its rivals, the public sector was comparable in size to some notably state-centred societies such as the Netherlands and France and, as Table 4.1 shows, economic development has seen convergence with the Japanese state, a notably different institution.

There would appear to be more to state building than ideology alone might suggest. Still, to the extent that ideology expresses a collective consensus, the privileging of exit should account for the state's minimal role in many interpretations of American economic development. In fact, the privileging of exit lends itself to a number of distinct (and in important respects opposing) interpretations of this role which should be separated from the outset. In broad terms, these fall under the headings of conventional and political economy interpretations of state–market interactions.

Adopting the most conventional definition of the economic problem as the optimal allocation of scarce resources, a particularly mechanical interpretation of the exit function proscribes a more active state role, a priori, from a system always at—or close to—equilibrium. This interpretation of the role of exit can probably explain the lack of a systematic discussion of the role of the state in the 'growth accounting' literature produced by a body of eminent American economists including Simon Kuznets, Robert Solow, Ed Dennison, and others (Maddison 1985: 58), as well as from those grander modelling exercises which drew extensively on Anglo-Saxon experiences, such as Rostow's 'stages of growth'.[5]

Although a constructive economic role for the state is written out of these conventional accounts of economic progress by their chosen assumptions, the historical limitations of a conventional economic perspective are perhaps even more apparent once the idea of an economy close to equilibrium is rejected and the possibilities of state intervention are actually contemplated. Recognizing various 'market failures' implies an economy where the restorative powers of entry and exit are weak or ineffective, justifies managing economic activity, and identifies a series of goals for which a competent economic bureaucracy should develop and apply appropriate policy instruments. This technocratic view of the state has also found an Anglo-Saxon lineage through the germination of Keynesian ideas under the disequilibrium conditions of the 1930s, their rapid adoption by an influential group of young economists on both sides of the Atlantic, and their steady influence over policy-makers in the decade following the publication of the *General Theory*, culminating in the broad commitment to fiscal activism as the basis for post-war recovery, full employment, and growth.[6] These histories have never satisfactorily described the rich comparative pattern of state intervention during the interwar years and beyond.[7] More recently, technocratic notions of state action have reduced the debate on industrial policy—in both the United States and Britain—to a question of picking winners or creating losers (Thompson (ed.) 1989; Scheiber 1987: 415–17).

[5] It is not the case that the state is entirely absent from this approach. Rather, the acceptable responsibilities of the state, such as a guarding against those activities—including its own—which could act as an obstacle to exit and, thereby, an optimal growth path and ensuring the rules of the competitive market game are respected, are conceived to be exogenous to the functioning of the economy itself. In the American context, this perspective might be appropriately labelled a Marshallian view of the state to reflect Talcott Parson's influential interpretation of Marshall (see Andreano 1965).

[6] See Winch 1969; Stein 1969; Sweezy 1972.

[7] Much of the discussion of the rise of a core Keynesian agenda has been weakly embodied in the appropriate institutional context. Thus, whilst undoubtedly correct that American economists were quick to adopt the new macroeconomic aproach to economic relationships, their resulting prescriptions had to be delivered through existing state structures which had long resisted the formation of a national bureaucracy with the ability to challenge regional and local interests and establish a national economic agenda (Weir and Skocpol 1986; Tomlinson 1985: 1–11). This institutional legacy proved to be a key factor in the subsequent influence and evolution of Keynesianism in the United States—most significantly on the final shape of the Full Employment Act of 1946. The essays in Hall 1989 provide an important comparative perspective on Keynesianism including in the United States.

These conventional histories of the American state clearly reflect our earlier criticisms. By assuming the primacy of markets, economic and political forces are kept completely separate or interact in a very mechanical fashion (see also Chapter 2) and the exclusion of significant change in all economic variables in order to achieve determinate results in the allocation of goods and resources (Ginzberg 1974; North 1994) deprives the state of the historical heritage that appears central to understanding its influence over the processes of economic development and change.[8]

The rich interplay of political and economic forces across time and embodied in different patterns of institutional evolution provides the broad framework for a more dynamic approach to economic development where the uncertain process of learning, searching, and innovating involves a collective effort of 'calling forth and enlisting for development purposes, resources and abilities that are hidden, scattered or badly utilized' (Hirschman 1987: 210). Rather than a spontaneous process, economic development appears as a continuous process of discovery involving both cumulative improvements to existing activities and radical departures into new markets and along unfamiliar technological trajectories. In such a world, the forces of competition are joined by increasing returns, uncertainty, cumulative causation, path dependence, as the context for policymakers and private entrepreneurs alike.[9] Indeed, it is precisely because of these discontinuities in the economic landscape that this world accords a central place to entrepreneurship as an agent of transformative growth and economic progress (North 1994: 361; Baumol 1968).

An alternative American economic perspective on the role of the state does incorporate both the interplay of economic and political forces and a role for entrepreneurship. The overriding feature of this political economy tradition has been its characterization of the state as an institution with a distinct capacity to waste scarce resources and distort productive policy goals. From this starting-point, American economic development is portrayed as a continuous struggle to contain the predatory behaviour of the state. Douglas North has provided one of the fullest accounts of this perspective.[10] North's analysis rests on three basic assumptions. First that economic development is the product of a robust and efficient structure of property rights. Secondly, in principle, the state, as an organization with a monopoly over violence, provides the surest means to establish and enforce such rights. Finally, because the state—like any other economic agent—is

---

[8] Kaldor, of course, owes much to Allyn Young's seminal work. However, Young's discussion contains a more nuanced role for entrepreneurship than sometimes appears in Kaldor's own writing. See further Chang and Kozul-Wright 1994. It is possible that this missing dynamic aspect explains why economists have been less influential in fashioning an American tradition than one might otherwise expect (Galbraith 1962: 67–79).

[9] Paul Krugman (1993) has recently expressed this opinion with considerable alacrity.

[10] Douglas North (1981) has wrongly, I believe, defined his theory as neoclassical. A more apt definition might be Smithian.

itself wealth maximizing, its own rational behaviour conflicts with its wider social responsibility resulting in a widespread tendency to generate inefficient property rights:

From the redistributive societies of ancient Egyptian dynasties through the slavery system of the Greek and Roman world to the medieval manor, there was persistent tension between the ownership structure which maximized the rents to the ruler (and his group) and an efficient system that reduced transaction costs and encouraged economic growth. This fundamental dichotomy is the root cause of the failure of societies to experience sustained economic growth. (North 1981: 25)

North found this tension to be a pervasive feature of American economic development; describing a slow descent from a golden age of nineteenth century constitutional restrictions on the power of government to one, from the 1890s onwards, of growing state control and accompanying reductions in contractual freedom, weakened competition, and various other 'symptoms of malaise' (North 1981: 192).

Mancur Olson's influential study, *The Rise and Decline of Nations*, reinforced North's assessment of the state as a threat to economic growth by extending the state's own predatory behaviour to include its support of 'distributive alliances'. The state nurtures a whole system of rent-seeking activity at the expense of more productive behaviour. Like North, Olson also describes an evolutionary descent in the economic development of the United States; from its egalitarian roots through much of the nineteenth and early twentieth century, and when the predominance of exit associated with an expanding frontier limited the formation of distributive alliances, to the steady accumulation of such alliances for the remainder of this century.[11]

The idea of a predatory state is not restricted to the rightward spectrum of the American political economy tradition. A strong institutionalist tradition has always been suspicious of the state as an agent reinforcing unproductive activities through its links to large corporations. Thorstein Veblen, for example, saw this link reinforcing those habits of thought which favoured leisure and redistribution—typical of the business community—at the expense of industry and creativity and J. K. Galbraith (1967), although affirming the state's productive contribution in a mixed economy, discerned an American industrial state embedded in a military industrial complex, where public waste wins out over rational public action. C. Wright Mills and William Appelman Williams saw a similar threat in the external ambitions of the American state (Stedman Jones 1980). An influential Marxist tradition has also seen the defining characteristics of

---

[11] In the 20th century Olson's picture is complicated by the strength and stability of regional coalitions but in general the mosaic of distributive alliances favours the southern and western states where predatory state behaviour is weakest.

American capitalism in the rent-seeking behaviour of the giant corporation, reinforced under monopoly capitalism by state actions (Baran and Sweezy 1966: 66).

The extent to which the idea of a predatory state has captured the imagination of American economists can be judged by some more mainstream accounts of American economic history. Thus Birdzell and Rosenberg (1986) recount a story of United States technological development which suggests that the limited capacity of the state to impose 'massive extractions' on the economy created an environment in which the private entrepreneur could stimulate technological dynamism, and Paul Krugman has assiduously avoided the implications of his own analysis of strategic trade policy in light of what he sees as the predatory nature of the American state.[12]

Our concern here is not to provide an exhaustive assessment of these contributions or to downplay their differences. However, important commonalities shape their histories of the American state. First, although the introduction of entrepreneurship implies a more dynamic market economy, the state remains an unhistorical and monolithic institution with fixed interests. This repeats the mistaken assumptions of the traditional economic approach by denying history to one group of institutional actors that affect economic activity. It would seem to be a particularly misleading description of an institution that has had to adapt to tremendous changes in its operating environment and in which the balance between federal and local powers and legal and executive authority has been in constant flux (Scheiber 1987).[13] Secondly, their emphasis on distributional struggles ignores the 'productionist' bias which has figured strongly in the American tradition (Galbraith 1962; Maier 1987), particularly through its agrarian legacy (Hobsbawm 1985: 167). This bias has been a particularly important influence on state ideology dating back to Alexander Hamilton—'the architect of much of the early economic policy' (North 1974: 63)—whose *Report on Manufactures* sketched a development process in which a technologically inferior agrarian economy with small manufacturing firms would never catch up with advanced European producers without government support. As an early supporter of the case for infant industries, Hamilton recognized

---

[12] See the exchange between Krugman (1992) and Stiglitz (1992).

[13] Robert Higgs (1991) has described the growth of the American state as a path-dependent process in which periods of crisis have nurtured new institutions and ideas encouraging the scale and scope of government activities. Expansionary bureaucratic tendencies—which Higgs traces to the state's asymmetric access to information during periods of crisis—have also been accompanied by important ideological changes—a reinforcing process of crisis, bureaucratic opportunity, and ideological change have thereby characterized 20th century American development. However, Higgs's description of the post-war mixed economy as 'participatory fascism' also reveals the absurd limit to which the predatory state idea can be taken.

[14] According to Bairoch (1993: 33), Hamilton was the first to use the term infant industry.

that tariffs and subsidies were instrumental to the developmental aims of the American state.[14] Hamilton's stress on institutional design and the constructive policies of the state in shaping a nation's chosen development were soon echoed by the small northern manufacturing class and divided policy-makers and academics struggling to guide the development of a still economically insecure nation (Reich 1991: 18–24). Louis Hartz's path-breaking study of pre-Civil-War Pennsylvannia notes that the state's leading economic theorists developed the notion of '. . . a positive profit-making state. . . . The concept of profit led to a concept of public service, and the state became a gigantic entrepreneur whose gains were to be publicly shared' (quoted in Levine 1988: 3) and politicians, such as Henry Clay of Kentucky, gave an even broader developmental role to tariffs as creating national markets and providing the revenues to fund national infrastructure projects.

However, as economics gradually forfeited its interest in building institutions to support economic development and Social Darwinism captured the American mood (Galbraith 1962: 73–6), the idea of entrepreneurship acquired its more familiar individualistic and popular character (Reich 1991) and Hamilton's vision found more support in the European challenges of late industrialization. Through Chaptal, List, Rother, Mevissen, and others, the challenge of catching up was heeded by policy-makers in Europe. More formally, Joseph Schumpeter's analysis of 'plausible capitalism', characterized by the challenge to established firms and industries from new products and technologies, rested on the entrepreneur as the agent of 'creative destruction' and the advantages of temporary rent-seeking activities. Although Schumpeter's own ideas were formed prior to his arrival in the United States, he was fully conscious of their germination, describing the early industrial development of the United States as 'an almost ideal case for the application of the (Hamilton–List) infant industry argument' (quoted in Clemence (ed.) 1989: 171).

However, if entrepreneurship is truly purposive activity in an uncertain world, institutions to support it must provide a more broadly enabling environment than suggested by Schumpeter's own analysis. Whilst including an appropriate incentive system to encourage risk-taking—'the creative role of markets' (Kaldor 1989)—effective institutional arrangements must also provide the preconditions by and through which change can be understood and implemented and purposeful activity thereby made possible.[15] To this end institutions must function to reduce uncertainty and regulate conflict, which to some degree surrounds all economic activity, and estab-

[15] In this respect, J. S. Mill's conception of technological progress was in advance of Schumpeter; 'Improvement [in the productive arts] must be understood . . . in a wide sense, including not only new industrial inventions, or an extended use of those already known, but improvements in institutions, education, opinions, and human affairs generally, provided they tend, as almost all improvements do, to give new motives or new facilities to production' (quoted in Abramovitz 1989: 7).

lish the linkages to ensure the flow of knowledge and capabilities between economic units.[16] In addition, the state appears to have an additional role in managing rent-seeking behaviour.

Institutional diversity and evolutionary change undercut many of the traditional assumptions about entrepreneurship which have been nurtured in the American tradition.[17] First, although the willingness to make bold commercial initiatives and take risks are necessary entrepreneurial capabilities, they are not sufficient. Entrepreneurship requires a bundle of 'social capabilities' (Abramovitz 1989) which make possible the continuous assessment and improvement of economic activity. In particular, searching out available information and creating new knowledge requires constant learning and experimenting by economic agents, either individually or as groups. Moreover, because these kinds of purposeful actions cannot be exclusively identified with one individual or firm, entrepreneurial capabilities will only be fully developed and made effective within a wider network of institutional relations at the national level and through such collective traditions as voice, loyalty, and trust (Hirschman 1970).[18]

Secondly, whilst the central aspect of productive entrepreneurship is the introduction of new knowledge or the combination of existing knowledge in novel ways that enhance economic competitiveness[19] such activity does not preclude unproductive types of entrepreneurship, where individuals or enterprises engage in profit-seeking activity by using asymmetric information, establishing legal barriers to entry, or reinforcing a monopoly position through political, financial, or other organizational constraints to the entry of potential competitors (Baumol 1990). Although rent-seeking is not antithetical to development when the resulting redistribution of resources fosters new areas of growth (Chang 1994), to the extent that unproductive entrepreneurship becomes entrenched in the routines of the enterprise, the tendency to seek redistributive rather than creative activities will eventually undermine the wider economy's growth potential (Olson 1982). This suggests that enterprise governance cannot be separated from entrepreneurship. In the light of rent-seeking behaviour, firms must be subject to 'external' monitoring—by government agencies, banks, or others—and selective pressures must be available to the monitoring agency to re-establish creative routines.[20]

Finally, productive entrepreneurship directly contributes to the destruc-

---

[16] This approach to institutions is discussed in Hodgson 1988; Johnson and Lundvall 1989; North 1994.

[17] For a useful overview, see Reich 1991.

[18] On the collective nature of entrepreneurship, see further Reich 1991; Lall 1991; Johnson and Lundvall 1991; and Jorde and Teece 1990.

[19] Nelson 1986: 1973; Baumol 1968: 65.

[20] Because the state continues to maintain credible coercive powers, its governance role remains of significance but other institutions—financial intermediaries, labour unions, or foreign enterprises—may often be more effective in carrying out this function.

tion of existing capabilities and institutional routines and threatens the livelihood of groups and individuals who have invested in particular jobs, fixed capital assets, specific skills, and local ties. Consequently, in the course of economic development, some (potentially large) groups will be at odds with a wider community interest whose real income would be raised by technological innovations, structural reorganization, or the introduction of new products. Resistance to the erosion of existing assets is likely to make conflict an unavoidable element of the development process which, if uncontrolled or persistent, will prove a powerful obstacle to change. Some means must be found to manage these conflicts and share the burdens arising from a successful development strategy.

There is a need to be clear about the consequences of this notion of entrepreneurship for state action (Chang and Kozul-Wright 1994). Even if markets are not assumed to hold institutional primacy and property rights are neither immutable nor beyond encroachment, this does not provide *carte blanche* for state intervention. Rather, it suggests that public policy can play a key role in promoting the creation of national economic assets and capabilities which complement the actions of firms,[21] and, as Karl Polanyi insisted, it sensitizes the economic historian to the role of government as one among a number of institutions in economic life whose 'role consists often of altering the rate of change, speeding it up or slowing it down as the case may be' (Polanyi 1957: 37). Together, the various kinds of institutional arrangements supporting continuous innovation through a network of public and private institutional linkages that encourage risk-taking, learning, imitating, and experimenting, and can manage the destructive components of entrepreneurship—both rent-seeking behaviour and the socio-economic conflict which accompanies creative destruction—have been described elsewhere as a *national system of entrepreneurship*.[22] The evolution of such a system in the context of American economic development will be addressed in the final section of this paper. The next section will sketch in broad outline the American path of catching up and forging ahead.

2. THE MYTH OF ANGLO-SAXON CAPITALISM

For much of the nineteenth century, Britain's status as a military super-power was matched only by its rise to global economic leadership; her

---

[21] There is the constant possibility that states 'fail' in their designated responsibilities. This is particularly because, in an economy where control over productive assets lies, to a large extent, outside the state, those responsibilities are continuously being redefined by a myriad independent actors. But also because effective public policy is path-dependent reflecting institutional competencies accumulated in the past and which may be badly adapted to current problems. Tension between the effective governance and flexibility of the state will almost certainly be an integral part of any process of economic development.

[22] Chang and Kozul-Wright 1994. The terms is adapted from Lundvall 1988.

Table 4.2 Relative shares of selected countries in world manufacturing output, 1830–1973 (percentages; triennial annual averages)

	1830	1880	1900	1953	1973
United Kingdom	9.5	22.9	18.5	6.4	4.9
United States	2.4	14.7	23.6	44.7	33.0
France	5.2	7.8	6.8	3.2	3.5
Germany	3.5	8.5	13.2	5.9	5.9
Sweden	0.3	0.8	0.9	0.9	0.9
Japan	2.8	2.4	2.4	2.9	8.8

Source: Bairoch 1982.

Table 4.3 Per capita income levels for selected economies, 1820–1950

	Real GDP per capita				
	1820	1870	1890	1913	1950
United Kingdom	1,405	2,610	3,279	4,024	5,651
United States	1,221	2,247	3,106	4,854	8,611
France	1,052	1,571	1,941	2,734	4,149
Germany	937	1,300	1,726	2,606	3,339
Sweden	947	1,316	1,651	2,450	5,331
Japan	588	618	813	1,114	1,564

Source: Bairoch 1976.

goods captured an increasing share of world markets, her capital flowed into new opportunities across the globe, and her technologies and labour force were universally envied, feared, and copied. The reasons for Britain's industrial start are, undoubtedly, complex, but there is little doubting that manufacturing dynamism propelled her early rise to economic leadership.

Tables 4.2 and 4.3 translate this dynamism into simple numbers. Trade policy and export growth were essential ingredients in Britain's early industrial lead. However, and despite this lead being already apparent in the early nineteenth century, significant reductions in trade barriers only began in the 1840s, as the representatives of industry gained an upper hand over agrarian interests;[23] the dismantling of tariff barriers had to wait for the repeal of the Corn Laws in 1846 but the pace accelerated thereafter. From a broad historical perspective, the importance of this new industrial dy-

[23] The 1840s represent a turning point, when industry's share of national output exceeded that of agriculture and the Corn Laws were repealed, see Bairoch 1993: 20–1.

namic was not its national origins, but rather the powerful set of mutually enforcing social, market, technological, and political forces which established a new international division of labour and set the context for catching up among those follower economies in the core of the world economy (Landes 1990; Cameron 1985).

Britain's global industrial dominance peaked in the closing two decades of the nineteenth century during which time it was caught by the United States, a former colony with close cultural, political, and economic links. The American economy was already growing quite rapidly in the first half of the nineteenth century, grew particularly rapidly during the period 1870–1900, and slowed only slightly in the period prior to World War I; for the period 1829–31 to 1909–11, Paul Bairoch estimates that United States per capita GNP grew at 2.4 per cent per annum, Western Europe at 1.2 per cent, and the fastest growing European economies at 1.5–1.6 per cent (Bairoch 1993: 52). Although growth rates fell after 1913, the United States maintained a respectable comparative growth rate *vis-à-vis* most competitors until the severity of the Great Depression; between 1913–29 annual per capita growth in Europe averaged only 0.4 per cent compared with 1.1 per cent in the United States; however the faster growing European economies averaged between 1.1–1.8 per cent (Bairoch 1993: 8). Economic growth accelerated with the expansionary conditions of a war economy and by the end of World War II, America's industrial leadership had reached new heights.

Thus behind the rising global share of US industry was an acceleration in its growth rate unmatched by all but a handful of small European economies (principally the Scandinavian economies). In this respect, the United States was the first modern industrial economy to forge ahead of its competitors (Table 4.4). Tables 4.3 and 4.4 are striking in two other respects. First, already in 1820 the United States was a comparatively wealthy economy; a situation confirmed by historical reporting from the period.[24] Secondly, the task of catching up which the United States began in the early decades of the nineteenth century was, as a consequence, far less daunting than that facing many post-colonial developing countries, or, indeed, facing the European late developers; it required, by contemporary standards, a very modest growth rate for the United States to overtake the United Kingdom.

The transfer of economic leadership and the divergence—at least by 1913—in per capita income levels between the United States and other late developing countries has reinforced the idea of a distinct Anglo-Saxon model of economic development. However, America's process of catching up was more complex than is revealed by growth figures alone. The process involved transformation both in the structure of economic activity and the

---

[24] See Baumol *et al.* 1989: ch. 3.

Table 4.4 Closing a gap and building a lead: rates of divergence between follower countries and leader countries, 1820–1950

	Annual average compound growth rates		Catching up[a]	Forging ahead[b]
	1820–1890	1890–1950	1820–1890	1890–1950
United Kingdom	1.2	0.9	—	−0.8
United States	1.4	1.7	0.2	—
France	0.9	1.3	−0.3	−0.4
Germany	0.9	1.1	−0.3	−0.6
Sweden	0.8	2.0	−0.4	0.3
Japan	0.5	1.1	−0.7	−0.6

[a] Difference from UK annual average.
[b] Difference from US annual average.
Source: Maddison 1992: table 1.

Table 4.5 Structural transformation; employment shares for selected countries, 1870–1950 (percentage share, I = agriculture, II = industry, III = services)

	1870			1900			1950		
	I	II	III	I	II	III	I	II	III
United Kingdom	22.7	42.3	35.0	9.1	60.0	31.9	5.1	42.3	35.0
United States	50.0	24.4	25.6	37.6	30.1	32.3	13.0	33.3	53.7
France	49.2	27.8	23.0	41.8	34.0	24.2	28.3	34.9	26.8
Germany	49.5	28.7	21.8	36.8	44.7	18.5	22.2	43.0	34.8
Sweden	53.9	—	—	53.5	23.5	23.0	20.3	40.8	38.9
Japan	72.6	—	—	70.6	14.8	14.6	48.3	22.6	29.1

Source: Bairoch *et al.* 1968.

geographical distribution of the population. From Table 4.5 it is clear that, whilst the period of catching up was marked by a relative decline in agriculture in the United States, the overall pattern of structural change was very different from Britain (and indeed the European late developers). Agricultural employment maintained a prominent position during the period of catching up, whilst manufacturing employment was comparatively small. Indeed, during this period, the United States moved from being the world's fifth largest agricultural producer to its largest, and employment in the primary sector grew at a correspondingly more rapid pace than in most other capitalist economies.[25] Thus in contrast to Britain, the rise to economic leadership did not see a dramatic increase in the share of industrial employment and, by the end of the period of catching up, the share taken by the service sector was still larger. This trend was reinforced during the period of forging ahead; industry's share changed only marginally, whilst the precipitous drop in the share of agriculture was matched by a rise in services employment.

Changes in employment structure were accompanied by changes in the geographical distribution of the population. During the period of catching up America became a more urban society. However, the pace of urbanization remained much slower than in Britain, an already highly urbanized society.[26] Towards the end of the nineteenth century the distinctly American urban metropolis emerged but it was not until well into the period of forging ahead—around 1920—that the urban population exceeded its rural counterpart. Whilst some convergence in the distribution of population with Britain is visible in this period, by the end of its period of forging ahead the geographical structure of the American population remained closer to that of the later developing economies in Europe.

Underlying the shift in the American growth trajectory from the late nineteenth century was a transformation in the structure of industry. Again the differences between the United States and British experience stand out. Britain's rise to economic leadership rested on the combined presence of two separate development blocs—textiles and iron—which were loosely connected through a common technological paradigm based on coal and strongly oriented to external markets, often kept open through colonial rule (Cameron 1985: 9).[27] By the time Britain lost her industrial lead, she was still accounting for 30 per cent of world exports, over half of which were textiles and clothing. The process of catching up in the United States rested on a far broader economic base and an expanding domestic market. Consumer goods industries ranged more widely than textiles, reflecting the more extensive resource base of the United States; seven of the ten leading industries in 1860 processed domestic resources (North 1974: 80) and together with the growth and transformation of the agricultural sector describe an important agro-industrial development bloc.[28]

Transportation, both railroad construction and shipping, dominated the

---

[25] In terms of absolute numbers employed, between 1840 and 1887, the United States moved from the seventh largest agrarian nation to the third largest, see Hobsbawm 1985: 365: table 4. These changes reflected a transformation in agriculture towards new products, such as wheat and livestock, and new production technologies. Hobsbawm (1985: 213) notes that the number of agriculture patents taken out in the United States rose from 191 in 1849–51 to 3,217 twenty years later.

[26] See Hobsbawm 1985: 246–7.

[27] The term 'development bloc' is due to Dahmén (1985).

[28] At the close of the period of catching up this bloc still accounted for close to two-thirds of the capital stock in manufacturing.

capital goods sector. This was part of an emerging engineering bloc, built around the search for labour-saving machinery (such as agricultural machinery) in response to already high labour costs as well as new machines suitable to meet the growing demand for standardized domestic goods such as clocks, guns, and sewing machines (Hobsbawm 1985: 60). But transportation also represented a crucial link between the two blocs. The railroads became the first billion-dollar industry in the United States, with obvious spillover effects on the growth of all industry. Between 1850 and 1880 the length of track grew by more than tenfold, and doubled again in the closing two decades of the century, closing geographical distances and opening markets for the new consumer industries, as well as creating a direct market for the iron and steel industry, machine building, and timber (North 1974: 105).

From the late nineteenth century, the agro-industry development bloc was going through a transformation with the discovery and commercialization of new products; in addition to oil, bauxite, manganese, cobalt, nickel, and phosphates were all an integral part of the newly emerging growth path (Wright 1990). New production and distribution techniques were also helping to transform this bloc.[29] But developments in transportation continued to be the most important influence on the growth path adopted by the United States economy as it forged ahead of its rivals; the length of railway track peaked during World War I as the automobile began its rise to pre-eminence, to be followed during World War II by air transportation. Distances were shortened by other technological breakthroughs as the telegraph gave way to the telephone and wireless. These advances were reinforced by new sources of power, both electricity and oil, which had an equally profound effect on the technological and organizational face of American economic leadership. By the outbreak of World War II, this more sophisticated engineering bloc dominated the structure of American industry.

This new growth path coincided with particularly high rates of domestic savings and investment (Panić 1992: 94). Gross fixed non-residential investment peaked in the United States in the two decades before World War I; the figure was far in excess of that achieved by the United Kingdom and was only exceeded by other late industrializing nations after World War II (Table 4.6); thus, whilst Britain's gross fixed non-residential capital stock per capita was in 1820 over 15 per cent higher than in the United States, by 1890 the United States figure was more than double that of Britain and by 1913 three-and-a-half times larger (Maddison 1992: table 10). Although financing only a small percentage of domestic capital formation, the United States also became, during this period, the largest host to foreign invest-

---

[29] It is worthwhile noting the diversity of the ten leading industries in 1939; food remained the dominant sector and textiles and clothing were still present.

Table 4.6 Ratio of gross fixed non-residential investment to GDP, at current market prices, 1871–1940

	1871–80	1881–90	1891–1900	1901–10	1911–20	1921–30	1931–40
United Kingdom	7.5	5.9	6.8	7.4	6.2	6.4	6.5
United States	11.5	12.2	15.8	15.7	12.5	12.7	9.7
France	9.0	10.4	10.4	10.4	—	12.1	11.1
Germany	—	—	—	—	—	11.9	10.1
Japan	—	8.9	11.2	11.0	14.9	13.9	14.7

Source: Maddison 1991: table 2.3.

Table 4.7 Export performance, 1820–1950: average annual compound growth rates and ratio of merchandise exports to GDP (in brackets for final year indicated) (at constant (1985) prices and exchange rates)

	1820–70	1870–1913	1913–50
United Kingdom	4.9	2.8	0.0
	(10.7)	(14.7)	(9.5)
United States	4.7	4.9	2.2
	(2.8)	(4.1)	(3.3)
France	4.0	2.8	1.1
	(3.4)	(6.0)	(5.6)
Germany	4.8	4.1	−2.8
	(11.9)	(12.2)	(4.4)
Sweden	—	3.1	2.8
	(8.0)	(12.0)	(12.2)
Japan	—	8.5	2.0
	(0.2)	(2.1)	(2.0)

Source: Maddison 1991.

ment, attracted particularly to infrastructure projects.[30] These inflows of capital were complemented by inflows of migrants—which peaked during the decade 1900–10—seeking work in the rapidly growing economy.

The growth of United States exports exceeded output during the period of catching up, with a corresponding rise in their share of domestic output. But this was not, in comparison with other countries including Britain, a significant determinant of economic growth. Although exports held up

---

[30] Of the worldwide $44 billion stock of foreign investment in 1914, $10.5 billion was in the United States. According to Panić (1992: 101), net capital flows represented 5.2% of gross domestic fixed investment between 1880–90. This compares with 50.5% in Australia and 47% in Sweden. From 1890, there was a net capital outflow from the United States.

Table 4.8 Average tariff rates on manufactured products in selected developed countries, 1820–1950 (weighted average; in percentage of value)

	1820	1875	1913	1931	1950
United Kingdom	45–55	0	0	—	23
United States	25–55	40–50	44	48	14
France	—	12–15	20	30	18
Germany	8–12	4–6	13	21	26
Sweden	—	3–5	20	21	9
Japan	—	5	30	—	—

Source: Bairoch 1993: 40.

better than for many other economies during the interwar period, the share of exports declined during the period when the United States forged ahead of its rivals (Table 4.7). Over the period of catching up and forging ahead as a whole, it is quite striking to what extent America's trade policy resembled far more closely that of other late industrializers than the liberalism of Britain (Table 4.8). Differences between the two economies were also apparent in the structure of trade and the profile of foreign investment. United States exports reflected the close interdependence of the leading development blocs. Well into the period of forging ahead US exports were dominated by primary resources and natural-resource-intensive manufactured goods (Wright 1990), but these increasingly came to include higher-value-added machinery, transport equipment, and chemicals, which by 1929 accounted for 70 per cent of total exports compared to only 40 per cent in Britain (Dosi *et al.* 1993: 10). The growing technological lead of the United States was also becoming apparent to overseas competitors as manufacturing firms began to seek rents from their leaderhip by expanding their production activities abroad through foreign direct investment (Wilkins 1988; Chandler 1980).

3. SKETCHING THE ENTREPRENEURIAL ROLE OF THE AMERICAN STATE

The previous sections have established a broad context for the state assuming various responsibilities arising from economic development as a process of transformational growth. Entrepreneurship has been given a central place in defining those responsibilities and, in contrast to the predatory notion of state behaviour, the state is an important agent of creating advantages for the private sector, not only through traditional public investments in human and physical infrastructure, but by managing rent-seeking

behaviour, absorbing the social and economic costs of change and strengthening the creative potential of markets.[31] The object of this final section is
to suggest that such state involvement has been a continuous feature of
American economic development, albeit one which has changed with the
rise of the United States to economic leadership.

The economic responsibilities of the American state have institutional
roots which date back to the founding of the country (North 1990: 133–4).
Three of these legacies are of immediate relevance to the issues under
discussion. First, it is again worth emphasizing that the United States was,
before embarking on its industrial development, a prosperous economy
with an expanding domestic market and a quite sophisticated business
class. In light of the research on economic backwardness these conditions
can be expected to limit the demands on the state's developmental role.
Secondly, the early opposition to centralized authority, the rapid geographical expansion of the territory, and the resulting size of the functioning
economic space have combined to produce state actors at different levels
and with varying degrees of competing political authority. Finally, and
partly as a consequence of this diversity, the legal structure has taken an
unprecedented role in mediating state and private-sector decision-making
over the use of economic resources (Scheiber 1981).

Recognizing these legacies does not, however, proscribe an active role for
the state. As property rights historians such as Douglas North and Morton
Horwitz have made abundantly clear, the legal arm of the state had a
profound impact on the transformation of economic activity in the nineteenth century, an impact which was often channelled through local state
structures.[32] But because the perspective adopted in this paper denies the
institutional primacy of markets, property rights are only part of the enabling institutional environment for transformative growth, and an entrepreneurial role for the state cannot simply be confined to the effectiveness
of the bureaucracy in creating and defending such rights or correcting the
market failures which stem from the inherent weaknesses of a system of
private property, but encompass a broader pattern of governance in support
of growth.[33]

The State as a Catalyst of Catching Up

Catching up did not simply involve a shift away from agriculture or increased rates of capital formation, it also implied closing a technological gap

[31] This is not to deny other economic responsibilities which may come under the auspices
of the state, or to suggest that the governance provided by the state is exhaustive and
independent of other (formal and informal) governance mechanisms (see Campbell et al.
1991). Rather the aim is to highlight some aspects of state governance denied or downplayed
in many accounts of American economic history.

[32] A series of important studies have traced the creative role of the local state in American
history, see Hartz 1948; Handlin and Handlin 1969; Heath 1954.

[33] Campbell et al. 1991 have made this their starting-point for discussing the organization
of modern American industry.

established by Britain's early industrial leadership. A number of writers have traced the incremental changes made by individual entrepreneurs and firms which facilitated the adaptation and spread of European techniques and the subsequent evolution of an American system of production (Nelson and Wright 1992; Rosenberg 1985). However, this was not simply the monumental efforts of individual entrepreneurs.[34] Despite the 'natural' protection afforded by transportation and information costs, America's infant industries sought and received considerable tariff protection. Alexander Hamilton's *Report on Manufactures* had made an early case for such protection and, following the end of the Napoleonic Wars in Europe, his ideas for industrialization through tariffs received increasing support. The woollen and textile industries were the first to receive protection, from the 1820s, but by the early 1830s the average tariff on all manufactures had reached 40 per cent, creating a steadily rising conflict with agricultural interests in the South which dominated domestic politics for the next thirty years. Victory for the industrial North in the American Civil War saw the introduction of high tariffs on most manufactured goods. As already noted earlier, for the remainder of the period of catching up, tariffs far exceeded those introduced by European late industrializers. The overall welfare impact of higher tariffs is not certain. However, the recent research by Paul Bairoch has shown that for the period from 1870–90, increasing protectionism coincided with a phase of very rapid growth; '. . . the best 20 years of American economic growth took place in a period when its trade policy was protectionist while that of the United States' major competitors was liberal' (Bairoch 1993: 53). What is more certain is that the accelerated development of a number of industries during the nineteenth century certainly owes something to the presence of tariff protection (McCraw 1983; Bils 1984; Edwards 1970; Allen 1981) and in particular to the accumulation of tacit knowledge under infant industry protection which was the driving force of industrial development during this period (Mowery and Rosenberg 1989). In addition to these direct efforts to nurture industrial development, the state was also in a position to reduce the uncertainty facing infant entrepreneurs through the creation of market demand. A 'Buy American' clause was introduced into appropriations legislation as early as 1844, providing a more secure market for such industries as cotton goods and firearms (Dell 1991: 60 and 506). At the local level, as previously noted, various forms of legal protection to employers effectively reduced the risks of new business enterprise and, in some cases, state funds were channelled to capital formation (Hammond 1957).

In the kind of dynamic context contemplated by Hamilton, tariffs alone are an inadequate (and in the long run a destructive) engine of growth. In this respect, the strong links between agriculture and industry added a uniquely American dimension to its process of catching up. During the

---

[34] Hobsbawm (1985: 174–7) notes that many of the well-known entrepreneurs from this period were not industrial pioneers.

early period of catching up, agriculture was a source of labour and other inputs to the emerging industrial sector (Gordon *et al.* 1984: 60) as well as providing a domestic market for most industrial goods. As Wright (1990) has shown, these linkages 'locked' American industry into a distinct technological path and organization of work. Of considerable interest to this paper is the way in which this legacy shaped wider economic and political relations through a particular type of state action.

Inevitably, the early consolidation of market relations through a securing and strengthening of property rights focused on the ownership of land. The geographical boundaries of the United States were secured through a series of territorial disputes and land purchases in the first half of the nineteenth century. Although the basic decision to privatize land was established by the Northwest Ordinance of 1787, the actual process of disposing of 'state' lands involved a complex legislative process, which culminated in the Homestead Act of 1862. The reasons for the disposal of land changed over time, as did the terms under which land could be acquired by private citizens (North 1974: ch. X), but throughout the period of catching up, the steady provision of new economic opportunities reinforced incipient entrepreneurship by stimulating risk-taking and investment activity.[35] Still, government activity did not stop wth disposal. Even as the private sector acquired entrepreneurial skills, a variety of federal programmes were being introduced to extend markets and cheapen their use, by providing the supportive infrastructure and expanding the information and research base through which productivity could be augmented and land-use activities upgraded (Davis and North 1971; Rausser 1992).

As early as the 1830s, the state was funding agricultural research. However, it was only after the Civil War with the establishment of the Bureau of Agriculture that a more concerted guidance was provided. The Morrill Act of 1862 provided grants of public land for the purpose of establishing agricultural colleges and, towards the end of the period of catching up, the state was sponsoring research and experimentation on a more extensive scale. The Morrill Act also provided a stimulus to engineering education and, in incipient form, the important linkage between industry and the university system. These efforts were expanded by the 1887 Hatch Act, introduced to provide experimentation in state colleges, and a series of government agencies, such as the Bureau of Animal Industry and the Bureau of Agricultural Chemistry were established with the intention of encouraging new crops and farming methods and disseminating this information as widely as possible.[36] Throughout the period, these targeted

[35] As Hobsbawm (1985: 167–8) has noted the absolute number of beneficiaries of the Homestead Act—less than 400,000 families—belies its ideological prominence. But Hobsbawm also notes its important—though difficult to measure—role as a stimulus to entrepreneurship.

[36] Such efforts led Schumpeter to note that by revolutionizing farming practices, the 'Department of Agriculture [that] acted as an entrepreneur' (Schumpeter 1949: 260).

programmes were complemented by broader efforts by the state in basic education among the American farming population, ensuring a more receptive audience for all these initiatives.[37]

The state's entrepreneurial efforts were not confined to agriculture. A series of legislative initiatives to promote natural resource development, following the Timber Culture Act of 1873, were designed not only to strengthen private property rights to ensure further exploration and exploitation, but also to restrict unproductive entrepreneurial behaviour in the form of excessive depletion (North 1974: 120). Again the Department of Agriculture, through its Division of Forestry, provided the necessary governance and sought to disseminate more scientific methods of production. In minerals production, the early actions of local states in carrying out geological surveys and establishing mining schools were expanded under the auspices of the United States Geological Survey founded in 1879 (Wright 1990: 664) and the country quickly rose to world leadership in the training of mining engineers (Nelson and Wright 1992: 1938). Although these government agencies forged closely co-operative links with industry, the major federal conservation and reclamation programmes begun in the closing decade of the century also indicated the willingness of the state to challenge unrestricted property rights when considered detrimental to a wider national interest.

The efforts of the entrepreneurial state to create and sanction property rights were not confined to the primary sector. The actions of local states, particularly in the area of transportation (see below) are perhaps familiar, but local regulatory powers over land holding and factory conditions provided wider powers for creating markets and attracting capital. Of probably greater long-term significance, the shift of resources into industrial activities after the Civil War—characterized by a tremendous increase in capital per worker—was facilitated by reform of the legal constraints on company formation (Birdzell and Rosenberg 1986: 194–204; Davis and North 1971: 251), and the actions of the judiciary in support of business were widened to include such areas as torts, contracts, and labour law.[38]

Probably the most important contribution of the entrepreneurial state during the process of catching up was the creation and expansion of an effective transportation system. In this case, the more blatant divergence between private and social returns provided strong justification for direct

[37] In 1840, less than half of the total investment in education was public. By 1900, almost 80% was public (Davis and North 1971: 27). According to Cameron (1985: 21), adult literacy in the United States (for whites) had, by 1900, reached 94%, a figure matched only by a small number of North European economies. Moreover, by 1850 enrolment in primary school education was already well in advance of all other countries.

[38] See Horwitz 1977. In this respect, legislative actions reflected a shift in power from the local to the central state, although it was not until the late 1880s that, 'the Supreme Court overturned a significant range of state legislation regarding railroad commissions, regulation of labour hours and working conditions, and health and tax matters' (Scheiber 1987: 427).

subsidy of private activity, but the linkages between the public sector and private entrepreneurs also involved a more creative process of institutional design. State support for improved modes of transportation began at the local level with the construction of the eastern network of canals. This local industrial policy involved a rich interplay between state entrepreneurship and infant industries (Miller 1962; Scheiber 1987). But it was the expansion of the railroad that revealed the full extent of public–private collaboration (Goodrich 1960). Together, the federal and local states provided close to 200 million acres in land (granted or given) to the railway companies and growing tariff revenues, particularly in the closing decades of the nineteenth century, allowed for dramatic increases in federal spending; the Union Pacific and Central Pacific railways received a grant of $68 million to connect the Atlantic and Pacific coasts. Just as important was the state's role in institution building in this sector. Franchised corporations, with the privilege of nullifying individual property rights in the wider collective interest of expanded transportation services, were the chosen vehicle to develop the rail network, albeit under regulatory constraints. This structure provided a stable institutional context to attract the large amounts of necessary capital, and the increased corporate activity revealed the potential of scale economies (Birdzell and Rosenberg 1986: 194–5). The success of these franchised corporations ensured their further use in the expansion of urban markets, providing water and other public utilities, early streetcar lines, and, towards the end of the period, telecommunication services. Given the importance of transportation as a link between the two key development blocs which emerged during its period of catching up, the state's efforts in this area are best seen as part of a wider industrial policy.[39]

America's path of catching up was the product of many creative private initiatives. Undoubtedly, the evolving structure of property rights secured a necessary degree of certainty as well as directing resources to facilitate growth. But it was also the product of state action, combining infant industry protection with a network of linkages in support of economic activity through enhanced transportation and education as well as new forms of institutional design. Indeed, towards the end of this period, a growing number of (often hostile) critics identified the first industrial development bloc—linking railroads, light manufacturing, and agricultural industries—as the product of an entrepreneurial state.

[39] It was also a regional policy. As Krugman (1993) has recently reminded economists, one of the most striking features of this process in the United States was its strong regional concentration along a mid-west/eastern seaboard corridor. In 1859 nearly 84% of the manufacturing labour force was concentrated in this region. In 1914, the figure was still over 76%. There was some intra-regional restructuring with employment shares declining in the New England states and rising in the Great Lakes states (see North 1974: 112).

Forging Ahead and the Growing Constraints on State Governance

America's process of catching up gave way to industrial leadership in the closing decades of the nineteenth century. The transition was not a smooth one. Even as alarmist voices in Europe were contemplating a new competitive threat, the American economy was itself preparing for a new and unprecedented technological and organizational transformation against a backdrop of economic and political uncertainty (David 1991; Kolko 1977). This environment posed new and difficult challenges for the state for which it was, in many respects, ill-prepared and to which it adapted with difficulty.

The most striking aspect of continuity in state governance was trade policy. Despite the maturing of infant industries, tariff levels remained high throughout the period of forging ahead (Table 4.8). However, the rationale changed in line with the new demands of economic growth and transformation. A central justification for the McKinley tariff of 1890 was in terms of protecting wage levels, a rationale very much in line with the creation of mass markets for the newly emerging mass production industries (Bairoch 1993: 36). However, adapting other policy measures to an era of mass production proved more difficult.

For much of the period of catching up, enterprises remained small in scale and operated within local or regional markets. The actions of the state, by helping to create and link a national economic space, were in advance of private capital. The accelerated accumulation of capital, after the Civil War began to close this gap, and the period of forging ahead opened with unprecedented rates of domestic capital formation (Table 4.6). The period was also one of technological revolution. New sources of power (electricity generation) and new and improved modes of transportation and telecommunications not only created new markets but described a 'paradigmatic' change which carried unique and systemic technical and economic opportunities (Freeman and Perez 1988: 47–58). The shift to higher-value-added activities was as characteristic of traditional resource-based industries where new exploration and processing techniques had a dramatic impact on the industrial potential of copper, nickel, zinc, aluminum, and above all oil, as it was for new industrial activities based on advanced engineering and metal-working skills. Along with the spread of national and (though less significantly) international market pressures, these technological revolutions and the growing scale of economic activity posed new and intricate institutional challenges.

Alfred Chandler has documented the importance of economies of scale and scope to the 'logic of industrial success' (Chandler 1977, 1990). Translating the advantages of size to industrial success was not automatic (David 1991) and the evolving rules of mass production contained new threats to corporate stability which required intra-firm governance and new types of state intervention (Best 1990: ch. 3). Indeed, the 'logic' of more hierarchical co-ordination, particularly through mergers and acquisitions, supplementing market-based governance, was in important respects the (unintended) consequence of the state's own internal tensions. From the mid-nineteenth century, the growth of manufacturing and the widening geographical reach of markets had given rise to trade associations to combat the uncertainty of price competition. Although the state was often instrumental in encouraging these types of new institutional design—as, for example, with the railroads—they were universally opposed by the courts as a constraint on trade. This legal opposition culminated in the Sherman Anti-Trust Act, passed in 1890. However, legislative actions merely reinforced organizational and geographical obstacles to effective collective action among firms where size and regional variation were already significant deterrents, and accelerated the trend to large hierarchical corporate structures.[40]

The organizational, financial, and technological pressures which accompanied the pursuit of scale were closely associated with new company strategies and the formation of new managerial capabilities. American firms pioneered many of these developments. The need to ensure cost competitiveness and expand market share involved a creative organizational response through measures to increase the speed and volume of production, improve internal efficiency, and enhance the technological responsiveness of firms. It also required a more hierarchical firm to co-ordinate the different phases of mass production and distribution. As the relative autonomy of the new corporation increased, the influence of existing state instruments of governance diminished. The dilution of traditional patterns of ownership structure complicated the economic importance of property rights and, despite an overriding concern to preserve competitive pressures, the momentum behind large-scale corporations was beyond the reach of legislative action. But equally, the state's own creative capabilities and its links with the productive sector were very much tied to a pattern of agrarian industrialization which was not necessarily suited to matching the actions of the new industrial corporations. However, these legal tools remained powerful enough to obstruct the emergence of other forms of state governance and in the absence of strong national bureaucracy—at least outside agriculture—the organization of mass production appeared to evolve independently of the state.[41]

---

[40] See Hollingsworth 1991: 38–41.

[41] It is of course true that the Progressive era—from 1900–20—witnessed the formation of a number of regulatory agencies, including the Federal Reserve System, saw unprecedented enforcement of anti-trust legislation, and spawned various efforts at a national economic agenda, such as through the corporatist National Civic Federation. But in all these respects, Weir and Skocpol's discussion of Progressivism is particularly apt; they note, '. . . the successes of the Progressive administrative reformers were scattered and incomplete, and their partial successes combined with the weakening of party competition in the early twentieth century

But state anti-trust action had another important influence on corporate governance by preventing options that had figured prominently in the rapid growth of other economies. This was true in the case of closer ties between finance and industry which had been instrumental in building linkages across the newly emerging development blocs.[42] As anti-trust action closed down this option, corporations relied increasingly on internally generated funds and the more short-term solution of the stock market.[43] The impact of anti-trust legislation was not confined to the links between finance and industry. Anti-trust legislation also acted to constrain the development of labour unions and the evolution of more corporatist governance structures. By the early years of the twentieth century, the relative autonomy of corporate management was becoming established as a characteristic feature of the American economic landscape. This marked a break with the national system of entrepreneurship of the nineteenth century and loosened the established avenues established by the state to influence the pace and direction of economic activity. However, the state continued its efforts to stimulate a more dynamic productive structure. In the emerging electrical engineering industries, the government was instrumental in creating new markets for electrical tramways and urban lighting. Somewhat later, government procurement created an early market for the aircraft industry and more advanced chemicals.[44]

The rise of larger firms provided the financial basis for independent research and development. Government efforts to curtail unproductive entrepreneurship also continued. Indeed, state involvement in the setting of national standards was critical to industrial dynamism under mass production. Because standards are very much a public good, they are open to abuse through free-riding which could threaten overall industry performance where the reliability of product standards, particularly for intermediate goods but also for the final product, is essential (Mowery and Rosenberg 1989: 35–8). American industry evolved a remarkable set of voluntary scientific and engineering associations to oversee this process of standard setting. However, the Bureau of Standards, established in 1902, also played a crucial role both through Federal Specifications and in setting scientific standards of physical measurement which are basic to commerce, industry, and learning (Booth 1960). Moreover, in some industries, such as the

United States to exacerbate tendencies toward dispersion of political authority within the American state structure as a whole. Conflicts increased among presidents and congressional coalitions, and the various levels of government in the federal system became more decoupled from one another' (Weir and Skocpol 1986: 135).

[42] The most powerful investment bank of this era was J. P. Morgan and Co., but other investment banks of importance included Kuhn, Loeb and Company, and National City Bank.

[43] In this respect the Anglo-Saxon model of industry–finance linkages (Singh 1993) had its roots in particular historical and institutional conditions.

[44] These initiatives were extended during World War I and, in the case of some chemical industries, the state not only created the demand but also owned the productive assets.

construction-related industries, government involvement (through safety standards) was more extensive and in some food processing industries, such as dairy products and meatpacking, government regulation was critical to the maintenance of product standards.

In a similar vein, but of perhaps greater importance, was the state's role in maintaining the learning and innovating capabilities of industry. The provision of public education continued at the high levels already established during the period of catching up.[45] However, the emphasis placed on education as a tool of national integration gave way to an emphasis on its contribution to the supply side of the economy (Maddison 1985: 61). Mass production coincided with the growing importance of formal scientific knowledge to industrial performance (Mowery and Rosenberg 1989). Higher-value-added industries, such as chemicals, rubber, petroleum, electrical machinery, tended to be more research-intensive than traditional industries, and during the period of forging ahead, this gap tended to widen (Mowery and Rosenberg 1989: tables 4.2 to 4.5). The newly evolving corporate structure quickly established its own formal technological skills in expectation of perceived market opportunities and first-mover advantages, and new corporate strategies—such as strategic patent—were developed to achieve an advantage over competitors. Still, state support in building linkages between industry and science was an important feature of this period. The earlier commitment to agricultural research and engineering training expanded significantly in the years before the World War I, through such initiatives as the Adams Act and public laboratories committed to applied experimentation and upgrading (Nelson and Wright 1992). The commitment of resources to college-level education—already in advance of most other countries—expanded during the period of forging ahead, particularly in the applied sciences, where close links with private firms created an effective network of highly trained workers. Moreover, local states which had often been ahead of the federal government and private business in some areas of scientific research continued to build educational ties with local industries (Scheiber 1987: 432).

During World War I, the state was again instrumental in redesigning governance structures to facilitate entrepreneurship. In a number of industries, trade associations were re-established to help co-ordinate the war economy. But more centralized co-ordinating structures such as the War Industries Board, the War Finance Corporation, and the Office of War Mobilization established a network of linkages with large corporations (Higgs 1989: 135–43). However, the lingering tension between these new patterns of governance and traditional notions of property-rights protection continued to obstruct the development of a more permanent state presence. Most federal agencies were rolled back after the war and, despite the

[45] From the figures provided by Douglas North the share of education in total federal and local spending fell slightly between the beginning of the century and 1950 (North 1974: 172).

unprecedented shock of the late 1920s and early 1930s, the institutional designs of the New Deal—which aimed to re-establish public governance to match those in the private sector—met a similar fate.

These institutional developments point to a more lasting failure of the period of forging ahead: the absence from the American national system of entrepreneurship of institutions to manage the more destructive features of capitalist development. By contrast to its long-standing commitment to education, the state's role in ensuring that other areas of social policy, such as welfare and housing, contributed positively to the overall growth path of the economy was noticeably absent. In the opening decades of this century, state governments passed social legislation (Skocpol and Ikenberry 1983). These initiatives culminated in a series of New Deal measures introduced during the 1930s. In this respect, the failure of the New Deal to tie its social legislation to the growth-enhancing capacities of the state was at least as important as the (emasculated) rise of Keynesian macroeconomic management. Whilst the Full Employment Act, eventually passed in 1946, could not hide the closer ties evolving between the state and industry, particularly through the strategic defence sector, the failure to construct a more permanent national system of social spending was perhaps the most damaging result of wartime recovery and the failure of a social-democratic trend to emerge from the American political economy (Maier 1987: 121–34).

CONCLUSION

The American economic tradition has played a leading role in publicizing the case of 'government failure' (see Chapter 2). The weight of the American economy in the global economy has ensured an attentive audience among policy-makers, particularly in developing countries and the economies in transition. Whatever the analytical limitations of this case, it contradicts America's own successful path to economic prosperity. The state has played a continuous, if uneven, role in the growth of the American economy. In this respect, the American economy has always been a mixed economy. However, the idea of mixture doesn't fully capture the extent of state involvement in institutional design, governance, and entrepreneurship and we have preferred to describe this evolution through a national system of entrepreneurship. This creative role of the American state has been obscured by the fascination among economic historians with an Anglo-Saxon pattern of economic development and by a distinctly American perspective of state action as predatory. Both these positions have been rejected in this chapter.

Rather, a national system of entrepreneurship has been defined through competing levels of state governance, technological and structural changes, and new opportunities for the private and public sectors which reflect

America's shift from catching up to economic leadership. Throughout this period, the state has sought to manage a process of creating and removing rents in support of economic development. The most consistent component of this was its willingness to create markets through its trade and procurement policies. During catching up, agricultural development and transportation gave a powerful forum for the state to express its creative role. However, by the late nineteenth century the very success of catching up gave way to a new period of rapid growth, the engine of which was in many respects beyond the institutional competencies and reach of the national state. Moreover, many of the state's more creative efforts in support of forging ahead—through procurement, standard setting, educational facilities, etc.—were in important respects obstructed by a legal system whose economic responsibilities had diminished significantly. As a result, the state was not able to create lasting institutions to match the new structures and strategies of private firms or to find appropriate social measures to offset the more destructive aspects of capitalist development. Although not discussed in this chapter, it seems realistic to contend that the tension between different aspects of state governance, and which only partially gave way during the 1930s, continued to shape the national system of entrepreneurship which evolved during and after World War II, as the United States economic leadership began to be challenged by other successful late developing economies.

REFERENCES

ABRAMOVITZ, M. (1989). 'Catching Up, Forging Ahead and Falling Behind', in *Thinking about Growth*. Cambridge: Cambridge University Press.

ALLEN, R. (1981). 'Accounting for Price Changes: American Steel Rails, 1850–1913', *Journal of Political Economy*, 89: 512–28.

AMSDEN, A. (1989). *Asia's Next Giant*. New York: Oxford University Press.

ANDREANO, R. (1965). *The New Economic History: Recent Papers in Methodology*. New York: Wiley Press.

ASHWORTH, W. (1985). 'Typologies and Evidence: Has Nineteenth Century Europe a Guide to Economic Growth', *Journal of Economic History*: 140–58.

BAIROCH, P. (1976). 'Europe's Gross National Product, 1800–1975', *The Journal of European Economic History*, 5/2.

—— (1982). 'International Industrialization Levels from 1750 to 1980', *Journal of European Economic History*, 11: 269–310.

—— (1993). *Economics and World History*. Brighton: Wheatsheaf.

—— et al. (1968). *International Historical Statistics*, i. *The Working Population and its Structure*. Brussels.

BARAN, P. and SWEEZY, P. (1966). *Monopoly Capitalism*. New York: Monthly Review Press.

BARDHAN, P. (1993). 'Economics of Development and the Development of Economics', *Journal of Economic Perspectives*, 7/2: 129–42.

BAUMOL, W. (1968). 'Entrepreneurship in Economic Theory', *American Economic Review*, 58, Papers and Proceedings: 64–71.

—— (1990). 'Entrepreneurship: Productive, Unproductive and Destructive', *Journal of Political Economy*, 98, 5: 893–921.

—— BLACKMAN, S., and WOLFF, E. (1989). *Productivity and American Leadership*. Cambridge, Mass.: MIT Press.

BEREND, I. and RANKI, G. (1974). *Economic Development in East-Central Europe in the 19th and 20th Centuries*. New York.

BEST, M. (1990). *The New Competition*. Cambridge: Polity Press.

BILS, M. (1984). 'Tariff Protection and Production in the Early U.S. Cotton Textile Industry', *Journal of Economic History*, 44: 1033–45.

BIRDZELL, L. and ROSENBERG, N. (1986). *How the West Grew Rich*. London: I. B. Taurus and Co. Ltd.

BOOTH, S. (1960). *Standardization Activities in the United States*. Washington, DC: Department of Commerce.

CAMERON, R. (1985). 'A New View of European Industrialization', *The Economic History Review*, 38 (Feb.), 1–23.

CAMPBELL, J., HOLLINGSWORTH, J., and LINDBERG, L. (1991). *Governance of the American Economy*. Cambridge: Cambridge University Press.

CHANDLER, A. (1977). *The Visible Hand: The Managerial Revolution in American Business*. Cambridge, Mass.: Harvard University Press.

—— (1980). 'The Growth of the Transnational Industrial Firm in the United States and the United Kingdom: A Comparative Analysis', *Economic History Review*, 32: 396–410.

—— (1990). *Scale and Scope: The Dynamics of Industrial Capitalism*. Cambridge, Mass.: Harvard University Press.

CHANG, H.-J. (1993). 'The Political Economy of Industrial Policy in Korea', *Cambridge Journal of Economics*, 17: 131–57.

—— (1994). *The Political Economy of Industrial Policy*. London: Macmillan.

—— and Kozul-Wright, R. (1994). 'Comparing National Systems of Entrepreneurship', *Journal of Development Studies* (July).

CLEMENCE, R. (ed.) (1989). *Essays on Entrepreneurship, Innovations, Business Cycles and the Evolution of Capitalism by Joseph Schumpeter*. New Brunswick, NJ: Transaction Publishers.

DAHMÉN, E. (1985). 'Development Blocks in Industrial Economics', *Scandinavian Economic History Review*, 36/1.

DAVID, P. (1991). 'Computer and Dynamo' in *Technology and Productivity: The Challenge for Economic Policy*. Paris: OECD.

—— (1992). 'Knowledge, Property and the System Dynamics of Technological Change', paper prepared for The World Bank Annual Conference on Development Economics, Washington, DC.

DAVIS, L. and NORTH, D. (1971). *Institutional Change and American Economic Growth*. Cambridge: Cambridge University Press.

DELL, G. (1991). 'Indirect Restrictions on Foreign Trade' in A. von Bogdany and E. Grabitz (eds.), *U.S. Trade Barriers: A Legal Analysis*. New York: Oceana Publications.

DOSI, G., FREEMAN, C., NELSON, R., SILVERBERG, G., and SOETE L. (eds.) (1988) *Technical Change and Economic Theory*. London: Pinter Publishers.

—— FABIANI, S., FREEMAN, C., and AVERSI, R. (1993). 'On the Process of Economic Development', CCC Working Paper 93-2. Berkeley: University of California.

EDWARDS, R. (1970). 'Economic Sophistication in 19th Century Tariff Debates', *Journal of Economic History*, 30: 802–38.

FREEMAN, C. (1992). 'Catching up in World Growth and World Trade', in M. Nissanke (ed.), *Essays in Honour of Alfred Maizels*. Oxford: Oxford University Press.

FREEMAN, C. and PEREZ, C. (1988). 'Structural Crises of Adjustment: Business Cycles and Investment Behaviour', in Dosi *et al.* (eds.).

GALBRAITH, J. K. (1962). *The Affluent Society*. London: Pelican.

—— (1967). *The New Industrial State*. New York: Mentor.

GERSHENKRON, A. (1966). *Economic Backwardness in Historical Perspective*. Cambridge, Mass.: Belknap Press.

GINZBERG, E. (1974). 'Government: The Fourth Factor', in P. David and M. Reder (eds.), *Nations and Households in Economic Growth*. New York: Academic Press.

GOODRICH, C. (1960). *Government Promotion of American Canals and Railroads, 1800–1890*.

GORDON, D., EDWARDS, R., and REICH, M. (1984). *Segmented Work, Divided Workers*. Cambridge: Cambridge University Press.

HALL, P. (ed.) (1989). *The Political Power of Economic Ideas: Keynesianism Across Nations*. Princeton: Princeton University Press.

HAMMOND, B. (1957). *Banks and Politics in America: From the Revolution to the Civil War*. Princeton: Princeton University Press.

HANDLIN, O. and HANDLIN, M. (1969). *Commonwealth: A Study of the Role of Government in the American Economy: Massachusetts, 1774–1861*. Cambridge, Mass.: Harvard University Press.

HARTZ, L. (1948). *Economic Policy and Democratic Thought: Pennsylvania 1776–1860*. Cambridge, Mass.: Harvard University Press.

HEATH, M. (1954). *Constructive Liberalism: The Role of the State in Economic Development in Georgia to 1860*. Cambridge, Mass.: Harvard University Press.

HIGGS, R. (1991). *Crisis and Leviathan*. Oxford: Oxford University Press.

HIRSCHMAN, A. (1970). *Exit, Voice and Loyalty*. Cambridge, Mass.: Harvard University Press.

—— (1987). 'Linkages', *The New Palgrave*. London: Macmillan.

HOBSBAWM, E. (1964). *Industry and Empire*. Harmondsworth: Penguin.

—— (1985). *The Age of Capital, 1848–1875*. London: Abacus.

HODGSON, G. (1988). *The Economics of Institutions*. Cambridge: Polity Press.

HOLLINGSWORTH, J. (1991). 'The Logic of Coordinating American Manufacturing Sector', in Campbell *et al.*

HORWITZ, M. (1977). *The Transformation of American Law*. Cambridge, Mass.: Harvard University Press.

JOHNSON, B. and LUNDVALL, B. (1989). 'Limits of the Pure Market', in *Samhällsventenskap, Economioch Historia—Festskrift till Lars Harlitz*. Göteborg: Daidalos.

JORDE, T. and TEECE, D. (1990). 'Innovation and Cooperation: Implications for Competition and Antitrust', *Journal of Economic Perspectives*, 4/3.

KALDOR, N. (1977). 'Capitalism and Industrial Development: Some Lessons From British Experience', *Cambridge Journal of Economics*, 1: 193–204.

—— (1985). *Economics without Equilibrium*. Cardiff: University College Cardiff Press.

—— (1989). 'The Role of Increasing Returns, Technical Progress and Cumulative Causation in the Theory of International Trade and Economic Growth' in F. Tagetti and A. Thirlwall (eds.) (1993), *The Essential Kaldor*. London: Duckworth.

KOLKO, G. (1977). *The Triumph of Conservatism*. New York: Free Press.

KRUGMAN, P. (1992). 'The Counter-Counter Revolution in Development Economics', in *Proceedings of the World Bank Annual Conference on Development Economics*, Washington, DC: World Bank.

—— (1993). *Geography and Trade*. Cambridge, Mass.: MIT Press.

LALL, S. (1991). 'Explaining Industrial Success in the Industrial World' in V. N. Balasubramanyam and S. Lall (eds.), *Issues in Development Economics*. London: Macmillan.

LANDES, D. (1990). 'Why Are We So Rich and They So Poor?', *American Economic Review*, 80.

LEVINE, M. (1988). 'Introduction: The State and Democracy in America—Historical Patterns and Current Possibilities' in *The State and Democracy*. London: Routledge.

LUNDVALL, B. (1988). 'Innovation as an Interactive Process: From User–Producer Interaction to the National System of Innovation', in Dosi *et al.* (eds.).

McCRAW, T. (1983). 'Mercantilism and the Market: Antecedents of American Industrial Policy', in C. Barfield and W. Schambra (eds.), *The Politics of Industrial Policy*. Washington, DC: American Enterprise Institute.

MADDISON, A. (1985). 'Origins and Impact of the Welfare State, 1883–1983', *Banco Nationale de Lavoro Review*, 55–87.

—— (1991). *Dynamic Forces in Capitalist Development*. Oxford: Oxford University Press.

—— (1992). 'Explaining the Economic Performance of Nations, 1820–1989', mimeo, University of Groningen.

MAIER, C. (1987). *In Search of Stability*. Cambridge: Cambridge University Press.

MILLER, N. (1962). *The Enterprise of a Free People: Aspects of Economic Development in New York State During the Canal Period, 1792–1838*.

MOWERY, D. C. and ROSENBERG, N. (1989). *Technology and the Pursuit of Economic Growth*. Cambridge: Cambridge University Press.

NELSON, R. (1986). 'Incentives for Entrepreneurship and Supporting Innovations' in B. Balassa (ed.), *Economic Incentives*. London: Macmillan.

—— and WRIGHT, G. (1992). 'The Rise and Fall of American Technological Leadership: The Postwar Era in Historical Perspective', *Journal of Economic Literature*, 30: 1931–64.

NORTH, D. (1974). *Growth and Welfare in the American Past*. Englewood Cliffs, NJ: Prentice-Hall.

—— (1981). *Structure and Change in Economic History*. New York: W. W. Norton & Co.

—— (1990). *Institutions, Institutional Change and Economic Performance*. Cambridge: Cambridge University Press.

—— (1994). 'Economic Performance Through Time', *American Economic Review*, 84: 359–68.

OLSON, M. (1982). *The Rise and Decline of Nations*. New Haven: Yale University Press.

PANIĆ, MIĆA (1992). *European Monetary Union: Lessons From the Gold Standard*. London: Macmillan.

POLANYI, K. (1957). *The Great Transformation*. Cambridge, Mass.: Belknap Press.

RAUSSER, G. (1992). 'Predatory versus Productive Government: The Case of U.S. Agricultural Policies', *Journal of Economic Perspectives*, 6/3: 133–58.

REICH, R. (1991). 'Entrepreneurship Reconsidered: The Team as Hero', in *Participative Management*. Cambridge, Mass.: Harvard Business Review.

ROSENBERG, N. (1985). *Inside the Black Box*. Cambridge: Cambridge University Press.

SCHEIBER, H. (1981). 'Regulation, Property Rights and Definition of the Market: Law and the American Economy', *The Journal of Economic History*, 41: 103–9.

—— (1987). 'State Law and "Industrial Policy" in American Development, 1790–1987', *California Law Review*: 415–44.

SCHUMPETER, J. (1949). 'Economic Theory and Entrepreneurial History', in R. Clemence (ed.), *Essays on Entrepreneurship, Innovations, Business Cycles and the Evolution of Capitalism*. New Brunswick, NJ: Transaction Publishers.

—— (1987). *Capitalism, Socialism and Democracy*, 6th edn. London: Unwin Paperbacks.

SINGH, A. (1993). 'The Stock Market and Economic Development: Should Developing Countries Encourage Stock Markets?', *UNCTAD Review*, 4: 1–28.

SKOCPOL, T. and IKENBERRY, J. (1983). 'The Political Formation of the American Welfare State in Historical and Comparative Perspective', *Comparative Social Research*, 6: 126–31.

STEDMAN JONES, G. (1980). 'The History of US Imperialism', in R. Blackburn (ed.), *Ideology in Social Science*. London: Fontana.

STEIN, H. (1969). *The Fiscal Revolution in America*. Chicago: Chicago University Press.

STIGLITZ, J. (1992). 'Comment on Krugman' in *Proceedings of the World Bank Annual Conference on Development Economics*. Washington, DC: World Bank.

SWEEZY, A. (1972). 'The Keynesians and Government Policy, 1933–1939', *American Economic Review*, 62: 116–24.

THOMPSON, G. (ed.) (1989). *Industrial Policy—USA and UK Debates*. London: Routledge.

TOMLINSON, J. (1985). *British Macroeconomic Policy Since 1940*. London: Croom Helm.

VEBLEN, T. (1979). *The Theory of the Leisure Class*. Harmondsworth: Penguin Books.

WADE, R. (1990). *Governing the Market*. Princeton: Princeton University Press.

WEIR, M. and SKOCPOL, T. (1986). 'State Structures and the Possibilities for "Keynesian" Responses to the Great Depression in Sweden, Great Britain and the United States', in P. Evans *et al.* (eds.), *Bringing the State Back In*. Cambridge: Cambridge University Press.

WILKINS, M. (1988). 'European and North American Multinationals, 1870–1914: Comparisons and Contrasts', *Business History*, 30: 8–45.

WINCH, D. (1969). *Economics and Policy*. London: Hodder and Stoughton.

WRIGHT, G. (1990). 'The Origins of American Industrial Success', *American Economic Review*, 80: 651–68.

5

Resolving the State–Market Dilemma in East Asia

Robert Wade

Bigger and better markets often need bigger and better states; but bigger states often seek to control, remove, or distort markets. This is the state–market dilemma, in Michael Lipton's elegant formulation.[1]

This chapter focuses on how Taiwan and Korea (with references also to Japan and Hong Kong) resolved the state–market dilemma. But before coming to this subject, we first discuss East Asian economic performance, and then the debate about the role of government in economic development. At the end we address some questions of replicability, and some more general conclusions about economic and political policy.

INDICATORS OF EAST ASIA'S ECONOMIC SUCCESS

Take as a performance measure the change in a country's per capita dollar GNP relative to the average of the long-term core countries (North-West Europe and North America). Though such a measure has many problems (it should be adjusted for purchasing power parity, or at least for fluctuations in exchange rates and terms of trade), it is useful enough for present purposes. Table 5.1 sets out the numbers for countries and regions of the world from 1938 to 1988.

Note three things about Korea's position. First, in 1960 Korea was very low in the world economic hierarchy—much lower than Latin America, lower than the Middle East and North Africa, lower than Southern and Central Africa, about the same as South-East Asia, but above South Asia and Western and Eastern Africa. Secondly, Korea has risen very fast, so that by 1988 its ratio was higher than that of all of the regions which it had been below less than thirty years before. Thirdly, Korea's gain has been especially dramatic during the 1980s, from 13 per cent in 1980 to 20 per

Much of the data and argument of this paper comes from Robert Wade (1990). 'Governing the Market: Economic Theory and the Role of Government' in *East Asian Industrialization*, Princeton: Princeton University Press. See also Wade (1992) 'East Asia's Economic Success: Conflicting paradigms, Partial Insights, Shaky Evidence', *World Politics*. (Jan.).

[1] Michael Lipton (1991). 'The State–Market Dilemma, Civil Society, and Structural Adjustment', *The Round Table*, 317: 21–31.

Table 5.1 Comparative economic performance

	1938	1960	1980	1988
Core:				
NW Europe, N. America, Australia, and New Zealand	100	100	100	100
E. Asia:				
Japan	21	23	76	118
S. Korea	n.a.	8	13	20
S. Europe				
Italy	32	37	61	75
Spain	42	19	48	43
Latin America	20	17	20	11
Middle East and N. Africa	n.a.	12	11	7
Sub-Saharan Africa				
West and East	n.a.	7	5	2
South and Central	25	11	n.a.	6
S. Asia	8	4	2	2
SE Asia	n.a.	7	6	4
Yugoslavia	41	28	23	14

Measure: GNP per capita, weighted by population as % of core.
Source: G. Arrighi (1990). 'World Income Inequalities and the Future of Socialism', mimeograph, Braudel Center, Binghampton, NY: SUNY.

cent in 1988 (that is, its dollar GNP per capita relative to the average of North-West Europe and North America rose from 13 per cent to 20 per cent in less than a decade). During this same decade the relative economic performance of most poor regions of the world deteriorated. Brazil, for example, rose from 12 per cent in 1960 to 18 per cent in 1980—and back to 12 per cent in 1988. Korea is about the only sizeable developing country to improve its position *vis-à-vis* the core during the 1980s. (Taiwan would show a similar rise from a higher base had it been in the sample.)

Another indicator is the number of hours of paid labour that an unskilled male labourer must work to earn the equivalent of 100 kilograms of the basic food-grain. This 'economic hardship' measure, like the gap measure, is also full of problems; most obviously it should include not just the cost of food but also the cost of shelter as well as the probability of employment. But it does allow rough and ready comparisons of hardship in one country across time and even between countries. Here are some results:[2]

- France and Germany from the seventeenth to the late nineteenth century inclusive (using the price of wheat and the wage of a plasterer's

[2] Source for European data: Fernand Braudel (1981). *The Structures of Everyday Life: The Limits of the Possible*. London: Collins: table 2.4. The other figures are my own calculations, based on data collected at each location. See further Wade (1990): 39–40.

or bricklayer's assistant as the standard): well above 100 hours; between 1700 and 1860 one-third of the observations are at or above 200 hours.
- France, 1920–30: 40–60 hours.
- India (Delhi), 1991: 140–170 hours.
- South Africa (Cape Town), 1991: 50 hours.
- Taiwan (Taipei), 1950s: 150–200 hours (a little lower, on average, than France between 1700 and 1850).
- Taiwan (Taipei), early 1980s, a quarter of a century later: 40–60 hours.
- USA (Washington), mid-1980s, using minimum legal wage: 15 hours.

These figures, like the first set on relative per capita GNP, underscore both the magnitude of the transformation that has occurred in East Asia, far larger than anywhere else in the world, and also the huge gap in mass living standards compared with the core that remains.

THE DEBATE

The Neo-Liberal View

What accounts for the outstanding economic success of East Asia? Among professional economists and the main international financial institutions, the standard view has been that the East-Asian economies succeeded mainly because their governments followed economic policies which did not obstruct the natural growth-inducing processes of capitalist market economies. Governments elsewhere in the developing world failed to exercise such restraint, and their citizens paid dearly for it.

This 'neo-liberal' view emphasizes the importance of East Asia's near free trade regime, undistorted exchange rates, conservative government budgeting, high real interest rates, and free labour market. Hong Kong is the paradigm.

But over the past decade much evidence has come in that questions this view. This evidence suggests that Taiwan and Korea (1) did not have unusually liberal trade regimes; that (2) in some respects their public sectors were unusually large; that (3) Korea's high real interest rates through the banking system prevailed for only a few years, 1967–71, after which they were very low or negative; that (4) both states operated tightly controlled financial systems (Korean banks were owned by the state until the early 1980s; Taiwan's are only now in the process of being nominally privatized); and that (5) both governments carried out policies to promote specific industries in succession, using subsidized and targeted credit, fiscal concessions, and protection to alter profit functions, and using quite a lot of arm twisting as well, in order to induce or cajole more resources into targeted sectors than would flow in the absence of such 'distortions'.

Faced with evidence of this sort, neo-liberal economists have revised the core interpretation in one of three ways. Some simply acknowledge that Korea, for example, had relatively high protection from, say, 1960 to 1985, but then pass on without attempting to say what implications this fact has for the neo-liberal prescription for nearly free trade. This is the simplest response.[3]

Other neo-liberals have come to agree that Korea and Taiwan were not cases of *laissez faire*, that the state did take an 'active role' in the economy; but then, in specifying the content of that active role, emphasize only the provision of public goods, like education, and say little about state policies which distorted prices or blocked market exchanges. This keeps the explanation consistent with the neo-liberal prescription of what governments should and should not do, while making a rhetorical concession to the new sympathy for intervention.

A third group acknowledges these various interventions and price distortions, but then says that the distortions were sufficiently balanced to cancel each other out in the aggregate. The distortions in effect 'simulated' a free market. This group further implies that if the whole array of distortionary policies were withdrawn at a stroke there would be no more than short-term effects on resource allocation. In World Bank economist Frederick Berger's words, 'I believe that the crux of the Korean example is that the active interventionist attitude of the State has been aimed at applying moderate incentives which are very close to the relative prices of products and factors that would prevail in a situation of free trade.'[4]

The trade theorist Jagdish Bhagwati combines the second and the third responses. 'The Far Eastern economies (with the exception of Hong Kong) and others that have come close to the EP strategy [export promotion strategy consisting of getting the average effective exchange rate for importables approximately equal to that for exportables] have been characterized by considerable government activity in the economic system. In my judgement, such intervention can be of great value, and almost certainly has been so, in making the EP strategy work successfully.'[5] What are the components of this 'considerable government activity' that has been 'of great value'? The interventions of great value are interventions that establish the necessary confidence in the minds of producers that the government's commitment to the EP strategy is serious (but Bhagwati gives no

---

[3] See e.g. James Riedel (1988). 'Economic Development in East Asia: Doing What Comes Naturally?' in Helen Hughes (ed.), *Achieving Industrialization in East Asia*, Cambridge: Cambridge University Press; Seiji Naya (1988), 'The Role of Trade Policies in the Industrialization of Rapidly Growing Asian Developing Countries', in Hughes.

[4] Frederick Berger (1979). 'Korea's Experience with Export-Led Industrial Development', in B. de Vries (ed.), *Export Promotion Policies*, Staff Wording Paper no. 313, Washington, DC: World Bank: 64.

[5] Jagdish Bhagwati (1988). 'Export-Promoting Trade Strategy: Issues and Evidence', *World Bank Research Observer* 3/1 (Jan.): 27–57, at p. 33, emphasis added.

indication of what precisely these interventions are). He mentions in passing that the EP strategy does not preclude import substitution in selected sectors, but gives no attention to this combination. In this way Bhagwati recognizes the fact of considerable government 'intervention' in the East Asian cases, but then implies that, in so far as those interventions helped more than they hindered, they did so by creating and reinforcing some of the neoclassical growth conditions. Interventions that do not meet this criterion are treated as by the first group: acknowledged but ignored as being of no consequence for the theorems or the recipe.

In one or more of these ways neo-liberal economists are able to say that (1) they know that Korea, Taiwan, and Japan have not been paragons of *laissez faire*; (2) state intervention was, however, mostly consistent with neo-liberal principles (it simulated a free market); and (3) any interventions that are inconsistent with those principles were unimportant enough to ignore; no more than 'window dressing'. But there is no evidence for this last proposition; it follows from an assumption that the theorems must be right, so that anything inconsistent with the theorems must (in the context of a successful case) be unimportant enough to ignore. In this way the paradigm is protected against data that would upset this way of looking at things (a form of protection its exponents are not anxious to eliminate). Nowhere is this nonchalance towards contrary data more evident than in the way that leading trade policy economists like Bhagwati, Anne Kreuger, James Riedel, and others have avoided a serious engagement with East Asian trade regimes, to which we come shortly.

Two Kinds of State–Market Interactions

Behind this neo-liberal interpretation—both the simple and the revised versions—lies a theory that views most of the interactions between states and markets as a *vicious* circle:

1. More and stronger state action subverts or distorts markets (other than the provision of public goods and, in Bhagwati's formulation, policies which enhance producers' confidence that the government will stick to an EP strategy).

2. The gainers in such subverted markets use their gains to subvert the state yet further.

The solution is a compressed state, with smaller shares of GNP flowing through state channels of allocation, allowing healthier markets. The East Asian and Latin American counter-cases are taken to show the truth of both sides of the argument.

Outside the mainstream is a more miscellaneous body of analysts, many of whom emphasize the role of the state. These 'statists' imply a theory of state–market interactions as a *virtuous* circle:

1. More and stronger state action aids more efficient and sustainable markets, by providing infrastructure, education, enforcement of property rights, commodities subject to both large economies of scale and diseconomies of private monopoly regulation, and early investments in high entry barrier industries important for the economy's future growth.

2. The incentives, rivalry, and feedback of these markets in turn help keep state actors effective and efficient.

The difference between East Asia and Latin America lies not in the size of the state, but in East Asia's more disciplined use of state power in line with criteria related to the national economic interest.

In the general case, there is clearly truth in *both* arguments: bigger and better markets do often need bigger and better states, while bigger states do often seek to control or remove markets.

The state-market dilemma directs our attention to two big questions about East Asia which may help us supersede the stale old 'states or markets' debate. (1) From the first horn of the dilemma, what have East Asian states done to widen and improve the workings of markets, especially in terms of the ability of markets to generate growth or new resources—as distinct from their ability to generate efficiency in the use of existing resources. And as a sub-question, how much of this is consistent with neo-liberal prescriptions as to what governments should and should not do? (2) From the second horn of the dilemma, what has disciplined the state in East Asia not to subvert or remove markets, at least not to the degree of impeding growth? Why hasn't there been massive 'government failure'?

STATE ACTIONS TO IMPROVE THE CAPACITY OF MARKETS TO GENERATE GROWTH

The key feature of industrial policy in Korea and Taiwan was a 'governed market'. This is a system of (1) mostly private enterprises competing and sometimes co-operating (2) under state supervision, in the context of (3) heavy investment in education.

In this system there were *both* large amounts of *dirigisme* and large amounts of competition. The competition came in large part in export markets, competition in the domestic market being (as we shall see) somewhat buffered by protection. The *dirigisme* was guided neither by the half-light of economic theory nor by the preferences of vote-seeking politicians. Rather, the technocrats paid close attention to (1) the industries needed to boost military self-sufficiency, (2) the Japanese model, down to quite specific organizational arrangements, (3) results in export markets, and (4) private demand for imports of capital and intermediate goods. With criteria derived from these sources, they did a lot of what neoclassical economists say bureaucrats cannot do well: they picked particular industries for special promotion, encouraging resources into them beyond what individual companies were prepared to risk. They treated particular industries at any one time (latterly within information, electronics, and biotechnology) as the natural successors of the bridges and lighthouses of Adam Smith's day, which he thought too critical for the general welfare to be left to market forces.

With governed markets, Korea and Taiwan managed to obtain (1) the economies of scale that come from acting in a wide economic space—the international market—plus (2) the innovations induced by competititon, plus (3) some buffering of domestic producers from international competition in the domestic market, and (4) some reduction of risks or increases in profits in industries which the government deemed important for the economy's future growth. Both countries were able to ride the wave of internationalization while at the same time imposing a politically determined directional thrust on resource allocation within the national territory, integrating and transforming the production structure faster than would have occurred had the controllers of capital been allowed to operate within an unconstrained logic of global profit maximization.

No other developing countries achieved this combination. China, India, and Eastern Europe, for example, had plenty of *dirigisme* (of a less strategically focused kind), but little competition; and apart from Eastern Europe they had much less of a sustained commitment to raising skill levels.

Let us consider two domains of state action in East Asia: education and protection. State regulation of and even supply of education is generally considered to be consistent with the neo-liberal recipe, because of its externalities and public good characteristics; protection is generally considered to be quite inconsistent.

Education

One of the most striking things about Korea, Taiwan, and even more Japan, is the increase in the ratios of skilled to basically skilled to unskilled people in the labour force over the past forty years. This is measured not just in terms of level of education attained, but in terms of the content of the education: a high proportion of the total is in engineering or science. In a population of 20 million, Taiwan's junior colleges have produced over 20,000 engineering diploma holders a year over the 1980s, the universities another 10,000 bachelor-level engineers a year (nearly twice as many as the USA in relation to population). About a quarter of all university graduates since 1960 have been engineers (law graduates, 1.2 per cent). Science and engineering students together accounted for over one-third of post-high-school graduates during the 1960s, and over a half by the 1980s.

The rapidly rising skill level is fundamentally important in the East Asia story. Its particular importance rests on some recent research on North-

South trade in manufactures, which concludes that this trade 'is based almost entirely on differences in the availability of human skills . . . [and] not on differences in the availability of capital'.[6] That is to say, comparative advantage, in the context of North–South trade in manufactures, rests largely on the skill composition of the labour force; and shifts in a country's comparative advantage in the direction of higher wage activities are dependent upon rises in the ratios of skilled to basically skilled to unskilled labour.

Behind this is the argument that product categories can be ranked in terms of the skill mix needed for their production, and the categories that are 'appropriate' to a country at any one time (in the sense of being in line with comparative advantage) can be read off by comparing the product's skill requirements with the skill composition of the labour force—because the ratios of skilled to basically skilled to unskilled people determine the scarcity and relative cost of different levels of skill, and therefore the viability of investments that require different combinations of these skill levels. So it was the onrush of technically educated people into the labour force of Korea, Taiwan, and Japan that lowered the relative cost of skilled labour, allowing investments in progressively more skill-intensive, higher wage activities to be viable.

What about government policy for education? The onrush of skilled people was not simply the result of citizen preferences. The government has steered the demand for education through a series of manpower plans. In Taiwan the actual results—in terms of expansion of enrolments in different subjects, the balance between private and public schooling, the overall rate of expansion, the proportion of GNP for education—have corresponded fairly closely to the targets of these plans.[7] Moreover, many of the targets have run *counter* to citizen demand. For example, post-junior-high school enrolments in *vocational* institutions expanded much faster than enrolments in academic institutions, raising the ratio of vocational to academic places from 40:60 in 1963 to 69:31 in 1986. Growth of the academic institutions has been deliberately restrained. But the rate of private return on education in the academic institutions has been calculated to be higher than that on education in the vocational institutions, suggesting that the restriction on expansion of the academic institutions runs counter to private demand. In sum, even within the domain of education the Taiwan government did not maximize the scope for individual preferences.[8]

---

[6] Adrian Wood (1990). 'A New–Old Theoretical View of North–South Trade, Employment and Wages', Discussion Paper. 292, Institute of Development Studies, Sussex University: p. ii. This paper is based on a chapter of his book, *North–South Trade, Employment and Inequality*. Oxford: Oxford University Press.

[7] Jennie Hay Woo (1988). 'Education and Industrial Growth in Taiwan: A Use of Planning', EEPA Discussion Paper 18, Harvard Institute of International Development.

[8] Another example of government forcefulness in the education field. In 1983 the Taiwan government launched an aggressive programme to induce more Taiwan-born students,

Protection

Still less did the East Asian governments allow consumer preferences to prevail in international trade. All three East Asian countries have had closely managed trade regimes (in Japan's case, most of the protection, or at least that part of it caused by state policies, was removed between 1970 and 1980). Their regimes are inconsistent in major ways with even a modified neoclassical account of a good trade regime. For example, Bela Balassa, a leading advocate of a modified neoclassical prescription, recognizes the case for giving some special encouragement to manufacturing on grounds of (1) externalities and (2) the excess of market wages over the economic cost of unskilled labour. He argues in favour of abolishing import quotas and setting a relatively low uniform rate of tariff protection of around 10 per cent. He accepts that on infant industry grounds there may be a case for granting a higher rate of protection to new firms, but at no more than 20 per cent with no distinction drawn between different infant industries or firms. This protection should last for no more than five to eight years.[9]

I shall concentrate on Taiwan, which is often presented as an exemplar of a liberal trade regime. The main evidence for this view is the study by Lee and Liang using data from as long ago as 1969.[10] This study does indeed show Taiwan as having, at that time, a relatively low average level of protection overall, and for manufacturing in particular. But there are two basic problems. (1) If we disaggregate even a little, we find that Lee and Liang's results show significant industry and trade bias between industries (that is, significant differences in the extent to which different industries are spurred on by policy-based incentives, and significant differences between industries in the balance of incentives to export or sell on the domestic market). (2) In any case, methodological problems mean that we have to be cautious about accepting the study's results at face value. In particular, certain assumptions and omissions have the likely effect of either making the amount of inter-industry incentive *bias* seem lower than it really is (that is, of concealing the true degree of incentive non-uniformity), or of making the average *level* of protection seem lower than it really is.

Some other evidence for later periods suggests substantial—not unusually low—protection. For example: (1) In 1984, after waves of much

engineers, and scientists abroad to return. Instead of waiting for them to contact it, it set about contacting all likely candidates. It built up a list of 10,000 Chinese students and graduates in high-tech fields whose skills would be of interest to Taiwan. It contacted every name on the list to explain the incentives to return. It keeps in touch with potential recruits and regularly reminds them of the opportunities. It administers a programme to bring them back for short-term assignments, so that they can test the waters at little cost to themselves. By these means, government helps to convert a 'brain drain' into a 'brain bank'.

[9] Bela Balassa *et al.* (1982). *Development Strategies in Semi-Industrial Economies*. Baltimore: Johns Hopkins University Press.

[10] T. H. Lee and K. S. Liang (1982). 'Taiwan' in Balassa *et al.* (1982): ch. 10.

vaunted 'liberalization', 54 per cent of Taiwan's imports by value were still covered by various non-tariff barriers. The most comprehensive required prior approval of the import by either the domestic producer of substitutes or a government department. All steel imports, for example, had to be approved by the big public enterprise steel-making company, China Steel until 1987. (2) The average legal tariff in 1984 was 31 per cent, about the same as the developing country average of 34 per cent for tariffs and other trade charges.[11] Yet, since Taiwan's tariffs had come down before this much faster than the developing country average, we can infer that Taiwan's average legal tariff before then had been higher than the developing country average.

In the neoclassical argument, protection has four main harmful effects. (1) High protection eases or removes pressure on domestic producers to lower their costs to international levels. (2) High protection makes for high dispersion in protection levels between industries, resulting in unplanned and undesirable differential incentives. (3) High protection harms exports and agriculture. (4) High protection induces rent-seeking, which causes social losses.

We consider just two of these effects here. How was protection arranged so as (1) not to eliminate international competitive pressure on domestic producers, and so as (2) not to harm exports? The key point is that protection policies operated in the context of a strong government emphasis on exports. The government (here I refer to both Korea and Tawain) created a special regime for exporters that enabled them to obtain imported inputs quickly and at near-world prices. This was supplemented by a facility that covered much or all of their working capital requirements at lower than normal bank loan rates. Both these facilities operated according to well-established rules, and were automatically available to exporters.[12]

More broadly, the goverment came to take export performance as a criterion for discretionary judgements. If a firm wanted help for one reason or another (perhaps to avoid penalties for building a factory outside the land zoning plan) its request would be more favourably viewed if it could point to good export performance. Exporting became what in the language of game theory is called a 'focal point' of government–business relations, with players on both sides knowing that export performance would be used as a principle for adjudicating unforeseen contingencies. Firms therefore sought to export not just to get the various export incentives, but also to build up 'credit' in their future dealings with government. In this sense there was a government-created export 'culture'.

[11] R. Erzan et al. (1988). 'The Profile of Protection in Developing Countries', Discussion Paper 21, Geneva: UNCTAD.
[12] See Robert Wade (1991). 'How to Protect Exports from Protection: Taiwan's Duty Drawback Scheme', The World Economy 14/3: 299–309.

Even firms enjoying protected domestic sales were under pressure to enter export markets. Indeed, the sheltering of their domestic sales allowed them to practise discriminatory pricing, charging higher prices on domestic sales and using the higher profits to subsidize scale-enhancing and competition-providing exports. In 1979 the average total cost of the Hyundai car, the Pony, was US$3,700; the domestic price was $5,000; the price abroad was $2,200.[13] Similar dual pricing continued at least to the late 1980s.[14]

Even in some heavy, upstream industries where firms directly exported rather little and where they have enjoyed substantial protection, firms have been under competitive pressure to lower costs to international levels. If their prices get much above the cost of import substitutes, exporters can petition the government to allow in more imports, and they will probably have some success. (The allowable proportion of imports in the total use of a specific chemical, for example, may be raised from 40 per cent to 60 per cent for a limited period.) In other words, the protection given through non-tariff barriers is not unconditional. The government often sponsors negotiations between upstream firms and downstream user firms (in petrochemicals, for example), aimed at balancing the interest of upstream firms in having a reliable base of domestic demand against that of downstream firms in getting inputs at world market prices. This balance expresses the compromises between the competitiveness of present-day exports and the government's conviction that the industrial structure should be changed towards higher value-added activities at a speed faster than unguided market forces alone would produce. To soften the trade-off between present and future, the government devotes considerable resources to assessing the long-run prospects of various technologies, goods, and foreign markets, as well as providing plenty of current market information for domestic producers and foreign buyers.

Still another use of quantitative trade management to aid industrial transformation is seen in the following case. A large multinational was producing on Taiwan a product which required an unusually high purity in a certain chemical. Domestic makers could not supply the chemical at this purity, and the company was allowed to import its requirement. At a certain point, the Industrial Development Bureau official who supervises that part of the chemical chain began to think that production at the higher level of purity was within the technological capability of the Taiwan-based makers. He discussed the possibilities with the makers, and he discussed them also with the multinational. He encouraged the latter to make a purchasing agreement with the domestic makers to guarantee them sales if they under-

[13] Yun-han Chu (1987). 'Authoritarian Regimes Under Stress: The Political Economy of Adjustment in the East Asian NICs', doctoral diss., Political Science Dept., University of Minnesota.

[14] *Automotive News* (1988). 'Hyundai Canada guilty of predatory pricing' (22 Feb.): 1, 37.

took the requisite investment in plant and skills. The multinational was doubtful. But after a while, it found that its applications to import the chemical, previously approved automatically, began to be delayed—and the delays began to lengthen. It got the message; it did enter into a purchasing agreement with the domestic suppliers, and they did upgrade their capacity. Replicated across many industries, this shows how the Taiwan industrial policy officials can nudge the production structure into more sophisticated activities. But note that the necessary condition for this to work is that the domestic makers be able, within not too long a time, to produce to the required standard of purity and at not much above the world market price.

In short, the procedures by which protection is administered suggest how the shape of Taiwan's protection regime and its integration into a wider export and industrial transformation strategy may have offset the predicted neoclassical costs of protection on domestic cost levels and on exports. Protection administered in this way may even have helped to accelerate the shift of comparative advantage into higher value-added activities, by means of a 'learning-by-doing' effect on skills.[15]

East Asian trade regimes, and their industrial policies more generally, gave government officials, often men and women in their thirties, much discretion. From the neo-liberal treatment of government-in-general, we would expect that this discretion would have been systematically misused.[16] Yet it would be hard to argue that, however we define 'misuse of discretion', it has happened on a significantly growth-retarding scale in Korea and Taiwan. This brings us to the second horn of the state–market dilemma.

WHAT HAS DISCIPLINED THE STATE?

Bigger states are often capable of and interested in removing, controlling, or intervening in markets in ways that obstruct growth. In neoclassical economics there are three broad arguments that explain such a tendency.

1. The information available to public officials is inherently more limited or inaccurate than for decentralized private agents. This questions the ability of government to carry out its intentions, whatever those intentions may be.

2. Government interventions create 'rents' for whose capture private agents use resources 'wastefully' or 'unproductively', in growth-inhibiting ways. This likewise questions the ability of government to implement its

[15] For more on Taiwan's trade management see Wade (1990): ch. 5; 'How to Manage Trade: Taiwan as a Challenge to Economics', *Comparative Politics* (1991); 'How to Protect Exports from Protection: Taiwan's Duty Drawback System', *The World Economy*. 14/3, 299–309.

[16] William Niskanen (1971). *Bureaucracy and Representative Government*. Chicago: Aldine-Atherton. David Colander (ed.) (1984). *Neoclassical Political Economy: The Analysis of Rent-seeking and DUP Activities*. Cambridge, Mass.: Ballinger.

policies with the intended net effects (because the costs, once broadened to include the unproductive use of resources to capture government-created rents, are likely to exceed the benefits).

3. Government officials tend to seek objectives only distantly related to the ostensible public purposes of their agencies, especially because their behaviour is less constrained by anything analogous to the profit imperative for business people. This argument questions the extent to which the real— as distinct from publicly stated—objectives of government actions are to correct market failure and promote the public interest.

In short, as government becomes bigger and more active, according to the neoclassical view, the net impact of its growing attempts to change the composition of economic activity is likely to be harmful to growth, for reasons to do with information, rents, and the discrepancy between ostensible and real bureaucratic objectives. What has checked these tendencies in East Asia? This is the jackpot question.

There is no simple answer. We can make some headway and avoid a completely *ad hoc*, regionally specific and historically unique kind of explanation (e.g. 'Confucian values') by looking at the East Asian facts through the lens of the three neoclassical arguments about 'government failure' given above.

Information

The information problem has been eased in several ways. First, the civil service is still an elite career, even today when the private sector pays much more, which helps to overcome compliance and asymmetric information problems within bureaucratic agencies. (English-language speakers take note: it is in the English-language countries—the UK, the USA, Canada, Australia, and New Zealand—where vigorous efforts have been made over the 1980s to move away from the concept of an elite civil service with lifetime employment.)[17] Secondly, the economic bureaucracy is staffed by people with high levels of technical expertise which reinforces the first effect.

Thirdly, central officials draw on expertise and information located in the forest of parastatal 'research and service' organizations surrounding the core economic bureaucracy. For example, when Taiwan officials need to make decisions about protection in one of the branches of electronics, they get advice from the Electronics Research and Service Organization (ERSO), with a staff of 1,700 in 1987. These research and service organizations are able to employ specialists more flexibly than the central government service can.

[17] Christopher Pollitt (1990). *Managerialism and the Public Services: The Anglo-American Experience*. Oxford: Blackwell.

Fourthly, the government invests substantially in acquiring information and making it available. Officials can know within forty-eight hours what is imported and exported from the country, for example. In Taiwan, Industrial Development Bureau officials responsible for monitoring particular sectors spend several days a month making factory visits up and down the country. The Export Quality Control scheme required that each exporting factory be inspected at least once a year by a team of experts in quality control, who grade the factory's quality control system (the higher the grade the lower the inspection fee). Through both channels (factory visits by Industrial Development Bureau official and by export quality control officials), governmental decision-making can be based on detailed knowledge of production conditions and capabilities—though not about finances, which firms keep much more secret. These devices were a kind of substitute for the government–industry 'deliberative councils' that were more common in Japan and Korea.

Finally, the architecture of the industrial policies themselves. Several kinds of public help are made conditional on performance, with relatively easy-to-monitor performance indicators (notably exports, or the gap between domestic and international prices). This too eases the information problem.

In short, information is abundantly available to central economic bureaucrats. And information asymmetries both between the top decision-makers and lower level officials, and between the state and target groups, are checked by the eliteness of the corps (which aids compliance within it), by performance indicators, and by the sheer variety of information sources.

Self-Seeking Officials and Rent-Seeking Private Agents

Other neoclassical preoccupations are that officials will use their discretion over budgets and permissions to pursue goals only distantly related to their ostensible public purposes, and that, even if well-intentioned, their interventions will generate rents to whose capture private agents will divert resources 'unproductively'.

Again, we find several factors at work in Taiwan which serve to inhibit these effects. The high level of talent attracted into government service, specifically talent with technical training, has already been mentioned. It means, among other things, that government officials are able to steer their conduct by norms of intellectual and technical integrity. At the same time, they are not caught between the pressures of rival interest groups lobbying for favours. Economic interest groups have little autonomy, while the civil service has a lot of autonomy from the legislature. On the other hand, officials are subject to monitoring from centres of expertise and influence outside the core bureaucracies, namely, the research and service agencies. And the press is fairly free to make economic (but not political) criticisms of the government. Industrial officials study the business press with care.

Moreover, the performance conditions attached to several kinds of government assistance discipline not only the recipients, but also the givers. Officials know that their own behaviour can be assessed in relation to the same performance indicators. If a firm or set of firms can show that its ability to meet performance conditions (e.g. exports) is being impaired by incompetent or bribe-seeking officials, it has a second channel of recourse. Indeed, the same performance conditions give officials clearer indicators of what they are meant to be doing, and give them an incentive to use their discretion in ways that help 'their' firms to meet those conditions. So performance conditions not only help the information problem, they also help the 'bureaucratic self-seeking' and 'private agent rent-seeking' problems.

So while officials have certainly conferred rents (by giving more help to some firms or industries than others), the resources devoted to rent-seeking have been quite limited because, in this particular political economy, the chances of modifying government allocations in line with kick-backs are not high.[18] Moreover, the industrial rents conferred by government have often facilitated higher productivity growth (a possibility hardly explored in the rent-seeking literature), because of the wider competitive–co-operative incentive structure facing rent-capturing firms and because the government has often (not always) been able to withdraw the rent-creating interventions when necessary.

This, then, helps to provide an understanding of why 'government failure' might be less in Taiwan and Korea than neoclassical theory would predict. But neoclassical theory is rooted in the institutional structure of the West, and takes for granted certain features that should not be taken for granted in a broader comparative context. For example, we need to be explicit that Taiwan and Korea have had economies based on markets and (mostly) private-property for centuries. Unlike Russia, China, Vietnam, and others, these states never took their undoubted admiration for the state to the point of having it make shoes and provide haircuts. The control of most of the economy's productive assets by private capitalists meant that government officials had to pay close attention to how their decisions affected profits if the government's military and catch-up objectives were to be achieved.

In another way, however, Taiwan and Korea are closer to the just mentioned 'socialist' cases than to the West. Until very recently their structure of government has not met even the minimal condition of democracy: one where the ruling party can, potentially, lose power through elections. And civil society has been kept deliberately weak, as a govern-

---

[18] See Wade (1990): chs. 7 and 9, esp. 286 ff.

ment imperative. In terms of civil and political rights, they came no higher than half-way down a ranking of middle-income countries by civil and political rights during the 1970s and early 1980s. The absence of democracy and civil society has made it easier for government officials to carry out their intentions. But what has kept those intentions in line with national economic growth objectives (in contrast to the case of Myanmar, for example)?

At this point in the argument we need to step back up the causal chain from the 'proximate' causes into the domain of historically more specific and contingent ones.[19] Taiwan and Korean officials operate with cultural models of power and authority generated by centuries of experience in the centralized polity and economy of the Chinese empire and the Korean kingdom.[20] The cultural models are reinforced more recently by Japanese colonialism, by the organizational exigencies of fighting wars, resisting siege, and (in the case of Taiwan but not Korea) being perceived as alien by the native population.

Taiwan and South Korea are both 'part countries' facing a credible threat to the continued existence of their torn off part.

The sense of external threat, and the urge to do better than the other side, may have compensated for the lack of internal competition with a domestic opposition party as a source of discipline on the rulers in their use of authoritarian powers. After all, the governments of most developing countries knew that they could fail economically without risking the survival not only of the government but the state and nation itself. These East Asian governments, by contrast, knew that without fast economic growth and social stability this ultimate horror might well befall them. This led them to make an unusually close coupling between national security and economic strength. As earlier in Japan, the economic bureaucracies were initially given responsibility for directing resources so as to enhance the war potential of manufacturing, an objective subsequently extended, with the same 'must do' mentality, to joining the club of advanced Western nations as fast as possible.

Here the 'neighbourhood' effect of being near Japan has been important. Japan provided a 'textbook' on how to catch up, with which the Taiwan and Korean rulers have been well acquainted. It provided them with a tangible model of what a disciplined state could achieve both militarily and econ-

[19] For analysis of the character of the Taiwan state, see the papers in Edwin Winkler and Susan Greenhalgh (eds.) (1988). *Contending Approaches to the Political Economy of Taiwan.* Armonk: M. E. Sharpe; and Edwin Winkler (1992). 'Taiwan Transition?', in Tun-jen Cheng and Stephan Haggard (eds.) (1992). *Political Change in Taiwan.* Boulder, Colo.: Lynne Rienner.

[20] Lucian and Mary Pye (1985). *Asian Power and Politics: The Cultural Dimensions of Authority.* Cambridge, Mass.: Belknap Press. Richard Whitely (1991). 'The Social Construction of Business Systems in East Asia', *Organizational Studies* 12/1: 1–28. Carter Eckert, Ki-baik Lee, Young Ick Lew, Michael Robinson, Edward Wagner (1990). *Korea Old and New, A History.* Seoul: Ilchokak Publishers, for Korea Institute, Harvard University.

omically, and that model contributed to the development of a mission-oriented organizational culture in key government agencies. And independently of government policies, the Taiwanese and Korean economies benefited from spillovers from Japan's high-speed growth, spillovers which, ink-blot-like, were spatially concentrated. How important this 'ink-blot' or neighbourhood effect was I do not know.

These various 'upstream' conditions of history and culture generate the pressure for a coherent national economic strategy, and also the ability to implement the strategy. Above all, they help to explain why Taiwan and Korea have met the central proximate condition of government 'success', that the persons intervening in the market on behalf of the national interest must have the national interest at heart, must be talented enough to translate between broad goals and policy specifics, must have a lot of accurate information at their disposal about the capacities and behaviours of private agents and their own subordinates, and must be embedded in organizational arrangements that make them take the goals and authority of the organization as the bases for their own actions.[21]

REPLICATION?

If this explanation is accepted as far as it goes, what does it suggest about the chances that other developing countries can transform their economies and raise incomes sufficiently fast to shoot up the hierarchy at something approaching the rates of Korea and Taiwan? It suggests that the chances are a good deal slimmer than the neo-liberal account would have us believe. For one thing, the key 'externality' of an expansive world economy is today less evident than when, in the 1960s and 1970s, Korea and Taiwan built up their momentum. For another, the political conditions needed to establish and sustain the key policy combination of compettiton, *dirigisme*, and education are too stringent to be met by many other states. The stringency of this combination is consistent with evidence on the *rarity*

---

[21] My account is obviously highly stylized. In a longer treatment we would have to deal with the dispersion around these central tendencies—such as bureaucratic corruption and in-fighting, the Rhee period in Korea, the early Chiang Kai-shek period in Taiwan. We might look at these questions in terms of the 'Migdal effect', the tendency for insecurely established leaders to pulverize the arms of the bureaucracy in order to prevent challenges to their rule from centres of power within the state, at the same time as they rely on those arms for policy effectiveness and legitimacy. See Joel Migdal (1986). *Strong Societies and Weak States: State-Society Relations and State Capabilities in the Third World*. Princeton: Princeton University Press. For further discussion, see Wade (1990): chs. 7–10, esp. 333–42; also Wade (1982), *Irrigation and Agricultural Politics in Korea*. Boulder, Colo.: Westview Press, last ch.; and Wade (1983), 'South Korea's Agricultural Development: The Myth of the Passive State', *Pacific Viewpoint* 24/1 (May): 11–28. Also Bruce Cumings (1989). 'The Abortive Abertura: South Korea in the Light of Latin American Experience', *New Left Review*, 173: 5–32.

of country mobility from periphery to semi-periphery or from semi-periphery to core over the past five decades.[22] As we saw, Korea (and Taiwan) have been exceptional in the magnitude of their upward movement.

On the other hand, we have to take note of some pointers to a more optimistic conclusion. First, several of the key institutional arrangements in East Asia are the result not of deep historical trends or 'culture', but of deliberate and fairly recent design. One thinks of Japan's industrial relations system, some parts of which were put in place in the 1920s and 1930s (plant unions, and gradual extension of white collar privileges—security of employment and incremental salary scales—to blue collar workers), but which was institutionalized as a national system only as recently as the early 1950s, in response to intense labour–management conflict. Japan's economic bureaucracy and other public sector organizations (such as police, post office, and navy) were designed after close study of Western models in the late nineteenth century.[23] Korea and Taiwan based many of their organizational arrangements for industrial policy on (modified) Japanese models in the 1950s and 1960s—Korea's deliberative councils, for example.

Secondly, these arrangements are now 'available' for other catch-up countries to copy. Of course, major organizational change is rarely voluntaristic, in the sense of coming about simply because policy-makers think such change would be to their country's advantage. It generally comes at a time of economic distress and social conflict. But when people seek resolution of conflicts they tend to choose from among alternatives already familiar to them, on the basis, partly, of their knowledge of how alternatives work elsewhere. The superior economic performance of the East Asia region gives legitimacy to efforts in other parts of the world to adopt some elements of East Asian organizational arrangements. Thirdly, Malaysia, Thailand, and Indonesia (population 270 million) and the southern coastal provinces of China (Guandong and Fujian, population 100 million)[24] have been growing at high speed over the 1980s, though from a very low base. Their growth is partly 'at the invitation of' the East Asians, who are investing heavily. Can it be sustained? Perhaps some Latin American countries, squeezed by debt and by Asian competition in potential export markets, are descending from the semi-periphery to the periphery, leaving space in the semi-periphery for some of the Asian newcomers to move into. Perhaps Britain, with the most ill-educated labour force of all the core

[22] Giovanni Arrighi and Jessica Drangel (1986). 'The Stratification of the World-Economy: An Exploration of the Semiperipheral Zone', *Review* 10/1 (summer): 9–74.

[23] Elenor Westney (1987). *Imitation and Innovation: The Transfer of Western Organizational Patterns to Meiji Japan*. Cambridge, Mass.: Harvard University Press.

[24] See Ezra Vogel (1989). *One Step Ahead in China: Guandong Under Reform*. Cambridge, Mass.: Harvard University Press.

countries'[25] and a long-standing commitment to an overvalued exchange rate, is steadily dropping out of the core toward the semi-periphery, leaving space for some others, such as Taiwan, Korea, Singapore, Spain, and perhaps parts of Eastern Europe.

Perhaps. But on the minus side, note two facts. One is the global recession, seen in the decline in annual rates of world GDP growth from 4.9 per cent in 1960–70, 3.5 per cent in 1970–80, to 2.9 per cent in 1980–9. This makes it more likely that increases in trade from countries newly integrating into the world economy will constitute trade diversion rather than trade augmentation; which is presumably more difficult to do. Growing protection in the West, induced by the global recession, reinforces this tendency. The second fact is that the South-East Asian industrialization is dominated by foreign investors, who have so far connected up with domestically based suppliers and users to a remarkably small degree. For example, Thailand's 'investment rush' of the late 1980s was driven largely by foreign investment; 75 per cent by value of the investment projects approved by the Thai Board of Investments were from foreign firms, half of those Japanese. The local content of consumer electronics goods produced by Japanese FDI firms in Thailand and Malaysia (1988) was only about 30 per cent, and of locally procured parts, most came from transplanted Japanese parts makers.[26] I do not have figures for Taiwan and Korea at an equivalent time in their industrialization. But it is clear that theirs was much less dominated by foreign firms, and that those foreign firms were more closely anchored in the domestic economy, thanks partly to government actions to make it happen (recall the case of the high-purity chemical in Taiwan).

If the prospects for 'large-scale' replicability are small, this does not mean that newly industrializing countries cannot learn a great deal from the successful East Asian cases. The most transferable knowledge is at the level of specific institutional design. For example, if some protection for domestic industries is to be maintained, it is essential to exempt imports of inputs into exports from having to pay tariffs, so that exports can get inputs at world market prices. Taiwan and Korea have much experience of how to organize such a tariff-rebate scheme, which it would be crazy for newcomers to ignore.[27] Or if government seeks to improve information exchange and consensus formation with private firms, it should look to Japan's and Korea's experience with deliberative councils. That experience suggests that such devices work when the councils can take actionable

---

[25] See the discussion between British economic policy-makers and academic analysts of British decline in 'From Clogs to Clogs: Britain's Relative Economic Decline Since 1851', P. Hennessy and C. Anstey (eds.), Strathclyde Papers on Government and Politics, Department of Government, University of Strathclyde.

[26] Etsuro Ishigami (1991). 'Japanese Business in ASEAN Countries: New-Industrialization or Japanisation?', *IDS Bulletin*, 22/2: 21–8.

[27] On Taiwan's and Korea's scheme, see Wade (1991).

decisions (when they are more than debating chambers) and when all parties are committed to carry out agreements, so that firms will go into repeated participation.

CONCLUSIONS

1. *Role of Industrial Policies* Korea, Taiwan, and Japan show that selective industrial promotion need not be *inimical* to rapid industrialization. Whether they show that selective industrial promotion ('picking winners') can itself *accelerate* industrialization in such a way as to bring net social benefits is a more open question. There is no conclusive evidence either way. My own judgement is that the balance of evidence is in favour of the argument that selective industrial policies as practised by Korea, Taiwan, and Japan did assist their (internationally competitive) industrialization.

To make the point more precise we need to distinguish between two types of government 'intervention': leading the market and fallowing the market.[28] Following the market means that the government assists (some of) the projects that private business people want to undertake at current prices. Leading the market means that the government initiates projects that private business people would not undertake at current prices. Leading in turn comes in two degrees: initiating projects that are *ex ante* unviable at current prices but viable at proper shadow prices (L1), and initiating projects that are *ex ante* unviable even at 'proper' shadow prices (L2). Looking at the role of government in East Asian industrialization, we see a pattern of government intervention shifting between these roles in some industries over time, while in other industries we find little if any intervention, not even regulatory. It seems likely that most of the government's leadership of the market was of type L1. But there *are* some cases of L2 which turned out, *ex post*, to be successful; the Korean steel industry being the most celebrated example. In any case, whether doing L1 or L2, the government's role in industrial promotion went far beyond the neo-liberal recipe.

Where the central proximate condition for industrial policy success, given above, cannot be even minimally met, it would be foolish for a government to try L2; and even L1 has to be done very selectively. The bulk of industrial promotion should be of the followership kind, with export performance or the gap between domestic and international prices being a dominant criterion of continued assistance.

---

[28] See Robert Wade (1990). 'Industrial Policy in East Asia: Does it Lead or Follow the Market?', in Gereffi and Wyman (eds.), *Manufacturing Miracles: Paths of Industrialisation in Latin America and East Asia*. Princeton: Princeton University Press.

2. *Education* Raising a country's ratios of skilled to basically skilled to unskilled people is the most effective way to shift its comparative advantage in the direction of activities which support higher incomes.

3. *Trade Policy* (a) Trade policy ('outward orientation', 'inward orientation') is of secondary importance in explaining trade patterns, relative to skill mix and natural resource endowment. (b) A trade regime which is, overall, 'trade neutral' (that is, which meets Bhagwati's EP condition) is quite consistent with substantial differences between industries in the extent to which they are spurred on by industrial policy incentives and in the extent to which they have incentives to sell abroad or in the domestic market. One of the most important topics for research is how, practically and theoretically, this combination can be achieved—and how reconciled with rules of a global trading regime. (c) The vast neoclassical literature on trade policy is wrong to treat protection as a unitary phenomenon. The costs of protection depend heavily on the organizational mechanisms and conditions with which it is granted. The incentive effects of different protection 'contracts' warrant more research attention, especially to identify the conditions in which protection can be expected to stimulate investment and learning-by-doing by more than enough to offset allocative inefficiencies and rent-seeking.

4. *Trade Protection and Social Protection* Protection in East Asia was used not only as an instrument of industrial promotion, but also as a means of buffering the population from the risks stemming from the international market (as well as for raising revenue). As these governments have reduced protection, they have also bolstered expenditure on domestic insurance in the form of welfare and transfer payments. All this is in line with David Cameron's finding from eighteen advanced industrialized countries that '[n]ations with open economies were far more likely to experience an increase in the scope of public funding than were nations with relatively closed economies', expenditures on income supplements and social insurance constituting a major source of the expansion of the public economy.[29] Robert Bates *et al.* find evidence in a sample of thirty-two low and middle income countries that 'the higher the level of terms-of-trade risk that a nation faces in international markets, the more likely it is to increase trade barriers', and that 'the greater the social insurance programs mounted by a nation's government , the less likely that government is to block free trade.'[30] The force of this point is reinforced by the new international competition, in which it has become possible for a set of industries located

---

[29] David Cameron (1978). 'The Espansion of the Public Economy: A Comparative Analysis', *American Political Science Review*, 72.

[30] Robert Bates *et al.* (1991). 'Risk and Trade: Another Exploration', *International Organization*, 45: 4.

in one country to wipe out competitors in another country within half a decade, posing enormous adjustment problems, a phenomenon of which Adam Smith and David Ricardo were entirely innocent.

5. *Organization of Dirigisme* Korea, Taiwan, and Japan all used 'pilot agencies' to exercise foresight and strategic planning, in a way that private business people could not afford to cultivate. These pilot agencies (MITI in Japan, Industrial Development Bureau in Taiwan, Economic Planning Board in Korea) were located in the *heartland* of government, where they acted as a lobbyist for a long-term perspective on national issues. They were staffed by some of the best talent available in the society (and most of their officials were not economists). They had control over only rather small amounts of resources, much of their influence coming from persuasion of the resource controllers, for which their position in the heartland of government was crucial. However, our knowledge of the organization and operation of the economic bureaucracies of East Asian countries is remarkably thin; especially knowledge about the incentives and motivations of officials, and the character of authority relations.[31]

6. *State–Society Relations* The pilot agency, in turn, formed part of a state apparatus which had a high measure of autonomy from the rest of the society (pre-1970 or thereabouts in the case of Japan). This is of course a stringent political condition. A more corporatist form of organization may be a more feasible and attractive substitute for state autonomy, and is still likely to be more effective than the 'free trade' of US-style political pluralism, which tends to produce the damaging immobilism seen in US domestic policy.

7. *Democracy and Human Rights* The East Asian states did not allow resource allocation to be determind only by decentralized business people operating in a logic of global profit-seeking. Above all they mediated the *external* transactions of the owners and managers of capital, in such a way as to generate an intense cycle of investment and re-investment within the national borders; and they further subjected this investment to priorities determined through a political process (a non-democratic one in the case of Korea and Taiwan, an anomalously democratic one in the case of Japan).

Against this experience, we should be concerned at the current uncritical embrace of 'democracy' and 'human rights' as the political correlate of the economic doctrine of 'free markets'. Not only the new European Bank for Reconstruction and Development but also the old and ostensibly 'non-

---

[31] But see Chalmers Johnson's classic (1982), *MITI and the Japanese Miracle: The Growth of Industrial Policy, 1925–1975*, Stanford, Calif.: Stanford University Press; also Wade (1982): chs. 6 and 8.

political' multilaterial financial institutions (World Bank, IMF) are now beginning to make 'democracy' and 'human rights' a condition of their loans, implicitly modifying their own previous notion of sovereignty.

The reason for concern is that political changes promoted under the banner of democracy and human rights open the way for the controllers of transnational capital to exercise still greater influence over national political outcomes. 'Human rights' are being taken to include rights to use one's economic assets almost however one wishes, so that restrictions on asset use of the kind that East Asian states routinely imposed come to be seen as violations of basic human rights. 'Democratic rules' readily allow outside groups to pour money into national electoral competition in an effort to determine the result (as recently in Nicaragua). These principles together can justify arrangements which, ironically, undercut the nation state as a political centre where compromises are hammered out between groups of people who live within the national territory. In particular, they can make it difficult to reach and enforce compromises that entail restrictions on the use of capital, especially transnationally mobile capital. Yet without some such restrictions, and without an effective political centre, it is unlikely that a particular nation in late twentieth-century conditions can make fast strides up the world economic hierarchy. That, at least, is what the East Asian experience suggests.

6

The State and Structural Change: What can be Learnt from the Successful Late Industrializers?

Juhana Vartiainen

1. INTRODUCTION

The role of public policies in the process of economic growth and industrial transformation is a classical controversy within economics and politics. The fact that the economic discussion on this issue almost always at least implicitly boils down to a generalized verdict about the right or wrong way to shape economic development testifies to the fundamentally normative endeavours of much of economics.

This chapter adopts the relatively modest aim of trying to learn from some cases of successful state-led industrialization. Whether these experiences are replicable or not, it seems to me that an interventionist strategy for industrialization and modernization has in some cases been very effective. Then it is at least instructive to try to understand these cases in the light of modern economics. The countries we have in mind include the Asian miracle cases of Korea and Taiwan, but one of the chapter's attempted contributions is the argument that surprisingly similar elements of the determinants and practices of successful state intervention are to be found in European countries such as Austria and Finland. The thrust of the chapter is moderately favourable to the interventionist case, and it can be seen as a collection of arguments which show how state interventionism can work. Yet much of the chapter is concerned with the determinants of success of state interventionism, and it will be clear from the discussion that many of these conditions do not easily accommodate the idea of social engineering and replication. Why some policies have worked at some times in some countries is a question distinct from the question of which policies might work for some countries at some other times.

Other and better papers will present contrary views. Yet I think it is important to make the interventionist case emphatically, especially so because so much of economic policy-making and thinking about economic

I am grateful for comments by Ha-Joon Chang, Bob Rowthorn, and other participants in the project.

policy reflects the basic instincts of *laissez-faire* liberalism, and the approaches adopted by the IMF and World Bank development programmes continue to pay much more attention to the creation of 'market conditions' than to the conception of feasible political and social institutions that may support industrialization programmes (see Biersteker 1990, 1992). The interventionist case should be treated with healthy scepticism; yet there is perhaps not enough of that scepticism on the other side of the trench. My suspicion is that the neoclassical policy strategy for developing countries chronically fails to understand how much collective action and how strong a state is needed to support the development of 'spontaneous' markets and private economic activity. To sustain the norms that are conducive to a well-functioning market economy and to encourage the buildup of new industries, there should be a competent state bureaucracy, the logic of which should precisely *not* follow the logic of individual utility maximization. Peter Evans[1] very nicely makes the point that a logic of the market and individual maximization is predominant within the administration of some weak African states that may be characterized as predatory.

The chapter starts by emphasizing the political implications of some modern economic theories. In contrast to the neoclassical competitive price theory, modern ideas of endogenous economic growth, dynamic externalities, and strategic action by organized agents all generate powerful implications and predictions about the potential role of state intervention in economic development. Whether the *Weltanschauung* of endogenous and non-convex growth theory is 'true' or not is a question safely outside the scope of this paper, but it is not a useless task to spell out the political implications of these theories should they convey a more or less correct picture of the economy.

The chapter then makes an attempt at analysing the determinants of successful state intervention. The basic contention is that the state should be autonomous and capable of disciplining the private agents of the economy, but that there should be a delicate balance, so that the fate of the state bureaucracy itself depends on the success of the economy. I have no grand theory on this issue, but the discussion emphasizes factors such as strong bureaucratic and administrative traditions and the role of external challenges. Indeed, it can be argued that many Third World countries need more bureaucracy, not less.

The role of future expectations and basic commitments to property rights is also underlined. Economic planning of many similar characteristics has been practised in countries as diverse as Korea, Taiwan, Finland, Austria, Norway, Chile, France, East Germany, and Cuba. That planning leads to good results in some countries and to disasters in some others may have

[1] Peter Evans has kindly let me see the draft of his forthcoming book on the positive role played by the state's 'embedded autonomy'.

much to do with basic ideological commitments and expectations of future political norms. Capital owners in a capitalist country may be willing to swallow a lot of planning provided they are convinced that a basic commitment to private property rights will ultimately be respected in the future. This is perhaps one reason why planning of some sorts has worked in Korea and Finland whereas it has failed in a regime like Cuba or that of Alan Garcia in Peru.

Section 4 summarizes the argument by presenting a verbal description of a stylized model economy. The next section uses the conclusions of the model to briefly review some concrete areas and instruments of state interventionism and then moves on to analyse the country cases of Korea, Taiwan, Austria, and Finland. Korea and Taiwan have been extensively discussed elsewhere and in other chapters of this volume, so that their treatment is relatively brief and concentrates on the arguments that have been presented in the earlier sections of the chapter. More space is devoted to the description of the Finnish and Ausrian cases, since the juxtaposition of these countries to the Asian NICs has probably more novelty value. I try to show that these countries share some characteristics and determinants of successful state interventionism with the East Asian miracles. The next section is a brief discussion of some failure cases. They have not been selected by a systematic method other than the will to illustrate the arguments of the chapter through negation: how the failure of some of the conditions for success leads to reverse results. The concluding section discusses the lessons for success.

2. THE SCOPE FOR STATE INTERVENTION

While a deeper understanding of incentive mechanisms and information economics has definitely discredited the feasibility of comprehensive central planning and public ownership as a viable economic strategy, the emphasis of most interesting modern economics has also shifted in a way that makes the interventionist case more appealing than it used to be.

First, new theories of endogenous growth have pointed out the potentially great significance of *dynamic externalities related to the accumulation of human capital and the level of technical knowledge*. This aspect of economic development is now seriously appreciated in growth theory.[2] There is as yet no single and unifying theory of endogenous growth, but it is already

---

[2] It is fair to say, however, that these basic ideas were already present in Nicholas Kaldor's writings (see Kaldor (1978): chs. 1, 2, and 7 in particular). Technical progress that is embodied in equipment investment and the importance of increasing returns to scale for endogenous growth play an important part in Kaldor's analysis: 'once, however, we allow for increasing returns, the forces making for continuous changes are endogenous—they are engendered from within the economic system' (ibid. 186).

possible to learn from this literature. The theory of endogenous growth focuses on externalities related to the accumulation of human capital and technological expertise. At the level of economic theory, many of the models share such assumptions as increasing returns to scale associated with the levels of various capital stocks. Models of endogenous growth can typically lead to several equilibria and the possibility of discrete jumps between accumulation regimes. In this way, they seem to make sense of observed differentials in different countries' growth performances better than the basic Solow growth model.[3] Empirical support for the idea that investment in comprehensive education is a major determinant for growth is provided by Azariadis and Drazen (1990).

Similarly, modern studies of successful industrial economies like Porter (1990) speak of clusters of industries which generate an environment and a system of linkages favourable for industrial growth. The notion of a cluster is a plausible empirical counterpart of the theoretical notion of externality. We may include Erik Dahmén's (1951) early idea of a 'developmental bloc' in the same cateogory.

Thus, it is fair to say that there is a growing consensus in mainstream economics that investment in education, research, and development should in some ways be publicly sponsored and subsidized. Whether these externalities 'exist' and how important they are will probably not be a question that allows a final answer. Yet there is a lot in the literature on economic growth and development which lends credibility to the modern interventionist view.

The second group of externalities that call for public policies are related to distribution and distributional conflicts. Economic theorizing on games has cast light on problems of distribution and strategic action in corporatist economies with powerful and organized agents. We may call 'corporatist' any economy in which some important actors are so large relative to the economy's size that they act strategically towards the relevant economic variables. Typical corporatist actors are big corporations, labour unions and their federations, and industrialists' and employers' organizations.

The problem with a corporatist economy is that it is *generically inefficient*. This is generally true of Nash equilibria of one-shot games, but it is also typical for repeated games and truly dynamic models. This is due to the fact that the future returns of today's investments depend on the strategic reactions of other agents. In other words, the social returns and costs of investments do not correspond to the private returns and costs. Nash equilibria of dynamic games typically exhibit the result that investments and other sacrifices for the future remain too low, because the agent in

---

[3] Yet the evidence is not conclusive and does not necessarily support the view that the 'Solow' long-term view of the world is inferior to the new growth theory view; see Crafts (1992).

question cannot be assured that he can privately enjoy a return that corresponds to the cost of the optimal investment.

Furthermore, the history of industrialism as well as reflection on theories of endogenous growth suggests that these externalities are related to each other. *If* it is the case that there are increasing returns to scale and externalities in the sense that social or industry-wide returns of R&D or equipment investment are larger than its private costs, *then* it will also be the case that successful economies will exhibit corporatist characteristics. Big oligopolistic or monopolistic firms will do better than small firms, and industrial associations which co-ordinate their members' research activities have a *raison d'être*. Industries will try to organize research activities on a collective basis, will try to obtain state support for the buildup of infrastructure, will seek the help of state diplomacy in their exploration of export markets, and will by and large depend on the state authorities in a myriad of ways. A 'Hayekian' reading of European economic history that would only emphasize the 'spontaneous' development of new productive activities and trade routes by innovative individuals is flawed; on the other side of the coin, state-sponsored infrastructure and research activity, encompassing export organizations, big mercantile companies, and political management of economic change have always been an integral part of economic history. This is of course particularly clear in the examples of successful late industrialization. In the Asian success stories, the large but diversified business groups, with close ties to the political decision-making, have been the most important engine for economic growth.[4] To take this speculative reasoning one step further, consider the implications of these arguments for the role of the state. Let us assume that there are indeed increasing returns to scale in some industries so that there is an optimal size to each industry. Suppose further that these industries have been able to successfully exploit these returns. In small countries like the Nordic ones, successful firms and industries will then be important and 'big' actors in the political and economic arena and will therefore also command a powerful bargaining position in the labour market (for more empirical arguments on this, see Katzenstein 1985). This in turn makes encompassing organization rela-

---

[4] Patterns of late industrialization are different from the experiences of the mature industrialized countries, because of their rapidity if for no other reason. This does, however, not mean that one should see industrialization of the mature countries as a 'spontaneous' process. Even the traditional view according to which the industrialization of the old industrial countries was an essentially market-driven process has now been seriously questioned by economic historians. The attitudes of economic historians are surveyed by Supple (1973), whose theoretical positions have been influenced by Alexander Gerschenkron and Friedrich List. Supple emphasizes that the role of the state in industrialization has not been limited to the provision of a basic legal framework, public order, and external security. Institutions favourable to industrialization have been actively encouraged, various public services organized, and the State has even undertaken direct organizational activities in production. The Hungarian historians Berend and Ranki (1982) arrive at essentially similar conclusions in their study of several peripheral European economies.

tively more attractive from labour's point of view. It is indeed typical for Finland as well as other Nordic countries that an encompassing corporatist mobilization of all the major agents of the economy was undertaken from the turn of the century onwards (for Finland, see Vartiainen and Pekkarinen 1993; for Sweden, for example, see de Geer 1992). When some groups organize, organization becomes more attractive from the point of view of other groups as well.

A successful open economy may then exhibit a corporatist strcture with a few important actors like the banks', agriculturalists', employers' and workers' fedrations. The conflicts of opposing interest groups will then automatically assume a political character. This is where the state has to step in again. The ideal role of the state is to act as a mediator or as a partner in the social concertation that should lead to acceptable bargains on income distribution.

Thus, the state's role is enhanced by the political consequences of both 'families' of externalities. To get industrialization under way, the state must mobilize and organize the economy, and act to build a coherent corporatist structure with which it can work and design growth-promoting policies. This means that it must also be able to deal with the inevitable distri-butional conflicts. The state must cope with the inherent paradox that rapid structural change requires more social organization and political co-ordi-nation of resources, which, at the same time, may aggravate problems of inefficient corporatism and unilateral interest group action aimed at redistributive rent-seeking.

Thus, very broadly speaking, all these phenomena can be seen as *externalities* related either to *human capital and technology* or to *strategic action and distributional issues*.

Now there is no need to be dogmatic about the specific institutional forms that will be or should be generated by these economic charateristics. Some countries such as Austria have relied more on corporatist concertation between organized agents, some have been more étatist in the Korean or Taiwanese way. But it is probably right to say that these exter-nalities point towards an extended role for the state in a normative as well as in a positive sense. In a normative sense, because they show that there may be an enormous scope for improving an economy's performance by state intervention; in a positive sense, because corporatist economies will need effective mediation of interests and the role of the state would ideally be the design of such compromises and social contracts that enhance economic growth and structural transformation.

What are then, in more concrete terms, the potential tasks of the state and why should they be left for the state? States exist for many reasons and in many forms, but I hope that the following discussion casts some light on why the state institutions typical of capitalist market economies are rela-tively well suited to the management of the tasks outlined above.

Much of economic theorizing is concerned with the question of whether the economic arrangements required by growth and industrialization can be generated by the market or by 'spontanenous' co-ordinated action by economic agents.[5] The Coase Theorem suggests that economic efficiency can be attained if all mutually beneficial bargains can be struck. Many economists seem to interpret Coase's result as a confirmation that a decentralized economy can always attain efficient outcomes without state intervention. Yet it is unrealistic to assume that real economies can organize all the necessary bilateral and multilateral exchanges without some kind of public bodies—and it is therefore precisely the job of the public bodies to organize this exchange. A down-to-earth view of the state is that the state is there precisely because of the need to organize these socially necessary bargains.

As argued above, the functions of the state in the successful management of the economy are related to the organization and co-ordination of investment (including the accumulation of human capital), and the management of distributional conflicts.

Co-ordination of investment. While it is perhaps possible to believe the Walrasian auctioneer story in the case of static markets, it is much less plausible that decentralized markets could always co-ordinate the investment decisions of an economy in a way that selects a path on a frontier of a dynamic production possibilities schedule. The functioning of markets in a static setting requires arbitrage and a matching of the supply and demand decisions of a large number of agents. Investment activities, in contrast, are unique in character, take time, and the profitability of one investment project may depend on the successful completion of some other project. At time zero, however, neither of the two may seem profitable on its own. The notion of a production possibility frontier is indeed elusive in the sense that the frontier really depends on the flexibility of social arrangements and on the costs and means of transmitting information about production possibilities. Public policy may be needed to map out an economy's productive potentials.

This input–output way of thinking about a national economy fits ill with dominant neoclassical economic theory, but mapping an economy's resources and growth potentials in various industries has often been an essential element of successful industrial take-offs. In the Nordic countries, for example, an extremely important aspect of economic development has been the creation of an institutional research structure to support the development of natural resources. In Finland, the management of the nation's most important resource endowment, the forests, was at an early stage organized on a half-public half-corporatist

---

[5] This research agenda legitimately reflects the powerful conclusions of equilibrium price theory—that a system of decentralized trading can co-ordinate activities in an efficient way— but also a basic neoclassical suspicion about the role of the state.

basis.[6] We can interpret this as the mapping out of the production possibility frontier by the public agents. It is hard to see how such progress could have taken place if entrusted to private entrepreneurs only. Large firms might have carried out some of the research, but they would not necessarily have had the incentive to make them public.

That *investment in education and research* is and should be publicly organized is not seriously questioned. The empirical literature on endogenous growth has convincingly pointed out the impact of education on economic growth (see Azariadis 1990).

Other functions of the state related to economic change are the *management of conflicts* and the unavoidable *uncertainty* related to economic change and structural transformations. These problems are linked with each other. Suppose that the agents of an economy want to embark on an ambitious industrialization programme. This will require sacrifices and investments now, co-ordination of investment projects, and new forms of social and political mobilization. It is impossible to see in advance all the positive and negative externalities and potential for distributional coalition-building.

Moreover, an economy undergoing modernization and structural change will at some stages present opportunities for rent-seeking and windfalls for somebody on the one hand and severe losses for some other agents on the other hand. When the capital stocks and other state variables of an economy change, the potential gains obtainable by distributional coalitions may change relative to the transaction costs associated with their formation. Similarly, new positive and negative externalities may emerge: the social cost of industrialization may turn out to be higher than expected or it may turn out that the returns due to capital accumulation and the spread of knowledge accrue at a slower tempo than was originally—implicitly or explicitly—agreed upon. Such contingencies may disrupt the original corporative contracts.

While it is theoretically possible to imagine a world in which transaction costs are so low that all efficient agreements can always be found, again and again, by any agents of the economy, it is much more plausible that the task of overseeing the economy should be entrusted to one or a few co-ordinators.

The state should therefore be seen as a *general co-ordinator* that can undertake at least some action in all kinds of originally unforeseeable contingencies. It is empowered with a usefully *wide* mandate to promote efficiency and resist socially harmful, unilateral collective action. The axiom is not that the state always will and always is able to carry out that task. But

---

[6] Similarly, in Sweden, the state was very active in developing similar institutions for other areas of productive potential as early as between 1870 and 1914. State-sponsored organizations were created to map the country's mineral resources by using geological surveys, and similar bodies for research in hydrography and water technology were established (see Södersten 1991).

of all institutions of liberal societies, it is the only one with an institutional and jurisdictional form which permits such an interpretation.

This is related to the state's economic capacity to act. All of these tasks of the state are such that they do not fit very well with the logic of individual utility maximization at the level where the policies are implemented. The state must have the economic potential to keep a buraucracy that is prestigious enough to be able to follow its own logic.

From the point of view of the state's 'principal', the citizen, the state in a modern society seems to be the only institution upon which everybody seems to have a claim. From the point of view of game theory, the state can be identified with the 'grand coalition'. In this sense, a functioning state is a precondition for efficiency: if for various reasons the grand coalition is unable to 'meet' and ensure that a prospective distribution cannot be improved upon by joint collective action by everybody, there is no guarantee that the economic outcome will be collectively rational.

One basic problem of collective action is that the cost of participation may be too high to induce an individual to participate, when the individual in question can realistically estimate that his voice will not alter the policy of the organization. The state with its institutions offers a relatively inexpensive way of participating. If there were no state and all externalities were taken into account by freely organized collectives, it is likely that the interests of small groups within which the marginal return of each member's lobbying activity is relatively high would be even better catered for than they are now, at the expense of the general interest.

So states can be 'relatively' impartial and enhance the general interest. This need not always be the case, but the basic understanding of state institutions in market societies is such that they should not be allowed to be completely hijacked by one party.

Publicity and information also play a role that has an economic interpretation. A basic idea of modern game theory is that dynamically efficient solutions can be sustained by playing trigger strategies whereby an agent behaves 'nicely' towards other agents as long as the others have not deviated from this 'nice' behaviour. A firm can count on the loyalty of its work-force as long as it is clear that the firm will go on investing in the long-term future of the workers. Similarly, in a national context (think of, say, Taiwan and Finland), consumers may be willing to accept low wages or high taxes as long as they have been convinced that this additional saving is being used to build the productive potential of the nation. Now, if such dynamically efficient arrangements are to be sustained as Nash equilibria, it is required that all parties can constantly monitor each other and observe each others' deviations in behaviour. This is precisely what one can in principle do with a reasonably democratic state: the running of its affairs is *public*, and this public character is affirmed in some way or another in most constitutions and fundamental political notions associated with the state.[7] If the national economic strategy were entrusted to a collective of organized groups, it is less clear how this public monitoring could be arranged.[8] One should bear in mind that an important ingredient in many traditional definitions of the State has been the idea that the State has to do with the running of public affairs in the sense that all concerned parties can present their claims to the state.

3. DETERMINANTS OF SUCCESSFUL STATE INTERVENTION

We have outlined general arguments about the potentially important and positive role of the state in economic development. If the *Weltanschauung* of endogenous growth theory and corporatist theories is correct, there is no way to evade the issue of state intervention in the economy. The state, on the one hand, can do a lot to improve an economy's performance, and, on the other hand, it will become an important actor in the mediation of conflicts, as argued in the previous section.

This section then asks the reverse, positive question: can the cases of successful and less successful state intervention teach us something on *when* this intervention is likely to work well. This is not a question of the simple 'design' of policies that 'should be' implemented as spelled out in pro-grammes of bodies such as the World Bank of the International Monetary Fund. Policies cannot simply be designed and transferred to the desks of bureaucrats and politicians. Economic and industrial policy depends on institutions and traditions, and the scope for social engineering is limited. For practical policies towards the developing countries, it is probably more important to foster democratic and representative political institutions which may in due time be able to generate economic change than to unilaterally emphasize the creation of 'market conditions'.

The student of the successful industrial policy experience of Korea, Taiwan, Austria, and Finland observes that all these countries encountered a very similar situation after World War II:

1. In all of them, there was an old bureaucratic tradition capable of providing competent administration.
2. In all of them, the outcome of the war had to a great extent shaken pre-war power blocs and disrupted the former distribution of power amongst the elites.

---

[7] This is not to deny that a lot of decision-making in East Asia and Finland and Austria (see Katzenstein 1984 for Austria) has not been public. But even in Korea and Taiwan, public criticism of economic management was treated with much more tolerance than political dissidence.

[8] Although such models are still very rudimentary, it is also one lesson of modern bargaining theory that bargaining set-ups where information is asymmetric can lead to inefficient outcomes.

3. For all of them, their external position in the international political system posed grave dangers which might even have led to the annihilation of these nation states.

4. Although all of them were poised geographically more or less 'between' the two major power blocs of international politics, the basic commitment to respect private property rights was never seriously questioned.

Heroically generalizing from these experiences, the view suggested in this paper is that successful state-led industrialization may have been associated with a *strong state* that is *autonomous* so that it can discipline the private economic agents and not succumb to particular interests. On the other hand, the state *must itself be disciplined*. It must be *dependent* on the performance of the economy and *endowed with formal and informal ties* with the organized agents of the economy.[9] Thus, the balance between the state and civil society is a delicate one. The state has to be strong to be autonomous and remain deliberately weak in some areas. Weak client states can act very strongly in some areas of social life, causing great social losses. The predator states of some African countries offer ample examples of this: they are certainly strong enough to murder their citizens while they are weak against the particular interests of the elites and the individual maximization strategies of the corrupted leaders and top civil servants.

Factors conducive to successful state action, furthermore, include at least coherent *bureaucratic* traditions and a *coherent corporatist network*. Furthermore, *external challenges* can play a positive role. A lot of state planning and political management of the economy may be acceptable for the owners of private capital as long as there is a *basic commitment* to the bourgeois legal order and respect for private property and entrepreneurship in the future.

The Bureaucratic Tradition

As emphasized by the Weberian tradition, rational management of the economy requires a meritocratic bureaucracy that is competent and autonomous enough to obey its own logic which is not one of individual utility maximization. The Weberian professional bureaucracy consists of career civil servants who are committed to their tasks and prestigious enough not to be easily corrupted by outside interests. Such a meritocratic civil service is also able to reproduce itself, since its prestige makes it possible to recruit from the best talents.

Thus, the quality of state institutions genuinely depends on history and traditions. In a political culture in which the public service is held in high

[9] In his forthcoming book (see n. 1), Peter Evans introduces the term 'embedded autonomy' to designate an autonomous state with well-working connections to civil society's agents and organizations. Evans's analysis of some African and East Asian cases is interesting and illuminating.

esteem, it is easier to recruit amongst the best minds. This has been emphasized by Wade (1989) for Taiwan as well as Amsden (1989) for Korea. In Korea and Taiwan, the industrial pilot agencies were continuously able to retain their prestige and recruit able personnel. Corruption and mediocrity are self-enforcing phenomena as well: mediocre administrations can at best attract mediocre people, and corrupt regimes attract corrupt people and encourage the corruption even of those who originally tried to enforce the common interest.

Our success cases have all 'enjoyed' the services of a competent and prestigious administrative bureaucracy able to design and carry out successful industrial policies. We argued above that a successful state must be able to formulate credible and consistent policies that do not change overnight. This is precisely what bold and insensitive bureaucracies are good at.

It is a characteristic of weak states that their bureaucracies' behaviour follows the economic logic of individual maximization. In its most extreme forms, this is seen in the militarily strong but otherwise certainly weak African states where even administrative behaviour is aimed at individual revenue maximization. In his manuscript, Peter Evans (1993) describes at length the Zairian state, where 'everything is for sale', and 'personalism and plundering at the top destroys any possibility of rule-governed behaviour in the lower levels of the bureaucracy, giving individual maximization free rein underneath' (Evans 1993: 6). As Evans points out, it is not bureaucracy but its absence that makes the state rapacious.

Another, less extreme case in point is related to the 'industrial organization of corruption', as analysed recently by Shleifer and Vishny (1993). The economy may tolerate a reasonable amount of corruption as long as this corruption is organized by a 'monopoly', so that an entrepreneur need not bribe a thousand officials to get a project completed. This is one more argument for a strong and centralized bureaucracy. A strong bureaucracy may harass the prospective entrepreneur with a lot of red tape, but if individual bureaucrats are well monitored within the system, the economic costs of corruption remain moderate. The monopolistic bureaucrat of the strong state expropriates a part of the economic surplus related to an investment project, but if the project is economically sound, it will be carried out anyway. The situation is very different with the uncontrolled bureaucracies of weak states: there the entrepreneur must bribe every official that can block the investment, and these competing bureaucrats together impose a much higher economic cost.[10]

The Historical Conjunction of Weakened Elites

All the success cases also exhibit the characteristic that old power blocs had been weakened by the political upheavals associated with the end of World

[10] For a formal analysis, see Shleifer and Vishny (1993).

War II. This may be one more important factor that explains the success of state activities. With the weakening of the ancient elites, the field of action for an enlightened bureaucracy might be greatly enhanced—if there is one. Old power blocs are almost by definition resistant to change. This may also be related to the argument of Mancur Olson (1982) about the beneficial consequences of political disruptions: in the course of time, interest groups become more perfectly capable of seeking rents at the expense of others, so that a shake-out of a society's power groupings also diminishes the scope for harmful rent-seeking.

External Challenges

If an obnoxious state bureaucracy and political elite is not sufficiently disciplined by internal political forces, the necessary balancing may come about because of an external challenge. It is remarkable that the success cases selected in this study have in common a stringent challenge of international politics.

The very existence of Korea has been dependent on the constellations of international politics and on the willingness of the United States to maintain its military presence in the area. A similar story might apply to Taiwan, the existence of which has been continuously put into question. Taiwanese rulers were faced with the challenge of mainland China and an outright economic failure could have meant the very end of the Taiwanese State. In addition, the Taiwanese political elite represented an immigrant minority on the island.

Finland and Austria also share a precarious international position. Both countries found themselves after World War II in a contested border zone between the two political power blocs, and both had a history of bitter internal conflicts and civil war. For Finland, successful industrialization and the integration of the productive structure into the Western European economies was a powerful political objective as well as an economic motivation. The buildup of state-led corporatist structures from the 1960s onwards was a conscious political mobilization project encouraged by the state as well as many employers (see Jakobson 1992). The international position of Finland was precarious even in the 1970s, and the buildup of a broad social democratic trade union movement was regarded even by many employers and the bourgeois parties as an insurance policy against communist influence. The encompassing nature of Austrian corporatism probably also owes something to a political project of national integration and mobilization (see below).

The interpretation of this is that an external threat to the very existence of the nation concentrates the minds of elites and policy-makers in a useful way. It may decisively change the pay-offs of the game. If there is no threat to the nation, elites may manage with less efficient management of the national economy. Humans are probably very much concerned with their relative position in society, and the prestige and income level of a member of the top elite probably does not depend very much on whether the nation prospers economically or not. A failure to industrialize and modernize does not necessarily mean a large decrease in the welfare of the super-rich. On the other hand, if a failure to industrialize and modernize leads to the collapse of the entire nation, successful economic management becomes a prime objective.

In this sense, external threats can be useful, since they reduce the incentive to seek rents if excessive rent-seeking effectively leads to a disaster.[11] The impact of external challenges may have been very important for the cases of Korea and Taiwan. It is indeed easy to imagine that everything would have gone very wrong in these countries: the economy was completely politicized and an authoritarian state exerted extensive control over all areas of economic life. For example, why did the authorities not become much more corrupted, since there was relatively little democratic control and discussion about the running of public affairs? When officials have been in charge of allocating credit for investment purposes, this must have created a huge potential for individual corruption and rent-seeking. That such activities did not become more widespread was perhaps due to the powerful external challenge.

Expectations and the Commitment to Private Property

The successful late industrializers have adopted very different policies in many important respects. Conversely, some policies seem to work in some countries and fail in others. This suggests that basic commitments and basic political will may be as important as specific policies. Paradoxically, a regime that is fundamentally committed to respect private property and the private ownership of productive assets may successfully use wide-ranging planning and other radical ways of political intervention. These are then accepted by capitalists as temporary measures. For example, after World War II, extensive political and corporatist planning of the economy has been practised in countries as diverse as France, Korea, Taiwan, Finland, East Germany, and Chile. The fact that planning was successful in the first four and a failure in the last two may have much to do with the fact that in the first four there was a clear commitment ultimately to respect the property rights of capital owners. Another example would be that of Brazil in the 1950s and 1960, where econmic planning was at least moderately successful.

A left-wing regime, on the other hand, keen in its anti-market rhetoric,

[11] This is not to deny, of course, that external challenges may entail other costs. Korea, for example, has used about 5–6% of its GDP for defence purposes.

loses the confidence of domestic investors even if the practical policy packages are not very radical and comprehensive. Thus, a planned route to a market economy may succeed, whereas market solutions within planning-oriented regimes look less viable. As pointed out by Katzenstein (1984), there was more planning in the Austrian economy than in some of its nominally socialist neighbours, and Korea and Taiwan at best were not much behind the GDR in overall *dirigisme*. Yet only Taiwan, Korea, and Austria were committed to and successful in becoming successful capitalist economies.

Another example which illustrates this comparison is that of Peru during the years of President Alan Garcia 1985–8. Garcia's aim was to mobilize domestic investors in a national programme of industrial restructuring. Although his policies would probably not have been more interventionist than those of Taiwan and Korea, his basic political orientation of anti-IMF rhetoric roused the suspicions of the national elites and his economic policy resulted in failure.[12]

4. SUMMARY: A STYLISED ECONOMY

To summarize some of the above ideas, consider a stylized model economy. The model amounts to a rudimentary economic theory of the state in a corporatist economy.

Suppose that the economy is based on a few manufacturing industries that are characterized by the typical assumptions of endogenous growth theory: there are increasing returns external to each producer but internal to each industry. These may depend on various kinds of 'linkages'; when one firm invests resources in the education of an engineer, this engineer may become very valuable for the other firms, too, because he may generate innovations in their production techniques as well. Similarly, investment in the development of a new product may open up new production possi-bilities for other firms as well. At the level of each individual producer, however, technology is characterized by a fixed coefficient (linear) pro-duction function, so that output is simply a multiple of the capital stock.

Then a completely decentralized allocation without coordination is of course inefficient, because it fails to take advantage of these positive exter-nalities. However, it will be advantageous for any particular industry to organize collectively some of its investment and research activities. Once

---

[12] Of course, Garcia's explicit political project of reneging on foreign debt was a clear breach of the market-oriented rules of the game. Although stopping the interest payments on foreign debt increased the scope for short-term industrial policy, a rational domestic investor in Peru must have pondered whether a regime not committed to the fundamental property rights of capitalism would in the future guarantee a fair return on his own investment.

this is understood, all industries will organize themselves and coordinate a part of their investment in fixed capital, education, and research. Thus, the economy is likely to exhibit a corporatist structure with a number (clearly less than infinity) of important corporatist actors.

However, the elimination of the first type of inefficiency and the coordination of investment activities within each industry may lead to a new type of inefficiency, precisely because of the institutional structure that is generated by the need to eliminate the inefficiency. Since the corporations are large relative to the size of the economy, they act strategically towards each other. The relative price of the product of a corporation is determined in the product market, so that a larger volume of output leads to a lower relative price for the product. Since the corporation can internalize this relation as well, it is likely to recommend to its members a level of investment that falls short of society's first-best optimum. The economic outcome will then be a Nash equilibrium in a strategic game between the corporations, and, as is well known from game theory, such equilibria will not in general be efficient. Thus, externalities in production may give rise to an institutional structure that in turn generates other externalities due to distribution.

The ideal role of the state is to use its means to overcome these distributional conflicts. A benevolent state can use taxation and investment subsidies or downward rationed interest rates to generate as much investment as a first-best equilibrium would require. Alternatively, it may just control the price structure and thereby eliminate the scope for the strategic action by organized corporations.

The first-best solution requires an uncorrupted state that is willing to maximize a weighted welfare function of all parties. Suppose, by contrast, that the state is weak and becomes a client of one corporation. In economic terms, this can be interpreted as an inability to commit itself to a specific policy. Instead of being a leader in the game, the state takes the action (investment in the model) of some corporation as given and then maximizes the welfare of the economy. This clearly leads to a suboptimal result.

The role of the external constraints can also be illustrated in a model like this. Suppose that it is politically unclear whether the state is able to commit itself to a policy that leads to a first-best optimum. Or, alternatively, one may suppose that the corporations themselves try to work out a national investment plan which stipulates a high level of output for each sector. In both of these situations, it may be highly unclear whether everybody will stick to the first-best policy. An external constraint, however, may change the pay-offs in such a way that nobody benefits from cheating. In economic terms, it may be interpreted as a constraint that says that everybody's welfare is very low (overthrow of the regime) unless a very high level of national product is achieved. Then it may become very easy for the state-cum-corporatist round table to implement a national investment plan.

5. CONCRETE FORMS OF INTERVENTION

Even a very simple model like this points the way to the instruments of intervention. In the model economy, the enlightened state can achieve its aims either by subsidizing investment, controlling prices or rationing credit, and keeping interest rates artificially low. Conspicuously enough, all of these means have been extensively used in our examples of successful developmental states.

Credit rationing of some sort has been practised in all of our success stories. Financial markets have been 'underdeveloped' by neoclassical standards. In Korea, all banks were nationalized in 1961 with the advent of the government of Park Chung Hee. This enabled the government to control very directly the allocation of investment. The banks were privatized in the 1980s, but the government maintained its control of commercial banking (Amsden 1989: 16). In Taiwan, the financial system has remained undiversified and dominated by the banks. Almost all banks have been owned by the government, and the government has appointed their senior staff (Wade 1990: 159–60). This has made it possible to exert very direct discretion about the allocation of investment funds to various projects. In Finland, banks have remained privately owned and have not been tightly controlled by the authorities. Yet a system of credit rationing and low interest rates was set up after World War II by a joint arrangement between the commercial banks and the central bank. Credit was rationed and the central bank issued orders about the preferential treatment of investment in manufacturing industry. Real interest rates were often near zero or even negative in the 1960s and the 1970s.

Low effective interest rates have been typical for most of our success countries. In Korea, the price of long-term credit has been negative with the exception of the 'liberal' experiment of the years 1965–72. Even during that time, the government arranged long-term international credit for favoured firms at terms that were more advantageous than those encountered by other domestic agents. In Taiwan, real interest rates have been higher than in Korea and Finland, but even there the effective price of long-term credit for exporters has been quite low because of various kinds of subsidies. In any case, the level of interest rates in Taiwan entailed continual excess demand for credit (see Wade 1990: 59), so that political intervention has set interest rates below their market clearing level.

A policy of low interest rates may thus be a straightforward way of taking advantage of externalities related to investment. De Long and Summers (1991) have pointed out the empirical correlation between equipment investment and growth. According to them, high rates of growth are statistically associated with high rates of equipment investment, and the causal connection runs from equipment investment to growth, because the relative price of investment goods has also been lower in the high growth countries.

Selective measures in the rationing of credit have been necessary to prevent the allocation of subsidized investment resources to speculative purposes or consumption. In a perfect world where information flows freely without transaction costs, speculative windfall profits are not possible. In the real world, information is costly and it can be worthwhile for some of the best minds to concentrate their efforts on financial arbitrage. These talents are then not available for productive purposes. The possibility of this kind of inefficiency has been demonstrated theoretically by Murphy, Shleifer, and Vishny (1991).

Low interest rates discourage saving, and it is also typical of the late industrialization cases that savings have been boosted by other means. Katri Kosonen (1992) has outlined a 'Nordic model of accumulation' in which the state provides an important part of the saving necessary for capital accumulation. In Finland, for example, the ratio of public saving to aggregate investment has been of the order of 20–30 per cent from the 1950s to the mid-1970s inclusive. In Korea, the cost of credit was low for exporters and manufacturers, but a system of multiple interest rates was in operation, so that domestic savers and other domestic debtors could transact at a higher interest rate.

Administration of prices is another potential instrument of the state. In Finland, the state in the 1950s used the price of agricultural products as a bargaining instrument to alleviate the potential conflicts of the labour market: the price of food was subsidized in order to achieve corporatist wage agreements which encouraged manufacturing investment. This is a reasonable enough empirical counterpart to the role of price rationing suggested in the model. Similarly, the newly industrialized Asian countries have been distinguished from other developing countries by a relatively low price for investment goods (see Wade 1990: 20). This has been achieved partly by low interest rates but also by direct subsidies to the domestic producers of investment goods.

It is, however, the *straightforward intervention in the allocation of investment* which has probably been the most important determinant of fast industrialization in the success cases. In Korea and Taiwan as well as in Japan, government officials have exerted huge discretionary power to determine the allocation of investment in different productive processes. In Finland, too, the central bank has given out loans to businesses and industries that it judged capable of growth, and manufacturing industries have received selective subsidies for investment on regional grounds.

In Korea, the main engine of industrial policy was subsidies offered by the state to private enterprise. As emphasized by Amsden (1989: 63) this involved a large amount of horse-trading and wheeling and dealing, but there was an essentially reciprocal balance of power: the state was strong enough to use its power to discipline business and required output, growth, and superior performance in exchange for the subsidies.

An additional conclusion based on Korea's and Taiwan's experiences is that industrial policies have been at least as concerned with the productive efficiency of industries as with the more general 'neoclassical' goal of fostering a competitive environment and an efficient allocation of resources.

In the Scandinavian countries, Finland included, industrial policies driven by the state have also been a key element of industrialization (see Hjalmarsson 1991). It is interesting to note that in the Scandinavian countries too the goals of industrial policy have been defined in terms of productive efficiency and economies of scale rather than competition, allocative efficiency, and anti-trust objectives. Scandinavian industrial policy has 'concentrated on structural efficiency of various industries and on policy measures that should be taken to promote more rational industrial structures' (Hjalmarsson 1991: 245). This strategy relies heavily on the assumption that there are important economies of scale in many production sectors (see Hjalmarsson 1991: 246, for references). The Swedish government concentrated its activities on trying to influence the speed of structural rationalization and investment in new plants. A variety of subsidies and other selective measures were used to enhance productivity. The growth of firm size was encouraged. A competitive environment as an objective *per se* was not altogether neglected, but rather taken as granted by a small open economy. The same can be said of Finland, where industrial policy has not until recently been much concerned with the creation of competitive conditions.

In terms of the model economy outlined above, one can say that the state has concentrated its efforts on finding efficient solutions to distributional conflicts, given the corporatist and oligopolistic nature of the economy. If the assumptions of technological externalities are true, this may indeed be a good strategy, because it is probably very difficult for the state to perceive all the economies of scale due to clusters and linkages within various industries.

If this (speculative) idea is correct, it vindicates the principles of 'Nordic–East-Asian' industrial policy. Notice the difference between this state-cum-corporatism policy outlined in the model and the application of the neoclassical prescription to the same model economy. The neoclassical recipe would of course be to set up a general subsidy scheme for investment in order to exploit the technological externality but otherwise prevent the formation of corporations. This solution may fail because of information constraints. It may be very difficult for the state to perceive the intra-industrial linkages and externalities whereas the management of conflicts is a much more natural task for the state. It may also fail because it may prevent the growth of firms to a size that would enable them to exploit economies of scale.

To sum up, there is an important common thread in the industrial policies of the Nordic countries and the Asian miracles. The growth of productivity has been actively enhanced by pragmatic and selective means and the creation of large manufacturing firms has been actively encouraged. This policy has involved a lot of pragmatic, selective, and administrative intervention, while it has always been clear that the basic division of roles in a capitalist economy will be respected: productive activity is to be undertaken by private entrepreneurs, and whatever 'planning' there is, its purpose is to influence the rate of investment and productivity growth without questioning the basic division of the tasks.

6. SUCCESS CASES: KOREA, TAIWAN, FINLAND, AUSTRIA

Let us now investigate in more detail how the 'matrix' of factors analysed above has been at work in the specific country cases.

Korea

The Korean experience has been analysed by Amsden (1989). Korea illustrates most of the elements outlined above. The Korean state has been very strong not only towards labour but also towards business. The Korean State has offered large rewards for successful entrepreneurs, but it has also had the ability to discipline business: 'where Korea differs from most other late industrializing countries is in the discipline its state exercises over private firms' (Amsden 1989: 14).

The historical roots of the strength of the Korean State have been analysed by Amsden (1989). The Japanese colonization of Korea left a power vacuum after World War II, and the state was able to establish its power in the 1960s because of the weakness of social classes. The landlord aristocracy had been dispersed by land reform, the working class was too small and too weak to pose a serious challenge, and capitalists had become dependent on government subsidies. The military government nationalized the banks in 1961, which gave the state the crucial power to determine the allocation and timing of industrial investment.

Thus there is no question of the strength of the Korean State. What is perhaps more problematic is what constituted the necessary balance of power. Why did the Korean state not degenerate into a circle of corruption? Amsden emphasizes the role of the student movement as well as that of external pressures and the US administration. The student movement was important because it presented the state with a constant danger of rebellion which in turn 'disciplined' the government against the worst excesses of power. The students were in a pivotal position because the Korean strategy of industrialization relied on the rapid education of a class of salaried engineers and other white collar workers.

The external challenge factor has also been present. The North Korean regime has provided a challenge which may have compelled the Korean rulers to pay more attention to overall performance and efficiency than what would otherwise have been the case. Korea has not been a real democracy until recently and it is instructive to ask what did prevent a degeneration of its economy in the hands of an authoritarian state apparatus which was not really controlled by democratically elected bodies. The student movement may have played a role in controlling the actions of the state, but the external challenge of North Korea and the dependency on the US military commitment are probably more important explanations.

Taiwan

Taiwan's performance has been analysed by Wade (1990), who characterizes Taiwan's industrialization from the 1950s to the 1980s as state-led. Industrial policies have emphasized sectoral promotion of productivity, which is in accordance with the 'Scandinavian–Asian' model.

Taiwan shares with Korea a past of Japanese colonialsm. The strength of the Taiwanese state derives from the 'invasion' of the island by the two-million military and civilian Nationalist mainlanders in 1949 after the defeat of the Nationalist army. The islanders had no army or powerful political structure to challenge the position of the Nationalist forces, and the Nationalist-mainlander government could enjoy an unusually wide room for manoeuvre (Wade 1990: 75). The monopolies originally owned by the Japanese colonialists passed to the incoming government. The government established multi-year development plans. They were not very detailed, but these government initiatives laid the basis for several branches of production (i.e. plastics, fibres, cement, and textiles). In the 1960s and 1970s, new sectors such as steel, automobiles, and shipbuilding were boosted, partly motivated by the idea of import substitution. Throughout this period, the government intervened heavily in favour of export industries. An impressive economic bureaucracy was set up to manage the governing of the economy.

The question of balance is more complicated. In Taiwan's case, too, the Nationalist rulers were faced with a strict external challenge. Being the claimants of legal rule in mainland China, they could ill afford a failure in economic management. A challenge, external to the Nationalist party but internal to the Taiwanese society, was constituted by the native Taiwanese islanders, whom the Nationalists excluded from power positions (Wade 1990: 237).

The role of the external challenge has probably been very important in Taiwan's case, too. Without that challenge it would be almost too easy to tell a hypothetical story which could have led to an altogether different conclusion: a corrupt dictatorial regime, repressed native islanders, and a huge and inefficient bureaucracy.

Finland

Finland provides an example of state-led corporatist industrialization where all the elements analysed in the above story have been present. Although Finland's severe crisis in the early 1990s has blurred the picture, it is clear that Finland's economic performance during the post-World War II period must considered very successful. The breakthrough of industrialization took place later than in the other Nordic countries. The economy was predominantly agrarian in the 1930s, and as late as 1950 more than half of the population and 40 per cent of output was still in the primary sector. Per capita GDP was only half of that of Sweden (Andersson *et al.* 1993). By the late 1970s, Finland had become a mature industrial economy.

Finland came out of World War II in a very vulnerable position between the power blocs of international politics. The victorious Soviet Union did not invade the country, but throughout the next forty years, Finland was within the sphere of influence of Soviet foreign policy and belonged to a contested border zone between the world's ideological blocs. Immediately after the war, the Soviet Union imposed a heavy war indemnity which required an extremely rapid buildup of industrial production. The way in which this challenge was tackled points the way to the organization of economic management that was to become prevalent for the entire period of state-led industrialization. The organization of industrial production was entrusted to a committee dominated by private industrialists and bankers. This happened at the same time as at the political level the right was discredited and the Social Democrats and Communists dominated the scene together with the agriculturalist Centre Party. It is remarkable that this leftist offensive did not really affect the 'pragmatic' running of the economy, which was entrusted to private agents and the central bank representatives (Vartiainen and Pekkarinen 1993).

This starting-point led to a conscious programme of state-sponsored industrialization and the buildup of a corporatist structure that was actively encouraged by the state. In the early 1950s, a key strategic decision was made not to decrease taxes to the pre-war levels but to use instead the surplus created by the subtraction of war expenditure from the budget to increase investment by state-owned as well as private companies.[13] As a result of this and a tradition of fiscal orthodoxy, the Finnish state became an important net saver for the economy. The structural budget surplus did not vanish until the 1980s, and public saving accounted for as much as 30

[13] A classical reference on this issue is the book by the future president Urho Kekkonen 'Onko maallamme malttia vaurastua' ['Has our country the patience to prosper'], 1952, where he endorses a state-led investment strategy.

per cent of aggregate saving during the 1950s and 1960s (see Kosonen 1992). Kekkonen also thought that the trade unions would moderate their wage claims if a larger share of savings and investment were undertaken by the state.

The first phase of industrialization in the 1950s and early 1960s was characterized by active and direct state participation in the diversification of the economy (see Andersson *et al.* 1993: 13). Several new state-owned companies were established and old ones were developed. The most important examples include Neste, which established a monopoly of oil refining and then continued into different lines of petro-chemicals and plastics.

As far as the decision-making institutions are concerned, we see at work both an efficient bureaucratic tradition and a powerful corporatist network. The prestige and strength of the civil service have been repeatedly emphasized by Finnish historians. This tradition dates back to the *autonomy* period from 1809 to 1917 when Finland was under Russia's rule. Throughout this period, the civil service was in Finnish hands and its legalistic tradition provided a protective shield against the more imperialistic aspirations of Russian politics. This is one important factor that explains the powerful and respected position of the Finnish civil service in comparison with the government and the parliamentary institutions. The civil service has played an important role in economic policy throughout the post-war years. In comparison with the East Asian countries, one may say that the Finnish state, if understood as the executive power of the government, has been relatively weaker while business corporations and the bureaucracy have been very strong.

The buildup of corporatist structures had already begun in the interwar years, but it was actively continued in the 1950s and the 1960s. If one speaks of state-led industrialization in the Finnish case, one must be willing to extend the legal meanings of statehood a bit. In a way similar to Austria, key economic decisions have been taken at informal, half-public half-corporatist meetings that have encompassed the powerful business corporations, the monetary authorities at the central bank, and the top civil servants as well as government officials.

These are typical ways of corporatist concertation in which the state is but one actor amongst many others. But there is no doubt about the essential mechanisms: Finnish industrialization was 'managed' by a handful of corporatist leaders, top civil servants, bankers, central bankers, and government officials. This half-official half-corporatist decision-making structure dates back to the very birth of the independent state. The victorious White side of the civil war of 1918 was an improvised organization of the military, bankers, industrialists, and right-wing politicians. Generally distrustful of republican democracy, they established a constitution which set clear checks and balances for a properly political intervention into the economy. The rights to private property in particular have enjoyed a strict constitutional protection. This can be seen as an important ingredient in the 'basic commitment' discussed above, a basic commitment that has probably been especially crucial for a country that has been situated in a contested zone between the world's ideological blocs.

The banks and the central bank have been an important centre of economic management. Theoreticians of the state have yet to appreciate the peculiar nature of Finnish statehood: it is clear that the regime of economic management has been very far from *laissez-faire* ideals; yet it is equally clear that political intervention into the economy has been limited in many important respects (see Vartiainen and Pekkarinen 1993). The credit markets were rationed until the 1980s and, in a similar way to Taiwan and Korea, credit was allocated to productive manufacturing investment while households' demand for credit exceeded supply. But most of this management took place in the banks and the central bank, and less at the hands of the government. From the 1930s onwards, the central bank became an authoritative agent of economic policy, largely insulated from government control, but sensitive to the demands of the organized business community. As an example of collective economic management yet outside the sphere of the democratic process, one may as well take the loan finance advanced by the central bank *directly* to certain types of business.

Thus, to use the phrase of Vartiainen (1991), the 'Finnish capitalists were innovative enough to socialise the investment function . . . between themselves'. The devaluation-prone nature of Finnish monetary policy can be understood in the light of this tradition: the central bank has provided an investment insurance for the Finnish export industries.

Thus, Finnish corporatism had from the outset acquired a clear pro-business bias. However, when the Finnish Left and the trade union movement were strengthened after World War II, they were gradually encompassed into the established decision-making institutions without revolution in those institutions. The buildup of a coherent corporatist structure on the 'labour' side, that is, the comprehensive unionization of Finnish workers, was not at all resisted by the state. On the contrary, it was actively encouraged by the authorities in the 1960s, when the unionization rate increased from under 40 per cent to almost 80 per cent (see Vartiainen and Pekkarinen 1993). This had its economic as well as political logic, both fitting well into the stylized story of managed industrialization of a small and vulnerable economy. From the point of view of the state authorities and the employers, the inclusion of workers in a corporatist structure was a protection against communist influence and a way to contain potentially dangerous political pressures.[14] A concrete expression of this official accept-

---

[14] Against this background, it is not surprising that the employers and the government have in the early 1990s adopted an attitude much more inimical towards trades unions as well as incomes policies: with the collapse of the Soviet Union and the threat of communism out of the scene, there is no similar imperative to integrate the workers' organizations into the state

ance of trade union organization was the introduction in 1967 of the tax deduction on the membership fee of a trade union.

Finally, we also see at work the phenomenon of old power networks being dissolved by the outcome of the war. Finland's defeat in the war against the Soviet Union discredited the bourgeois parties, and from then on the business community felt much more insecure and more in need of political support. This facilitated the practical management of the economy. The industrial policies of the time were a perfect illustration of the 'mapping out an economy's production potential' argument outlined above. This was understood on a regional basis: the industrial policy of the 1950s and the 1960s aimed at a balanced exploitation of the natural resources of all the major areas of the economy.

These étatist aspects of Finnish economic management were greatly enhanced by trade with the Soviet Union. This was organized politically, and close ties with the political elites became a source of lucrative business contracts as well. This entourage of President Kekkonen was sometimes jokingly referred to as 'red magnates'.

Austria

The Austrian economy also underwent a process of late industrialization after World War II. In contrast to Czechoslovakia, Austria had never been part of the industrialized core area of Central Europe, and the outcome of the war left Austria with an economy that still relied to a great extent on agricultural output and primary production. Furthermore, the Potsdam agreement of 1945 gave the Soviets the right to seize German assets in their occupation zone and many Austrian factories were effectively dismantled and the machinery parts sent to the Soviet Union (Mjöset 1992: 164).

However, the period running from the late 1940s to the 1970s became one of heavy expansion for manufacturing industries. Iron and steel production as well as output of aluminium products expanded particularly rapidly.[15]

Most of the mechanisms discussed above can be seen at work in Austria. The legal and formal institutions that have carried out the political intervention into the economy have been more similar to Finland's than those of the East Asian cases: the Austrian state has been relatively weak in comparison with the power of the various semi-official corporations. The Austrian state and the corporations of civil society have merged with each other in a

and the rest of society. This effect is not confined to Finland. De Geer's (1992) account of Swedish industrial relations shows how strongly the buildup of Swedish corporatism was motivated by the employers' perceived need of taming the potential radicalism of the working class.

[15] Pig iron and raw steel production, for example, rose more than threefold in three decades.

remarkable way. In broad terms, the Austrian and the Finnish cases are reminiscent of each other. Austria, too, had to struggle for survival from 1945 to 1952. After the liberation from Nazi rule, the economy was in chaos and the country did not enjoy full sovereignty. Austria was occupied by the Allied (including Soviet) forces until 1955. As in the other cases treated in this section, it is fair to say that an economic failure could have led to further losses of sovereignty.

This critical starting-point led to a remarkable mobilization of the nation's resources and the adoption of an industrialization strategy that depended on state action and corporatist concertation. This was a response to the external challenge as well as a reflection of the country's history. There had been a tragic civil war in 1934, when the Social Democrats, having been subjected to increasing provocation by the Nazis, took to arms. The victory of the conservative forces led to an authoritarian government, and the Austrian state's half-hearted attempt to counter Nazi-German infiltration was unsuccessful. The country was annexed to Germany in 1938. Thus, there were ample lessons for Austrians about the dangers of internal strife and external dangers. With reference to the discussion of Section 2, one can say that the outcome of the war certainly produced a situation where established internal power blocs were disrupted. 'Denazification' laws passed in 1946 and 1947 formally eliminated Nazi influence from the public life of Austria, and the labour movement had to reconstruct itself after years of repression.

This organizational mobilization was a rational response to the weakening of the state authority which had been formally subjected to Allied sovereignty (see also Katzenstein 1984: esp. p. 59). As able political leaders have known throughout history, a danger of loss of sovereignty is lessened by powerful organizations within civil society. The very management of the Austrian economy has typically taken place in an informal border zone of public decision making and private concertation. Yet there has been a strong centralization of power in economic policy making, which, as far as the practical results are concerned, has been almost equivalent to a strong state. Whether all these decisions have been taken within the formal jurisdiction of state activities is then of secondary importance. As emphasized by Katzenstein (1984: 66), this concentration of power occurs 'in a political setting that does not recognise a distinction between public and private. Lines of formal authority are typically blurred. As bodies of public law, some of Austria's major interest groups exercise, in addition to their normal, autonomous operations, administrative powers delegated by the state.' A typical institution in this respect is the Joint Commission, which joins both state representatives and industrial organizations in deliberations about incomes policies and other economic policies.

The political management of the economy included, firstly, nationalization of a large part of the Austrian economy. At the end of World War II, the newly established Parliament decided to nationalize most of the assets seized by Germans after the Anschluss of 1938. Similarly, when the Soviet Union withdrew its forces from Austria in 1955, many of the enterprises formerly in the Soviet zone of influence fell to the hands of Austrian state. This vast nationalization might at first glance seem at odds with the hypothesis that successful state intervention should not aim at full-scale public ownership. Yet it reinforces the argument that state-led economic management can be perfectly acceptable from the point of view of private capitalists as long as it is not motivated by a socialist ideology: it was clear in Austria that these nationalizations were not a reflection of ideological class struggle but instead an expression of the striving for national independence.[16] This hypothesis is also indirectly confirmed by the fact that the Austrian state let the public enterprises be managed in accordance with profit maximization and withdrew from more extensive planning.

However, there have been important elements of planning and political intervention within Austrian economic policy. There has been extensive regulation of prices and wages by political–corporatist bodies. The first wage/price agreements in 1947 were immediate responses to the inflationary chaos of the immediate post-war period. This co-ordination was institutionalized in 1951. The political–corporatist determination of prices has, remarkably, been by and large accepted even by the business community.

Finally, the public ownership of a large part of the banking sector and rationing of credit markets has 'socialized' a large part of investment decisions. This political determination of investment has introduced one further instrument which has made it easier to conclude corporatist agreements and to socialize risk due to economic restructuring.

Many authors have emphasized the weakness of the Austrian state with respect to corporations of the civil society. We have argued above that this weakness is somewhat illusory, since the state and corporations have merged with each other and power has been centralized. Furthermore, Austria, too, has enjoyed a strong administrative tradition that dates back to the mercantilist unification of the most important German parts of the Habsburg empire in the eighteenth century (see Katzenstein 1984: 63). The Austrian civil service has the reputation of great competence and is intimately involved in relations with business and trade unions. Measured by the number of officials per capita, Austria's welfare bureaucracy is larger than that of any other Western European country (Katzenstein 1984: 63). So, we see, again, a competent bureaucracy richly endowed with formal and informal ties with organized economic agents. The East Asian one-party state is substituted in Austria with a network of corporatist arrangements and a state influenced by two remarkably stable political parties.

[16] In this respect it is important to note that the nationalization laws were passed unanimously by the Austrian parliament (Katzenstein 1984: 49).

5. SOME FAILURES AND WEAK STATES

We have claimed above that success in late industrialization can in some cases be traced back to a strong bureaucratic state which is committed to economic development and autonomous enough to conceive efficient industrial policies but also endowed with strong ties with a corporatist civil society. This section in turn considers some phases of economic failure in certain countries. Although these cases have not been selected in a systematic way, their point is to illustrate how the absence of such a state has adversely affected a country's economic performance. This description is not representative in the statistical sense, but it suggests some causal connections. Economic failure is often associated with a state

- too weak or unwilling to organize economic development;
- too dependent on particular interests to set its own agenda;
- too poorly endowed with connections with organized economic interests;
- without external challenges that would have required a good performance.

In Chile, the government's perennial strategy has been to tax the export industry, but the state has not been able or determinate enough to build the industry on a domestically owned basis (see Meller 1991). This meant that the financial position of the state was much consolidated already during the first 'nitrate boom' of 1880–1930, but the state did not become dependent on the overall performance of the economy. The failure to develop industries on a national and domestic basis was one factor that led to political instabilities after World War II. The Chilean government subsequently leant more heavily on copper, but was equally uncommitted to a domestic industrialization strategy. The economic role of the state increased without clear purpose, and the political practices of taxing exports and granting selective protection for the ablest lobbyists encouraged the development of a rent-seeking society. In this way, the role of the state in the Chilean economy gradually strengthened without it being the case that the position of the state was heavily dependent on the development of the entire economy.

The historical roots of this role of the state lay in the oligarchic nature of Chilean elites. The layer of domestic entrepreneurs was thin and closely related to the agrarian aristocracy. There was no effort to create a large indigenous class of entrepreneurs, and the political process concentrated on the contest about the distribution of tax income that the basically foreign-owned mineral production was able to generate. The weakness of domestic entrepreneurship contributed to the fact that, once the state's role was extended in the late 1930s with the election of a worker-oriented government, the state assumed a very direct role in the productive process. The socialist experiment starting in 1970 did not have time to show its ability to mobilize national resources.

In Uruguay, the period reaching from the early 1950s to the late 1960s can also be characterized as an economic failure during which per capita output declined by more than 10 per cent. Rama (1991) has suggested that this decline was closely related to a progressive weakening of the Uruguayan state, with the loss of autonomy for the relevant policy decisions (Rama 1991: 111). According to Rama, the state could not contain the social groups whose strength was of its own creation: the civil servants, manufacturers, and wage earners.

The number of civil servants increased dramatically between 1941 and 1969, from less than 3 per cent of the population to almost 8.5 per cent. The efficiency of the public sector was reduced as new public sector jobs were allocated on a cliental basis. Education became a means of getting access to the public sector while technical education was neglected. In a way not very different from Chile, the affluence due to temporarily high export earnings was exploited by a state bureaucracy not committed to the development of the economy. What we see at work here is indeed bureaucracy without an established bureaucratic tradition: a career in the civil service became a handy way of personal advancement, without the constraints and incentives posed by a meritocratic system where achievement is compensated.

The manufacturers, on the other hand, were not very numerous, and to lobby for protection became an activity of very high marginal returns. In contrast with the Korean and Taiwanese cases, the state did not really require much in terms of industrial performance in exchange for the protectionist policies. The strong trade unions, undisciplined by the weak state, were in turn capable of extracting high wage increases incompatible with profitability and growth. This vicious circle ultimately ended by the close of the 1960s with very high social costs and the end of democracy.

Ireland is an interesting European case of relatively unsuccessful economic performance. The Irish case can be characterized as one of a relatively strong state and bureaucracy but without commitment to rapid industrial modernization and without sufficient vertical and horizontal links towards organized economic actors.

As is apparent from Lars Mjöset's extensive survey (1992), these facts have much to do with the strong influence of the Catholic Church. Irish nationalism has been organized and mobilized by religious organizations, whose predominant goals have not been economic. Many characteristics and social implications of industrial modernism for modern industrial societies have even been inimical for the church, which has been opposed to individual profit-seeking, consumerism, and materialism. The Asian cases show how nationalism played a positive role within a bureaucracy whose aims were set chiefly in economic terms. By contrast, Irish nationalism was from early on blended with assertive Roman Catholicism instead of economic modernization (Mjöset 1992: 224). The church has also controlled education, with the result that the educational system has not put an emphasis on technical and engineering skills.

The absence of linkages and networks has also been related to the fact that Ireland's collective values were primarily articulated through religious organizations. This has meant that the other corporatist structures conducive to agro-industrial linkages remained underdeveloped. Mjöset (1992: 242–5) compares the structure of Irish agriculture with the Danish one and emphasizes the role of the co-operative movement in Denmark. The Danish co-operatives played an important role in the introduction of new processing machinery and the transformation of production towards products with more value added. Thus, they fostered links between industrial and agricultural production. There was no co-operative movement of similar importance in Ireland. Whether such a corporatist structure emerges is not formally associated with state activities, but the economic success cases (cf. the discussion on the Asian miracles and Finland above) show that the buildup of such corporatist structures has been actively encouraged by the interventionist state. Thus, their existence cannot be seen as wholly external to the state. In Ireland, such encouragement of an autonomous civil society organized in economic terms hardly took place. The Irish state, church, and civil society have been linked together (ibid. 250), but these links have been built on religious and traditionalistic values and not on the hope of rapid industrial growth.

Furthermore, the intellectual traditions of the Irish civil service have been of British origin (ibid. 258), and have therefore reflected an economic liberalism natural for an older industrial nation. There has been an important and influential 'deflationist central bank' faction within the bureaucracy, opposed to active industrial policy and reluctant to put in place powerful Asian-type development agencies. This was reflected in the fact that the Industrial Development Authority, founded in 1949, became more interested in attracting foreign investment than in fostering and planning for national industrial policies.

Finally, while Ireland's economic well-being has been constantly in doubt, there has certainly been no external challenge to the nation. Ireland's geographical position binds the country to Britain, a major European power, which however does not any more represent a threat of outright political imperialism. Being in Britain's backyard probably lets one away with a cosier existence than being located in the trenches of the cold war.

7. CONCLUSIONS

This paper has made an attempt to understand the experiences of some successful state-led industrialization policies. There is no presumption that these case studies should prove that the interventionist school of development policies is ultimately right. Many of the factors that have been singled out in the paper are indeed such that they are not or should not be replicable. A long tradition of competent meritocratic bureaucracy is not to be chosen from any supermarket of social institutions. Social upheavals that lead to the disruption of established elites are dangerous and cannot be engineered at will. Finally, even if it is true that the threat of international conflicts concentrates the minds and compels the nation to organize its economy efficiently, nobody would want the cold war to continue or wish that the system of international politics remain so threatening that this function would play a significant role in economic development.

Furthermore, the policy models of the success stories are not presented as timeless solutions. The late industrializers have been in a catch-up position in which it has been relatively easy to copy the achievements of forerunners. Not everybody can imitate, however, and there is a similar danger of composition fallacy in the policy of protecting local industries and subsidizing exports. If everybody protects and subsidizes, the markets for the hoped-for export growth may not be there.

Yet these studies show that state intervention and corporatism can work well in some places and in some times. On the basis of the foregoing analysis, one may at least present some tentative points to the neoclassical orthodoxy of international development policies:

1. While an overall orientation for exports and international trade is important, a certain degree of economic nationalism may be a good thing in the mobilization of an economy's resources.

2. State bureaucracies are not bad *per se*; what matters is that they are competent, meritocratic, and endowed with sufficient resources. Employment in the bureaucracy should not be the sole objective of talented young people, but nor should public bodies be seen as necessarily useless and corrupt institutions (if this is the general appreciation, they will probably attract useless and corrupt individuals).

3. A structure of corporatist organizations may be a very useful partner for the state bureaucracy to deal with. Inasmuch as there are externalities in investment (in infrastructure, human capital, and equipment), a public-planning industrial-policy agency is probably a good place to deal with them.

REFERENCES

AMSDEN, ALICE H. (1989). *Asia's Next Giant: South Korea and Late Industrialization.* Oxford: Oxford University Press.

ANDERSSON, JAN OTTO, KOSONEN, PEKKA, and VARTIAINEN, JUHANA (1993). 'The

Finnish Model of Economic and Social Policy—from Emulation to Crash', Research Report A:401, Abo Akademi University, Department of Economics.

AZARIADIS, COSTAS and DRAZEN, ALLAN (1990). 'Threshold Externalities in Economic Development', *Quarterly Journal of Economics*, 105/2 (May), 501–26.

BEREND, IVÀN T. and RÀNKI, GYÖRGY (1982). The European Periphery and Industrialisation 1780–1914.

BIERSTEKER, THOMAS J. (1990). 'Reducing the Role of the State in the Economy: A Conceptual Exploration of IMF and World Bank Prescriptions', *International Studies Quarterly*, 34: 477–92.

—— (1992). 'The "Triumph" of Neoclassical Economics in the Developing World; Policy Convergence and Bases of Governance in the International Economic Order', in J. A. Rosenau and E. O. Czempiel (eds.), *Governance without Government*. Cambridge: Cambridge University Press.

BLOMSTRÖM, MAGNUS and MELLER, PATRICIO (eds.) (1991*a*). *Diverging Paths: Comparing a Century of Scandinavian and Latin American Economic Development*, Inter-American Development Bank, distr. by the Washington, DC: Johns Hopkins University Press.

—— —— (1991*b*). 'Lessons from Scandinavian–Latin American Comparisons', in Blomström and Meller (1991*a*).

CALMFORS, LARS and DRIFFILL, JOHN (1988). 'Bargaining Structure, Corporatism and Economic Performance, *Economic Policy*, 6.

CRAFTS, NICHOLAS (1992). 'Productivity Growth Reconsidered', *Economic Policy* (Oct.).

DAHMÉN, ERIK (1951). *Entrepreneurial Activity and the Development of Swedish Industry 1919–1939*. Stockholm: Industriens Utredningsinstitut.

DE GEER, H. (1992). *The Rise and Fall of the Swedish Model*. Stockholm: Carden Publications and the FA Institute.

DE LONG, J.B. and SUMMERS LAWRENCE (1991). 'Equipment Investment and Economic Growth', *Quarterly Journal of Economics* (May).

HJALMARSSON, LENNART (1991). 'The Scandinavian Model of Industrial Policy', in Blomström and Meller (1991a).

JAKOBSON, MAX (1992). *Vallanvaihto havaintoja ja muistiinpanoja vuosilta 1974–82.* [Shift of power. Observations and notes from years 1974–82.] Helsinki: Otava.

KALDOR, NICHOLAS (1978). *Further Essays in Economic Theory*. London: Duckworth.

KATZENSTEIN, PETER (1984). *Corporatism and Change: Austria, Switzerland and the Politics of Industry*. Ithaca, NY: Cornell University Press.

—— (1985). *Small States in World Markets: Industrial Policy in Europe*. Ithaca, NY: Comell University Press.

KEKKONEN, URHO (1952). *Onko maalamme malttia vaurastua?* [Does our country have the patience to prosper?]. Helsinki: Otava.

KOSONEN, KATRI (1992). 'Saving and Economic Growth from a Nordic Perspective', in Pekkarinen, Pohjola, and Rowthorn.

LANDESMANN, MICHAEL and VARTIAINEN, JUHANA (1992). 'Social Corporatism and Long-Term Economic Performance', in Pekkarinen, Pohjola, and Rowthorn.

MATSUYAMA, KIMIONORI (1991). 'Increasing Returns, Industrialisation, and Indeterminacy of Equilibrium', *Quarterly Journal of Economics*, May.

MELLER, PATRICIO (1991). 'Chilean Economic Development 1880–1990', in

Blomström and Meller (1991a).

MJÖSET, LARS (1992). 'The Irish Economy in a Comparative Institutional Perspective', National Economic and Social Council, no. 93. Dublin.

MURPHY, K. M., SHLEIFER, ANDREI, and VISHNY, ROBERT (1991). 'The Allocation of Talent: Implications for Growth', Quarterly Journal of Economics (May).

OLSON, MANCUR (1982). The Rise and Decline of Nations. New Haven: Yale University Press.

PEKKARINEN, JUKKA, POHJOLA, MATTI, and ROWTHORN, BOB (eds.) (1992). Social Corporatism—A Superior Economic System?, WIDER Studies in Development Economics. Oxford: Clarendon Press.

PORTER, MICHAEL (1990). The Competitive Advantage of Nations. London: Macmillan.

RAMA, MARTIN (1991). 'Economic Growth and Stagnation in Uruguay', in Blomström and Meller (1991a).

SCHLEIFER, ANDREI and VISHNY, ROBERT W. (1993). 'Corruption', Quarterly Journal of Economics, 108/3 (Aug.), 599–618.

SUPPLE, BARRY (1973). 'The State and the Industrial Revolution 1700–1914', in Carlo M. Cipolla (ed.) (1973), The Fontana Economic History of Europe, iii. The Industrial Revolution. London: Fontana/Collins.

SÖDERSTEN, BO (1991). 'One Hundred Years of Swedish Economic Development', in Blomström and Meller (1991a).

VARTIAINEN, JUHANA (1991). 'Suomalainen korporatismi ja talouspolitiikan vastuu'. [Finnish corporatism and the sharing of responsibilities in economic policy] Kansantaloudellinen aikakauskirja [Finnish Economic Journal] 4.

VARTIAINEN, JUHANA and PEKKARINEN, JUKKA (1993). Suomen talouspolitiikan pitkä linja [History of Finnish economic policy]. Helsinki: WSOY.

WADE, ROBERT (1990). Governing the Market: Economic Theory and the Role of Government in East Asian Industrialisation. Princeton: Princeton University Press.

7

The State and Industrialization in India: Successes and Failures and the Lessons for the Future

Ajit Singh

1. INTRODUCTION

Among the non-socialist developing countries, the Indian economy has long been regarded as being a classical case of heavy state intervention. In the eyes of the powerful and influential neo-liberal critics of the country's economic development, particularly the Bretton Woods institutions, this intervention, if not disastrous, has certainly been inefficient. It is thought to have resulted in a sluggish pace of industrialization and a relatively slow growth of the economy. The majority of India's indigenous economists on the other hand, although critical of many aspects of the state-planned economic regime, generally regard it in a more favourable light.

The classical Indian state-directed industrialization model held sway for three decades, from 1950 to 1980. The model began to erode in the 1980s.[1] After the elections of 1991, the new Congress party minority government of Narasimhan Rao was faced with an acute external short-term liquidity crisis. The government sought assistance from the IMF to cope with the situation and to restore confidence. It also announced at that time its intention more or less to abandon altogether the traditional model. This chapter, however, concentrates on this traditional model which has dominated Indian economic development over most of the post-independence period. The chapter sets out the main lines of the arguments of the critics as well as the proponents of the model, and provides and assessment of their relative merits.

Section 2 outlines the main features of the Indian industrialization model. Section 3 considers various indicators of the success or failure of the model. Section 4 examines the case of the critics. Section 5 outlines the counter-arguments of the proponents. Section 6 provides an overall conclusion. Also, in addition, it briefly examines the question whether (*a*) the

I am very grateful to Ha-Joon Chang and Rathin Roy for helpful comments on an earlier draft. The usual disclaimer applies.

[1] For an analysis of the reasons for, and the implications of this erosion, see Singh and Ghosh (1988).

country would have done better under an alternative industrialization model and, (b) whether such a model was feasible in the Indian circumstances. This discussion is specifically directed towards the practicality and wisdom of the East Asian model for India. Such counter-factual speculation is not simply an intellectual exercise, but has an important bearing on the industrial policy issues confronting the Indian economy in the changed circumstances of the 1990s.

2. THE INDIAN MODEL OF PLANNED ECONOMIC DEVELOPMENT

Among the mixed economy Third World nations, India pioneered development planning and instituted, beginning in 1952, a set of five-year plans for planned economic development of the country.[2] The inspiration for Indian planning came from the Soviet Union which was thought to have successfully achieved industrialization of the country in a relatively short span of time. The 'Fabian socialist' leadership of the newly independent India, personified by Nehru, sought to adapt the Soviet model to the requirements of a mixed economy and a democratic polity in order to provide a 'third' way of economic development for nations emerging from colonial rule.

In keeping with the ideals of the top leadership, the Indian Plans were designed to bring about economic and social development within a 'socialist' framework. The plans pursued multiple objectives of industrialization, raising per capita incomes and equity in the distribution of gains from economic progress. They also sought to reduce the existing concentration of economic power and to achieve a better regional distribution of industrial development. As far as economic strategy is concerned, the following elements were the most important during the 1950s, 1960s, and most of the 1970s:

• First, The Indian planners emphasized the role of heavy industry in economic development and sought to build up as rapidly as possible the capital goods sector.
• Second, the plans envisaged a leading role for the public sector in this structural transformation of the economy. Not only was the government to play a dominant role in infrastructure investments (railways, electricity, etc.), but many industries, particularly in the capital goods sector, were exclusively reserved for development by the state.
• Third, major investments in the private sector were to be carried out, not by the test of private profitability, but according to the requirements of the overall national plan. For example, car production might have

---

[2] There is a large extensive literature on Indian planning. Notable recent contributions have been Chakravarty (1988) and Gupta (1989). For an important earlier contribution, see Streeten and Lipton (1968); see also the original five year plan documents of the Planning Commission (1952, 1956, 1963, 1970, 1976, 1981, 1985).

been highly profitable, but the manufacturers were prohibited from expanding output since the use of scarce resources for the production of such luxuries was socially less beneficial than, say, for the production of tractors or ploughs.

• Fourth, the plans emphasized technological self-reliance, and for much of the period, an extreme inward orientation in the sense that if anything could be produced in the country, it should not be imported.[3]

As is well known, the economic rationale for this capital-goods-biased industrial strategy was provided by P. C. Mahalanobis. In the Mahalanobis (1963) model, essentially that of a closed economy, the development of the capital goods industry emerges as the main constraint on economic growth. This model of internal technological and heavy industry development could be rationalized for an open economy of the size of India if one envisages slow rates of growth of the world economy and trade, and, perhaps, falling commodity prices in world markets. Alternatively, it could also be justified in more orthodox terms along the lines that India's dynamic comparative advantage was in industries like steel, for which the country has available the necessary raw materials in close proximity to each other (thus reducing the costs of transportation).

An important drawback of the heavy-industry-biased industrial strategy is that it conflicts with the employment objectives embodied in the five-year plans. The plans sought to square this circle by providing external *and internal protection* to a number of small-scale and cottage enterprises for which the capital–labour ratio was very low. Thus, for instance, modern textile factories were limited in how much they could expand their output so that they would not compete with the high-cost products of the cottage industries.

In implementing this industrial strategy, and particularly in making the private sector conform to the requirements of the plans, the government used a wide variety of measures. The most important of these were:

• Industrial licensing. For much of the period, this entailed that any enterprise which wished to manufacture a new article or sought a substantial expansion of its existing capacity had to obtain a licence from the relevant government authority.

• Strict regime of import controls. A 'red book' listed the whole range of items for which imports were prohibited altogether, usually to provide protection for new infant industries. In practice, it often meant that as long as there was 'indigenous availability' of a particular manufactured product in the country, it was protected from foreign competition whatever the costs of domestic production.

---

[3] During the late 1970s and in the 1980s, the concept of self-reliance was redefined in less stringent terms. It was interpreted to mean an 'economic base that is sufficiently strong and internationally competitive to generate the export earnings required to pay for needed imports of goods that cannot economically be produced domestically'. See further Byrd (1990).

• Subsidization of exports through special measures. The adverse effect of import quotas and tariffs on the exporting industries was sought to be alleviated by a variety of special provisions and subsidies for exporters (e.g. the import entitlement scheme).
• Administered prices. In addition to the licensing requirements for industrial production and expansion, the government also fixed market prices for a range of 'crucial' or 'essential' products, for example, steel, cement, sugar, aluminium, etc.
• Foreign investment policy. Investments by multinationals were generally subject to strict controls—much more stringent than those for the national companies.

Finally, it is important to observe that considered in technical or economic terms alone, the above economic strategy chosen by the Indian leadership was by no means the only feasible one available. In the public debate that took place at the time of the formulation of the early five-year plans, two leading Indian economists, Vakil and Brahamananda (1956) advocated an alternative, more orthodox, strategy. This involved building on India's competitive advantage in textiles. After the war, the country had emerged as one of the leading exporters of textiles in the world. Vakil and Brahamananda favoured concentration on textile exports, on the development of light industries, and reliance on market forces to achieve industrial development. This kind of alternative strategy was deliberately shunned by the Indian leadership in favour of state-planned industrialization.

3. ECONOMIC AND INDUSTRIAL PERFORMANCE

There is a large debate on the question of how the overall results of Indian planned development over the last four decades should be assessed. The proponents of Indian planning argue that in the 1970s and 1980s, when the world economy was subject to severe turbulence, the overall economic performance of the country was very creditable. India has recorded a trend increase in its rate of economic growth since 1973. Between 1963 and 1973, India's rate of growth of GDP was about half as high as that of other Asian and Latin American countries (see Table 7.1). During the 1980s, the Indian growth rate rose to the average level of the Asian countries and was way above that of the Latin American countries, most of which suffered a sharp setback to their economic prospects. Because it was able to significantly increase its trend rate of growth, India could be regarded as having been strikingly successful in coping with international economic fluctuations. The proponents of the Indian development model argue that this ability of the economy to withstand world economic shocks has largely

Table 7.1 GDP in Asian and Latin American countries (real rates of growth)

	1963–1973	1973–1979	1980–1990
ASIA			
China	8.6	4.9	9.5
India	3.4	4.3	5.3
Indonesia	6.9	7.1	5.5
Korea	9.6	9.8	9.7
Malaysia	6.6	7.3	5.2
Pakistan	6.2	5.0	6.3
Philippines	5.2	6.4	0.9
Sri Lanka	4.5	5.0	4.0
Taiwan	10.7	9.2	—
Thailand	8.0	7.7	7.6
Median	6.7	6.7	5.3
LATIN AMERICA			
Argentina	4.8	1.8	−0.4
Bolivia	4.7	4.7	−0.1
Brazil	8.3	6.9	2.7
Chile	3.6	2.7	3.2
Colombia	5.9	5.0	3.7
Ecuador	7.2	6.8	2.0
Mexico	7.8	5.7	1.0
Peru	3.9	2.4	−0.3
Venezuela	5.2	5.6	1.0
Median	5.2	5.0	1.0

Source: World Bank, various issues.

been due to the country's long-term strategy of import substitution and technological self-reliance.[4]

In contrast, a far harsher assessment of the overall Indian record comes from *The Economist*: 'The hopes of 1947 have been betrayed. India, despite all its advantages and a generous supply of aid from the capitalist West (whose "wasteful" societies it deplored), has achieved less than virtually any comparable third-world country. The cost in human terms has been staggering. Why has Indian development gone so tragically worng? The short answer is this: the state has done far too much and far too little. It has

---

[4] The liquidity crisis of 1991 cannot be ascribed to external shocks. Nor did it arise from any inherent features of the planned industrialization model. It was primarily due to uncharacteristically lax fiscal control exercised by weak minority governments at the end of the 1980s. The crisis was abetted by the uncertain political situation in the country and the state of turmoil caused by the 'anti-reservation' agitation. This led to withdrawal of capital by non-resident Indians, thus precipitating the liquidity crisis.

Table 7.2 Actual and targeted rates of growth of industrial output

Plan period	Target (%)	Actual (%)	Deviation (%)
First Plan (1951–56)	—	7.3	—
Second Plan (1956–61)	8.3[a]	6.6	−25.75
Third Plan (1961–66)	11.1[a]	9.0	−23.33
Fourth Plan (1969–74)	8–10	4.7	−51.49
Fifth Plan (1974–1979)	7.0	5.9	−18.64
Sixth Plan (1980–85)	8.0[b]	6.4	−25.00
Seventh Plan (1985–90)[c]	8.0	8.5	+5.88

[a] Envisaged increase in index of industrial production.
[b] Average rate of growth for the first four years of the plan.
[c] The target for the Sixth Plan as given in the seventh plan document, however, is 7%.

Source: Mani (1992): table 1.

crippled the economy, and burdened itself nearly to breaking point, by taking on jobs it has no business doing.'[5]

One way of assessing the record of state-planned industrialization in India is to compare the actual outcomes with the planned targets. This comparison (see Table 7.2) shows that the actual rate of growth of industrial production in each five-year plan was below the target rate except for the seventh plan. The average industrial growth rate over the whole period, 1950 to 1990, is about 6.2 per cent relative to the average of approximately 8 per cent, projected in the plans. Mohan (1992) estimates that, had the planned industrialized targets been consistently achieved, the Indian overall per capita annual economic growth would have been 1.2 to 1.4 percentage points higher than it otherwise would have been.

Despite the improved performance of the Indian economy after 1973, in comparative international terms, the overall long-term Indian economic and industrial record does not compare favourably with that of the successful Asian countries. The speed of Indian industrialization has been much slower than that of countries like Korea, Taiwan, or China. The relatively slow growth of the economy has also meant that the pace of structural change has been much slower in India than in these other economies (Singh and Ghosh, 1988). Equally significantly, the critics of Indian development rightly point out that the country's performance in terms of literacy, education, and health has been much worse than that of many other developing countries, not just the leading Asian economies. The critics also point to the fact that, in comparative terms, India has not performed at all well with respect to the eradication of poverty—which was one of the major

[5] *The Economist*, 'A Survey of India', 4 May 1991: 9. For more academic assessments of the Indian economic performance along the same lines, see e.g. Lal (1987), Ahluwalia (1985, 1991).

goals of the whole Indian development effort. Similarly, it is argued that the five-year plans have not been successful either in reducing concentration of economic power or in bringing about a more equitable regional distribution of economic and industrial development (Mani 1992; Byrd 1990).

However, as Singh and Ghosh (1988) note, it is inadequate to consider India's industrial progress in purely quantitative terms. The quality and the depth of Indian industrialization has been impressive in a number of ways. Despite all its shortcomings, the concept of technological self-reliance has meant that the country has one of the largest pools of trained technical manpower in the world. Among the Third World semi-industrial countries, by the 1970s India became a leading exporter of technology. Lall (1984) assembled the best available information on technology exports of the leading NICs. This data shows that in industrial project exports, the leading exporter was India, followed at a large distance by Korea and Brazil. In non-industrial civil construction project exports, by far the most important country was Korea, followed by India and Brazil. Similarly UNIDO (1984) statistics on the comparative development of the key machine-tool industry in the leading NICs reveal that India has been more successful in this area than most other NICS. In 1979–80, India exported a greater proportion of its machine-tool output than either Mexico, Brazil, or Korea. Although in relative terms, India's exports were lower than Argentina's, its machine-tool imports were considerably smaller than those of the latter country. A good indication of the depth of India's industrial development is indicated by the fact that it is able to build nuclear power stations on its own. As the *Financial Times* noted, in the mid-1980s, India was one of only six countries in the world which possessed that capacity. The country also had substantial capacity for building thermal and hydroelectric stations.

4. PLANNED INDUSTRIAL REGIME AND ECONOMIC PERFORMANCE: THE CASE OF THE CRITICS

An important analytical question which arises in assessing the success or failure of India's state-led economic development is to ask to what extent the country's observed economic performance is due to the characteristics of the development strategy as opposed to factors external to the developmental model. What, in other words, is the nature of the links between the overall economic performance and the industrial regime? Isher J. Ahluwalia, the leading contemporary critic of India's planned industrialization, ascribes what in her view is the country's poor overall industrial record to particular features of the industrial regime. Specifically, she calls attention to the following adverse consequences of the Indian model.

(a) barriers to entry into individual industries that limited the possibility of domestic competition;
(b) indiscriminate and indefinite protection of domestic industries from foreign competition;
(c) the adverse effects of protecting small-scale industries and regional dispersal of growth on the choice of the optimal scale of production;
(d) barriers to exit by not allowing firms, even when they were non-viable to close down, and the failure to move the resources to an alternative growing industry;
(e) administrative hurdles inherent in a system of physical controls;
(f) increased incentives for rent-seeking activities that resulted in dampening entrepreneurship;
(g) little or no incentive to upgrade technology.

Other critics (for example, the World Bank) have added to this formidable list:

(h) adverse effects of universal credit rationing through the nationalized banking system;
(i) poor performance of public sector enterprises.

The critics suggest that these factors are largely responsible not only for the low, long-run growth of India's industrial economy but, more importantly, for the deceleration in the manufacturing growth rate between 1965 and 1975. Manufacturing expanded at an average rate of 6.2 per cent per annum between 1955 and 1965; however, the corresponding average growth rate in the following decade (1965 to 1975) was only 3.3 per cent. Since 1975, manufacturing production has increased at a much faster pace: the growth rate rose to 4.5 per cent in the period 1975-6 to 1980-1 period and to nearly 8 per cent during the 1980s. The critics of the traditional industrial regime have ascribed this improvement to the gradual relaxation of industrial controls that began in the late 1970s.

In the view of the critics, the precise link between the industrial policy regime and the deceleration in industrial growth between the mid-1960s and mid-1970s is provided by the increases in capital–output ratios and a reduction in the growth rates of labour and total factor productivity in Indian industry during this period (Ahluwalia 1985, 1991; World Bank 1985, 1986). Ahluwalia suggests that with the relaxation of the planned industrial regime, these microeconomic indicators of economic efficiency have shown significant improvement during the last decade.

5. EXTERNAL AND INTERNAL SHOCKS, GOVERNMENT MACROECONOMIC POLICY, AND INDUSTRIAL GROWTH

It is nominally conceded by the critics of the planned industrial regime that weaknesses in areas other than trade and industrial policy may also be

responsible for the observed decline in the rate of growth of Indian manufacturing industry in the decade from the mid-1960s to the mid-1970s.
Following the extensive literature on the subject, the critics do call attention
to the role of such factors as (a) the slow rate of growth of demand for
industrial output and (b) the low rate of investment in infrastructure (e.g.
railways, power) during the relevant period, which too could cause poor
industrial performance. Nevertheless, they seem to regard the industrial
and trade policy regime to be the main culprit.

Singh and Ghosh (1988) argue, however, that the two factors (a) and (b)
above, rather than the trade and industrial policy regime, may be entirely
responsible for the deceleration in industrial growth during 1965–75. The
period coincided with at least three major shocks to the economy: the Indo-
Pakistan war of 1965 and its aftermath, the Bangladesh war, and the 1973
oil price increase. The Indo-Pakistan war led to the suspension of foreign
aid which was only resumed after the devaluation of the rupee in 1966. To
cope with the inflation arising from the droughts and bad harvests of 1965–
6 and 1966–7, the government had adopted a restrictive fiscal policy. The
consolidated government deficit was reduced from Rs 4 billion in 1965–6
to Rs 0.7 billion in 1969–70. This, together with the reduction in aid, led
to a trend fall in investment, particularly in transport and communication,
power, and water supply (Joshi and Little 1987).

The Bangladesh war of 1971 involved a rise in defence expenditure, a
costly government programme to help with the ten million refugees from
East Pakistan, and another suspension of aid. Moreover, agricultural production, which had increased substantially during the 1960s, faltered in the
early 1970s. Unfortunately for India, the harvest failures coincided with the
huge rise in world wheat prices which began in the summer of 1972.

Thus, the first oil shock, which led to a fourfold increase in the price of
oil between September 1973 and April 1974, came at a time when the
economy was already in serious difficulties. As the Indian economy is
relatively closed, the impact of the change in the terms of trade on GDP was
comparatively small; however, the balance of payments and financing re-
percussions were very large. As a proportion of GDP, the current deficit
increased from an average of 0.45 per cent of GDP during the three years
1971–4 to 1.4 per cent of GDP in 1974–5. More relevantly for a low
trading economy, the deficit as a proportion ot total exports of goods and
services rose over the same period from about 8 per cent to 25 per cent. In
order to cope with the pre-oil-shock inflation and the effects of the oil shock
itself, the government introduced a highly deflationary fiscal and monetary
policy. A number of measures were taken in 1974 to reduce private disposable income and to cut the central and the state governments' fiscal deficits.
The public sector investment in real terms fell slightly in 1973–4, and by
more than 10 per cent in 1974–5 (Ahluwalia 1986).

In view of (i) the leading role of the public sector in Indian industry and (ii) the deflation and macroeconomic fluctuations arising from the shocks of the two wars and the oil price rise of 1973, it is not surprising that there should have been a trend fall in the rate of growth of Indian manufacturing production between the mid-1960s and the mid-1970s. The relatively slow and fluctuating rate of growth of demand, which was the consequence of these macroeconomic shocks, would in itself be adequate to explain the poor industrial performance without invoking the alleged microeconomic inefficiencies of the trade and industrial policy regime. Moreover, to the extent that the slow rate of growth of demand affects capacity utilization and capacity creation, the macroeconomic shocks outlined above clearly have an adverse effect on these microeconomic variables as well.

With respect to the second broad area of the critics' argument—namely, that the improvement in Indian industrial performance during the 1980s is due to the gradual introduction of internal and external liberalization measures—Singh and Gosh (1988) point out that the stance of fiscal and monetary policy after the second oil shock was rather different from that following the oil price increase of 1973–4. Instead of deflation, the government deliberately followed an expansionary fiscal and monetary policy and tried to increase public investment. As M. S. Ahluwalia (1986) observed:

The behavior of public investment after the second oil shock was in marked contrast to the experience after the first oil shock and reflects a basic difference in the stance of macroeconomic policy. On the earlier occasion there had been a shift to a restrictive macroeconomic policy principally because of perceived dangers of inflation and this policy had depressed public investment in real terms . . . However the approach to controlling inflation on this occasion [i.e. after 1979] placed much more emphasis on removing short-term and medium-term supply bottlenecks. One reason for this change of emphasis is that the balance of macroeconomic policy was set in the light of priorities outlined in the Sixth Five-Year Plan which covered the period 1980–81 to 1984–85. The plan emphasized the importance of investments in several critical areas, especially in the energy transport infrastructure.

By traditionally prudent Indian standards, the government's fiscal stance was overly expansionary for most of the 1980s, culminating in a budget deficit of about 8 per cent of GDP by 1990. Singh and Ghosh note that the significant acceleration in Indian industrial growth during the last decade was achieved, unlike in the second half of the 1970s, at the expense of a serious deterioration in the current balance and a sharp increase in the country's debt-service ratio. They warned that such a fast pace of the rate of growth of demand could not be maintained for very long.

Osmani (1993) provides powerful support for the foregoing analysis which stresses the role of internal and external shocks and their macroeconomic policy consequences in generating the observed time pattern of Indian industrial growth over the last four decades, that is, high growth in the Nehru–Mahalanobis period (to use Osmani's phrase), 1952–65, followed by relative stagnation in the middle period, 1965–75, followed further by high growth again in the 1980s. He complements the Singh and Ghosh study by considering not just the time path of overall industrial growth but also its composition by industry. The deceleration in industrial growth in the middle period did not uniformly affect all industrial sectors. Osmani notes that, compared with the first period, the average growth rate of the capital and intermediate goods sectors fell by more than half in the second period. The consumer durables fared only a little better, but the consumer non-durables slowed down only marginally from 5 per cent per annum to 4.8 per cent. However, the recovery in the third period was led by the consumer goods sectors, both durables and non-durables. Consumer durables reverted back to the growth rate of the first period; the non-durables reached an all-time high. In contrast, capital and intermediate goods sectors recorded only marginal improvement in the 1980s; as a result their growth rates have remained well below those attained in their heyday during the Nehru–Mahalanobis period.

Osmani's examination of these changes in the overall, sub-sectoral, and individual industry growth rates leads him to the conclusion that the variations in the government's macroeconomic policy stance provides the only consistent explanation for the observed facts. Other theories, not just the 'microeconomic inefficiencies' ones of the mainstream critics outlined earlier, but also those of the Marxist economists (which usually run in terms of inequalities in income distribution generated by the political economy of growth under the Nehru–Mahalanobis mode)[6] simply do not accord with the data.

6. CONCLUSION: THE INDIAN INDUSTRIALIZATION MODEL VERSUS THE EAST ASIAN ALTERNATIVE

In the light of the foregoing analysis we can arrive at the following overall assessment of the Indian state-led industrialization model. First, over the last two decades, the Indian economy has shown an impressive ability to withstand external economic shocks. Although India suffered a decline in its rate of growth between 1965 and 1975 as a result of the two wars and the first oil shock, the disruption in the tempo of economic activity was nowhere as great as that experienced by the Latin American economies during the 1980s. The latter were much more integrated with the world economy in terms of trade, and particularly finance, than the Indian economy (Singh 1993a).

Secondly, if we take a long-term view of Indian economic development

[6] There is a large literature here. For a recent review, see Sandesra (1992). See also a discussion in Ahluwalia (1985).

over the last four decades as a whole, contrary to *The Economist*, the record is far from being disastrous. It is clearly not outstanding—it is about average for the developing countries of Asia (the most successful of the three developing continents). The central analytical question which this raises is: could India have done better under a different economic or political regime? Although there cannot be any conclusive answer to such a question, the intellectual exercise is interesting and important, as it bears on the future policy lessons of the Indian story so far.

The orthodox response to the above question is an unequivocal 'yes'. It is argued that the country has enormous entrepreneurial talent and the role of the state has essentially been to thwart this talent from achieving its full potential. So, if the state had not been heavily interventionist, but instead had assumed a 'market friendly' night-watchman status, the economy would have done much better. Similarly, it is suggested that keeping the Indian economy relatively closed to the international product and financial markets has been a costly mistake. This has resulted in myriad inefficiencies, slow technical progress, and hence, 'inefficient' and sluggish growth.

This line of reasoning is unconvincing since recent scholarship[7] shows quite conclusively that in the outstandingly successful East Asian economies of not just socialist China, but also capitalist Taiwan, South Korea, and Japan, the state has played a pivotal role, in a wide variety of ways, in bringing about rapid industrialization. It has pursued in each of these countries a vigorous and aggressive industrial policy to carry out the required structural transformation of the economy. The government has 'guided' the market, and not followed a hands-off market friendly approach. Moreover, these highly successful East Asian economies did not attempt a deep and unconditional integration with the world economy. Rather they sought a strategic integration, that is they integrated in the direction and to the extent that it was necessary for promoting national economic growth.[8]

So then the relevant question becomes: could the Indian state have acted to foster economic development in the same way as did the state in Taiwan, Korea, or Japan? Many Indian intellectuals answer this question in the negative on the grounds that the Indian state lacks the 'autonomy' to implement a Korean or Japanese style of industrial policy.[9] Bardhan (1984, 1992) for example, characterizes the Indian polity as being in a class stalemate between the dominant classes. In the pluralistic Indian democracy, it is argued that none of these classes—landlords, businessmen, and

---

[7] See e.g. Wade (1990), Amsden (1989), Singh (1994).

[8] For a fuller discussion of these issues, see Singh (1993*b*).

[9] Although Japan, Korea, and Taiwan differ in some respects in the economic policies that they have followed, there are also important similarities. Taiwan and Korea have tried to emulate the Japanese model in significant ways. See further, Singh (1993*a*).

professional and technical elite—is strong enough to capture the state for itself, or to enforce its will on the others. The net result is a plethora of state subsidies and handouts to various political groups and special interests, rather than a purposive attempt at rapid industrialization or faster economic development. In economic terms this means that the Indian economy is confined to a low level equilibrium trap.[10]

This theory undoubtedly contains important insights into the Indian political economy. However, it is also not without shortcomings, and is therefore not fully persuasive. Today, the Indian government is indeed very weak but it is not a static situation. There were periods of greater autonomy—for example, the Nehru era of the 1950s, when there was a national consensus on certain developmental goals. Similarly, at different times, Rajiv Gandhi and Indira Gandhi had overwhelming majorities in the Indian parliament, allowing them in principle to push through and implement a better developmental programme. After all, Indira Gandhi, despite the class stalemate, did manage to nationalize the Indian banks.

In view of the rather different history and the institutional circumstances of India, clearly not all aspects of the East Asian model could have been replicated in that country. Nevertheless, important and useful lessons could have been learned from the East Asian experience and implemented in the country during various phases of strong government in the last forty years. Once implemented and sucessful, they could have generated positive feedback dynamics of their own leading to further autonomy for the state. To illustrate, an outstanding feature of the East Asian economies like Japan and Korea is that, although they protected their industries from external competition, they also greatly encouraged exports. During the high growth periods in these two countries (Japan 1950–73; and Korea 1970–82) the government, in return for the protection being afforded to the firms, set them various performance standards, most notably in relation to exports and world market shares. Thus the Japanese and Korean firms were obliged to use their profits from the protected home market to invest and to capture export markets. Companies in these countries came to recognize that to move forward, to have access to foreign technology, licences, etc., they had to export. Lal (1987) and Bhagwati (1988) suggest that all that the East Asian governments did was to provide a neutral trading regime, that is, one in which the incentive to sell in the home market was the same as to sell abroad. This view is, however, contested by a number of economists who suggest that in fact what the East Asian governments did was to discriminate positively in favour of exports.[11]

In contrast, the incentive system for the large Indian firms with potential to export has pointed in the opposite direction for most of the last four

---

[10] In Bardhan's (1992) words: 'The Indian public economy has thus become an elaborate network of patronage and subsidies.'

[11] See e.g. Chang (1994), Amsden (1989), Scott (1992).

decades. As noted earlier, to offset the biases of protection and import controls, the Indian government periodically provided special incentives and subsidies for exporters. However, until the 1980s they were never adequate to fully offset the bias of the protectionist trade regime.

The important question is, why were exports not given the attention and the incentives accorded to them in the East Asian countries? For had exports been given proper priority, in view of India's past history of exporting and the existence of large business groups, there is no reason to believe the country would not have been able to maintain its pre-war share in world manufactured exports even if it had not been as spectacularly successful as the East Asian NICs. Quite apart from the advantages for exporting provided by the ready availability of large private business groups (they did not have to be created almost from scratch as in Korea, for example), India's historic links with the Middle Eastern countries (one of the fastest growing markets in the 1970s) and the large Indian diaspora abroad provided the country with special opportunities for exporting. Had such opportunities been realized and India been able to achieve a trend increase in exports, it would have helped alleviate the chronic balance of payments constraint. This in turn would have allowed the economy to move along a higher growth trajectory compared with its actual record. It would also have provided the potential for the positive feedback mechanism referred to earlier.

So the important question is, why were exports neglected or not given the attention that they deserved? It will be difficult to argue that it was interest groups or the class stalemate which prevented the Indian planners from vigorously pursuing exports. There are, however, other reasons which are more likely and are more persuasive.

The first is clearly the large country syndrome—that India is a big country with a large market. It does not have to worry about exports. The second reason is India's colonial past and the popular perception, widely shared by the ruling elite, that foreign trade was exploitative and was the precursor to the British colonial domination of the country. Thirdly, it is important to take into account the anti-private-business bias and the ideology of the Fabian socialist leadership of Nehru and the later Indian leaders. This made them emphasize public enterprise and seizing the 'commanding heights' of the economy under public ownership. At a deeper level, this ideology also prevented the Indian leadership from forging a genuine partnership with private business in the way that the East Asian economies did. Such a partnership is clearly essential for the successful functioning of a mixed economy. There is no reason to believe that the leadership could not have created such a partnership and won public support for it during periods of large parliamentary majorities and strong government. However, for this to have happened would have required a wide measure of ideological flexibility which the Indian ruling elite clearly did not possess. The contrast between the post-Mao Chinese leadership and the Indian ruling circles, in this respect, could not be more striking.

The neglect of exports is one, but a very important example, of the intellectual failure of the ruling elite to correctly appreciate the world around it, rather than a problem which arose from the lack of autonomy of the state. There are other similar examples concerning technology imports, foreign direct investment, etc., which, it can be shown, also point in the same direction. Of course, it is possible to plead extenuating circumstances for these failings in terms of Indian colonial history as mentioned above (see also Mohan 1992), but that does not alter the fact of these failures. Similarly, it may be that the Indian state did not have the autonomy to orchestrate oligopolistic investment races or to set export targets for firms in the the East Asian manner—even that is not certain—but it definitely could have learned other useful lessons from, for example, the Japanese MITI, particularly the latter's role in continuously building a social consensus around the required developmental policies as world circumstances changed. In other words, the essential point is not that a subset of MITI-type sensible policies could not have been implemented because of lack of autonomy of the state, but simply that they were not implemented because of intellectual failings on the part of the ruling elite.

REFERENCES

AHLUWALIA, ISHER J. (1985). *Industrial Growth in India: Stagnation since the Mid-Sixties.* Delhi: Oxford University Press.

—— (1991). *Productivity and Growth in Indian Manufacturing.* Delhi: Oxford University Press.

AHLUWALIA, MONTEK S. (1986). 'Balance of Payments Adjustment in India 1970–71 to 1983–84', *World Development,* 14/8.

AMSDEN, A. (1989). *Asia's Next Giant.* New York: Oxford University Press.

BARDHAN, P. K. (1984). *The Political Economy of Development in India.* Delhi: Oxford University Press.

—— (1992). 'A Political Economy Perspective on Development', in B. Jalan (ed.), *The Indian Economy: Problems and Prospects.* Delhi: Viking.

BHAGWATI, J. (1988). *Protectionism.* Cambridge, Mass.: MIT Press.

BHAGWATI, J. N. and DESAI, P. (1970). *India Planning for Industrialization: and Trade Policies since 1951.* Oxford: Oxford University Press.

BYRD, WILLIAM A. (1990). 'Planning in India: Lessons from Four Decades of Development Experience', *Journal of Comparative Economics,* 14/4, Dec.: 713–35.

CHAKRAVARTY, SUKHAMOY (1988). *Development Planning: The Indian Experience.* Delhi: Oxford University Press.

CHANG, H.-J. (1994). *The Political Economy of Industrial Policy.* London: Macmillan.

ECONOMIST, THE (1991). *A Survey of India* (4 May).

GUPTA, S. P. (1989). *Planning and Development in India: A Critique.* New Delhi: Allied.

JOSHI, V. and LITTLE, I. M. D. (1987). 'Indian Macro-economic Policies', *Economic and Political Weekly,* 22/9, 28 Feb.

LAL, D. (1987). 'Ideology and Industrialization in India and East Asia', in Helen Hughes (ed.), *Achieving Industrialization in East Asia.* Cambridge: Cambridge University Press.

LALL, S. (1984). 'Exports of Technology by the Newly Industrialising Countries', *World Development.*

MAHALANOBIS, P. C. (1963). *Approach of Operational Research Planning in India.* London: Asia Publishing House.

MANI, SUNIL (1992). 'New Industrial Policy: Barriers to Entry, Foreign Investment and Privatisation', *Economic and Political Weekly* (29 Aug.): 86–100.

MOHAN, RAKESH (1992). 'Industrial Policy and Controls', in Bimal Jalan (ed.), *The Indian Economy: Problems and Prospects.* Delhi: Penguin Books India.

OSMANI, S. (1993). 'Growth and Poverty in South Asia', mimeo. Helsinki: WIDER (July).

PLANNING COMMISSION (1952). *First Five-Year Plan.* New Delhi: Government of India.

—— (1956). *Second Five-Year Plan.* New Delhi: Government of India.

—— (1963). *Third Five-Year Plan.* New Delhi: Government of India.

—— (1970). *Fourth Five-Year Plan.* New Delhi: Government of India.

—— (1976). *Fifth Five-Year Plan.* New Delhi: Government of India.

—— (1981). *Sixth Five-Year Plan.* New Delhi: Government of India.

—— (1985). *Seventh Five-Year Plan.* New Delhi: Government of India.

SANDESRA, J. C. (1992). *Industrial Policy and Planning, 1947–91.* New Delhi: Sage Publications.

SCOTT, BRUCE (1992). 'Economic strategy and economic performance', Harvard Business School Case Study, no. N9-792-086, 24 Nov.

SINGH, AJIT (1993a). ' "Close" vs. "Strategic" Integration with the World Economy and the "Market-Friendly Approach to Development" vs. an "Industrial Policy": A critique of the *World Development Report 1991* and an Alternative Policy Perspective', paper presented at the Joint World Bank/UN University Symposium on Economic Reform in the Developing Countries: Issues for the 1990s. Washington, DC. 6 Feb.

—— (1993b). 'Asian Economic Success and Latin American Failure in the 1980s: New Analyses and Future Policy Implications', *International Review of Applied Economics,* Sept.

—— (1994). 'Openness and the Market Friendly Approach to Development: Learning the Right Lessons from Development Experience', *World Development,* 22/12: 1811–23.

—— and GHOSH, JAYATI (1988). 'Import Liberalisation and the New Industrial Strategy. An Analysis of their Impact on Output and Employment', *Economic and Political Weekly,* special number (Nov.): 2313–42.

STREETEN, PAUL and LIPTON, MICHAEL (eds.) (1968). *The Crisis Of Indian Planning: Economic Planning in the 1960s.* London: Oxford University Press.

UNIDO (1984). *Industry in a Changing World*. New York.

VAKIL C. N. and BRAHAMANANDA P. R. (1956). *Planning for an Expanding Economy*. Bombay: Bombay University Press.

WADE, R. (1990). *Governing the Market*. Princeton: Princeton University Press.

WORLD BANK (1985). *The Country Report on India*. Washington, DC.

—— (1989). *World Bank Country Study (1989)*. *India: An Industrializing Economy in Transition*. Washington, DC: The World Bank.

8

The State and Economic Change in Africa

Brian Van Arkadie

1. INTRODUCTION: AN APPROACH TO THE CURRENT PREDICAMENT

This chapter concerns the role of the state in economic management in contemporary sub-Saharan Africa. It starts by describing the ongoing crisis of the African state, the depth of which leads to the question of whether, or in what sense, states exist in many parts of Africa. The origins of the deep crisis are explored, and the factors which have conditioned the responses of governments and of other actors in African society to the crisis are touched upon. The ways in which the character of the state has changed as a result of crisis and response are examined. The essay concludes by examining some possible responses to the current predicament, both by African governments and donors.

1.1. Are there 'States' in Africa?

Discussion of the role of the state in economic change in Africa involves a major, but typically implicit and unexplored, premiss—that a state exists. Disagreements about the use of policy instruments and the appropriate degree of state intervention presuppose the possibility of state action. For the economist, this implies that there are a set of working institutions—government, judiciary, and bureaucracy—capable of carrying out certain economic tasks and determining and adjudicating the 'rules of the game' which guide and constrain non-official actors in the economy. At a minimum, this might include the capacity to maintain a satisfactory degree of civil order and to secure the boundaries of the state in question. Beyond that, it would also involve the capacity to provide public services, issue a currency accepted for transactions, and raise public revenues.

Doubts about the capacity of the state in Africa are most obviously justified where government has actually disappeared, or where as a result of civil war the national government controls only part of its territory. A number of countries are now without governments capable of implementing coherent policy or providing basic services, in some cases with such political disorder (e.g. Somalia, Liberia) that there is no government and therefore neither policies nor public services, while in other cases the geographical writ of governments is so limited that they are unable to implement national policies in a meaningful sense (e.g. Angola and Mozambique). The depth of the crises facing some of these societies, and the resulting lack of political or administrative coherence, is such that any discussion of the economic role of the state seems irrelevant. Such states, facing deep crisis, provide a miserable life for their citizens and pose particularly difficult demands on the international community in terms of humanitarian relief, refugee support, and peace-keeping operations. The logic of current international initiatives is such that in some cases a period of internationally supervised colonialism appears to be on the agenda, the appeal for humanitarian intervention having set the international community on a path towards some sort of international trusteeship (as currently in Somalia), as anti-slavery agitation and appeals to the White Man's Burden spurred nineteenth century colonialism.

In a number of other countries extended and unresolved political crises have rendered government increasingly ineffective. In the face of political stalemate (e.g. Zaire and Togo) or political transitions of uncertain outcome, the scope for coherent policy-making is severely constrained. Even countries which were being touted not so long ago as possible models for African success (e.g. Côte d'Ivoire and Kenya) are faced with unresolved political and economic crises.

In addition to the obvious manifestations of the erosion of state authority, the high degree of external dependence also limits state action. Key economic policies, such as exchange rate, fiscal, and monetary policies, depend on the initiative of the Bretton Woods institutions, and even in relation to project choice, design, and staffing, the various donor agencies often play the leadership role. In noting this point, appeal is being made neither to the Latin American 'dependencia' literature nor to earlier African discussions of neo-colonialism, which sought to establish dependence in subtle and hidden relationships between centre and periphery, but rather to the stark and overt realities of policy-making in contemporary Africa, in which considerable power has accrued to the bureaucrats of the international aid community. As a consequence of this dependence, any discussion of the role of the state in contemporary Africa must address the role of donors, as much as discussions of policy in Africa before the 1960s would have had to address colonial policies.

The first question to be addressed is the historical origin of the current predicament.

1.2. Post-Independence Planning: Change and Continuity

Most African countries came to independence about three decades ago. The first decade of independence was, by and large, a period of considerable optimism.[1] The independent states adopted medium-term development plans, which typically sought to increase national participation in the economy, to invest heavily in 'human capital' and to begin a process of structural change. If anything, international conventional wisdom at the beginning of the 1960s was more bullish about Africa than Asia. In most of the British and French colonies the transition to independence was carried through in a remarkably orderly fashion. The new African governments were led by figures with the authority and legitimacy gained at the head of national independence movements, whose task was to reap the economic fruits of political independence.

The initial era of self-confident planning in Africa came to an end in the 1970s, with the onset of the economic decline which still engulfs the continent. One view is that failure resulted from over-ambitious exercises in macroeconomic planning, including unrealistic commitments to industrialization (through import substitution) and an excessive belief in the efficacy of state intervention, and undue scepticism about the market. This is a widely held view with some credibility; certainly most of the plans failed in terms of their chosen objectives. However, although criticism is justified, it should be based on the historical record, rather than mythology, and should therefore be founded in a more nuanced interpretation of the record.

In fact, early planning efforts were quite limited in scope, modest in technical ambition—in the 1970s there was little elaborate modelling, and, despite sometimes grandiose vocabulary in plan documents, there was little serious effort to introduce the comprehensive planning of the command economy. Even talk of industrial strategy was little more than rationalization of the hodgepodge of projects offered by promoters of one sort of another.

The decisive influence on the content of the early plans was more typically early World Bank mission reports[2] than socialist aspirations, and there was more continuity in approaches to policy with colonial precedents than the rhetoric of change implied. Indeed, many of the policy instruments identified with the post-independence regimes were colonial inventions—

---

[1] Which was not universal however; besides the reservations of the unreformed colonialists, Rene Dumont was already in the early 1960s decrying A False Start in Africa (the title of his widely read book, London: Earthscan, 1966), and critics from the left as well as the right were questioning the directions chosen by the new states (e.g. R. Fitch and M. Oppenheimer 'Ghana: The End of an Illusion', Monthly Review, 18/3 (1966), New York, and Issa G. Shivji Class Struggles in Tanzania (1976), London: Heinemann, from the left, and any one of a number of diatribes from Peter Bauer on the right).

[2] For example, the World Bank mounted substantial missions to Uganda, Tanganyika, and Kenya just prior to the independence of each of the countries and produced published reports. These reports drew heavily on available colonial materials and the projects identified in the reports were mostly included in the post-independence developments. Thus, the case of Tanzania, the 'transformation' approach to rural development through village settlements, one of the antecedents to the Ujamaa village programme, was adopted in the World Bank report.

such as the export crop marketing boards, developed by the British in the 1940s and used by them to defend sterling,[3] the multi-purpose state development corporation,[4] and even import substitution industrialization.[5] And despite the rhetoric of diversification and structural change, planned growth remained largely dependent upon expansion of the traditional export base. The continuities with the pre-independence colonial economy are worth noting, as in its economic aspect the contemporary African crisis is arguably a crisis of the colonial economic inheritance as well as of the post-independence project.

In those colonies without a significant settler population (which in the British case was all the colonies, but for Kenya and Rhodesia), the colonial state had been staffed by a small expatriate civil service elite, financed by the surplus generated by an export trade based on peasant crop production or the exploitation of minerals. The aspirations of the colonial state were constrained by cautious financial policies. The pace of economic growth and the size of the state budget was more or less determined by the trends and cycles of exports—thus the 1930s was a time of government retrenchment and minimal investment, while the Korean War commodity boom financed a late burst of colonial investment.[6]

In a simple but realistic model of early colonial policy, the main task of the colonial state was to use tax policy and more direct pressures, as well as the incentives provided by the availability of imported commodities, to push the peasantry into production for export, or where there were mines, settlers, or plantations, to ensure a sufficiently cheap supply of labour by direct and indirect means to sustain the expatriate-owned enclave.[7] The economy grew, depending on the real output growth of the export sector and the terms of trade in international markets.

The rhetoric of post-independence planning was very much directed at structural change, to diversify away from dependence on traditional ex-

[3] And, indeed, the marketing boards were a matter of considerable controversy among economists during the colonial period—see the controversies in the pages of the *Economic Journal* in the 1950s.

[4] The Uganda Development Corporation was one of the most successful examples of colonial state enterprise.

[5] In East Africa, for example, protection was granted both to the Kenyan industrial sector which emerged during and after World War II and to the state-sponsored industrialization programme in Uganda, adopted in the first development plan, written by Worthington just after the World War II under the influence of the Commonwealth Development and Welfare Act, and implemented by Governors Sir John Hall and Sir Andrew Cohen.

[6] Thus the somewhat bizarre adventure associated with John Strachey, the Groundnuts Scheme, was a quite exceptional effort by the metropolis to fund accelerated colonial development—albeit to deal with the then 'dollar problem'. It is of some continuing interest, as it incorporated many of the mistakes which have been subsequently faithfully reproduced in failed agricultural projects by later development funding agencies.

[7] The classic theoretical exploration of that model was by W. Arthur Lewis in his article 'Economic Development with Unlimited Supplies of Labour', *Manchester School*, 22 (1954)— an extraordinarily fertile exploration of the economics of the colonial economy, if somewhat reticent about the role of the colonial state in creating the 'unlimited labour supplies'.

ports. The failure to achieve such a transformation left Africa peculiarly susceptible to the vicissitudes of the international economy in the 1970s and 1980s.

The inadequate economic inheritance from the colonial era was not enhanced by post-independence developments which contributed to the crisis, for the 1960s brought change as well as continuity.

The growth in public spending accelerated. This was not merely the result of the understandable ambitions of the new governments; two other developments enabled governments to translate ambition into practice. The availability of substantial amounts of development aid funded the expansion of development budgets with too little regard to the ability of the domestic resource base to sustain the expanded activities—aid broke the link which had existed between domestic savings and investment. Secondly, the monetary restraints of the colonial financial system were ended, as the colonial currency boards[8] gave way to the new central banks, allowing for monetary and fiscal flexibility and a break in the link to sterling.[9] At the same time, the fiscal discipline of British Treasury controls over colonial finance also ended.

However, despite the greater short-term fiscal and monetary flexibility, over the longer term the real resources available to government remained constrained by the growth of export earnings, which remained subject to the vagaries of international markets and the limits of technology in the primary production sector. As state budgets expanded beyond those limits, the export sector was increasingly squeezed and export production faltered. In the more extreme cases, kleptocratic regimes squeezed the export sector for the direct benefit of the leadership and to fund a patronage system which supported the regime (e.g. Sierra Leone and Zaire).[10] In those cases in which there was a serious intent to use resources from the export sector to fund structural change, crisis was fuelled by the failure of investment programmes to generate either sufficient export diversification or real import substitution.

The second area of decisive change related to control over the economy. With independence, a lack of congruence emerged between political and

<hr>

[8] The colonial monetary boards had in their early days issued currency against foreign exchange reserves, with the results that colonial currency had been virtually 100% backed by sterling assets; only towards the end of the system were modest holdings of public debt countenanced.

[9] In the case of the East African currencies, parity with sterling was maintained until the sterling devaluation of 1967, when the East African governments decided not to follow sterling, and maintained the existing dollar exchange rate.

[10] There is a paper to be written on the economics of kleptocracy. It seems characteristic of kleptocratic regimes that greed pushes the rate of extortion beyond that which would maximize the total illicit revenue accruing to the regime, to the point of the erosion of the economic base of the regime. This seemingly economically irrational behaviour may either be explained by the short planning horizon of such regimes, or by the internal dynamics of competing interests within such regimes.

economic power. When political power was transferred to populist independence movements, it was no longer acceptable that Africans should be limited to the roles of peasant and worker. Either strategies of expanded public ownership (as in Ghana and Tanzania) or the public support for transfer of wealth to an emerging African property-owning class (as in Kenya) were placed on the political agenda, in an effort to rapidly create a class of national entrepreneurs—in the public or private sectors. This was combined with moves to restrain or displace powerful minority economic interests (the white settlers in Kenya, the Lebanese in parts of West Africa, the Asian traders in East Africa—most dramatically in Uganda, more subtly in Tanzania).

One focus for change was the public service. Initially the new political authorities took over a bureaucracy still largely expatriate staffed. The rapid localization of bureaucracies, with a salary structure carried over from the expatriate colonial service, was one of the priorities of the new governments.

The third related area of change was in the provision of social services. In the first decade of independence there was an impressive expansion in social service provision: in Tanzania, for example, the second five-year plan (1969–74) set out a strategy similar to what some years later became known in the donor world as 'basic needs'. The one area in which African countries performed well by international comparison was in expansion in education at all levels. However, meeting the demand for education added to the pressure for expansion in public employment both on the supply and demand side of the labour market.

The fourth change was the expansion of military expenditure. The imperial regimes enjoyed economies of scale resulting from their capacity to move their forces from colony to colony, an efficiency lost through independence, so that each newly independent country faced the need to form a national army. The rise in military expenditures was subsequently driven by the use of the military in many countries for purposes of civil control (a continuity with the colonial period) and, particularly in southern Africa, by external threats. Larger armies, once created, have needs which must be met, particularly by weak regimes of precarious legitimacy.

While there was a diversity of performance in the two decades after independence, by the end of the 1980s virtually all African economies were in decline, irrespective of the vocabulary of policy and planning chosen in the previous two decades, and the era of structural change and planning gave way to that of structural adjustment. But structural adjustment did not replace planning—planning had already died. For planning to have any meaning at all, however modest, there has to be some degree to which government has control over events—has real choices in manipulating policy instruments. If in the optimistic decade of the 1960s one of the failures of planners was to exaggerate the degree to which governments could control their nations' economic destiny, nevertheless there was some room in which governments could manoeuvre. A significant part of the development budget was locally financed, balance of payments were in reasonable order, exchange rates were not out of line, and inflation appeared only occasionally and then in modest form. An indicator of the orderly macroeconomic environment was the cosy relationship between the IMF and most African countries before the first oil shock.

The combination of ambitious fiscal expansion and the costs of not very successful attempts to promote African entrepreneurship (public or private) placed a heavy burden on the export sectors, while such industrial investments as were implemented signally failed to reduce import dependence (in practice, import substitution industrialization often increased structural dependence on imports, as industries were created with little or no real domestic value added, which could only operate using imported inputs). At the same time, donor-financed projects, on which heavy reliance was placed, had on average extremely low productivity.

The African economies were therefore vulnerable in the face of the new international economic disorder. The weakness and inflexibility of the export base demonstrated the validity of the shared premiss of many policy-makers in the 1960s, that fundamental structural change was needed—it was just that Africa had neither the means nor the time to effect the transformation before the onslaught of hard times. As declining export performance and negative shifts in international terms of trade reduced foreign exchange earnings, the initial response was largely defensive of the interests of the state apparatus and urban groups. Controls were increased to defend the flow of increasingly scarce resources to the state sectors. There was also considerable inertia, shared by donors and national governments alike, in persisting with investment programmes which were no longer viable in the new economic conditions. The continent is littered with failed projects which should have been stopped, once it was evident the economic assumptions of project appraisal were no longer valid.

Faced with crisis, efforts were made to shield the domestic economy from the full force of the changing conditions, by defending existing exchange rates and budget levels, when in retrospect it would have been better to have made a quicker response to new, harsher realities. The failure to respond adequately also meant that phantom exercises in planning continued long after they had real meaning, even to those undertaking them.

1.3. Explanations of Ineffective State Interventions

There are two useful viewpoints from which to approach the emergence of the economic crisis of the African state: by exploring the *capacity* of the state to intervene in the economy and the factors which determined the *willingness* of the state to take one line of action or another. Thus the state can be viewed as an organization, more or less effective in undertaking assigned tasks, or the state can be viewed as a terrain over which competing interests struggle for influence.

Viewing the African state as an organization, one source of its poor performance was the limited initial human capital stock in the administration, the army, the judiciary, etc. At independence, in many African countries the scarcity of trained nationals was severe, countries in many cases having a stock of university graduates below 1 to 10,000 of the population. This was at its most extreme in the ex-Portuguese colonies, where the abrupt flight of the colonialists left a professional vacuum, but even such countries as Tanganyika and Kenya approached independence with totally inadequate cadres of national manpower. Even the British colonies of West Africa and some of the French colonies, which had a longer tradition of university training and metropolitan exposure, had a very thin elite. This was in striking contrast to the situation in most Asian and Latin American countries. There was a pressing need to train nationals to take over posts at all levels of state administration, above the most junior, and that was given a high priority by national governments and donors.

The vast amount of technical assistance which flows into Africa is ostensibly based on the premiss that there is still a missing component in the state apparatus which can be made good by additions to the human capital stock from outside. No doubt many of the difficulties faced in the first decade of independence had their origins in the sheer weakness in the ranks of the national bureaucracy—inadequate numbers of qualified personnel, limited experience, and over-accelerated promotion. But if that provided a plausible explanation of weaknesses in state capacity in, say, the early 1970s, it was much less convincing a decade later. By then the situation had been transformed by one of the real successes of independence, the implementation of ambitious education programmes. While gaps remained in particular technical and scientific skills, in most countries the stock of human capital, at least as measured by formal qualifications, had been transformed. While in the 1960s, it was often necessary to draft scarce graduates into the public service through bonding schemes, by the 1980s disguised graduate unemployment was widespread in the public service, with many graduates employed well below their formal qualifications and in excess of need. More recently, open graduate unemployment has emerged.

Even if it can no longer be claimed that administrative incapacity reflects the paucity of national trained cadres, there is a systemic failure to effectively utilize trained staff. Part of the explanation for this is that in the post-independence decade too many tasks were loaded onto a bureaucracy still handling a process of transition from the colonial authorities, over-stretching administrative capacity in a period in which it might have been wiser to consolidate, and contributing to a deterioration in performance which accelerated under the impact of economic difficulties. Donors contributed to this. New departments of government and parastatals were funded with little concern for their eventual sustainability, either in manpower or financial terms. The flow of technical assistance itself contributed directly to a cancerous proliferation of bureaucracy, as development projects spawned new sorts of bureaux and planning capacities. For the planners and technical assistance nothing succeeded so well as failure—the failure of macro-planning led to the creation of sectoral and project planning units, failure at the centre motivated the development of regional and district planning, and failures in aid implementation led to the creation of project implementation and monitoring units.

And, of course, post-independence expectations that higher education would guarantee access to a government post created its own pressures for the over-expansion of the public service. Over-expanded civil services found it increasingly difficult to assimilate new staff, leading to a decline in morale, which accelerated with the decline in real incomes as the real resources at the disposal of the state were squeezed. The result has been a decay of administrative systems to the point that disinvestment in human capital takes place, as new entrants into a decaying bureaucratic milieu are exposed to a process of *unlearning by not doing*.

The problem was compounded by donors who continued to respond to perceived weaknesses in administrative capacity through technical assistance approaches developed in the 1960s to handle a quite different set of problems, inserting highly paid foreign advisers or consultants into systems which suffered, not from a lack of trained nationals, but rather from an incapacity to utilize them effectively. This has bred resentment and frustration on both sides.

Although a diagnosis of contemporary ills should recognize administrative weaknesses, and part of the solution lies in administrative reform, that in itself is only part of the story. It is also necessary to address the forces at work which mould the economic behaviour of the state.

One view of the political aspects of the economic débâcle in Africa which has gained a certain currency recently among Western commentators is that the root cause of weaknesses in 'governance' (a not very meaningful term promoted in World Bank literature) is the absence of pluralistic politics based on an open electoral process, reinforced by views currently popular within Africa that the continent has been ill-served by its politicians and by politics. It is not difficult to have sympathy with such sentiments which respond to the widespread failure of political regimes to deliver what they promised. It is necessary to be honest about those failures and one would particularly not wish to be an apologist for the nastier regimes in Africa. Nevertheless, it is not obvious that poor economic performance in Africa can be explained by the undemocratic nature of regimes nor that the solution will lie in pluralism. It has not been established that pluralistic democracy is either a necessary or sufficient condition for successful economic growth. The tigers of East Asia were long on aggressive development policy and short on democracy. And it is not evident that governments subject to popular pressures in very poor countries can make effective economic policy (the same donors who preach the pluralistic message, being practical men, seem to be particularly sympathetic to 'strong men' such as Rawlings and Museveni, who clothe their authoritarian rule with the merest fig-leaf of democratic practice).

Democratization may be necessary to break the entrenched interests and to create the necessary political impetus in support of reform, and decentralization of economic power through the market may provide a basis for decentralization of political power. However, and sadly, it seems unlikely that current economic conditions combined with the breakdown of existing political authority provide very fertile ground for the growth of pluralistic democracy, while pluralist politics could well make administrative and economic reform difficult to implement, emphasizing the play of regional, religious, and ethnic interests.

Surely the issue to be confronted is not why Africa has had one-party states, military rulers, and corruption, but why these institutions in the African context have so far proved incapable of generating effective economic performance. After all, Latin America has had its one-party states (e.g. the PRI in Mexico), its military rulers (e.g. Pinochet and the Brazilian military), and corruption, all of which have been arguably associated with periods of economic success, even if undesirable in other respects. The case is even stronger in Asia, where regimes led by the military, innocent of much in the way of democracy and not unsusceptible to corruption and rent-seeking, have been the most successful performers in the world economy in recent decades.

One line of explanation, maybe more widely held than openly expressed, is cultural (racial?), implicit in views not only of non-Africans but also in the auto-critic of many Africans of their lack of seriousness, lack of discipline, etc. There is not the space to treat such views here, except to state a robust scepticism, noting that cultural (and racial) stereotypes, in so far as they have any basis in reality, tend to reflect an *ex post* response to observed performance and have little *ex ante* accuracy in predicting the future.

A more fruitful avenue of analysis relates to the weak foundations of the new states, in three different senses: the lack of connections between the political superstructure and well-articulated economic interests bent on aggressive accumulation; the absence of a strong bureaucratic tradition; and the limited historical roots of the nation states.

The weak articulation of national economic interests coming to bear on the state permitted a high degree of apparent relative autonomy of state action following independence.[11] By the same token, there was an absence

---

[11] Thus in Tanzania, following the Arusha Declaration in 1967, the TANU government was able to engage in widespread nationalization, and in latter years President Nyerere was

of pressure groups agitating for effective performance from the state, or of entrepreneurial groups capable of manipulating the state to support their own schemes of accumulation. The colonial authority itself had been relatively free from pressures from local interests, except in the case of the settler colonies and, from time to time, the need to respond to popular resistance to onerous colonial impositions. It was, however, subject to the pressures and interests of the metropolis, as defined by colonial policy, which might, in turn, have responded to particular metropolitan economic interests, or have reflected the more abstract influences of colonial ideology and Colonial Office conventions. With independence, the colonial power was replaced by populist nationalist movements, with support among the broad mass of workers and peasants, but unattached to the local concentrations of economic power, which were largely non-African (e.g. Asians in East Africa, Lebanese in West Africa, and European firms throughout). The mass of the population could not be expected to play an active role in influencing policy—the peasantry expressed its discontent mainly by the passive resistance of withdrawal from the market;[12] and workers could mobilize to defend a particular interest (e.g. subsidized staple food prices), but neither group could demand effective economic performance of the state.

The only groups with the potential to articulate their interest within the national politics were the new middle class elites—the political class and the bureaucracy. While individual members of this emerging middle class were often able to use their positions in the state apparatus as a base for personal accumulation, and therefore had an interest in expanding state activity and funnelling resources to the state bureaucracy, as a group they lacked the interest or coherence to push for the sort of state intervention which would be effective in promoting economic growth.

The lack of coherence of the bureaucracy is partly explained by the absence of a deep-rooted tradition; the imperial bureaucracies of Africa had a history which was too brief, and locals were inducted into the system too late to have created anything like the Indian Administrative Service, or to have laid down the deep historical roots of the Mandarin tradition which has had its influence in many parts of East Asia. A bureaucratic elite swiftly emerged following independence, which became a focus of power and interest, and was often professionally competent, but only to a very limited degree did it have the self-confidence and coherence to hold the state together in the face of strong political centrifugal forces or to frame and implement a viable national development project.

The weakness of the nation state is to be contrasted with the surprising

able to mount apparently profound experiments in rural social transformation ('Ujamaa'), with remarkably little opposition.

[12] A point elaborated at length by Goran Hyden, e.g. in his book *Beyond Uiamaa in Tanzania: Underdevelopment and an Uncaptured Peasantry* (1980), London: Heinemann.

degree to which national boundaries have remained inctact, despite their exogenous and sometimes almost whimsical colonial origins.[13] However, rather than providing evidence of the depth of legitimacy of the new states, it may be the very lack of deeper historical significance of most boundaries which acted as an incentive not to adjust any. And although national boundaries have remained largely sacrosanct, the authority of state institutions within those boundaries has come increasingly into question.[14] In the competition for political power and access to the economic resources at the disposal of the state, tribal and clan loyalties and patron–client networks have proved more potent than class or other national interests.

The resulting political economy can be seen in the history of agricultural marketing.[15] In the colonial period the primary function of the export crop marketing boards was to squeeze the peasantry in the interests of the colonial power (e.g. to build up sterling balances) and the colonial state (transfer of surplus to fund colonial development expenditures). Following independence the burden of the marketing system on the peasantry increased, but no longer to the benefit of sterling—there was no longer an accumulation of sterling deposits—nor the state, as transfers to the state budget dried up (indeed, in many instances the state found itself subsidizing loss-making marketing institutions which, nevertheless, were unable to offer a reasonable price to the peasant). The marketing authorities became a sort of bureaucratic black hole, into which vast resources flowed from farmers and from public funds, partly to the benefit of the functionaries of the institutions and partly dissipated through inefficiency.

However, while in their early years the independent states could be viewed as vehicles for sustaining the incomes of the new elites, as resources dried up it became increasingly difficult for the state to deliver reasonable incomes to its own employees, so that increasingly they had to defend their own living standards through moonlighting activities or through 'informal' incomes derived from the use of their state positions. Moreover, in a poorly functioning political and economic system, those requiring services from state institutions often found it easier to buy favours from functionaries, than to bring pressure to bear for a more general improvement in performance.

[13] The first substantial redefinition of national boundaries occurred while this chapter was being written, with the independence of Eritrea from Ethiopia.

[14] Basil Davidson has emphasized this point, going as far as to identify the national state in Africa as a black man's burden, imposed as a result of the colonial experience. (*The Blackman's Burden*, London: Currey, 1992). While Davidson is no doubt correct to point out the weak historical foundations of most African states, it is less clear what flows from that view, as even if a return to pre-colonial political formations were placed on the political agenda, and might even seem feasible in such areas as Buganda and Ashante, in many parts of Africa there is no coherent base for political units based on pre-colonial boundaries.

[15] See Robert Bates (1981), *Markets and States in Tropical Africa*, Berkeley: University of California Press.

2. STRUCTURAL ADJUSTMENT AND SYSTEMIC REFORM

2.1. The Structural Adjustment Package

The conventional, donor-driven response to the mounting crisis which became evident in Africa by the late 1970s was policy reform, under the banner of 'structural adjustment', so that the past fifteen years could be described as the economic era of structural adjustment in Africa.[16] The story is familiar enough, and a summary of certain broad features of the structural adjustment experience is all that is attempted here. Structural adjustment can be characterized as a mixture of economic stabilization, liberalization, and pruning of state economic activities. On the one hand, it represented conventional, pro-market donor thinking, supported by many within Africa faced with the obvious débâcle of the existing policy regimes. On the other hand, it might be seen as a defeat for the state systems, which, no longer able to command the resources required to sustain themselves, had to accept a retreat, not only in the face of donor pressures, but also in reponse to spontaneous (parallel or informal) developments in the indigenous economy: structural adjustment replaced structural change in the rhetoric of public policy.

Structural adjustment emerged as a policy response in shattered economies among the debris of collapsed development efforts. National governments had to accept that their attempts to mould the pattern of economic growth and to shield themselves from the impact of economic decline had failed; donors had to recognize that the main thrust of their support should no longer be directed to increasing the capital stock, but should instead provide the minimal resources required to sustain recurrent activity and to rehabilitate key elements in the decaying infrastructure.

A number of countries have implemented packages which have, to varying degrees:

(a) changed the macroeconomic policy environment (the exchange rate regime, interest rates, price policies, and, typically less successfully, the budgetary stance);

(b) transformed the regulatory regime and improved incentives to the private sector;

(c) accepted a commitment to privatize significant segments of the public sector (although the actual extent of privatization in practice has been quite limited so far).

---

[16] The structural adjustment agenda was set out in the World Bank study *Accelerated Development in Sub-Saharan Africa: An Agenda for Action* (World Bank, 1980). This report is commonly know as the 'Berg Report'—the team producing the report was led by Elliot Berg, who could claim a reasonable degree of consistency, as he had already been a critic of etatist development strategies in Africa in the mid-1960s.

As the overall tone of this chapter is gloomy, three achievements of structural adjustment in a number of countries which have implemented programmes should be recorded:

(*a*) In many countries there has been a re-vitalization of private economic activity, as domestic actors in the economy have responded to new market opportunities. The positive response has been greater than suggested by conventional GDP data, which incorporate most of the activity in the official, public economy and underestimate that of the unofficial, private (often informal) economy. As it is the official economy which has borne the brunt of stabilization, and the private economy which has mainly benefited from liberalization, the GDP data have a downward bias in measuring recovery under structural adjustment.

(*b*) It seems unlikely that structural adjustment has had a regressive income impact (the very real deterioration in the condition of many of the poor resulted from the crisis which gave rise to the need for policy change, rather than from structural adjustment policies as such, which, if anything, have a pro-rural bias and particularly hit the formal incomes of the urban middle class).

(*c*) The policy reforms have received more widespread popular acceptance than politicians themselves expected, although there has been understandable public opposition to some measures (e.g. to changes in food price policy) and resistance from particular pressure groups.

The collapse of the existing economic system because of foreign exchange famine and pressures from external funding agencies demanded a shift in the internal terms of trade in favour of the exporting sectors. As this involved some loss of privilege for state functionaries, some policy changes were (and in some cases still are) resisted. However, the conditional availability of external financial support cushioned the impact, so that while some privileges were lost, the funding of increased imports allowed for a general revival in living conditions. After more than a decade of structural adjustment there has been significant change in the prevailing policy regimes and, perhaps more important, a sea change in the way policy options are perceived.

However, despite success in promoting policy reform, the hard economic benefits achieved so far have been less than projected. Nowadays a certain fatigue can be observed throughout the region, both on the part of national governments and in the donor community, as the economic results of policy reform have been disappointing, in comparison, for example, to projections incorporated into adjustment programmes. If, on the positive side, some evidence can be offered that the structural adjustment medicine is working and that a number of near-moribund African economies are showing signs of life, the recovery so far is less than complete. Sustained success stories are hard to find. Donors tend to point to the prodigal sons—

the economies which fell so far and whose repentance therefore seems so much more dramatic. The modest successes of Ghana and Uganda look impressive against the sorry background of the depths to which those economies sunk, although it is chastening to realize that in both cases they have a way to go till they return to the levels of thirty years ago. Although markets are working and life in general is improving in such countries as Ghana, Uganda, and Tanzania, it is not yet evident that the material and institutional basis has been laid for sustained growth over the longer term.

While there has been widespread revitalization of the indigenous economies in a number of countries, partly as a consequence of deregulation and liberalized trade and payments regimes, perhaps the most challenging area for economic policy relates to continuing weakness in African export performances. This is partly a result of the deplorable state of the world markets for leading traditional exports; however, the persistence of the vulnerability of African economies to the performance of international markets for a few traditional crops demonstrates their continuing structural weakness, a problem for which a solution has yet to be found. The assault on 'inward-looking' trade policies, which has its intellectual origins in the theory of comparative advantage, is often supported by appeals to examples of successful export-led growth in East Asia. However, the success of the Asian tigers was based on dynamic adjustment of their comparative advantage, with the state playing an active role in support of the private exploitation of export markets, whereas the export trade of Africa continues to concentrate on primary commodities.

In the pre-structural adjustment period, government interventions to alter the location of African economies in the international division of labour were signally unsuccessful. Under structural adjustment, in a number of countries, diversification into new export areas has made a small beginning, but weak export performance still remains an important negative factor and reforming economies are heavily aid-dependent. There is, at the moment, no plausible vision of how the African continent can earn its way in international markets. Even if market stimulus is a necessary ingredient for economic success, it is far from obvious that it will be sufficient to generate lively export growth across the continent. The best that can be said is that, despite the lack of dramatic breakthroughs in export growth, the response to new economic opportunities by actors in the domestic economy has been significant, and given time this may have a cumulative impact and provide the institutional basis for export diversification.

Continuing weakness in performance as measured by such key indicators of sustainability as export earnings and savings cannot be ignored, as policy reform is not an end in itself, but a means to achieving higher income and output. A 'freely' operating market may be a beauty to behold, but its justification has eventually to rest on performance in terms of output and incomes. Even such improvement as can be observed is at least in part the result of a self-fulfilling donor hypothesis: policy reform is necessary; therefore increased donor support is conditional on reform; but increased support following reform itself results in improved performance—that is, output revival in a number of countries following introduction of structural adjustment has been as much a result of aid increases as the positive impact of policy reform.

2.2. Structural Adjustment and Capacity Building

Economic crisis set in train events which, with the additional push coming from the donor community, led to the dismantling of ineffective instruments of state policy and a shift of resources from parasitic state institutions. However, it is far from clear that sustained growth will emerge from market forces, unaided by state intervention, while the capacity of state institutions has definitely not been restored in the structural adjustment process. As a result, the policy discussion in Africa is shifting from structural adjustment to capacity building. In terms of the discussion above, that involves seeking means to increase the capacity of the state to make and implement policy and exploring whether the emerging political economy will be conducive to effective policy making.

Both in the adjusting economies of Africa and the 'transitional' ex-communist economies it has become evident that the effective operation of market economies needs to be backed up by reasonably strong state institutions, to provide a stable macroeconomic setting, a positive institutional environment, and those economic and social services which are necessarily the responsibility of the state. Some characteristics of the political economy of the reform process impede the development of such an effective state.

One difficulty is that the specifics of structural adjustment, as promoted by donors in the 1980s, were flawed in not taking account of the impact of crisis and the reform package on the morale and performance of the public service. It could be argued that a major weakness of policy in the 1970s was to assume that peasants would go on increasing production in the face of falling prices—they didn't; it could equally be argued that in the 1980s it was assumed that civil servants would go on working in the face of falling incomes—and they haven't. One result was that informal economic activity became the order of the day for public servants. In the 1960s, transfers from public servants contributed through the extended family network to the welfare of those outside the official system; by the 1980s the direction of flows reversed as the bureaucracy had to seek sustenance in informal activities. In the face of economic crisis and failed state intervention, it was perhaps reasonable to view the bureaucracy as largely parasitic, and its euthanasia as of little consequence. However, with the revival of private activity, weaknesses in the state apparatus have quickly become a constraint on development.

Other basic contradictions arise from the ways in which the political economy of the post-structural adjustment era is conditioned by the process of economic and social change under structural adjustment, including the spontaneous reactions of actors in the economy to the economic crisis and to adjustment policy. With the decay of systems of government control, the informal rules of the game change even before the first attempts at policy reform. With the growth of the parallel economy, activities which had been marginal in the past become more central to the economy.[17] The parallel system in economies in the throes of reform deserves attention, as it is a crucial aspect of the transition—it feeds on the failure of the old system and may provide the genesis of the new.

The term 'parallel' economy encompasses diverse activities which become more or less accepted by society (and even by the authorities) while remaining illegal or quasi-legal. Two differing types of activity can be distinguished. Some activity is genuinely 'parallel' to the official economy, in the sense that it is made up of a circuit of activity quite separate from the official economy, such as small-scale agriculture and petty craft production. The failure to 'capture' this activity in the official circuit or to impose the intended control reflected the weakness of the state apparatus and unrealistic ambitions to extend state controls (e.g. over local trade in food), but had no particularly negative consequences for the internal working of state institutions. The thriving market in smuggled exports, a response to a persistently over-valued exchange rate, was more ambiguous in its effects, as it subverted the operation of key policy instrument (i.e. foreign exchange controls and trade revenues).

Other 'parallel' activities were very much an outgrowth of the official system, ranging from 'black marketeering', where scarce products of state enterprise were sold under the counter at above official prices, to the diversion of state property to private uses. This sort of activity might better be described as 'orthogonal' rather than 'parallel' to the official economy, in that it involved using access to the state as a basis for private accumulation, and set in motion changes in the state system. Characteristic examples of this process of change, also observable in centrally planned economies in crisis or in the early stages of reform, include managers of state enterprise using profit from access to scarce commodities to accumulate capital needed to launch their private ventures, managers of state enterprises beginning to operate in most essential respects as if they were managing a private business, and new ventures using machinery and materials purloined from state enterprises to feed their own operations.

[17] The importance of the parallel or hidden economy in Tanzania is captured in the book by T. L. Maliyamkono and M. S. D. Bagachwa, *The Second Economy in Tanzania* (London: Currey, 1990).

Widespread breaking of rules is typically necessary for any rigid bureaucratic system to operate; survival in a supply-constrained economy depends as much on technical 'know-who' as technical know-how. However, 'black marketeering' is often not only against the formal rules, but is also socially unacceptable; for example it subverts a system of distribution which, even if ineffective, provides the public with certain rights of access. For the consumer in the queue, black marketeering which diverts already limited official stocks to benefit privileged groups in the system, is unacceptable. The resulting cynicism in Tanzania led to the popular usage describing black market prices as 'party prices' in the early 1980s. This provided a popular basis for official campaigns against 'black marketeers'.[18] The dilemma is that the black marketeer who is the criminal of the old system can also be seen as the hero of the new. The 'black market' not only acts to break the old system but also begins to provide a working basis for a new system of distribution.

However, the genesis of market activity in an environment of 'black markets' generates unfortunate business ethics on which to base the emerging system (e.g. the ubiquitous Russian mafia). While parallel economic activity makes a positive contribution to the transition, it also institutionalizes a disrespect for the law, giving rise to a pattern of individual behaviour which carries over into the reformed system, including a disregard for the legal requirements of business and a disrespect for normal fiscal obligations (e.g. lessons learnt in avoiding the exchange control system are readily applied to customs avoidance and fiddles in reimbursement of import support allocations). Businessmen became wise in the avoidance of all forms of government controls and impositions, implemented with increasing feebleness by a decaying state apparatus. The resurgence of private economic activity has therefore only limited fiscal benefits. There is a tension between the need to relax government interference and the need to impose the disciplines necessary to expand the tax base.

At the early stages of structural adjustment, institutional reform was neglected by reform-mongers, who tended to concentrate on reform of the incentive system—'getting prices right'. That in itself was difficult to achieve, but proved to be far from the whole task. For a price system to work, prices have to be operative (i.e. act as working constraints or incentives influencing actors in the economy). Of course, if prices are not 'right' (e.g. if they are set well below market-clearing levels), then they cannot function, and some other mechanism must dominate (e.g. queueing or

[18] In 1983, when the Tanzanian economy was in the depths of crisis, the campaign against the 'walanguzi' virtually closed down the economy in some parts of the country, as by then in many parts of the country the parallel economy was the only effective marketing system, but was initially quite popular. Similarly, in the early stages of Soviet reform, there was a strong popular distrust of the 'mafia', which somewhat surprisingly seemed to be shared by Western donors, who claimed to be taking steps to ensure that aid went through 'proper' channels to the 'right' destinations.

rationing). But to create an effective market, institutional behaviour must also change, so that transactions are completed at the market price and enterprises respond to the consequences. As the literature on East European reform emphasizes, it means little to an enterprise to be faced with 'realistic' prices if it faces a 'soft' budget constraint. The difficulty of imposing hard budget constraints in practice is partly a question of political will, but there are also deeper institutional barriers. Financial discipline will be achievable only if it extends throughout the system. Otherwise when budgetary support is withdrawn it is quickly replaced by bank credits from state-owned banks. Public enterprises also finance themselves through growing debts to other public enterprises. And in the absence of a strong assertion of ownership interest, wage and salary bills have been met by cannibalizing the real assets of the enterprise.

The difficulty of enforcing discipline on public enterprises provides one argument for privatization. Slow implementation of privatization is partly because of opposition from vested interests in the parastatals, but also reflects the weakness of the indigenous business sector, which is too poorly developed to take over large-scale enterprises *en masse*. One solution is to call in foreign capital, but the wholesale transfer of public assets to foreign or minority community ownership is politically controversial, particularly as the desire to reduce foreign and minority community dominance of the economy rather than socialist doctrine provided much of the impetus to public sector expansion.[19] Enterprise policy needs to address not only the shift in the balance between public and private enterprise, but also the need for greater national participation in the ownership of private larger-scale economic activities.

With structural adjustment, there has been a flowering of private economic activity, both from small-scale producers who benefit from the recognition that their activities cannot (and should not) be subjected to state restrictions and from the new entrepreneurs emerging from the parallel economy. The internal dynamics of policy reform can be interpreted as a process in which the state accommodates these new groups, first implicitly by tolerating widespread practices which were in principle illegal, and then explicitly by adjusting the rules. Thus the Tanzanian government accepted large-scale imports financed outside the official foreign exchange system (so-called 'own account imports'), financed by foreign exchange which was largely acquired by illegal means, for about seven years before officially legalizing the parallel foreign exchange market.

The political economy which will emerge from structural adjustment is far from clear, and such questions as where the support for continuing reform of state institutions is to come from and what sort of politics is likely to encourage effective performance by the state remain open. The politics

[19] See my article at the time in Dharam P. Ghai (ed.), *Economic Independence in Africa* (East African Literature Bureau, 1973).

of Africa is in a state of flux and it is quite unclear how the economic groups strengthened under liberal economic policies will participate in the political process, how a lively small-scale sector, and fledgling indigenous capitalists, operating through the new multi-party populist politics will impinge on enfeebled state institutions. The dynamic small business sector could well provide support for some aspects of liberalization. It is more problematic in many African economies whether a class of indigenous entrepreneurs will emerge in the near future which can play an important role both in larger-scale economic sectors and in the political process.

There is no shortage of entrepreneurial talent in Africa in small-scale activities; one source of optimism is the widespread evidence of small-scale entrepreneurial initiatives in agriculture, trade, transport, construction, and craft activities. However, one important contrast between Africa and East Asia is the lack of large-scale national capital in the former and its active presence in the latter. This having been said, it is far from evident what is to be done about it; public support of private business only too readily generates rent-seeking rather than entrepreneurial behaviour.

It is not clear, either in countries such as Tanzania, Uganda, and Ghana in which structural adjustment has profoundly changed the system, or in countries such as Kenya, which have followed a more capitalist policy since independence, whether a national capitalist class is emerging that is capable of working with the state to develop a project for a more advanced stage of capitalist development.

3. WHAT IS TO BE DONE?

A number of countries have implemented policy reform with some vigour. Structural adjustment has had some modest successes in reviving private economic activity, particularly in economies such as Ghana and Tanzania in which the private economy was almost moribund a decade ago. However, structural adjustment has been singularly unsuccessful in restoring the capacity of the state. The erosion of real incomes and the collapse of morale and morality in the public service, the leeching of the self-confidence of state institutions as funding and therefore control increasingly fell into the hands of donors, and the decay of public infrastructure after two decades of underinvestment and neglected maintenance leaves a wreckage of state institutions, still a source of employment but not of realistic salaries for large numbers, able to deliver less and less by way of services. In this situation, even the maintenance of order is spontaneously privatized—the wealthier protected by private security services and the less well-off through the activities of self-help vigilante groups (in Tanzania, the 'sungu-sungu'). Thus even those economies where there are modest indications of economic revival are in most cases still subject to the decay of public institutions.

Structural adjustment shifted resources away from the government, loosened controls over the economy, and legalized market activities which had already developed in response to the failures of earlier policies. For the moment, the only plausible basis for the next stage of African development appears to lie in the decentralized initiatives of private economic actors. But as private economic activity revives, it becomes increasingly obvious that the state no longer has the capacity to undertake those basic tasks necessary to support the private economy. The expanding private economy faces new constraints because of the inadequate provision of those services which remain the responsibility of the public sector. One of the continuing costs of crisis, to which structural adjustment policies provided no solution, is the erosion of the capacity of the state.

True, one of the main thrusts of structural adjustment has been to trim the role of the state—the removal of exchange controls, price controls, and the reduction in all sorts of state intervention have dramatically reduced the tasks the state undertakes. These policy changes in part came to terms with a reality in which an enfeebled state apparatus was increasingly unable to enforce its rules and regulations. Economic reform has, by and large, narrowed the range of government intervention and should have left government with a more manageable set of tasks, but transfer of activities to the private sector has limits, on grounds of economic efficiency, social desirability, and political feasibility.

The tasks left with government are, however, not only critical, but also in some ways complex—the manipulation of market-related policy instruments, the implementation of public investment programmes and the management of public infrastructure, and the delivery of social services. There is little sign of restoration of governments' ability to handle essential tasks effectively.

In extreme cases, the state has withered away, although not quite as intended by Marxist visionaries. Societies in such deep crisis are not faced with issues of 'development'. Before issues of development policy can be addressed, a certain minimum degree of social order is necessary. Short of that, the population must focus on the requirements of bare survival, while international concern is likely to be peace-keeping, relief efforts, and refugee support. But the extreme cases of disorder and collapse of civil authority can be seen as part of a continuum in which a large number of countries have governments which can effectively perform few of the functions expected of them by their citizens.

Real salaries in the public service have collapsed, and the performances of many employees precisely match their vestigial incomes ('the government pretends to pay us, and we pretend to work'). Senior civil servants survive on the perquisites of office. Roads are not repaired and public power supplies fail, unless funded by donors. Health authorities are unable to cope with such basic public health problems as cholera outbreaks, while there is inadequate capacity to respond to the Aids epidemic, which is still gathering momentum. Such public investment as takes place is donor financed, so that public investment planning is almost entirely a matter of donor co-ordination.

It could be argued that what is required is nothing less than the reconstruction of the state. Even if an essentially private economy is to be the model for the post-structural adjustment era, a more effective set of state institutions is required. Assuming structural adjustment has some further success, and in a significant group of African countries the private economy expands, the state will need to be reformed to be able to meet the needs of that development, including the provision of essential infrastructure and social services and, as the private sector grows, the implementation of appropriate public actions to accommodate and orchestrate private economic activity. Even a minimalist state needs to fill gaps in the institutional arrangements for the private economy, including modifying the legal framework in such areas as land law and corporate law, sponsoring the development of new markets, such as financial markets, and encouraging co-ordinating agencies, such as trade councils and chambers of commerce.

The view developed in this chapter is that effective government participation in development has both a bureaucratic and political dimension; 'reconstructing the state' in Africa will require movement on both fronts. In principle the definition of the agenda for bureaucratic reform is straightforward. The short-term need is for a careful definition of the responsibilities of government in the emerging economic situation and a systematic effort to put in place a reformed bureaucratic structure to tackle the identified tasks. The agenda for the reconstruction of the state includes clarification of the required institutional structure, identification of appropriate manpower requirements, and the definition of an effective incentive system for the public service, involving fewer, but better paid public servants. In principle, it is not particularly difficult to formulate a blueprint for reformed systems of government administration; in practice, however, very little gets done as the existing systems, for all their weaknesses, operate as a subsistence sector for large numbers of employees.

In the longer term, it will be necessary to again address issues of economic structural change, learning lessons from the failures of the earlier efforts of the 1960s and 1970s.

The state also has responsibility for the provision of services to the mass of the population. The deterioration in the delivery of social services has persisted, reflecting stringent resource constraints and a failure to implement new strategies of delivery and cost recovery. Macroeconomic structural adjustment did nothing to improve the situation in the social sectors; while there is little evidence that structural adjustment had a regressive impact on the primary distribution of income, fiscal stringency has had a strong negative impact on the public provision of social services. Formulation of new sectoral strategies has been partial, support for the social sectors has not been informed by a coherent strategy to promote institutional reform, and progress in implementing new strategies has been limited. In light of the fiscal debility of central governments, the most plausible way forward is through local initiatives and control, either through local government or self-help NGOs (non-governmental organizations), even though this feeds regional inequalities and can give local interest groups control over access. Given the importance of investment in human capital, the continuing decay in education and health delivery systems may prove to be, over the longer term, the most debilitating of the weaknesses currently observable in the region.

If the technical requirements for good 'governance' can be addressed in a straightforward fashion, the political dimension is much more murky, if only because it involves interpretative analysis of political economy more than technocratic designs of social engineering. It is inevitable that the changing structures of African economies will unleash new political forces, resulting in new political alignments. At this point in time, predicting the likely political outcomes over the medium term would involve an exercise in social science fiction; the best that can be done is to monitor the new politics now emerging, to identify whether or not new coalitions of political forces could provide the basis for more coherent state interventions in development than in the past.

An essay on the role of government in economic change in any continent other than Africa would probably discuss the role of foreign aid agencies in a brief paragraph, if at all. It is part of the current African predicament that it is not possible to cast donors in a merely subsidiary role. Even if there are signs that some donors wish to disengage and even if it can be argued that past donor interventions have had, at best, a questionable impact, given the current reality it is too often the donor community which takes the lead in defining the policy agenda and, to be fair, donor support which in many countries has ensured that at least some public services have been maintained. Therefore this discussion concludes with some comments about the future donor role.

Emphasis has been placed increasingly on the importance of improved 'governance' in donor rhetoric. Reform of the public administration—of the budgetary system, of the civil service (its size, recruitment, salary and career structure), of the government decision-making system, etc.—have been dealt with in numerous studies by the World Bank, by various parts of the UN, by bilateral donors and national governments. However, so far there has been little success in achieving comprehensive public sector reform. The most important steps in structural adjustment involved changes in key macroeconomic policies and decisions to dismantle various government controls; as such, the programmes could be implemented by a small cadre of officials in the economic co-ordinating ministries and the central banks, and donor conditionality could focus on a few macroeconomic policy instruments. Reform of the institutions of government is a more complex task, and donor promotion of such reform faces the contradiction that their own role has been one source of the erosion of governmental capacity.

In the 1980s, what is somewhat euphemistically known as 'aid dialogue' was reasonably successful in promoting policy reform where the policy objective could be interpreted in terms of quantitative targets to be incorporated in aid conditions. There has been much less success in promoting reforms in the machinery of government. Reform of government is most likely to be achievable by a process owned by and embedded in the national government structure, with the understanding and eventual support of the top leadership. Such UN programmes as MDP and Natcap address aspects of administrative reform, as do World Bank public expenditure reviews and numerous bilateral technical assistance exercises. However, an effective donor strategy for promoting the required degree of reform in public administration has not yet been put in place.

Piecemeal efforts to improve performance of parts of government have had some success, but often at the expense of making the overall system more confused (e.g. the provision of *ad hoc* donor incentives to public servants in priority areas which render the overall incentive system even less coherent). To achieve more success in administrative reform, donors may need to make more ambitious and co-ordinated efforts than they have done to date. So far donor efforts have involved promoting an ineffective mix of ceilings on public expenditures and employment, programmes to ease the hardships of 'redeployed' civil servants to soften opposition to reform, and piecemeal and uncoordinated interventions to bolster particular parts of the public service.

Could donors do more to promote administrative reform? A note of scepticism should be sounded regarding the possible donor contribution. The organization of government is necessarily primarily a national matter, and there is little evidence that donors have a comparative advantage in providing government services.

A possible approach could be to set aside over a number of years a significant proportion of funds currently devoted to technical assistance, consulting, and so on to fund a new incentive structure for national professionals, which could be introduced *pari passu* with reforms to improve working conditions, to raise standards of performance, to improve the quality of recruitment, and to enhance training opportunities. This would compare with attempts at reform so far which have emphasized cuts in the public service (which are, of course, necessary) without generating noticeable benefits to the staff remaining in place. Such a donor initiative would require modification of long-standing donor thinking constraining the role of aid in supporting local costs; however, given the *de facto* contributions donors have been making to recurrent budgets through import support programmes, this would primarily involve an effort to think through the logic of existing practice. Perhaps the most alarming implication of such proposals is that donors are taken further down the road to becoming the meaningful government in Africa.

Certainly an alternative has to be found to the continuing support for expensive technical assistance, which can only substitute for weaknesses in local institutional capacity to a very limited degree. Technical assistance has increasingly responded to the failure to utilize trained nationals effectively, rather than filling needs resulting from gaps in the availability of local trained personnel. Not only is that response wasteful, because the cost of a foreign expert is so much more than the payments which would be required to effectively mobilize nationals, but the insertion of highly paid foreign experts to work alongside qualified, but underpaid and demoralized national staff has proved a recipe for misunderstanding and frustration on both sides. Donors should not continue to shore up an ineffective administrative and fiscal structure, but should be ready to underwrite reform over the medium term. The offer of substantial financial packages could be used to encourage profound reforms in civil service practice.

Much of the 'dialogue' regarding institutional performance in Africa has addressed the weaknesses in the performance of African governments. What of the performance of donors themselves? The power which has accrued to donor agencies in Africa suggests the need to consider another aspect of the 'governance' question, which has so far not been placed on the donor agenda—namely the governance of the donor agencies themselves. Applying the criteria by which African governments are found wanting to many donor agencies themselves suggests that they have their own weaknesses. By such criteria as accountability, transparency, and competitiveness, the agencies themselves perform badly. Agencies are not democratically accountable to those affected by their policies and agency officials are themselves typically insulated from being affected by any consequences of their actions—either from being directly affected by the performance of the programmes or by having their incomes or career prospects connected to programme performance. When agencies, either national or multilateral, are subjected to democratic pressures, these are more likely to reflect the concerns of the lobbies currently fashionable in the First World than the agenda and concerns of the Third World.

The conclusion has to be that donors may be able to help, but that the eventual revival of African fortunes will depend on the reassertion of the initiative by Africans—a new decolonization—but to be successful, that will have to be based on a political process which articulates national goals and supports a policy-making and implementation process that is more successful than the first decolonization of the 1960s.

PART III

SOCIALIST ECONOMIES IN TRANSITION

9

The State under State Socialism and Post-Socialism

Michael Ellman

1. THE STATE UNDER STATE SOCIALISM

1.1. The Initial Hostility to the State

Both Marx and Lenin displayed in some of their writings substantial hostility to the state as a social agent. On the theoretical level, Marx rejected the Hegelian analysis of the bureaucracy, which saw the bureaucracy as a universal class which represented the will and interests of the community as a whole. In his *Contribution to the Critique of Hegel's Philosophy of Right* (1843) Marx (1975 edn.: 50) argued that the police, the judiciary, and the bureacratic administration 'are not deputies of civil society itself, in and through whom it administers its *own* general interest, but representatives of the state for the administration of the state over [and] against civil society'. He also pointed out that the bureaucracy, far from being the universal class, was actually a group with its own interests which it defended against other groups in society with other interests. Furthermore, the relations within the bureaucracy are the result of the interaction of the interests of particular bureaucrats, or groups of bureaucrats, who use manipulation of information and other methods to advance individual and group interests. In his 1842–3 articles 'Debates on Freedom of the Press' and 'Comments on the Latest Prussian Censorship Instructions' he argued that freedom required that all information about public business be made available to all citizens. Censorship, he argued, was a means whereby the bureaucracy preserved politics as the exclusive domain of a dominant clique. The basic thrust of Marx's analysis of the bureaucracy in 1842–3 has much in common with the neo-liberal analysis of the 1960s and 1970s, although it lacks the formal analysis and recognition of the costs of political participation of the latter.

On a practical level, in *The Civil War in France* Marx praised the Paris

I am grateful to Jos de Beus, Anthony Hemerijk, Geert Reuten, Peter Wiles, and the participants in the conference in Cambridge in April 1993 for helpful suggestions, comments, and ideas.

Commune for destroying the old state apparatus and replacing it by elected recallable citizens. Its key acts, according to Marx, were the dismantling of the standing army, the bureaucratic administrative apparatus, the police, and the appointed judiciary and their replacement by a people's militia, an elected working body of councillors, recallable watchmen, and elected judges. This meant, in Marx's view, that central government through the state apparatus, standing above civil society, should be replaced under socialism by a restructured civil society with its own institutions which guarantee the participation of citizens in political life. In this way the national central government can be subordinated to society and to the self-government of civil society. Hence, in his *Critique of the Gotha Programme* (1875) he wrote that 'Freedom consists in transforming the state from an organ dominating society into one completely subordinate to it, and even at the present time the forms of State are more or less free to the extent that they restrict the "freedom of the State".'

According to Lenin, in his *State and Revolution*, democracy under capitalism is a fraud because it excludes the mass of the population from real political influence. 'Marx grasped this *essence* of capitalist democracy splendidly when, in analysing the experience of the Commune, he said that the oppressed are allowed once every few years to decide which particular representatives of the oppressing class shall represent and repress them in Parliament.' Under the dictatorship of the proletariat, the political form which would emerge from the socialist revolution, on the other hand, there would be 'an immense expansion of democracy, which *for the first time* becomes democracy for the poor, democracy for the people, and not democracy for the money-bags'. Nevertheless, democracy and freedom would not be general because of the need to repress the enemies of the revolution. Under the future communist society which would follow the dictatorship of the proletariat, however, the state would wither away, because 'freed from capitalist slavery, from the untold horrors, savagery, absurdities and infamies of capitalist exploitation, people will gradually *become accustomed* to observing the elementary rules of social intercourse that have been known for centuries and repeated for thousands of years in all copy-book maxims. They will become accustomed to observing them without force, without coercion, without subordination, *without the special apparatus* for coercion called the state.' For the state, Lenin, following Engels, had a very negative evaluation. 'So long as the state exists there is no freedom. When there is freedom, there will be no state.'

1.2. The State as the Driving Force of Development

Marx and Engels stressed the role of the state, and of force, in capitalist economic development. Orthodox economists treat the market economy as one in which various parties freely enter into mutually beneficial contracts.

Marxists treat it as an arena, structured and maintained by state power, in which unequal groups are forced into relations of dependence and exploitation. In his famous analysis of the origins of industrial capitalism (*Capital.* i. ch. 31) Marx wrote:

The discovery of gold and silver in America, the extirpation, enslavement and entombment in mines of the aboriginal population, the beginning of the conquest and looting of the East Indies, the turning of Africa into a warren for the commercial hunting of black-skins, signalised the rosy dawn of the era of capitalist production. These idyllic proceedings are the chief momenta of original accumulation. On their heels treads the commercial war of the European nations, with the globe for a theatre. It begins with the revolt of the Netherlands from Spain, assumes giant dimensions in England's Anti-Jacobin War, and is still going on in the opium wars against China, etc.

The different momenta of original accumulation distribute themselves now, more or less in chronological order, particularly over Spain, Portugal, Holland, France and England. In England at the end of the 17th century, they arrive at a systematical combination, embracing the colonies, the national debt, the modern mode of taxation, and the protectionist system. These methods depend in part on brute force, e.g. the colonial system. But they all employ the power of the State, the concentrated and organised force of society, to hasten, hot-house fashion, the process of transformation of the feudal mode of production into the capitalist mode, and to shorten the transition. Force is the midwife of every old society pregnant with a new one. It is itself an economic power.

Furthermore, in the writings of the Marxist classics, in particular those of Engels, the embryo can be found of the idea of the state as the key motor which, under socialism, will ensure rapid and successful economic development. For example, in the *Communist Manifesto* Marx and Engels wrote that, '[t]he proletariat will use its political supremacy to wrest, by degrees, all capital from the bourgeoisie, to centralize all instruments of production in the hands of the State, i.e. of the proletariat organized as the ruling class; and to increase the total of productive forces as rapidly as possible.' In *Anti-Dühring* Engels wrote that an efficient economic system is only possible in 'a society which makes it possible for its productive forces to dovetail harmoniously into each other on the basis of one single vast plan'. For Engels, the socialist revolution would enable the means of production to break free from inefficient bourgeois control, be rationally organized in accordance with a plan, and rapidly develop. 'With the present development of the productive forces, [he wrote in *Anti-Dühring*] the increase in production that will follow from the very fact of the socialization of the productive forces, coupled with the abolition of the barriers and disturbances, and of the waste of products and means of production, resulting from the capitalist mode of production, will suffice, with everybody doing his share of work, to reduce the time required for labour to a point which, measured by our present conceptions, will be small indeed.' According to the same book, the capitalist mode of production tightly bonds the forces of production and stops them developing rationally. 'Their deliverance from these bonds is the one precondition for an unbroken, constantly-accelerated development of the productive forces, and therewith for a practically unlimited increase of production itself.'

The Bolsheviks were influenced both by this inheritance from the classics and also by the Russian economic and political environment. They came to power in a war economy in which state determination of grain prices had been introduced by the Tsarist government (in 1916), a state grain monopoly was introduced in March 1917 and was defended by Kadets and Mensheviks (Lih 1990), and in a country whose political culture was much more pro-state than that of the UK or USA. It was in accordance with both Marxist and Russian traditions and the experience of five years of war, that the Russian Communist Party (Bolsheviks) in its programme adopted in March 1919 stated that after the socialist revolution, 'the State Power ceases to be a parasitic apparatus nourished upon the productive process. There now begins its transformation into an organization directly fulfilling the function of administering the economic life of the country.' A similar formulation can be found in Stalin's well-known *Economic Problems of Socialism in the USSR* (1952) where he wrote, 'The specific role of the Soviet government was . . . that in view of the absence in the country of any ready-made rudiments of a socialist economy, it had to create new, socialist forms of economy, "starting from scratch" so to speak. That was undoubtedly a difficult, complex and unprecedented task. Nevertheless, the Soviet government accomplished this task with credit.'

More generally, one can say that since the Bolshevik victory in the civil war, a voluntaristic faith in the possibility of reshaping society by state action was an integral part of communist thinking throughout the world. It was thought that the state could ensure economic growth, technical progress, full employment, an equitable income distribution, and all other desirable goals through appropriate institutional arrangements and economic policies. The statization of the whole economy and society was a means to abolish the anarchy of the market and ensure the fulfilment of social goals.

Outside the Marxist tradition, the role of the state in economic development has also been analysed by economic historians. In a famous presentation, based on the experience of Central and Eastern Europe, Gerschenkron (1962) argued that latecomers to industrialization, trying to catch up with the leaders, develop alternative economic institutions. One such institution is the active state which pushes development along. The same idea has also been formulated on the basis of the experience of East Asia (Johnson 1982).

1.3. The State and Society

The relationship between civil society and the state has taken a variety of forms. On the one hand, there are cases such as the USSR under Stalin where the state apparatus towers above society and reshapes it. On the other hand, there are cases, such as the USA between the Civil War and World War I, where the state apparatus is weak and fragmented and simply a subordinate element in a dynamic civil society. Under state socialism, although the situation differed between countries and over time, the state was normally closer to the former end of this spectrum than to the latter.[1] The institutions of state socialism are created and maintained by the party–state apparatus. It is the party–state apparatus that collectivizes agriculture, nationalizes industry, imposes a state monopoly of foreign trade and foreign exchange, introduces national economic planning, and so on. For the party–state apparatus to lose its power is the fundamental precondition for a transformation of state socialism into a different economic system.

1.4. State Failure

State socialism started off with the ambition to create a social system more advanced than capitalism which would demonstrate its superiority in competition with the latter. In this it entirely failed. This can be characterized as a dramatic and very important case of state failure. In the 1970s, empirical study of the situation in various European countries revealed the existence and importance of state failure (Cornford 1975). Soon after, by analogy with the Pigovian theory of market failure, which for a long time dominated much of the welfare economics and microeconomics literature, attempts were made to develop a theory of 'non-market failure' (Wolf 1979) or 'collective failure' (Peacock 1980). Within a short time it became standard to treat 'market failure' and 'public failure' as

[1] Przeworski (1991: 140–2) has argued that the states in Eastern Europe were weak states, similar to those in Latin America. It is correct that bargaining was important in East Europe, that the role of the state relative to society declined over time, that in some countries in some periods the totalitarian model was not applicable—in certain periods in certain countries (e.g. the USSR in 1989–91) the state clearly was weak—and that the two countries specified by Przeworski (Hungary and Poland) did differ significantly for a long period from the other CMEA members. On the other hand, the bargaining was normally between central *state* bodies, branch ministries which were an integral part of the *state* apparatus, and *state* enterprises. The central bodies could, and sometimes did, appoint and dismiss the functionaries with whom they bargained. The subordinate bargainers did not enjoy the independence conferred by private property and the world market. Furthermore, activist national leaders (such as Andropov, Ceausescu, and Gorbachev) played a much bigger role in their countries than would have been the case had there existed social and economic organizations independent of the state apparatus. In addition, the party–state apparatus played a crucial role in the functioning of the whole system.

symmetrical problems requiring correction (Stiglitz 1989). The most important areas in which state failure can be observed in the state socialist countries are economic, political, social, ideological, environmental, and international.

In the economic field, state socialism introduced an entirely new type of economic system, one in which the state was the owner of virtually all the means of production and bureaucratic co-ordination was the dominant allocation mechanism. This new system, however, despite the high hopes of its founders and ideologists, entirely failed to catch up with capitalism in labour productivity, living standards, or technical progress.[2] As far as the level of labour productivity is concerned, if one looks at the USSR one sees that this was always relatively low and in the last decade before the collapse of the USSR, it stagnated. As far as living standards are concerned, the gulf between standards of living in state socialist countries and comparable capitalist ones (Estonia versus Finland, East Germany versus West Germany, Hungary versus Austria, North Korea versus South Korea) played an important role in the collapse of state socialism. The failure of the state socialist countries to close the technology gap, and its growth in the 1970s and 1980s, was another important factor contributing to the collapse of the system.

In the political system, the Communist Parties aspired to introduce a system that would be more democratic than the capitalist one because it would represent the interests of a larger part of the population and extend real freedom to them. This failed. The communist parties introduced police states. Once repression was relaxed, these states collapsed since they had no strong social basis outside the repressive apparatus. Where they have survived (e.g. China), it is largely because of the resolute use of repression against their opponents.

Socially, the Communist Parties aspired to create just and efficient societies. They turned out to be neither just nor efficient. They were stratified, unequal, corrupt, repressive, lacked independent social organizations and free access to information, and their social relations were marked by subordination, servility, and negative selection of cadres. Although some aspects of these societies were widely attractive (full employment, relative equality, free education and medical care, child care), even here each

---

[2] It did, however, make substantial progress in certain periods. For example, the USSR in the 1950s and China in the Dengist period both experienced rapid economic growth which resulted in sharply rising living standards. In these periods the system was successful. Kornai's (1992b: 202) sceptical comment that 'the price for forcing growth is very high' is not very applicable for these periods. (Kornai's comment is applicable for those countries and those periods where rapid growth was accompanied by restructuring the national economy away from the needs of consumption or economic policies which had an adverse effect on consumption or welfare.) Furthermore, the system generally provided a substantial measure of security to its citizens.

achievement was accompanied by a problem. Full employment went with the obligation to work in the state sector, low wages, shortages, and low productivity. Relative equality was accompanied by 'closed' distribution and other privileges for members of the elite, and substantial interregional, inter-gender, and other inequalities. The free education and medical care was often of a low standard and sometimes required under-the-counter payment. Child care was often scarce and frequently of low quality.

The Communist Parties came to power with the belief that the ideas of their opponents were mere ideologies, but that their views were a science—scientific socialism. For some time there were many people who did believe in part or all of the beliefs of the Communist Parties. Eventually, however, the discrepancy between actual state socialist development and the expectations engendered by their beliefs became so great that their beliefs came under attack and were ultimately rejected by almost everybody as a mere ideology designed to conceal the reality of an unattractive and doomed social system.

State socialism was expected to avoid the destruction of the environment practised by capitalism. In *Ante-Dühring* Engels explained that 'The present poisoning of the air, water and land can be put an end to' only under socialism. Experience has shown, however, that state socialism has poisoned the air and the water, and destroyed the fauna and flora, at least as vigorously as capitalism.

Socialism was expected to spread over the whole world as people came to see its manifest advantages. Although by the mid-1980s it had spread to cover about third of the world's population, it never advanced any further. In addition, it was never able to spread to the most advanced countries, despite the expectations of Marx and Lenin. Comparison between really existing socialism and really existing capitalism showed the people of the capitalist countries the enormous advantages of their system. It was precisely this comparison of the two systems that was one of the bases of the rise of the New Right in the 1970s.

1.5. State Failure and the Collapse of State Socialism

The collapse of state socialism in Eastern Europe and the USSR in 1989–91 can be seen as a result of state failure. The economic, political, social, ideological, environmental, and international state failures led, via their effect on the leaderships and peoples, to the collapse of the whole system. At one time this system had seemed very strong, and even a threat to the advanced capitalist countries, but prolonged state failures led to its collapse.

2. THE STATE UNDER POST-SOCIALISM

2.1. The Liberal Revolution

In 1989–93, Eastern Europe and the USSR/Russia experienced liberal revolutions, analogous to those in Western and Central Europe in 1848. Repressive regimes were overthrown and new elites came to power determined to reduce the role of the state and expand that of the market economy and civil society. The liberal revolutions of 1989–93, however, differed in one important respect from those of 1848—and from the liberalization and democratization processes in post-Franco Spain and post-Salazar Portugal—and in this respect were similar to the state socialist revolutions. The victorious liberals could not simply leave the economy to *laissez faire*. Because of the absence of a working capitalist system they had to 'build capitalism' (Bauer 1991). Balcerowicz, the Polish Finance Minister in 1989–90 and the 'father' of the Polish shock therapy, correctly stated that 'in our conditions the state is responsible for the construction of the new economic system' (Wojtyna 1992: 173). Similarly, Kornai (1990) in his popular exposition of his programme for the transition devoted a section (pp. 206–9) to 'The Need for a Strong Government'. It was obvious to him that his stabilization-cum-transformation programme required a strong executive to implement it. In the same vein, the radical Russian economist Yavlinsky (one of the authors of the 500-days plan) in an early 1993 discussion (Yavlinsky 1993) of the political crisis in Russia, stressed that 'a strong political power is necessary... In other words—a state is necessary.' The need to 'build capitalism' implied a major role for the state in destroying the former system, creating the institutions of the new system, and generating and maintaining political support for the transition to capitalism.

The liberal revolutions of 1989–91 were associated with the disintegration of several previously existing states (USSR, Yugoslavia, Czechoslovakia, GDR), the enlargement of one existing state (Federal Republic of Germany), and the creation of a large number of new states (the successor states of the former USSR, Yugoslavia, and Czechoslovakia). Furthermore, the process of liberalization destroyed some essential instruments of effective state action under the old regime (the official ideology, the Communist Party, the state security apparatus, the old central economic bureaucracy) without automatically putting anything in its place (Ellman and Kontorovich 1992; Kornai 1992b: 570–4). As Brus (1992) has pointed out, the retention of the old political system has played a key role in the effectiveness of the Chinese economic reforms. Both the breaking up of previously existing states, and the elimination of what were previously key instruments of state action, had at any rate the short-term effect of reducing the possibilities open to the state for the implementation of economic policies. The importance of this depended on the speed with which new states could emerge as independent actors and on the extent to which new policy institutions (e.g. parliaments, political parties, anti-monopoly offices, a legal system able to cope with commercial disputes) developed and new policy instruments (e.g. monetary policy, fiscal policy, exchange rate policy, trade policy) were utilized.

Although the liberals aimed at transforming and reducing the role of the state, it would be a fundamental mistake to suppose that they saw no role for the state, or one confined to the transition period. Like Lord Bauer analysing economic policy in developing countries, or Eucken and Röpke laying the theoretical basis for the 'social market economy', they envisaged that, after their project to build capitalism had been successfully completed, the state would have a very important, but limited, role. The debate between the liberals and their critics which followed the revolutions, did not concern the need for a strong state (even Hayekians advocated the protection of private property and contractual rights by state action), but was about the goals appropriate for the state to pursue (e.g. whether or not this or that structure of the economy was a legitimate goal of the state), the methods that governments should use to attain their economic objectives, and the degree of freedom which business firms and business people should have to pursue their economic objectives. As Crouch (1986: 180) has pointed out, 'The state has vital functions within liberal market capitalism . . . a pure liberal market economy requires a state that is not only limited and restrained but which is, within its proper sphere, sovereign. It is the clarity of state–society boundaries that distinguishes this kind of political economy rather than state restraint as such.'

The liberal revolutions of 1848 led to roles for the state which differed sharply between countries. The institutional outcome depended on a wide variety of factors, such as whether or not the revolution was defeated (as in Germany and Austria); the role of the church/churches; the role of labour, capital, and agriculture; the level of development; the relationship to the world market; and so on. It seems likely that the liberal revolutions of 1989–93 will also lead to institutions which differ significantly between countries.

2.2. The Gains from the Liberal Revolution

The liberal revolutions brought a number of solid gains, both to individuals and organizations. They were: freedom of speech and of opinion, of the press, of association, of religion, of internal and external travel, freedom to work outside the state sector, freedom to work for oneself or to run one's own business, freedom to spend one's own income as one wished, freedom to buy a wider range of goods and services. These freedoms were attractive and widely used, both by individuals and by organizations (e.g. churches, trade unions, political parties).[3] People were no longer afraid to express their own opinions, new media came into existence, political parties and trade unions expressing their members' interests were formed, foreign travel grew, foreign consumer goods were enjoyed.

2.3. The Costs of the Liberal Revolution

The liberal revolution turned out to have two types of costs, the costs of revolution and the costs of liberalism. It is well known that revolutions bring with them substantial costs of revolution (Bukharin 1920: ch. 6). The 1989–91 liberal revolution was no exception. The destruction of existing states, and of some essential instruments of state action under the old regime, together with some of the revolutionary actions of the triumphant liberals (such as price liberalization), led in the revolutionary phase to a situation in which the state was unable to fulfil even such classic functions as the provision of stable money, the maintenance of law and order, and the enforcement of a stable and 'enterprise friendly' regulatory and taxation framework (Naishul' 1993b). Although the Czech republic quite quickly reduced inflation to West European levels, for other transition economies such an achievement remained just a dream even some years after the revolution. In all countries crime increased and introducing and enforcing a stable and 'enterprise friendly' taxation and regulatory regime turned out to be very difficult.

A particularly important cost of revolution resulted from the formation of new states which accompanied the liberal revolutions.[4] This turned out—at any rate in the short run—to be an expensive process, both economically and politically. Economically, its immediate effect was to reduce mutual trade and hence contribute to general impoverishment. Politically, it led to a large number of conflicts, varying from the civil war in Tadjikstan, the virtual war between Armenia and Azerbaidjan, the conflicts in Moldova, and the wars in the former Yugoslavia.

Liberalism itself turned out to have extensive costs, which were not foreseen by many of the crowds which welcomed the collapse of state socialism. Unemployment grew rapidly and became a major social problem in many of the post-socialist countries (but not in the Czech republic where up till now it has remained very low by EC standards). Crime grew rapidly and in many countries people began to worry about their vulnerability, no longer to arbitrary arrest by the state security service, but to arbitrary

---

[3] For economic freedom as an evaluation criterion for the reform process see Kornai (1988).

[4] This was a striking corroboration of North's (1979) stress on 'the inherent instability of all states'. It was also a striking criticism of those who theorize about the state and its role without recognizing the fluctuating territory and transitory nature of all states.

assault by criminals.[5] In some countries, poverty worsened and became a major social evil. Inequality frequently grew rapidly and reached a level many found undesirable. The 'high culture' formerly supported by the state was driven out and replaced by commercial culture, i.e. what many thought of as offensive sex, violence, and loud noises. As the UN Economic Commission for Europe sensibly observed of the situation in 1991–2 (*Survey* 1992: 53):

The abandonment of central planning and the switch to a market economy was generally supported by major groups of the population: workers, farmers, intellectuals. But this broad coalition, which brought about the revolutionary change, contains the seeds of its own destruction. The platform of national unity has essentially been built not on common future goals but rather on common past experience: all coalition groups were dissatisfied and frustrated with their lives under the socialist regime, especially against the backdrop of western consumption standards. Their desire to replace the traditional centrally planned system with the market economy and political democracy stemmed from a firm belief that they would *all* be quickly better off under the market system. But this proved to be *the big illusion*: because the transformation into a market economy includes, *inter alia*, a temporary decline in average standards of living due to a fall of production, and a radical departure from traditional egalitarianism and paternalistic interventionism, some important social groups, like wage-earners and farmers, are bound to lose, not win, at least in the short run.

Furthermore, not only did the liberal revolution have costs which many of its original supporters had not foreseen, but there was also an important potential contradiction between its two chief objectives, a market economy and a democratic political system (Brucan 1992). Given the initial weakness of the capitalist class, the costs of the liberal revolution, the strength of the egalitarian and paternalist legacy, and the absence of strong political parties, in many countries it seemed that only authoritarian methods were likely to establish a firmly based market economy.[6]

2.4. Towards a New Evaluation of the Role of the State

The liberals came to power with the intention of replacing the dominant role of the state under state socialism by a much more limited role for the state. They hoped to 'build capitalism' by establishing market institutions

[5] According to Przeworski (1991: 31) 'democracy does offer one fundamental value that for many groups may be sufficient to prefer it to all alternatives: security from arbitrary violence.' This is a generalization of Latin American experience and is not universally valid. Democracy may lead both to military conflicts on the territory of the former multinational states, and to a huge growth in private violence. It is quite likely that, for the politically conformist, democracy has led to a substantial decrease in security from arbitrary violence in most or all of the transition economies (as also happened to some extent in Spain in the transition from Francoism).

[6] For a discussion of the relationship between the transition to the market and democracy see Przeworski (1991: ch. 4).

(private firms, a free price system, a capital market, free international trade, etc.) and leaving economic development to be determined by these new market institutions. They were hostile to state intervention which exceeded the creation of market institutions. Writers of this school tend to begin from the standard supply-side critique of interventionism and then stress the system-specific inheritance of the transition economies which, in their opinion, makes efficient interventionism even less likely than in the OECD countries. For example, the Russian Hayekian Naishul' (1990) argued that in the USSR the absence of an efficient bureaucracy meant that an efficient economic system in that country required a smaller role for the government than in the USA. In Naishul' (1993a: 40) he argued that 'Russia no longer has efficient bureaucratic organisations and bureaucrats capable of carrying out their duties in a clear, consistent and honest way or, if need be, demanding that the higher authorities change existing regulations . . . That is why the restoration of bureaucratic order in the country can only be achieved if we have a minimum degree of state intervention in the economic sphere and rely on the market to a far greater extent than is the case in the traditional market economies. There should be few laws, which, in turn should be simple and have no exemptions . . . The few bureaucrats should be highly paid . . . Their work should be governed by rules and regulations, as clear-cut and as detailed as military manuals.' Similarly, according to Dabrowski (1992), who was First Deputy Minister of Finance in Poland in 1989–90, in addition to the standard liberal arguments against interventionism in the economy, there are some additional arguments which apply during the transition to a market economy. These are: the danger of continuing the planning mentality inherited from the former system, the danger of benefiting old sectors of the economy at the expense of new ones, the undermining of the possibility of enforcing a hard budget constraint for firms, the negative fiscal effects, and the lack of a good civil service. Hence his conclusion is that '[t]he attempt to use interventionism as a substitute for the market mechanism in the transition period can only delay the end point of the reform process without giving any significant benefits.' A Keynesian-type demand stimulation policy, according to Dabrowski is 'bound to lead to a return of inflation rather than to an increase in output'. The reason for this is that the fall in output is primarily a supply-side problem to be tackled by privatization, free entry, de-monopolization, and free trade. Similarly, Gomulka (1992: 360–1) has contrasted the Keynesian-type and structuralist analyses of the transitional depression and suggested that the depression should be seen as a 'Schumpeterian "creative destruction" phenomenon, similar in type (though larger in scale) to the Western recession of the early 1980s, following the oil shock of 1979'. Similarly Kornai (1993) ascribes the 'unique phenomenon' of 'transformational recession' mainly to supply-side factors. Hence he warns that the countries suffering from this unique problem cannot simply apply expansionary macroeconomic policies of the familiar Keynesian type. They should not 'go back to pursuing an expansionary policy and re-establishing old structures to keep alive loss-making firms and maintain obsolete jobs. They must move forward and continue the parallel processes of destruction and creation, eliminating unprofitable product lines and unproductive jobs while encouraging the evolution of profitable ones.'

Experience soon showed that simply establishing market institutions was often inadequate, given the (unexpected) outcome of liberal policies, the reality of a democratic political system, the economic and institutional structure inherited from the old regime, and the relatively slow adjustment of a market economy to major structural shocks. For Poland, Slay (1993: 23) has noted that, 'By mid-1991 the effects of recession, tight money, and fiscal discrimination against state firms had made the liberals' industrial policy a political and economic nonstarter. This opened the field for other policies.' In Russia, the need for an industry policy was accepted already in the summer of 1992, only about half a year after the liberals had come to power. In the Gaidar government's *Programme for Deepening the Economic Reform* submitted to the Supreme Soviet on 3 July 1992 there is a section on industry policy (*Programme* 1992: 107–17). Shortly afterwards the Russian Ministry of Industry was replaced by a state committee for industrial policy. At the beginning of 1993 the Chernomyrdin government's economic policy attempted to combine three elements, financial-monetary stabilization, privatization, and industrial policy/structural policy (Ellman 1993*a*: 43, *Osnovnye* 1993). It is important to realize that 'industry policy', as that is understood by the Russian Ministry of Defence, is largely concerned with preserving the capacity of Russian industry to produce military equipment and to develop new weapons systems—a fact which is an important part of the context of the Russian debate about 'industry policy', Hence the absence of a coherent Russian industry policy up till now has a very positive aspect from a welfare perspective.[7] In Czechoslovakia, the Prague government's liberal economic policies (which in the Czech lands were popular and successful, but which in Slovakia were less popular) were one of the factors contributing to the breakup of Czechoslovakia.

The need for an active Government policy soon came to be widely accepted, both among academics and international agencies. Abel and Bonin (1993) criticized the Hungarian government for 'state desertion'.

---

[7] In 1993 a debate took place in Russian government circles about economic restructuring. One group argued in favour of 'industry policy', i.e. a policy of state support (in particular, credits, orders, and protection) for industry carried out by one or more of the central economic agencies, having an important military component and having much in common with traditional central economic management. Another group argued in favour of regional restructuring funds, partly financed from abroad and partly managed by foreign fund managers, which would finance some of the investment needed to adapt the newly privatized enterprises to compete at home and abroad. (This would be analogous to the activities of the regional development bodies which exist in many West European countries.) The outcome of this debate was unclear at the time of writing.

They defined this as an abrupt and discontinuous decrease in the state's involvement in any particular sector of the economy. They argued, on the basis of the experience of Hungary's financial sector, that state desertion may be dysfunctional. Similarly, Kornai (1993: 4) argued that, 'Hungary and other transition economies cannot rely exclusively on market forces. Private business and the market are still weak, and these countries would likely suffer low-level economic activity and high unemployment—in a word stagnation. Governments must therefore provide carefully designed recovery packages. These programs must not generate further inflation by injecting more money in the economy; rather they must focus on stimulating private investment.' An important reason for this change in emphasis in Kornai's thinking was to placate the population and prevent popular dissatisfaction with poor economic performance derailing the whole liberal project.

The need for at any rate some minimum programmes of transfer payments (a 'safety net') to protect defendants (the old, invalids, and the sick) and the victims of liberalization (the unemployed) has long been a part of IMF orthodoxy. The importance of this in preserving social stability and legitimizing the new social order has recently been argued, in an essentially Bismarckian way but in Hegelian-Marxist terminology, by Williams and Reuten (1992).

Similarly, IMF staff economists with experience of the post-Soviet economies soon came to see that there is a transition-specific additional task for government that would not exist in a pure market economy. This is to restructure the large state enterprise sector. In 1993 Peter Isard of the IMF research department argued (IMF 1993: 11) that '[i]n transforming the large state enterprise sector, government has to play a fundamental role . . . unless government is able to become involved and take an active interest in getting other people involved in dealing with the large state enterprise sector early, the transformation process is going to be very difficult indeed.'

Naturally, the re-evaluation of the role of the state is likely to lead to significant institutional differences between countries (such as exist between OECD countries). Countries differ, in position in the transition process, size, importance and attitudes of organized labour and capital, existence and role of dominant religious community, economic success and level of economic development, and relationship to the world market. Furthermore, states differ with respect to the extent to which they meet the conditions for the state to intervene efficiently in the economy.

2.5. Conditions for Efficient Interventionism

Economists, in particular those from the OECD countries, who discuss the role of the state in the post-socialist countries, often make the hidden assumption that these countries have major possibilities for autonomous policy-making. They are analysed as if they were large OECD countries (e.g. Japan, the UK) with effective institutions and a wide array of instruments to achieve their objectives. Such economists pay little attention to the prior question of whether there exist in the countries concerned real possibilities for effective state action, since in their own country such possibilities were created a long time ago and need no discussion today.

Skocpol (1985: 16–17) has listed three preconditions for the state's ability to implement its policies. They are: sovereign integrity, that is, stable administrative–military control over a given territory, adequate financial resources, and loyal and skilled officials. With respect to these three preconditions, the situation varies sharply between the transition economies.

Some of them, such as Bosnia-Herzegovina, Moldova, and Russia do not have control over the whole of the territory which they purport to rule. This greatly reduces the possibility for the state to implement economic policy. For example, Yugoslavia introduced shock therapy in December 1989 to stabilize the economy. Although initially quite successful (in May and June 1990 the monthly inflation rate fell to 0% and the reduction in inflation between 1989 and 1990 was much greater in Yugoslavia than in Poland), and supported by the IMF, this programme collapsed within a year and a half since the Yugoslav federal government, which introduced it, did not have control of Yugoslavia.[8] The constituent republics refused to accept the programme and its consequences and were stronger than the federal government (*Survey* 1991: 138).[9] In April 1990 the IMF concluded that (*Survey* 1990: 127) ' . . . Yugoslavia's prospects for noninflationary growth in the medium run, with external viability, appear to be good.' In fact, however, due to the lack of control by the Yugoslav federal state over Yugoslavia, this stabilization programme was a failure.

Others, such as Poland, Hungary, Romania, and Bulgaria do have control over their national territory. These are states with a long tradition and in some cases (Poland, Hungary) are ethnically quite homogeneous. Hence the Polish government, which launched its shock therapy at almost the

---

[8] For the Slovene economist Zizmond (1992) the lesson to be drawn from the failure of shock therapy in Yugoslavia is not that the weakness of the central government had harmful economic effects, but that the harmful policies of the central government damaged the economies of the republics. He argues (Zizmond 1992: 108–9) that the 1990 Yugoslav policies 'failed' because of mistaken fiscal, incomes, and monetary policies by the Yugoslav authorities. This ignores the fact that in 1990, considered from the point of view of inflation control, the Yugoslav shock therapy was much more effective than the Polish one. (Yugoslav inflation fell from 2,700% in 1989 to 122% in 1990, whereas Polish inflation only fell from 640% to 250%.) Naturally this successful policy led to a decline in production in Slovenia (and elsewhere in Yugoslavia) but the subsequent Slovene policy of independence also led to a decline in production in Slovenia.

[9] e.g. in December 1990 it emerged that the Serbian national bank, on instructions from the Serbian government, had granted credits for $1.8 billion to finance wages and pensions in Serbia in order to buy support in the republican elections, in defiance of the restrictive credit policy of the Yugoslav central bank. Under such conditions, effective monetary restraint by the Yugoslav authorities was impossible.

same time as the Yugoslav one, *was* able to implement it and attain such important objectives as the abolition of shortages and a sharp reduction of inflation.[10] Naturally, the effectiveness in achieving economic policy goals of states still at the stage of state-forming under difficult initial conditions (e.g. Serbia/Federal Republic of Yugoslavia, Russia) is likely to be less than in long-standing states with stable borders and control over the whole of the national territory. Many of the new states are likely to experience a long and complex process of state formation. This may often involve military conflicts.

As far as finances are concerned, the situation also varies between the transition economies. Nevertheless, they share the fiscal problems described by Kornai (1992a). They are suffering from a major depression, which naturally has negative fiscal effects. They are giving up what was previously their main source of revenue (control over the state-owned enterprises). In addition they are encouraging the rapid growth of an economic sector (the private sector) whose willingness to pay taxes is much lower, and whose ability to evade them is much higher, than the state-owned sector it is replacing. Accordingly, all the post-socialist economies will find lack of financial resources constraining their ability to achieve economic policy goals. Furthermore, this lack of money, combined with the wish to attain cerain social and economic goals (e.g. to provide pensions and other social benefits, or to subsidize industry) may generate actions (such as large-scale monetary financing of the budget dificit) which have a very negative effect on economic development (e.g. by causing very high inflation).

One of the system-specific inheritances of the transition economies, to which liberal writers such as Naishul' and Dabrowksi correctly drew attention, is the lack of an efficient bureaucracy which can implement the measures required. There are four reasons for this. *First*, many of the more able officials have left state service to enjoy the higher salaries and possibilities for enrichment offered by the new private sector. Similarly, the ablest young people naturally strive to make the best of the glittering prizes held out to the successful by the private sector, rather than enter the poorly paid and non-prestigous public service. *Secondly*, the measures required are new for the countries concerned and officials have no or very limited experience in implementing them. Their expereience is of the *ancien régime* and a type of intervention which contributed to permanent backwardness. For example, a major need is to stimulate investment. This will often be private or foreign investment. The design of effective measures to stimulate private investment, however, is an area in which the countries concerned have little experience since their private sectors are so recent. *Thirdly*, the

[10] For a comparison of the Yugoslav and Polish shock therapies see Coricelli and Rocha (1991). For another discussion of the Yugoslav shock therapy in comparative perspective see Koldko, Gotz-Kozierkiewicz, and Skrzeszewska-Paczek (1992: ch. 3).

human and institutional inheritance makes 'normal' market behaviour less likely than in long-standing market economies. For example, many wealthy private individuals and businesses may be reluctant to invest in productive activities in view of the depression, the rapid inflation, the general uncertainties, such as the lack of demonstrable and unambiguous property rights because of the absence of a registration system for real estate ownership, and the superior attractions of arbitrage or Western bank accounts. Hence effective policy packages have to take account of the specific institutional environment in which they have to operate. *Fourthly*, the apparatus inherited from the old regime is unsuitable to implement the appropriate policies. As Fehér, Heller, and Márkus (1983: 107) sensibly argued, the party–state officials of the old regime 'cannot be conceived as bureaucracy in the proper, narrowly Weberian sense of the word'. Furthermore, many of its features, such as servility, negative selection of cadres, priority of obedience and political loyalty over professional competence and ability, and corruption are positively harmful from the standpoint of implementing effective economic policies. Hence a major aspect of policy in the transition economies must be to train and promote to high positions capable officials who are able to implement a policy of supply-side economic stimulation. Another aspect must be to take vigorous measures to stamp out corruption (e.g. by paying decent salaries and by eliminating the scope for administrative discretion in awarding lucrative licences/quotas, e.g. by eliminating the licence/quota system where possible). 'Replacing the old officialdom with an efficient civil service' (Ellman 1993b: 17) is in fact one of the most important, and difficult, measures of institutional change in the transition process. Efficient interventionist measures should take account of the capabilities of the officials who will administer them and should not assume the existence of an efficient and incorrupt bureaucracy where this is manifestly not the case.[11] Training a new bureaucracy, eliminating superfluous bureaux, creating necessary new ones, and effectively relating central and local bureaux are key issues in an effective transition.[12]

Given the financial situation and the actually existing bureaucratic apparatus, the absence of state policies to restructure the economy may be a positive development. Csaba (1992: 954), in a discussion of Hungary's 'Italian' path of development, has argued that 'the lack of a "clearly defined industrial policy" or a "clearly defined agricultural policy" etc. is a strong

---

[11] On a recent visit to Washington DC, the chairman of the economic reform committee of the Moscow regional soviet was asked to which level (central, regional, municipal, etc.) of the Russian bureaucracy aid should be sent. He replied that no aid should be given to any level of the Russian bureaucracy. 'Russian bureaucracy is bad bureaucracy at all levels. Any method [of distributing aid] that deals with the Russian bureaucracy is a bad method.' Rather than distribute aid within Russia, he recommended that the US government sponsor risk insurance for American businessmen who seek to invest in Russia. Any risk insurance agency, he emphasized, should be directed from the United States (*Meeting Report*, Kennan Institute for Advanced Russian Studies, 10/14).

[12] For a discussion of the attempt to establish a Russian civil service, see Yasmann (1993).

point rather than a weak point in the Hungarian context, as blueprints of individual ministries would never add up to an integrated concept, whereas their disregard for financial consequences is notorious indeed.'

The transition economies often lack, at any rate at the beginning, other important institutions necessary for pursuing an effective economic policy. For example, the liberal ministers who were appointed to head the economic ministries in Russia in November 1991 took over economic policy in a country which had neither a national currency nor effective customs frontiers. This naturally gravely limited the possibilities of monetary and trade policy. Other transition economies (e.g. Estonia) have voluntarily abandoned—at any rate initially—the possibility of implementing both monetary and exchange-rate policies, by introducing a currency board system.[13] In this way they hope to attain the important policy goals of reducing inflation and restoring macroeconomic stability. In many countries the initial lack of strong political parties created major difficulties in uniting the various components of the state apparatus (e.g. president, government, parliament) round a coherent economic policy which could be implemented over a prolonged period of time. In all the post-socialist economies the autonomy of the state is limited by the need to take account of the wishes of external creditors and their organizations (e.g. the IMF, the international capital market). In some cases, the latter play a major role in policy formulation. The autonomy of the state is also constrained by the wish of many of the transition economies to join various economic organizations (GATT, the EC) which have rules about what is, and what is not, acceptable economic behaviour. Even established market economies are constrained in their actions by the growing international economic integration (Smith 1986). In many of the transition economies the possibility of pursuing independent national policies is limited because the countries are small open economies and the usual limitations of national policy-making in small open economies (Katzenstein 1985) apply to them.

Moreover, all the post-socialist countries inherit from the previous regime substantial scepticism by the public and by intellectuals about state activities. Hence, at any rate initially, the legacy of state failure prevents imitation of the active role played by the state in East Asian development. It is well known that in East Asia an active state development policy has played a major role in stimulating the economy and gradually creating the conditions for a market economy. Drawing on the experience of Taiwan, Li (1988: 104) argues that, rather than seeing the market as a packet of institutions which can be introduced comprehensively and suddenly, '[a]

---

[13] The monetary system introduced in Estonia in 1992 is usually referred to as a currency board system since the intention (and apparently also the practice up till now) is that the domestic money will always be 100% backed by foreign currency. If, however, a 'currency board system' is defined so as to include the requirement that the currency concerned also has unlimited convertibility for current and capital account transactions, then the Estonian system is not a currency board system (Hanke, Jonung, and Schuler 1993).

free market is not a given in the social calculus. It must be constructed, slowly, through a process of changes in policy focus.' The legacy of state failure, combined with the wish to 'join Europe' made repetition of this experience impossible. As Przeworski (1991: 159) has noted, 'In several capitalist countries in which private entrepreneurship was feeble—Brazil, France, Mexico, South Korea—the state not only led the accumulation of capital but in time created a local bourgeoisie. Eastern European countries have no local bourgeoisie, and the prevailing mood is so radically antistatist that the state cannot play the same role in the near future.' Similarly, Kornai (1992a: 13–14) has observed that, 'The suspicion, indifference and even antagonistic feelings towards the state which are very prevalent among citizens are a legacy from the old order. A sizable part of the population does not consider tax evasion to be immoral. For a long time it was a form of civil courage to defy the state, and that attitude cannot be altered by ceremonial pronouncements alone. Experience has to prove that the state will be a good steward of the taxpayers' money; it must win the public's trust by its actions.'

Hence it can be seen that there are a substantial number of important factors, such as lack of sovereign integrity (in some cases), shortage of money, lack of a suitable bureaucratic apparatus, lack of the necessary institutions or the voluntary adoption of certain institutions, pressure from creditors, the rules established by international organizations, the general constraints faced by small open economies (in many cases), and the relations between the state and its citizens that greatly limit the possibility open to the state to pursue independent policies.

3. CONCLUSION

The failure of state socialism is a dramatic and very important state failure. This failure is a striking demonstration that the category of state failure is not an empty economic box but an important part of reality. This state failure led to liberal revolutions. Most of the liberal revolutionaries argued for—and attempted to institute—a strong state which would construct a market economy. The need to 'build capitalism' created a number of transition-specific tasks for the state. It also led to a potential contradiction between the two chief objectives of the liberal revolution, a market economy and a democratic political system. Experience soon showed the inadequacy for the transition economies of confining the role of the state to that of establishing market institutions. The precise functions of the state in the transition period, and in particular the extent to which it should be responsible for restructuring the economy, overcoming the depression, and social integration, gave rise to a lively debate. Effective state action, however, requires the existence of a number of preconditions. The most important of these are sovereign integrity, adequate financial resources, an effective bureaucracy which is capable of implementing efficient economic policy in a market economy and liberal democratic polity. Establishing these preconditions, however, is not easy, given the system-specific inheritance of the transition economies and the need for a long and complex process of state-forming in the successor states which frequently involves military conflicts. The possibilities of effective state action vary considerably between the post-socialist countries. Where the preconditions were lacking (as in the former Yugoslavia) realization of the liberal project was impossible. The outcome of the liberal revolutions of 1989–93, like that of the liberal revolutions of 1848, is likely to be a spectrum of roles for the state, differing between countries, depending on structural and conjunctural factors.

REFERENCES

ABEL, I. and BONIN, J. P. (1993). 'State Desertion and Convertibility: The Case of Hungary', in D. Newbery and I. P. Szekely (eds.), *Hungary: An Economy in Transition.* Cambridge: Cambridge University Press.

BAUER, T. (1991). 'Building Capitalism in Hungary', mimeo., IRSES, Paris.

BRUCAN, S. (1992). 'Democracy at Odds with the Market in Post-Communist Societies', in M. Keren and G. Ofer (eds.), *Trials of Transition.* Boulder, Colo.: Westview.

BRUS, W. (1992). 'Marketization and Democratization: The Sino-Soviet divergence', working paper no. 63. Stockholm Institute of Soviet and East European Economics.

BUKHARIN, N. I. (1920). *Ekonomika perekhodnogo perioda.* Moscow.

CORICELLI, F. and ROCHA, R. R. (1991). 'A Comparative Analysis of the Polish and Yugoslav Programmes', in P. Marer and S. Zecchini (eds.), *The Transition to a Market Economy,* ii. Paris: OECD.

CORNFORD, J. (ed.) (1975). *The Failure of the State.* London: Croom Helm.

CROUCH, C. (1986). 'Sharing Public Space: States and Organized Interests in Western Europe', in J. A. Hall (ed.), *States in History.* Oxford: Blackwell.

CSABA, L. (1992). 'Macroeconomic Policy in Hungary: Poetry versus Reality,' *Soviet Studies,* 44/6.

DABROWSKI, M. (1992). 'Interventionist Pressures on a Policy Maker during the Transition to Economic Freedom (Personal Experience)', *Communist Economies and Economic Transformation,* 4/1.

ELLMAN, M. (1993a). 'Russia: The Economic Program of the Civic Union', *RFE/RL Research Report,* 2/11 (12 Mar.).

—— (1993b). 'General Aspects of Transition', in M. Ellman, E. Gaidar, and G. Kolodko (eds.), *Economic Transition in Eastern Europe.* Oxford: Blackwell.

—— and KONTOROVICH, V., 'Overview', in M. Ellman and V. Kontorovich (eds.) (1992). *The Disintegration of the Soviet Economic System*. London and New York: Routledge.

FEHÉR, F., HELLER, A., and MÁRKUS, G. (1983). *Dictatorship over Needs*. Oxford: Blackwell.

GERSCHENKRON, A. (1962). *Economic Backwardness in Historical Perspective*. Cambridge, Mass.: Harvard University Press.

GOMULKA, S. (1992). 'Polish Economic Reform, 1990–91: Principles, Policies and Outcomes', *Cambridge Journal of Economics*, 16/3.

HANKE, S., JONUNG, L., and SCHULER, K. (1993). 'Estonia: It's Not a Currency Board System!', *Transition* (Feb.).

IMF (1993). *IMF Survey* (11 Jan.).

JOHNSON, C. (1982). *MITI and the Japanese Miracle: The Growth of Industrial Policy 1925–1975*. Stanford, Calif.: Stanford University Press.

KATZENSTEIN, P. (1985). *Small States in World Markets: Industrial Policy in Europe*. Ithaca, NY; Cornell University Press

KOLODKO, G. W., GOTZ-KOZIERKIEWICZ, D., and SKRZESZEWSKA-PACZEK, E. (1992). *Hyperinflation and Stabilization in Postsocialist Economies*. Boston: Kluwer.

KORNAI, J. (1988). 'Individual Freedom and Reform of the Socialist Economy', *European Economic Review*, 32/2–3 (Mar.).

—— (1990). *The Road to a Free Economy*. New York and London: Norton.

—— (1992*a*). 'The Postsocialist Transition and the State: Reflections in the Light of Hungarian Fiscal Problems, *American Economic Review*, Papers and Proceedings, 82/2 (May).

—— (1992*b*) *The Socialist System*. Oxford: Oxford University Press.

—— (1993). 'Anti-Depression Cure for Ailing Postcommunist Economies', *Transition*, 4.1 Washington, DC: World Bank.

LI, K. T. (1988). *The Evolution of Policy behind Taiwan's Development Success*. New Haven: Yale University Press.

LIH, L. T. (1990). *Bread and Authority in Russia, 1914–1921*. Berkeley: University of California Press.

MARX, K. and ENGELS, F. (1975 edn.). *Collected Works* iii. London: Lawrence & Wishart.

NAISHUL', V. (1990). 'Will the Soviet Economy be able to stay Left of the American?' *Communist Economies*, 2/4.

—— (1993*a*) 'Liberalism, Customary Rights and Economic Reforms', *Communist Economies and Economic Transformation*, 5/1.

—— (1993*b*) 'Perspectives of Economic Reforms', paper presented at Conference on the economic transformation in Russia, Stockholm School of Economics, 14–15 June.

NORTH, D. C. (1979) 'A Framework for Analyzing the State in Economic History', *Explorations in Economic History*, 16.

Osnovnve (1993). 'Osnovnye polozheniya i kriterii gosudarstvennoi selektivnoi strukturnoi politiki v 1993 godu', *Rossiiskie vesti* (4 May).

PEACOCK, A. T. (1980) 'On the Anatomy of Collective Failure', *Public Finance*, 35.

PROGRAMME (1992). 'Programma uglubleniya ekonomicheskikh reform', *Voprosy ekonomiki*, 8.

PRZEWORSKI, A. (1991). *Democracy and the Market*. Cambridge: Cambridge University Press.

SKOCPOL, T. (1985). 'Bringing the State Back In: Strategies of Analysis in Current Research', in P. B. Evans, D. Rueschemeyer, and T. Skocpol (eds.), *Bringing the State Back In*. Cambridge: Cambridge University Press.

SLAY, B. (1993). 'Evolution of Industrial Policy in Poland since 1989', *RFE/RL Research Report*, 2/2 (8 Jan.).

SMITH, R. (1986). 'Britain and the International State Apparatus', in P. Nolan and S. Paine (eds.), *Rethinking Socialist Economics*. Cambridge: Polity Press.

STIGLITZ, J. (1989). 'On the Economic Role of the State', in J. Stiglitz *et al.*, *The Economic Role of The State* (ed. A. Heertje). Amsterdam and Oxford: Blackwell.

SURVEY (1990). 'Yugoslavia Launches Bold Reforms to Combat Hyper-Inflation', *IMF Survey* (16 Apr.).

SURVEY (1991). *Economic Survey of Europe in 1990–1991*. New York: UN.

SURVEY (1992). *Economic Survey of Europe in 1991–1992*. New York: UN.

WILLIAMS, M. and Reuten, G. (1992). 'After the Rectifying Revolution: The Contradictions of the Mixed Economy?', *Capital & Class*, 49.

WOLF, C. Jr. (1979). 'A Theory of Nonmarket Failure: Framework for Implementation Analysis', *Journal of Law and Economics*, 22/1.

WOJTYNA, A. (1992). 'In Search of a New Economic Role for the State in the Post-Socialist Countries', in W. Blaas and J. Foster (eds.), *Mixed Economies in Europe*. Aldershot: Edward Elgar.

YASMANN, V. (1993). 'The Russian Civil Service: Corruption and Reform', *RFE/RL Research Report*, 2/16 (16 Apr.).

YAVLINSKY, G. (1993). 'Vmesto referenduma nuzhen vremennyi konstitutsionnyi akt', *Izvestiya*, 33 (20 Feb.), 8.

ZIZMOND, E. (1992). 'The Collapse of the Yugoslav Economy', *Soviet Studies*, 44/1.

10

Politics, Planning, and the Transition from Stalinism: The Case of China

Peter Nolan

The way out of the present problems lies not in giving up planning but in giving it new content (Chakravarty 1987: vii).

INTRODUCTION

After the collapse of communism in Eastern Europe and subsequently in the USSR, the conventional wisdom about economic and political reform was initially simplistic. Political democratization and economic liberalization were widely regarded as recipes for prosperity. This reflected the mainstream, neo-liberal political and economic thinking in the West in the 1980s.

The leading international institutions, especially the IMF, drew on their experience in 'stabilization' and associated 'liberalization' programmes to argue for rapid moves towards a market economy and a greatly reduced role for the state in the economy. Moreover, in large areas of the developing world, the condition for economic aid had come to include political democratization. The attitudes of Western governments were not homogeneous. However, domestic political pressures meant that mostly they were not interested in assisting the former communist countries to turn themselves into competitor industrial powerhouses. The advanced economies in the late 1980s faced large problems in coping with the structural adjustment consequent upon the explosive growth in newly industrializing countries, especially, but not exclusively, those of capitalist East Asia. It was unrealistic to imagine that the OECD countries could make their goal in assisting reform of the Centrally Planned Economies (CPEs) the creation of a powerful state which would lead the industrialization process in the fashion of the Meiji Japanese government, or subsequently, the government of Taiwan, South Korea, or Singapore. Their goal was a more neutral one of assisting the former CPEs to create a framework of property rights and accompanying law, producing an environment in which private enterprise could flourish, and from which their own economies also might benefit

I am grateful to the editors of this volume, Ha-Joon Chang and Bob Rowthorn, as well as to my colleague Geoff Harcourt, for their comments.

through increased trade and capital flows. Of course, many Western experts did indeed believe that a free market environment with a minimal role for the state would produce the most rapid pace of economic advance.

The leaders of the former communist countries were extremely hostile to the notion of 'planning', which they identified with their own experiences under the Stalinist 'administered' economy. Leadership attitudes in these countries arose from a deep-rooted hostility to the politics of a strong state and from a shattering crisis of intellectual confidence, which led the policy-makers to turn to 'Western' expertise for advice and intellectual inspiration. This was expressed dramatically by Janos Kornai:

[My approach to reform is that of] liberal thought (using the term 'liberal' in accordance with its European tradition). Respect for autonomy and self-determi-nation, for the rights of the individual, is its focus . . . [I]t advocates a narrowed scope for state activities. It recommends that citizens stand on their own feet, and rely on their own power and initiative. Perhaps the role of the government will be reconsidered at a later stage. *But right now, in the beginning of the transformation process, . . . it is time to take great steps away in the direction of a minimal state.* Perhaps later generations will be able to envisage a more moderate midway.' (Kornai 1990: 22) (My emphasis, P.N.)

The experience of China (and, indeed, that of almost all the Asian former Stalinist countries) calls into question these initial crude propositions about the transformation from Stalinist political economy. The Communist Party has remained in power. This authoritarian, nationalist state may well have provided a better opportunity successfully to build a powerful economy than the overthrow of the Communist Party would have done. The contrast between China's experience and that of Eastern Europe and the former USSR raises profound ethical and philosophical issues about the relation-ship between the rights of individuals and their duties towards enabling the attainment of common goals of the community or nation.

This chapter analyses the striking economic success that China has achieved since the mid-1970s. It argues that this is, in part, due to special factors that cannot be replicated elsewhere. However, to a considerable degree it is due to a comprehensive, experimental approach to political economy in a time of rapid structural change that does indeed have lessons for the other former CPEs. This chapter argues that the reforming former Stalinist economies need to re-understand the economic function of the state, shifting from the crude formulations of Stalinist 'planning' (in reality 'administration' rather than true planning) towards a renewed vision of planning which views its economic function as a creative interaction with the market to produce instrumental interference towards goals which can-not be precisely predicted because they release the creative power of mar-kets, but shape and guide the setting within which market forces operate. The former Stalinist economies should be reflecting on the reasons why some economies are so much better than others at instrumental intervention. They should seek to understand why state intervention often is corrupt and wasteful, but sometimes is strikingly successful.

The careful analysis in recent years of the reasons for rapid growth in the Asian Newly Industrializing Countries has contributed to a rethinking of the role of the state in economic development. The huge contrast between the outcomes in Eastern Europe and Russia on the one hand, and the Asian CPEs, China in particular, will provide further large impetus to this process. It is likely that economics will become much more sensitive to the importance and complexities of the role of the state.

1. POLICY ENVIRONMENT

1.1. Politics

From Totalitarianism to Authoritarianism

Despite maintaining a monopoly of control over political life, and tightly controlling the boundaries of freedom, a large range of socio-economic decisions was removed from the direct control of Party administrators. China's development strategy moved closer to that of Taiwan and South Korea in the 1960s and 1970s, than to China under Mao or the USSR pre-Gorbachev. The 1980s saw a clash between two different forms of 'new authoritarianism' in Chinese politics. One branch saw this as the vehicle to lead forward towards a rapid transition to a free enterpise economy based on privatization of assets, the 'hard state' being necessary to enable the beneficiaries from this process to control mass discontent at the uncertainty, unemployment, and inequality it produced. However, the view of the most powerful of China's leaders was that authoritarianism enabled the government to have a controlled move towards a market economy: economic change and popular consciousness could move forward in some sort of balance, with 'social tolerance' for change given a high weight; 'fairness' (*gongping*) and maintenance of living standards for the bottom segments of society could be sustained.

Political Stability

Economic life disintegrates without political stability. Neither foreign nor domestic investors have confidence. If politics is unstable, the state apparatus will be less able to guide economic development. The Chinese pro-democracy movement in the 1980s disagreed that a rapid move towards democratic institutions might produce *da luan*—great disorder. Table 10.1 suggests the different paths that China's politics might have taken in the late 1980s and early 1990s, their relative likelihood and desirability. The

Table 10.1 Alternative scenarios for China's politics in the 1990s

Possibilities	Desirability (rank)	Likelihood (rank)
(1) Overthrow of the CCP		
(a) Great turmoil (*da luan*)	Extremely undesirable (4)	Quite likely (2)
(b) Populist indecision	Very undesirable (3)	Quite likely (2)
(c) Purposive, reforming, democratically elected government	Extremely desirable (1)	Very unlikely (4)
(2) CCP remains in power		
(a) Indefinite quasi-Stalinism	Very undesirable (3)	Unlikely (3)
(b) Rational, secular, reforming authoritarianism	Desirable (2)	Very likely (1)

risks attached to pushing for rapid growth of democracy in China are high. Even though option 1(c) is much the most desirable this is not a likely outcome. The initial post-communist experience of the advanced Eastern European countries suggests that the likely outcome of an attempt to establish a Western-style democracy in China is much more likely to be 1(b) than 1(c). Indeed, for China, 1(a) is at least as likely an outcome as 1(b), with a sustained period of poltical turmoil, which one might loosely call the 'South-Eastern European' path to post-Stalinist political evolution. With successful economic development, it is inconceivable that widespread popular pressure would not in time push the system towards a firmly rooted democracy based upon high levels of income and all the associated cultural attributes.

In the 1980s, despite growing international and domestic pressure from liberal reformers, the Communist Party retained a firm grip on its monopoly of political power. He Xin's comments reflect the dominant view among China's leaders: 'Is it feasible to transplant [American-style democracy] into China? . . . If practised in China, this type of system would result in the creation of a politically weak, lax government, unable to unite the nation. Can such a 'feeble' government resolve the current complicated and tough social problems in China? Can it prevent internal strife and the country from dividing? . . . If the [Chinese Communist] Party was terminated now, China would be thrown into serious political chaos and there would be no unity of the people. This would bring certain disaster to China' (He 1990). China's elderly leaders consistently talked of China as analogous to a 'sheet of loose sand', which had a high propensity to lapse into the kind of political anarchy that had existed over much of the country for most of the late nineteenth and early twentieth century.

Professionalization of the Bureaucracy

The attempt to modernize the bureaucracy began early in the post-Mao period, spearheaded by Deng Xiaoping,[1] to create a professional bureaucracy. The intention was to dismiss into retirement the old guard of party officials in the government administration who did not possess high technical qualifications. This effort parallels those of Bismarckian Germany and Meiji Japan in the late nineteenth century, or Taiwan and South Korea in the 1950s, in which a key point of the modernization drive was the creation of a professional government administration which was responsible to an unelected executive authority rather than to an elected parliament. Slow, but important progress was made in the 1980s: '[T]he speed of organizational turnover, and the relative ease with which it has occurred, has been impressive. . . . [T]he Chinese bureaucracy now has a greater ability and willingness to bring technical competence to bear on competing policy alternatives' (Harding 1987: 208–9).[2] However, China in the 1980s remained a one party state, with the CCP (Chinese Communist Party) firmly in control of political life. The challenge to its authority in Tiananmen Square was repressed brutally.

Decentralization

China is a huge country, and there are large problems in trying to coordinate planning decisions from a central authority. The decentralization of important aspects of economic decision-making to lower levels of government has made a large contribution to improved economic performance. Self-evidently, local governments have much closer knowledge of local conditions than do central planners. Under appropriate revenue-sharing arrangements, they have a strong incentive to improve the performance of the economy over which they have responsibility. China's reforms in this sphere were broadly successful: 'Local government objectives are to enhance their revenue base and to develop an investment strategy that will foster growth. Both can be met by developing profitable industries' (World Bank 1990: 95).

1.2. Economics

Economic Ideology

In the 1980s China's policy-makers shifted decisively away from the Stalinist model. However, the Chinese leadership insisted upon a powerful role for the state in guiding market forces. Unlike their Eastern European

---

[1] The need to professionalize, reduce in size, and make more youthful China's government bureaucracy was a central theme of Deng's speeches in the early 1980s (Deng 1984).

[2] Harding (Harding 1987: 204–11) provides a careful account of the large increase in the proportion of technically qualified bureaucrats and the substantial decline in their average age during the early/mid-1980s.

counterparts in the wake of the anti-Stalinist revolutions of 1989, the Chinese leadership in the 1980s was deeply interested both in investigating the ways in which market forces could improve the functioning of their economy as well as in learning from the planning experience of Japan and the East Asian Newly Industrializing Countries. Few people in China, even among its leaders, now believe that a non-market economy is a feasible way to bring prosperity to any society.

Price Reform

By the mid-1980s, the Chinese government came to the conclusion that price reform was 'the key to the reform of the entire economic structure' (Central Committee 1984: 684). However, social stability was given a high priority. The government resolved to proceed cautiously since 'the reform of the price system affects every household and the national economy' (Central Committee 1984: 684).[3] Moreover, it was regarded as dangerous to conduct sweeping price reform before enterprises were accustomed to operating in a competitive market environment. The two reforms had to be synchronized.

After much internal debate and considerable advice to reform prices rapidly, the government decided to do so only gradually and in a controlled fashion. The method adopted to move relative prices towards market-determined prices was the dual-track system, with the proportion sold at free or floating prices gradually expanding in relation to those sold at state-fixed prices, and with the latter gradually moving towards the former. In the late 1970s virtually all prices were directly controlled by the state. By the mid-1980s there had been a large growth in the role of free markets, but even by 1990 it was still the case that no more than around one-half of the value of marketed goods was sold at free market prices (Table 10.2).

Agriculture

The institutional structure of post-Mao agriculture in China strongly re-sembled the modern 'Japanese' path in its balance between activities under-taken by individual households and those undertaken by the collective or the state. The Chinese government, through the Communist Party, re-mained substantially in control of the de-collectivization of farmland in the early 1980s. Equity considerations were paramount, with locally equal per capita distribution of land use as the dominant form. This egalitarian land

---

[3] 'There is much confusion in our present system of pricing . . . This irrational price system has to be reformed . . . otherwise it will be impossible to assess correctly the performance of enterprises . . . As the reform of the price system affects every household and the national economy as a whole, we must be extremely prudent, formulate a well-conceived, feasible programme based on the growth of production and capability of the state's finances and on the premise that the people's real income will gradually be increased, and then carry it out in a planned and systematic way' (Central Committee 1984: 683).

Table 10.2 Proportion of products sold at different types of prices (%)

	1978	1986	1990
Share of total retail sales sold at:			
state-controlled prices	97	n.a.	29.7
state-guided prices	0	n.a.	17.2
market-regulated prices	3	n.a.	53.1
Share of total sales of agricultural products sold by farmers at:			
state-controlled prices	94.4	37	25.2
state-guided prices	0	n.a.	22.6
market-regulated prices	5.6	n.a.	52.2
Share of ex-factory means of production for industrial use sold at:			
state-controlled prices	100	64	44.4
state-guided prices	0	23	18.8
market-regulated prices	0	13	36.8

Source: Li 1992: 17, and Tian 1990: 143.

reform tended greatly to increase socio-economic stability. It provided an asset which gave security to the weakest members of the village. It made public action easier to organize, since villagers shared a common relationship to the principal means of production. It provided a hugely egalitarian underpinning to rural, and indeed national, income distribution. Land ownership remained firmly in the hands of the village government, despite urgings from many economists that land ownership should be truly privatized. Community land provided an important basis of local government power. The terms on which land is used is determined by the community's government, and it is within the community's power to obtain more or less of the rental income for itself to be used for community purposes, whereas under a private-ownership, free-market system the rental income would accrue to private landlords. In so far as the need for land concentration develops, this should be realizable with the community acting as the landlord.

There were only small risks for Chinese peasants in de-collectivization. The managerial aspects of the new arrangements were simply an extension of the work already undertaken on the private plot: most farm work was unmechanized.

Despite rapid growth in the role of individual households, collective and local state activity remained a fundamentally important component of rural capital accumulation. Indeed, alongside the growth of individual households' accumulation went a large absolute growth in input provision by village (*cun*), township (*xiangzhen*), and co-operating households, providing inputs that were beyond the capacity of individual households.[4]

In most poor countries a large part of the rural population relies on informal, high-interest credit, thereby inhibiting the level of investment, especially among poorer but potentially efficient farmers, as well as making poor people dependent upon traditional money lenders. In the 1980s Chinese peasants saved roughly 13–15 per cent of their current income (ZGT JNJ 1990: 312), which resulted in a rapid increase in accumulated savings. This was deposited mainly in official institutions, notably the credit co-operatives and the Agricultural Bank. These institutions provided security, and 'usury' was still discouraged. A massive growth of institutional credit occurred in rural China in the 1980s with outstanding loans per peasant from the two institutions together increasing fourfold in real terms from 1980 to 1988 (ZGNCT JNJ 1989: 293–5).[5]

China feeds around 24 per cent of the world's population from just 7 per cent of the world's arable land. In the long term there is little doubt that it will be to China's advantage to import much larger amounts of land-intensive farm produce than it does at present. However, there are large risks involved in greater integration with world food markets, especially for a country of China's size and income level. If China was much more dependent upon world markets for its food supplies and some exogenous shock sharply reduced its ability to import foodstuffs, the results would be catastrophic. Until China can be confident of access to the main markets for its manufactured exports and of the state of world grain markets, it would be unwise to progress too far towards organizing its international food trade along the lines of comparative advantage.

Although in the 1980s private trade in farm produce was legalized, an important part of farm produce remained under compulsory procurement, notably a large share of grain, cotton, and edible oil marketings. Moreover, the state and the quasi-state 'supply and marketing co-ops', remained the dominant channel for the sale of farm inputs, which provided an important channel of control through which rural cadres could exercise sanctions over peasants in order to induce compliance with policies which were in the interests of the wider local or national community.

State Industry

China's reforms of state industry in the 1980s were cautious and experimental. A large body of informed opinion considered that in the early 1980s China should have liberalized industrial prices, eliminated the industrial

---

[4] Still in 1990 individual households were supplying only an estimated 23% of machine ploughing, 30% of drainage and irrigation services, 15% of plant protection, 48% of seed supply, and just 3% of veterinary services (Department of Agriculture 1991).

[5] Figures in current prices deflated by the national retail price index.

material balance planning system, opened the industrial economy to the forces of international competition, and rapidly privatized state industry.

In the post-Mao period China went to great lengths to attract foreign capital, being able to assure foreign investors of the 'good investment environment with 'stable social order and cheap labour' (*Beijing Review* (1991) 33/44). Local governments pushed central government regulations to the limit in order to attract foreign investment. Around three-quarters of the total inflow of capital in the 1980s came from Taiwan and Hong Kong, and was strongly concentrated in the coastal provinces of south-east China, especially Guangdong and Fujian. In addition to direct foreign investment, much overseas capital went into loans to indigenous factories to help them to upgrade their technical level through the import of new machinery (Sung 1991). These factories then undertook processing and assembly operations for the overseas Chinese capitalists. China's export growth was assisted greatly by Hong Kong capitalists' marketing activities on behalf of Mainland enterprises. China's political stability and booming economy, especially in the face of the world economic downturn in the late 1980s/early 1990s, made China an attractive haven for foreign, and especially Far Eastern, investment, soaking up the large capital surpluses that several of the region's economies had accumulated in the 1980s, with a further positive effect on China's growth.

China's instrumental attitude towards international trade in the 1980s had a lot in common with that of South Korea: 'In foreign trade our principle is to encourage exports and organize imports according to needs' (*Beijing Review* (1990) 33/44). A wide array of measures was adopted to promote exports, including foreign exchange retention rights for priority export sectors, tax rebates and direct rewards to exporters. At least a part of China's manufactured exports in the 1980s was being produced with zero or even negative net value-added at world market prices (Hughes 1991, and Vogel 1989). China maintained a battery of import controls, including state allocation of much foreign exchange and a wide array of quantitative restrictions (Vogel 1989). Priority was given in allocating rights to import to those products which it was judged would most rapidly raise China's labour productivity.

A superficial view of Chinese state industry in the late 1980s might conclude that nothing had changed in the nature of property rights compared to pre-1976, since the 'state' was still the 'owner' of the bulk of the industrial capital stock. However, property rights do not simply provide an alternative between 'state' and 'private' ownership. Rather, there is a whole gradation of property rights from comprehensively unrestrained individual property rights through a wide gradation of controls on the rights to sell assets, produce and market output, employ labour, and dispose of the income from assets. Within the texture of apparently unchanged 'state' ownership, important changes did in fact occur in the 1980s.

Following extensive experiments, the government widely introduced profit retention schemes in the early 1980s. By the mid-1980s, over two-fifths of fixed investment undertaken by state enterprises was financed from the enterprises' self-raised funds, so that a growing share of 'state' enterprises' capital stock was its 'own', since nominal ownership of fixed and working capital was assigned to the party which was the source of the initial investment (World Bank 1990: 149). By 1989, 21 per cent of fixed investment by 'state-owned' units was financed by domestic loans (ZGT JNJ 1990: 154), mainly from banks. Indeed, it was possible to perceive in embryo similarities between the Chinese system and that of Korea and Japan, in which industrial corporations maintain close ties, cemented by equity holdings, with the principal banks (World Bank 1990: 149).

In the second half of the 1980s, a number of industrial enterprise groups began to emerge. The state began to push important parts of state industry along Japanese and South Korean lines, with a succession of mergers, acquisitions, and joint ventures encouraged by the central and local governments (*Far Eastern Economic Review*, 5 Sept. 1990, and Yi 1992). These changes were intended to overcome the narrow product range and limited capacity for technical progress in single enterprise companies. The attempt to create in a planned way the corporate structure of advanced monopoly capitalism, based around huge conglomerates, stands in stark contrast to the *laissez-faire* approach adopted for enterprise privatization in Russia and Eastern Europe.

For example, in electrical appliance industry in the early 1980s China did not have any modern large-scale producers. The government began to build large combines out of related industries, giving them priority in the import of foreign technology, which grew very rapidly due to China's export success, importing numerous complete production lines from different countries. Through mergers, acquisitions, and joint ventures, several large industrial conglomerates were established.[6] For example by the late 1980s the Wanbao Group had several dozen enterprises with a total of 10,000 employees, annual output of over one-million refrigerators (among other products), and had become the eighth largest manufacturer of refrigerators in the world. In 1990 China's electrical appliance industry exported 200 million US dollars worth of goods, and the scope of its exports had broadened to include increasingly sophisticated products. China had begun to penetrate some of the world's most competitive markets. In 1988, for example, China exported 800,000 electric fans to the USA.[7]

China in the 1980s had an exceptionally high savings rate: China's households saved no less than 23 per cent of their disposable income in 1981–7, compared to 18 per cent in Taiwan (1965–81), 21 per cent in

---

[6] These included the Wanbao (in Guangdong), Jinxing (in Shanghai), the Panda Group (in Jiangsu province), and the Peony Group (in Beijing).

[7] The information in this paragraph is from *Beijing Review*, 34/23 (10–16 June) 1991.

Japan (1976–82), and just 8 per cent in the USA (1976–82) (World Bank 1990: 126). The main channel through which these reached industry was via banks and government bonds rather than shares. Share ownership systems developed only slowly, confined to an experimental role.

The right of state enterprises to determine their product mix was extended gradually. By the late 1980s only about one-fifth of industrial products was allocated directly by the State Planning Commission (Dong 1990: 66).

State enterprise managers became selected increasingly for their business skills since this would increase the likelihood of the enterprise earning profits for the government unit to which it was subordinate. In the absence of welfare benefits provided by the state, as opposed to the enterprise, the establishment of competitive labour markets would have been socially explosive. In the 1980s, the Chinese government began to reform the system of welfare and housing provision in the state sector but it was a complex process.[8]

The rate of growth of money wages in state enterprises in the 1980s was rapid in relation to China's history since 1940[9] but was well below the rate in most Latin American countries over the same period. China's work-force still lacked an independent, defensive trade union movement, and was unable to bargain for wage increases in the way that occurs in countries with democratic institutions.

Rural Non-Farm Enterprises

In former communist countries the IMF/World Bank recommends 'the rapid privatisation of small enterprises through outright sales to individuals, co-operatives and others' with the assets sold 'as quickly as possible' (IMF 1990: 2 and 27). China followed a different path. In the 1980s it once again became legal to set up and run small businesses, and the private sector grew extremely rapidly. None the less, within the overall structure of the rural non-farm sector, the 'collectively'-owned sector, i.e. *xiang* (township) and *cun* (village)-run enterprises, remained massively dominant (ZGJ JNJ 1985: v, 19 and 1989: v, 15).

China's 'collectively'-owned enterprises are not co-operatives in the normal sense of the word. Rather, they resemble national state-owned enterprises, with the 'state' being the local community (*xiang* or *cun*). The 'rural enterprises department' of the local government monitors the enterprises' operation.

[8] The most important sign of movement towards a competitive labour market in the state sector in the 1980s was the rapid rise in the number (10 million in 1978 to 24 million in 1988) and proportion of 'non-fixed' workers (from 14% in 1978 to 24% in 1988) (ZGLDGZT JZL, 1949–85 (1987: 28 and 33) and ZGLDGZT JNJ (1989: 203)), who had less rights and lower average wages than did existing state enterprise employees (on wage differentials, see ZGLDGZT JZL 1949–85 (1987: 171)).

[9] Around 11% per annum in state enterprises from 1978 to 1989 (ZGT JZY 1990: 41).

Poor transport in rural China provided a large degree of protection to rural enterprises from competition from the urban enterprises. Moreover, the rural non-farm sector, like the urban sector, benefited from substantial protection from other countries' potentially competitive labour-intensive industries. The rural non-farm sector was more flexible than partially reformed state industry in adjusting its product-mix to rapidly changing markets.

In the rural non-farm sector in the 1980s competitive factor and product markets were quickly established. Trade unions hardly existed and the large reserve army of surplus labour placed considerable downward pressure on rural wages. Whereas in the state sector the work-force was long established and used to a low pace of work, the work-force in rural non-farm enterprises was mainly first generation, lacking the privileges or organizational capacity of the state sector worker. Most workers in this sector were recruited on a contract basis, which made it possible to dismiss workers or terminate a contract for individual shortcomings, as well as to cut back staff in response to changing market conditions. In 1986, 70 per cent of the main material inputs of the rural non-farm enterprises were obtained from the market (Economics Research Institute 1987: 11). In the same year over two-thirds of rural non-farm enterprises' marketings were sold at prices determined by the enterprises themselves (Economics Research Institute 1987: 13).

The incentive structure for the management of the rural 'collectively'-owned non-farm sector changed dramatically. The most important insitutional innovation was the contract between the enterprise and local government. The most important part of the contract was the profits target.

Rural collectively-owned enterprises became the key to prosperity for Chinese local governments in the 1980s. While agriculture grew rapidly over the decade, the explosive growth of the non-farm sector meant that its share of total rural output rose quickly (from 31% of the gross value of rural output in 1980 to 55% in 1989 (ZGT JNJ 1990: 33)). Their capacity to absorb surplus labour was high, and the greater its success in this respect, the more approval local leaders won from their community, or from the governments at higher levels. Non-farm enterprises were vitally important, too, as the most dynamic contributors to local government revenue. It was strongly in the interest of local governments to ensure the expansion of profits from enterprises within their jurisdiction.

Local governments played a large role in the growth of the rural community enterprises. The most important decisions in local capital markets were taken either directly by the local government or, typically, by them in collaboration with the local managers of financial organizations (Byrd 1990: ch. 9). The local government's rural non-farm enterprises department identified new opportunities for profitable investment and took to risks involved in setting up new enterprises. They also made the final decision to close down collective enterprises and transfer the human and physical resources to other uses within the community. The World Bank's own study concludes: 'Without the deep involvement of community governments, China's rural non-farm sector could not have grown as rapidly as it did in the late 1970s and early 1980s' (Byrd 1990: 358).

An important consequence of the rapid growth of competitive small business, especially in the countryside, was that it provided a spur to the state sector. Markets were truly becoming contestable. This affected all markets, not just that for final products. Labour and capital were increasingly attracted towards the sector with higher returns, which frequently was the non-state sector. In the labour market, for example, the structure began to resemble the traditional Japanese pattern of a dual labour market. Employment in the modern large-scale sector, with *de facto* lifetime employment for most employees, expanded relatively slowly (from 36 million in 1984 to 45 million in 1991), while employment in industry outside this sector, where market forces operated much more powerfully in the labour market, grew explosively (employment in rural industry grew from 10 million in 1984 to 33 million in 1991) (ZGT JZY 1985: 26, and ZGT JZY 1992: 17).[10]

2. CRITICISM

2.1. Politics

The view that democratic politics in poor countries is positively and causally related to economic growth has gained widespread currency in recent years. Dasgutpa's influential article (Dasgupta 1990: 4 and 27–8) argues: 'The choice between fast growth in income and negative liberties is a phoney choice . . . Political liberties are *positively* and significantly correlated with per capita income and its growth. Nations whose citizens enjoy greater political liberties and civil liberties also perform better in terms of . . . improvements in life expectancy at birth, per capita income, and infant survival rates.' This is most gratifying, because one can kill two birds with one stone, and feel virtuous in one's support for greater 'democracy' because this will not only not harm growth but will improve it. Supported by 'reasoning' and 'statistical analysis'[11] such as Dasgupta's, the IMF began

[10] In the collectively owned segment of rural industry, it would be incorrect to describe the labour market as precisely analogous to that in the traditional small-scale sector in Japan. While the security of employment might be less than in the modern, large-scale sector, in advanced areas, at least, there is a well-developed system of community welfare and commitment to retraining workers rather than simply declaring them redundant as businesses cease to be competitive.

[11] In fact, Dasgupta's selection of developing countries is bizarre, omitting a large number of fast growing authoritarian ones (e.g. Chile, Peru, Brazil, Singapore, Hong Kong, Mexico,

to make 'democratization' of political institutions a third aspect of conditionality alongside 'stabilization' and privatization.

This approach was supported strongly by the apparent inability of East European communist countries to make progress in their economic reform beyond a certain point. The notion that gradual reform of the planned economy was infeasible due to the authoritarian nature of the Communist Party was a central plank of Kornai's extremely influential criticism of the 'Third Way', Kornai (1986) is scathing in his criticism of the 'naive reformers' who believe that a Communist Party can preside over a process that the considers will inevitably lead to its own demise.

A chorus of trenchant criticisms was made of the Chinese Communist Party in the 1980s, arguing in the same fashion as Kornai that the introduction of a market economy was impossible under communist rule: 'To survive and successfully evolve as a living social organism, the system of free markets, private property, and contractual buyer–seller transactions must operate within a legal order and in a politically democratic environment' (Prybyla 1990: 188). It was felt widely that the CCP could not itself make the transition to secular rational rule. It had the double burden of highly centralized traditions of Leninism plus millenia of centralized rule in China. The conventional wisdom, espoused in article after article and conference after conference, was that the CCP had to be removed from its monopoly of political power if the move to a market economy was to be put into effect:

Deng Xiaoping tried to restart China's economy without affecting the dictatorship of its entrenched vanguards . . . Although the term had not yet been invented, Deng sought *perestroika* without *glasnost*. This is not a particularly unusual project. There are innumerable examples of similarly placed monopolists of political power who wanted economic modernisation without political reform . . . It does not work . . . instead of duplicating South Korea and Taiwan, China seemed to have taken as its model Ferdinand Marcos's Philippines. (Johnson 1990: viii–x)

In the euphoria of post-communism, it was very hard to believe that such a brutal, undemocratic regime as China's could perform well economically. In the wake of Tiananmen it was felt to be morally repugnant to dare to suggest that such a brutal regime as the Chinese could possibly lead the economy forward successfully, let alone attract wide popular support. In fact, such violent repression of protest movements as that at Tiananmen is normal rather than exceptional in developing countries. Similar actions in recent years include that in Thailand in 1976 (Thammassat University), in South Korea in 1980 (Kwangju), and in India in 1990 (Srinagar). None of these received remotely as much publicity in the West as the Chinese

and Taiwan are all excluded) as well as most of the communist countries (North Korea, Algeria, Mozambique, Angola, Cuba, Yietnam, Burma, and Cambodia are all excluded). Moreover, his 'statistical analysis' consists of a series of rank correlation coeficients between pairs of variables, among which much the weakest relationship is that between growth and political freedom.

massacre, despite their great ferocity, and none of them had any lasting negative impact on the respective countries' economic performance.

2.2. Economics

In the post-Mao period, China put into practice a form of market socialism and, indeed, by 1992 the term 'socialist market economy' had become the official description of the system. A fundamental tenet of the advice received by East European reformers after the 1989 revolution, and subsequently by Russian reformers, was that the Third Way of 'market socialism' with a combination of strong planning and market, and a gradual reform of the Stalinist system, cannot work.

An important part was played in this argument by the apparent failure of China's reforms, which it was argued fitted the same pattern as the 'failed' reforms of Eastern Europe: 'In Hungary, and also in a number of the other socialist countries, the principle of "market socialism" has become a guiding idea of the reform process . . . Under this principle, state firms should remain in state ownership, but by creating appropriate conditions, these firms should be made to act as if they were a part of a market . . . I wish to use strong words here, without any adornment: the basic idea of market socialism simply fizzled out. Yugoslavia, Hungary, China, the Soviet Union, and Poland bear witness to its fiasco. The time has come to look this fact in the face and abandon the principle of market socialism' (Kornai 1990: 58).

Jan Prybyla was one of he most articulate critics of China's incremental reform strategy (Prybyla 1990 and 1991): 'To make the socialist system economic and modern at least three comprehensive measures have to be taken simultaneously. First, all markets—for consumer goods and factors of production—must be freed . . . Second the bulk of property must be privatised . . . [Third] the bureaucratic class must be *denomenklaturised*. Its allocative prerogatives must be abolished' (Prybyla 1990: 190). He, in common with a large body of analysts, argued that China's post-Mao reforms had 'failed'. Writing after Tiananmen he called the Chinese economy a 'broken system, which had crucial negative lessons to teach Eastern Europe: *The sad chronicle of China's post-Mao attempt to introduce a modern economic system contains a useful lesson which others, notably the East Europeans are taking to heart.* The lesson is that to address the economic problem in a modern way in the context of a low calibre, inefficient, slothful, wasteful, cronified socialist system, one must go all the way to the market system, do it quickly, and not stop anywhere on the way. To go part of the way slowly, "crossing the river while groping for the stones" as the Dengists put it, is to end up the creek to nowhere' (Prybyla 1990: 194) (emphasis added).

There was a remarkable degree of unanimity among advisers to the ex-communist governments of East Europe and Russia in the aftermath of the

defeat of communism. The idea that China's reforms had 'failed', powerfully reinforced by the Tiananmen massacre, played an important role in
bolstering their view of the necessary requirements of successful reform.
The common view was that the pace of the transition from central planning
should be rapid.[12] Anders Aslund, a close adviser to the Yeltsin government, argued: 'Common sense suggests that if you are sliding into a chasm,
you should jump quickly to the other side . . . and not tread cautiously.
There is no theory supporting a gradual switch of system' (Aslund 1990:
37).

The IMF/World Bank/EBRD (European Bank for Reconstruction and
Development)/OECD combined view of reform in Russia best reflects the
Western conventional wisdom about reform in the former communist
countries. Their view was that enterprises would not respond in desirable
ways to market signals unless private property rights were established:
'Stabilisation and price reform together will only set the scene for a meaningful supply response if they are accompanied by the establishment of
private ownership rights and the elimination of the panoply of controls
which currently prevent competition and discourage the efficient use of
resources' (IMF 1990: 2). They argued that enterprises' attempts to make
profits produce undesirable outcomes unless prices were determined by
market forces: 'Markets cannot begin to develop until prices are free to
move in response to shifts in demand and supply, both domestic and
external . . . Price decontrol is essential to end the shortages that . . . afflict
the economy' (IMF 1990: 17). They argued that economic progress would
be greatly inhibited unless there was full integration into the world
economy: 'It is . . . essential to move as rapidly as possible to a transparent
and decentralised trade and exchange rate system, in order to hasten the
integration . . . into the world economy . . . The exchange rate [needs] to be
moved to market clearing levels. [Only] a few sectors [need to be shielded]
for a short time from intense competition of international markets' (IMF
1990: 17). They put their combined weight of opinion behind a rapid
transition towards a market economy, despite explicitly acknowledging the
risks involved: 'The prospect of a sharp fall in output and rapid increase in
prices in the early stage of a radical reform is daunting . . . *In advocating the
more radical approach we are well aware of the concerns of those who recommend
caution*' (IMF 1990: 16–19) (my emphasis, P.N.).

3. RESULTS

The most important criterion by which governments in all settings, but
especially in poor countries, are judged by their own populations is their
success in economic affairs, and particularly in providing employment and

---

[12] One could add a very long bibliography of economists who advocated high speed as the
only 'logical' way to achieve a successful transition. Kornai's account (Kornai 1986) of the
'failure' of Hungarian reform was deeply influential in the early days of thinking about reform
in the post-communist countries.

Table 10.3 Comparative economic performance of the Chinese economy in the 1980s

	China	India	Low income countries[a]	Middle income countries
Av. annual growth rate, 1980/9 (%):				
GDP	9.7	5.3	3.4	2.9
Agriculture	6.3	2.9	2.5	2.6
Industry	12.6	6.9	3.1	3.0
Services	9.3	6.5	4.4	2.8
Av. annual real growth rate of exports, 1980/9 (%)	11.5	5.8	0.8	5.5
Av. annual growth rate of population, 1980/9 (%)	1.4	2.1	2.7	2.1
Av. annual rate of inflation, 1980/9(%)	5.8	7.7	14.9	73.0
Debt service as % of exports of goods and services: 1980	4.6	9.1	11.4	26.1
: 1989	9.8	26.4	27.4	23.1
Index of av. p.c.[b] food consumption, 1987/ 9 (1979/81 = 100)	128	113	103	101
Daily calorie intake p.c.[b]: 1965	1,931	2,103	1,960	2,482
: 1988	2,632	2,104	2,182	2,834
Crude death rate (no/1000): 1965	10	20	21	13
: 1989	7	11	13	8
Infant mortality rate (no/1000): 1981	71	121	124	81
: 1989	30	95	94	51
Life expectancy at birth (years): 1981	67	52	50	60
: 1989	70	59	55	66

[a] excluding India and China.
[b] p.c. = per capita.
Source: World Bank 1983 and 1991.

raising incomes. In the former communist countries in Eastern Europe and in Russia, the reforms since 1989 have produced desperately poor short-term economic results.

A detailed consideration of the performance of the Chinese economy in the reform period is beyond the scope of this paper. However, the broad outlines of this are provided in Tables 10.3–10.5. China's incremental path

Table 10.4 Changes in the standard of living in China, 1978–89

	1978	1989
Index of real p.c.[a] consumption	100	210
Consumption p.c. of:		
grain (kgs)	196	242
edible oil (kgs)	1.6	5.4
pork (kgs)	7.7	15.6
fresh eggs (kgs)	2.0	6.0
sugar (kgs)	3.4	5.4
cloth (metres)	8.0	11.6
Ownership of consumer durables (no/100 people):		
sewing machines	3.5	12.2
watches	8.5	50.1
bicycles	7.7	32.8
radios	7.8	23.6
TVs	0.3	14.9
Housing space p.c. (sq metres)		
cities	3.6	6.6
villages	8.1	17.2
Doctors per 10,000 people	10.7	15.4

[a] per capita.

Source: ZGT JZY 1990: 40–2.

produced outstanding economic advance over the course of a decade and a half.[13] In the first decade or so of economic reform China outperformed almost all developing countries in terms of output growth and export performance (Table 10.3). Moreover, compared both to most developing countries and to most of the reforming former Stalinist economies, it remained relatively unburdened by foreign debt and had achieved fast growth with relatively low inflation. China's system of authoritarian political control enabled her, in contrast to most other developing countries, to be able to control population growth, despite the bulge in the reproducing age cohorts in the 1980s. The improvement in economic performance was achieved through a sharp improvement in overall economic efficiency, reflected in the fact that the growth of output was accompanied by an extraordinary surge in popular living standards (Table 10.4) and remarkable reduction in absolute poverty (Table 10.5). China's economic performance in the 1980s was much better than that in the most relevant comparator country, namely India, and was vastly better than virtually anyone in the late 1970s could have hoped. Were Eastern Europe and the former USSR to achieve comparable advances (beginning from a much

---

[13] The reforms began the moment Mao Tsetung died in 1976.

Table 10.5 Poverty in China, 1978–1990

	1978	1985	1990
Total population (m.)	963	1,059	1,143
Urban	172 (17.9%)	251 (23.7%)	302 (26.4%)
Rural	790 (82.1%)	808 (76.3%)	841 (73.6%)
Average per capita income (1978 yuan)			
Urban	—	557	685
Rural	134	324	319
Poverty line (current yuan/year)			
Urban	—	215	319
Rural	98	190	275
Incidence of poverty (million)			
Total	270 (28.0%)	97 (9.2%)	98 (8.6%)
Urban	10 (4.4%)	1 (0.4%)	1 (0.4%)
Rural	260 (33.0%)	96 (11.9%)	97 (11.5%)

Notes: After three years of apparent stagnation in real rural per capita consumption, a substantial further growth occurred in 1991 (State Statistical Burean, ZGT JZY 1992: 42). Had the 1991 data been made available to the World Bank, it is likely that there would have been some further reduction reported in rural poverty.

The poverty line used in this table was calculated by revaluing for each year at current prices a constant 'poverty line' bundle of goods and services.

Source: World Bank 1992, v.

higher base, of course) in the 1990s, their reforms would be regarded as immensely successful.

4. A CHINESE PUZZLE

The fact that the Chinese system of political economy in the 1980s was 'market socialist' and yet was one of the most dynamic in terms both of output and income growth that the modern world has seen, presents economists with a puzzle: why did it perform so well in the first decade and a half of reform, despite the fact that the economic institutions and policies were gravely inadequate in relation to mainstream Western economic theory and policy? There are a number of possibilities, of different orders of difficulty for mainstream Western economics to digest.

The 'easy' answer for economists reflecting on the shambles of post-Stalinism in Eastern Europe and the former USSR is that China entered its reform programme with important advantages compared to Eastern Europe and Russia. These include China's low level of international debt, the special role of Hong Kong (and, increasingly, Taiwan), and the fact that China enjoys a strong 'capitalist' tradition stretching back at least a thousand years. It may be argued also that it is easier to reform a low income, predominantly rural CPE.

A more worrying possibility is that China's incrementalist approach to economic reform may have been correct and the attempt in most of Eastern Europe and in the former USSR to move rapidly towards a market economy may have been a serious mistake.[14] The correct economic advice to the former Stalinist economies may have been to stress that their structural transformation would require a lengthy period of extensive state intervention to cope with probable large areas of market failure. The enthusiasm of post-communist 'capitalist triumphalism' among advisers to Eastern Europe and the former USSR may have caused a major mistake in assessing not only the required speed of the transition but also the desirable economic functions of the state over an extended period. The huge tasks of structural transformation in an atmosphere of great uncertainty in the reforming CPEs is precisely a situation in which it is likely in principle that market failure will be especially large, with private agents tending, more than under other circumstances, to look towards the short term and speculation rather than towards longer term investment, so that the gap between private and social benefits may be especially wide.[15] The early stage of development economics in the 1940s and 1950s, and indeed, the practical experience of the Newly Industrializing Countries of East Asia,[16] may have been more relevant to the enormous tasks of transition that these economies now face than mainstream economics of the 1970 and 1980s which stressed the shortcomings of the state as a vehicle for achieving socially desirable goals.[17]

An even more worrying possibility for mainstream economics is that a main part of the reason for the contrast may lie in the realm of politics. A successful reform strategy may require a comprehensive perspective of

[14] This kind of 'Great Leap Forward' into a new socio-economic system which, allegedly, will bring great benefits was exactly that, paradoxically, against which Popper warned in the late 1950s in respect to the communist experiment: 'Every version of historicism expresses the feeling of being swept into the future by irresistible forces . . . Contrasting their "dynamic" thinking with the static thinking of all previous generations, [the historicists] believe that their own advance has been made possible by the fact that we are now 'living in a revolution' which has so much accelerated the speed of our development that social change can now be directly experienced within a single lifetime. This story is, of course, sheer mythology' (Popper 1957: 160).

[15] This applies a fortiori in so far as the reforms are accompanied by socio-economic instability to which they may have themselves contributed.

[16] See especially, Amsden 1989, and Wade 1990.

[17] Writing in respect of the economics profession's view of the role of the state in development economics Stern comments: 'The apparent swing in the profession from whole-hearted espousal of extensive government intervention to its rubbishing seems to be an example of unbalanced intellectual growth . . . There are problems and virtues with both state intervention and the free market' (Stern 1989: 621–2).

political economy. A more successful transition away from a communist economy may be easier to achieve with a strong state which is able to place the overall national interest above that of powerful vested interest groups. A self-reforming Communist Party may be the least bad vehicle available to accomplish this. The causes for China's success may lie above all in the set of historical factors which allowed the Communist Party to survive in China whereas it was overthrown in Eastern Europe and Russia, and to preside over the introduction of an increasingly competitive economy.

The most worrying thought of all is the possibility that China's explosive growth (and, increasingly, a wider growth process in former Stalinist South-East Asia) since the 1970s reflects a huge inherent catch-up and overtaking possibility which may have been latent in all the former Stalinist economies on account of the vast under-performance in relation to their huge physical and human capital inheritance. The reform of the Stalinist economies may be seen by history to have been a knife-edge situation in which correct choices in political economy could produce explosive growth and incorrect ones could send the system spinning backwards at high speed for an extended period.

CONCLUSION

The Stalinist vision of a development path without markets and competition is dead. After 1989 there was extraordinary unanimity among Western economists as to the desirable path that the former Stalinist systems should take, and great optimism about the results that might be achieved. The revolutions in East Europe were widely felt to offer the possibility of a swift construction in those countries of free market capitalism under the auspices of liberal democratic institutions. In the wake of the Tiananmen massacre, China's communist leadership was felt to be close to collapse. China's post-Mao reforms were widely felt to be cosmetic and uitimately to have achieved little. China was argued to demonstrate to the USSR and East Europe the danger of taking the half-way house path of incremental reform. Now it is time to take stock and consider soberly the lessons that may be learned about reforming Stalinist systems. Ultimately, this involves reflection on the nature of economics itself. This period has revealed how little the subject typically has to offer in considering grand questions of systemic change. Far too often, economic advice has been little more than slogans. Too rarely has it consisted of careful, pragmatic political economy.

Throughout the 1980s critics both inside and outside China argued that meaningful economic reform required a prior political revolution, involving the overthrow of the Communist Party, as occurred in Eastern Europe in 1989 and in the USSR in 1991. The argument that rapid political change in China might lead to chaos (da luan) which would prevent any serious economic strategy being followed, and would therefore be harmful to the interests of most Chinese people, was regarded widely as an immoral attempt to defend a 'fascist' regime. The creation of a stable, effective political system following the collapse of communism is a long process. Economic life atrophies without stable politics. The counter-factual question which must be posed is: would China's economy have advanced as rapidly as it did in the 1980s if the Chinese Communist Party in the late 1970s had been overthrown as those in Eastern Europe and the USSR were in 1989–91? Is it likely that a stable political system would have emerged quickly under whose guidance the Chinese economy could have prospered? Rather, is it not the case that the descent into political turbulence in the USSR and in much of Eastern Europe, especially the impoverished South-East shows the possible path that China might have followed? It is extremely difficult to organize a careful release of the political 'safety valve', with a controlled transition from Stalinist to democratic politics.

Throughout the 1980s China's incremental economic reform strategy came under fierce criticism from foreign economists and increasingly from China's own economists, allowed greater freedom to speak out until 1989. The implicit counter-factual proposition at the heart of much of the criticism is that China could have grown more successfully if she had early on taken a risk and dared to reform with 'one cut of the knife'. Whether one's hope is that China will have unrestrained capitalism or, as this essay has argued is desirable, that it will establish some form of market socialism, the dangers of trying to cross the river in one leap can now be seen with much greater clarity. The collapse of national output in the former GDR and USSR, and the serious decline in much of Eastern Europe, has produced great social tension. However, few people are likely to starve to death as a result. The same would not be true for China. The Great Leap Forward and the Soviet collectivization drive during the First Five-Year Plan showed vividly the price that could be paid in a populous poor country for a misguided attempt to leap into a new socio-economic order which would allegedly solve a vast array of problems at a stroke. The construction of a post-Stalinist economy is a long and complex process. The experience of the former GDR and Poland illustrate the risks involved in too rapid an attempt to move away from the Stalinist economy.

China's experience with incremental reform since 1978 confirms that this path brings great tensions, not least those associated with corruption. However, it shows that large gains in economic performance can be made even by a communist government which is determined to cling to power, and with extensive state ownership. For this to be so, the government must have recognized that the Stalinist system of economic organization had failed to improve people's living standards in a satisfactory way. It must be committed to forcing former Stalinist institutions to operate in a truly competitive environment. In the USSR in the 1920s the market socialist model of NEP was, indeed, overthrown. However, in the modern world once the process has gone beyond a certain point it is virtually impossible that the economy can revert to Stalinism. China had gone well beyond that point by 1991. A striking characteristic of the Chinese economy in the wake of the Tiananmen massacre was the fact that the move towards a market economy continued powerfully.

With hindsight, it seems most unlikely that some form of radical political democratization and associated 'big bang' programme of economic reform could have produced as successful an economic performance as China achieved since the late 1970s. Almost all China's citizens now have gained experience of markets, but unlike in the USSR and East Europe, the concept of a large state, working in the national interest to harness the market for common goals, remains a respected concept in the popular mind.

China still faces difficulties in progressing towards a market economy, and it has to do so against enormous difficulties arising from pressure of population upon natural resources. It is conceivable that a combination of pressure from the collapse of the Communist Parties in the USSR and Eastern Europe, and the disruption stemming from the death of Deng Xiaoping might yet lead to a loss of nerve by the Party in the face of a mass popular demonstration in the capital and to the overthrow of the Communist Party of China. It is still an open question whether the Party can make further progress towards transforming itself from a totalitarian into a 'rational authoritarian' party, which legitimates its tenure of office for the period of transition towards a more prosperous society in non-'Marxist', non-quasi-religious terms. Accepting the need for and managing political change may yet prove to be more of a stumbling block for the post-Mao regime than the management of a programme of incremental economic reform towards a market economy.

A simple homogeneous policy package of political economy cannot be recommended to all reforming socialist countries regardless of their size, location, income level, and historically bequeathed political conditions. The slogans 'free market' and 'democracy' do not provide a panacea for the complex problems of transition out of Stalinism. Nor is it possible to recommend China's politically authoritarian, economically incremental path of transition from Stalinism to other former socialist countries. The dangers of a wild attempt to leap out of a Stalinist and into a capitalist economy ought now to be clear enough. However, an incremental path of economic reform may be much more difficult to effect in countries which lack as strong political leadership as China possessed in the 1980s. Faced with the desperate economic collapse in large parts of the former communist world in Eastern Europe and the former USSR, a new authoritarian, political leadership based upon cultural and economic nationalism becomes increasingly probable. This is perhaps the most likely in Russia, the first socialist country and the once proud leader of the world socialist movement, in which the sense of national humiliation is the most intense.

REFERENCES

AMSDEN, A. (1989). *Asia's Next Giant: South Korea and Late Industrialization.* Oxford: Oxford University Press.

ASLUND, A. (1990). 'Gorbachev, Perastroika, and Economic Crisis', *Problems of Communism* (Jan.–Apr.), 13–41.

BYRD, W. (1990). 'Entrepreneurship, Capital, and Ownership', in W. Byrd and Q. Lin (eds.), *China's Rural Industry*. Washington, DC: World Bank.

CHAKRAVARTY, S. (1987). *Development Planning: The Indian Experience.* Oxford: Oxford University Press.

Central Committee of the CCP (1984). 'Decision on Reform of the Economic Structure', reprinted in S. N. Liu and Q. Wy (eds.), *China's Socialist Economy.* Beijing: Foreign Languages Press.

DASGUPTA, P. (1990). 'Well-being and the Extent of its Realisation in Poor Countries', *Economic Journal,* 100: 1–32.

DENG, X. P. (1984). *Selected Works of Deng Xiaoping. (1975–1982).* Beijing: Foreign Languages Press.

Department of Agriculture (1991). 'China's Land Contract Management System and the Operation of Co-operative Organisations in China in 1990', *Problems of Agricultural Economics* ['*Nongye jingii wenti*'], 8 and 9.

DONG, F. (1990). 'Reform of the Economic Operating Mechanism and Reform of Ownership', in Nolan and Dong (eds.).

Economics Research Institute (1987). *Report on the Organisation and Growth of China's Township Enterprises, Economic Research Materials,* 7.

HICKS, G. (ed.). (1990). *The Broken Mirror.* Harlow: Longman.

HARDING, H. (1987). *China's Second Revolution.* Washington, DC: The Brookings Institution.

HE, X. (1990). 'Scholar Discusses Democracy and Other Issues', *Beijing Review,* 33/4 (20–6 Aug.).

HUGHES, H. (1991). 'Constraints on Export Growth: Foreign or Domestic?', unpublished ms.

IMF, World Bank, OECD, and EBRD. (1990). *The Economy of the USSR: Summary and Recommendations.* Washington, DC: World Bank.

JOHNSON, C. (1990). 'Forward', in Hicks (ed.).

KORNAI, J. (1986). 'The Hungarian Reform Process: Visions, Hopes, and Reality', *Journal of Economic Literature,* 24: 1687–737.

——— (1990). *The Road to a Free Economy.* London: Norton.

LI, P. (1992). 'Price Reform the Progressive Way', *Beijing Review,* 35/18, 4–10, May.

NOLAN, P. and DONG, F. R. (eds.) (1990). *The Chinese Economy and its Future*. Cambridge: Polity Press.

POPPER, K. R. (1960). *The Poverty of Historicism*. London: Routledge and Kegan Paul.

PRYBYLA, J. (1990). 'A Broken System', in Hicks (ed.).

—— (1991). The Road from Socialism: Why, Where, What and How', *Problems of Communism*, 40 (Jan.–Apr.).

STERN, N. (1989). 'The Economics of Development: A Survey', *Economic Journal*, 99 (Sept.): 597–685.

SUNG, Y. (1991). 'The Reintegration of Southeast China', unpublished ms.

TIAN, Y. (1990). 'Prices', in Nolan and Dong (eds.).

WADE, R. (1990). *Governing the Market*. Princeton: Princeton University Press.

VOGEL, E. (1989). *One Step Ahead in China*. London: Harvard University Press.

World Bank (1983, 1985, 1987, 1991). *World Development Report*, Washington, DC: World Bank, and New York: Oxford University Press.

World Bank (1990). *China: Mecroeconomic Stability and Industrial Growth under Decentralised Socialism*, Washington, DC: World Bank.

World Bank (1992). *China: Strategies for Reducing Poverty in the 1990s*. Washington, DC: World Bank.

ZGJ JNJ (1985, 1989). *Chinese Economic Yearbook* [*Zhongguo jingii nianiian*]. Beijing: Economic Management Magazine.

ZGLDGZT JZL (1985). *Statistical Materials on Chinese Labour and Wages 1949–1985* [*Zhongguo laodong gongzi tongji ziliao*]. Beijing: Zhongguo tongji chubanshe.

ZGLDGZT JNJ (1989) *Chinese Yearbook of Labour and Wages* [*Zhongguo laodong gongzi tongji nianjian*]. Beijing: Zhonguo tongji chubanshe.

ZGNCT JNJ (1989). *Chinese Rural Statistical Yearbook* [*Zhongguo nongcun tongjinianjian*]. Beijing: Zhongguo tongji chubanshe.

ZGNYJ JGY (1982). *Chinese Agricultural Outline* [*Zhongguo nongye jingii gaiyao*]. Beijing: Ministry of Agriculture.

ZGT JNJ (1990). *Chinese statistical Yearbook* [*Zhonguo tongji nianjian*].

ZGT JZY (1985, 1986, 1990, 1991, 1992). *Chinese Statistical Outline* [*Zhongguo tongji zhaiyao*]. Beijing: Zhongguo tongji chubanshe.

11

The State and Economic Reform in Vietnam and the Lao PDR

Brian Van Arkadie

1. LESSONS FROM ASIAN TRANSITION

In the growing literature on the transition from planned, command economies to the market, a theme which needs to be addressed is the comparison and contrast between developments in the Eastern European and CIS economies and those in the transitional planned economies of Asia. This chapter attempts to throw some light on the theme by considering the experience of Vietnam and Laos.

In some respects, their liberalization can be interpreted as parallel to the dramatic changes taking place in Eastern Europe and the CIS. Certainly, there are many similarities in the issues which have to be faced in the reform process—the construction of the instruments of macroeconomic policy, for example, and the choice of options in enterprise reform. However, in important respects their experience is distinct and, by comparison with Eastern Europe and the successor states to the Soviet Union, the achievements have been impressive. Deep changes in systems of economic management have been implemented without a sustained decline in economic activity. In Vietnam, the economy grew despite the sudden collapse of Soviet aid, the US boycott and the absence of financial assistance from the multilateral aid institutions.

One distinctive feature of reform in these economies relates to the interplay between political and economic reform. While changes in economic policy in Vietnam and Laos have, of course, been associated with shifts in

The material on Vietnam and Laos is largely based on a study prepared by the author for the Asian Development Bank, which formed the basis for Part III of the *Asian Development Outlook 1993* (pp. 181–249). In turn, that study was based on reports prepared for the ADB by Adam Fforde and Steffan de Vylder on Vietnam and by Richard Vokes and Armand Fabella on the Lao PDR, shortly to be published by the ADB, which can be referred to for comprehensive bibliographies. Most of the detailed description of the evolution of policy in the two countries is drawn from those studies. The author also drew on work he had undertaken in Vietnam intermittently over 1989–92, including leading the mission which produced the UN–Govt. of Vietnam, *Economic Report on Vietnam* (prepared in 1989 and published 1991), working as a UN part-time adviser to the Vietnam government (1990–2) and producing a review of the reform process in Vietnam, jointly with Vu Tat Boi of the Office of the Council of Ministers, for the UN Management Development Programme in 1992.

political position and balance of forces within their respective regimes, there has also been substantial continuity in the political systems, processes of profound change in economic life being introduced and managed by ongoing political regimes. The comparative success of reform might be taken as evidence that, far from political change being a prerequisite of economic reform, economic reform may be more readily implemented under conditions of political continuity.

There may be a number of reasons why economic reform may be carried through more effectively in the absence of dramatic changes in the political system. At its simplest, the complex and sometimes painful decisions to be implemented in the economic reform process may be more than a fledgling political system can handle. More subtly, it may be the case that a political regime which has not made an abrupt ideological break with its past may be more pragmatic in exploring economic policy options and in so doing may be more likely to nurture an institutional framework well adapted to local conditions, than a regime which seeks to impose a blueprint of a new economic order following a sharp break with its political past.

A second feature of these economies is the relative importance of their rural sectors and the limited development of heavy industry. With rural economies based on relatively labour-intensive technologies and with a significant degree of self-sufficiency, they are technically less advanced and have lower incomes than Eastern Europe and the CIS economies, but, demonstrate greater resilience in the face of change and dislocation in the macroeconomy. Despite collectivization, the household remained an important element in the production system and technology in use remained consistent with the requirements of family farming. It has proved relatively easy to shift the agricultural systems in the direction of market-orientated family-based farming. Moreover, decentralized rural economies provide a useful base for the development of small-scale trading and craft activites, the local arteries of an emerging market system.

The relatively minor importance of large-scale, heavy industry contributed to the greater flexibility of the economies. Heavy industry, at the core of the central planning system, depending on allocated inputs and markets, with a committed and inflexible capital stock, was ill-adapted to the requirements of reform, but was of small relative weight. By comparison, light industry, smaller in scale and with technologies much more attuned to the underlying factor endowment, was much more responsive to the opportunities provided by the market economy.

The third distinguishing characteristic is geographical location. Adjacent to the fastest growing region in the world economy, with its exciting models of economic success, there is a spillover of capital and entrepreneurial energy from dynamic neighbours—this is already important for Vietnam and could become so for Laos.

Another factor may be the nature of the pre-reform planning systems. They were both part of the CMEA (Council of Mutual Economic Assistance) system and were heavily influenced by Soviet approaches to planning. However, the systems of socialist planning and administration were in practice more flexible and decentralized than in the Soviet case, making change easier. Although the form and rhetoric of Soviet central planning was adopted, the same degree of comprehensive and tight control as in the Soviet Union was never achieved, partly as a result of the rural nature of the economies. In Vietnam there was a high degree of economic autonomy exercised by the various political levels below the central government; this creates problems for macroeconomic management, but has also accommodated a remarkable diversity of behaviour by publicly owned enterprises, providing opportunities for genuine entrepreneurship particularly at the provincial and more local levels.

There have also been more intangible, social factors affecting the supply of entrepreneurship, with a latent potential for commercial entrepreneurship once opportunities became available and a lively commercial response of management which transformed segments of the publicly owned sectors. The reform process therefore had a strong spontaneous element, with fledgeling entrepreneurs taking the initiative ahead of policy changes.

2. EARLY STAGES IN THE REFORM PROCESS

In the two economies, the role of prices has been greatly enhanced, issues of enterprise ownership, management, and control are being confronted, the relationship with international markets transformed, agrarian systems reformed, and first steps made to put the machinery of fiscal and monetary policy in place. Change has been fast; it is not easy to capture and reflect an accurate picture of a fast moving process, in which description can be out of date as it is being set on paper.

Between 1954 and 1965, North Vietnam adopted an orthodox Soviet industrialization strategy and during the war with the USA, the basic approach was maintained. Private economic activity was largely forbidden, with the exception of private plots of land within the agricultural co-operatives. Industrial companies were owned by the state, either centrally or through provincial or local governments. The Vietnamese economy was—on paper—a classic 'command economy', although during the US war attention was more focused on the exigencies of the war economy than the implementation of economic plans. However, the severe economic difficulties experienced at the end of the 1970s, following the cessation of Western and Chinese aid, prevented the consolidation of the centrally planned system. As early as 1981, a decisive shift in agricultural policy was formalized, when the end-product contract system was generalized. A significant move towards autonomy for the farm household production unit was instituted, with households farming collective land under contract and marketing produce in excess of contracted deliveries. The role of the informal private sector in such areas as retail trade, handicrafts, and artisanship was also officially recognized. This began a process of liberalizing agricultural and small-scale trade and craft activities which fundamentally changed the character of the Vietnam economy, adding to the resilience of the economy during the subsequent decade of economic difficulties.

Following unification, the government had initially relied mainly on *ad hoc* measures to direct the economy, concentrating initially on the formidable tasks of reconstruction. The Interim Three-Year Plan (1978), drawn up with assistance from Soviet advisers, was intended to lay the foundations for subsequent socialist transformation, and in spite of the first reform efforts in 1979 the First Five-Year Plan (1981–5) set out to impose a strict central planning system. Production was based on state allocations of capital and inputs, even labour being allocated centrally within the modern sector. There was large-scale investment in cement factories, steel mills, and hydroelectric power plants. Material inputs and capital were extremely cheap, sometimes almost free of charge, Soviet assistance supplying cheap inputs which made the system of subsidy possible. Virtually all consumer goods were rationed and prices played a subordinate role in the allocation of resources.

The imposition of exaggerated targets on a war-torn economy was devastating. In the pursuit of unrealistic targets, enterprises sought to maximize their allocations of capital and inputs. The resultant hoarding amplified the imbalances caused by the over-ambitious macro-level targets. Difficulties in implementing the plan created the setting for the birth of the reform process.

Reform involved an incremental process, which can be interpreted both as a learning process, with the leadership responding to successes and failures of policies in practice, and also as the outcome of an ongoing debate within the political system regarding economic strategy. In the early 1980s, before the launching of *doi moi*, there were already high rates of open inflation, government exercising less control over the economy in practice than in most centrally planned economies. The fact that the centrally planned economy was not consolidated and never worked effectively in its own terms made the process of *doi moi* easier than reform of centrally planned systems which had operated more effectively.

For South Vietnam the experience of central planning was relatively brief, central planning only being applied with full vigour between 1976 and 1980. The private sector, although illegal, was never fully suppressed.

Even in the north, control by planners was in practice reduced from the start of the 1980s by the *de facto* de-collectivization of agriculture and the growth of extensive parallel markets. In the first half of the 1980s policy-making was subject to contradictory influences, as the commitment to central planning was tempered by pragmatic responses to difficulties in implementing central controls. Experiments with decentralized decision-making in selected state enterprises and price, wage, and salary reforms were introduced in 1984 and 1985, but there was also a renewed drive to collectivize agriculture. The Second Five-Year Plan (1986–90) emphasized the need to broaden the collective economy and to restrict the negative aspects of the private economic sectors, but was overtaken by the launch of further reforms in 1986.

While the increased autonomy of the farm household and the widening range of small business activity meant that a growing amount of economic activity fell outside direct state control, a number of key issues regarding the legal status of private economic activity remained unresolved (e.g. longer-term security of access to agricultural land) and many important policy issues related to the management of the emerging economic system had still be to addressed (e.g. price controls, exchange rate management). The state sector was left in a sort of half-way house. A good deal of autonomy was granted, central plan targets and instructions not being rigorously enforced. However, state enterprises were not yet subject to market discipline. Prices were not market determined and state enterprises were still, in principle, subject to the planning mechanism. Targets were set, and many prices centrally determined, but the central authorities lacked the instruments to enforce plan discipline.

In the Lao PDR, the period 1945–75 had been dominated by conflict, first against the French, and then, following independence in 1953, by civil war. Following the proclamation of the Lao People's Democratic Republic in 1975, socialist economic transformation was initiated, an attempt was made to introduce central planning, and the banking system and all large industrial plants were nationalized. In many cases, nationalization simply involved taking over enterprises abandoned by their former owners. Some attempts were made to establish agricultural co-operatives, although initially a low-key approach was adopted, focusing on the formation of solidarity groups and labour exchange teams rather than fully fledged production co-operatives. However, the country was firmly within the socialist camp, receiving external assistance from the former Soviet Union and its allies.

Despite the commitment made to central planning after 1975, effective state control was largely confined to the country's small modern sector. The economic situation of much of the population and even the organization of production changed little. Restrictions on private trade did make life harder for farmers involved in the money economy, leading many to retreat into subsistence. But collectivization met with some resistance, and even by 1985 co-operative farms were reported to cover only 40 per cent of the cultivated area, and many co-operatives did little more than share labour. Central planning had little time to get established; the regime was faced with deep economic problems from its foundation. The continuing crisis led to debate within the Party over economic policy and in 1979 the leadership embarked on a reappraisal, followed by the introduction of a radical reform programme aiming to accelerate growth, boost exports, and increase budgetary resources. Earlier restrictions on private-sector activity were reversed with the recognition that all sectors had a role to play in the country's transition to socialism. Also in 1979, there was a sharp increase in farm incentives and the collectivization campaign was suspended. Price levels were adjusted and a currency reform implemented. In 1981 steps were taken to improve the efficiency of state enterprises by increasing management autonomy and material incentives.

In spite of the reforms, parallel efforts continued to impose a central planning framework on the economy, setting out specific targets for the various sectors and state enterprises. As in Vietnam, early reform efforts were seen as temporary measures designed to make the emerging system of central planning work better. Further experiments with decentralized decision-making in selected state enterprises were continued through 1983 and 1984 and further price, wage, and salary reforms introduced in 1984 and 1985, but there was also a renewed drive to collectivize agriculture.

In Laos, the Fourth Congress of the LPRP in 1986 was the watershed in the country's economic reform programme, the Congress endorsing a programme that has since become known as the New Economic Mechanism. In 1987 controls on trade were reduced, allowing the private sector to compete on equal terms with state trading enterprises even in agricultural marketing, ending the state's monopoly on the import and export of a range of commodities, and removing price controls on all but eight 'strategic' commodities. The kip was devalued from K10 to the dollar to K350, close to the then free market rate. In spite of some continued resistance to the reforms and the acute shortage of experience of the market, the implementation of the NEM was re-emphasized in 1988. Sweeping measures covered financial and fiscal reform, price policy, state enterprise autonomy, the rights of the private sector, and a foreign investment code. This was followed in June 1988 by a new approach to agriculture with the breakup of collectives and a return to family farms. The reform process was consolidated in the new constitution in August 1991. Whilst one-party rule remained, the role of the private sector was recognized in a 'multi-sectoral economy' managed through the mechanism of the market and legal ownership guarantees provided for all sectors.

3. STEPS IN THE REFORM PROCESS

3.1. Agrarian Reform

Agrarian collectivization was intended to be an important part of the socialist strategy in both countries, but in recent years a decisive shift has been made to the family farm as the basic production unit.

In Vietnam, prior to the 1981 reforms, co-operatives in the densely populated north were organized on the basis of farmers working in brigades for work points. There had, however, been considerable illegal expansion of 'own-account' activity. The south-centre was collectivized rapidly after 1975–6, its institutional development parallel to that of the north. The experience of the Mekong was somewhat different. The Mekong delta is less densely populated than the Red River delta in the north and prior to 1975 commercial smallholder agriculture was more developed. Although collectivization in the Mekong was declared to have been successfully completed in 1985, doubts remain about the depth of influence of the co-operatives. Even in north and central Vietnam, households remained an important element in the system of production, although subject to collective control through producer co-operatives.

The 'output contract system' was introduced into the agricultural co-operatives as early as 1979–80, awarding the farmer more rights within the co-operative and the co-operative more rights vis à vis the state, compulsory deliveries being replaced by a 'contract' under which plots of land were allocated against the obligation to supply a certain amount of rice to the co-operative, any surplus being disposed of in any way the farmers wished. Reforms in 1981 and 1988 increased the autonomy of the farming household, the latter decisively shifting most economic power from the producer co-operatives to households, essentially returning agriculture to a family basis and greatly increasing the autonomy of the farming household. In 1989, further measures greatly reduced the direct involvement of the state in input allocation; procurement at prices below those on the free market formally ended, and the share of the available surplus procured by the state declined considerably. Under the 1988 reforms, co-operatives were still meant to exist to form a focus for various rural activities, but probably in the majority of cases were reduced to only a minor role, acting as local tax collectors and as the holder of residual property rights, and as an element of the formal state structure. A small group of co-operatives managed to shift successfully to a profitable service function and others retained some support from farmers, but were greatly diminished in importance.

Land use rights remained confused, but, while the formal legal framework remained ambiguous, in practice there had been a decisive shift in favour of family farms. Other farm assets had generally been privatized.

Livestock, machinery, brick-kilns, and other important sources of co-operative revenues had been sold to farmers. With no effective barriers to local private rice marketing, the secular rise in the dollar value of retail rice since the mid-1980s is striking evidence of increasing rural incomes. There is no reliable data on the aggregate terms of trade facing agriculture, but it appears that they have improved.

The breakdown of the state trading system at local level permitted private traders to develop local markets. Large-scale wholesaling, often based upon access to foreign exchange and other key inputs (such as transport facilities), generally remained under the control of state agencies. However, these usually compete with each other, and state trading companies utilize private retailing networks when operating away from their home areas. The end of price control meant that inputs were allocated to the state sector at prices close to those paid by other units.

The development of the rural economy since 1988 has occurred with little direct assistance from the central government, whose main contribution has been to assist in the development of national markets for rice. The reforms have increased economic efficiency resulting in gains in output, accompanied by greater social differentiation which has increased savings capacity. There has been a reduction of the number in the poorest income categories, whose living conditions appear to have eased, but a substantial proportion of the population has negative savings suggesting that they may lose control over productive assets.

Although output of staples and rural real incomes have increased under the impact of reform, there has been no great improvement in input availability to agriculture. Fertilizer supplies, credit, and better infrastructure are all lacking. This suggests that growth will slow in the mid-1990s, as it did in the mid-1980s, as the positive incentive and efficiency effects of the reforms are exhausted. The productive capacity of the system is constrained by the absence of a rural support network of the kind familiar in many market economies, such as rural credit, agricultural extension, and effective communications and transport. In turn, the main barrier to meeting these needs is the weakness of the state apparatus.

Agricultural reform in the Lao PDR has followed a similar path to that of Vietnam. Important rural reforms were initiated after 1986, when the promotion of co-operatives was de-emphasized and encouragement given to a return to family farms. Co-operatives were to transform themselves into co-operative marketing and trading units. However, the direct impact of reform on the farming community was limited, since collectivization had not progressed beyond the establishment of low level co-operatives, so that reforms essentially formalized arrangements already prevalent, with farmers having occupier status on the basis of traditional usufruct rights. Due to the mainly subsistence nature of production and the recognition, at the community level, of traditional usufruct rights, the lack of clear individual title has not yet been a significant constraint on agriculture development. Even in the absence of legal ownership rights, it is widely accepted that land 'sales' do occur.

Trade and pricing reforms since 1987 have had a significant impact on the rural community. In 1987 the private sector was granted the right to compete with state enterprises in agricultural marketing, while state enterprises involved in distribution were granted autonomy under the New Economic Mechanism. With the end of the rice ration for public employees in 1989, government paddy procurement ended, although it continued to purchase some cash crops, notably coffee. Higher up the marketing system, state enterprises remained dominant, although there was increased private investment in agro-processing, in particular in rice milling. The private sector also began to import and distribute fertilizer and other agro-inputs following the end of the state monopoly. Coupled with the 1987 exchange rate reform, these measures resulted in fundamental changes in agricultural incentives. By 1988 there had been dramatic increases in the prices of key agricultural commodities. Coffee prices increased about 50 per cent; maize, soy bean, and cassava by over 100 per cent, and paddy by between 80–200 per cent from a year earlier, with prices moving towards border parity.

Although the net effect of price changes in both the rural and urban economy was to turn the terms of trade in favour of the rural sector, there were a number of factors that limited supply response. Poor transport infrastructure reduced the local impact of improved terms of trade observable in national markets. The lack of irrigation limits the scope for dry-season cropping, and leaves the wet-season crop vulnerable to weather conditions.

3.2. Price Reform and the Emerging Market System

Price reforms have been thoroughgoing. Commodity prices are now largely market determined, the economies opened to the influence of international prices, and direct subsidization virtually eliminated. Two central issues in the shift to a market system of economic co-ordination are (i) the manner and timing of the shift from administrative to market prices, and (ii) the strategy for introducing a new set of 'rules of the game' whereby actors in the economy, particularly publicly owned enterprises, are constrained to respond to market prices by the discipline of a hard budget constraint. Administrative control of prices, with the prices of many products far from their scarcity values, is incompatible with an efficient decentralized market economy. Considerable success has been achieved in the speed and depth of the transformation of the price system, both in terms of the move towards market-determined prices and the shift in enterprise behaviour in responding to market opportunities and constraints. Despite the persistence of some 'distortions', these economies already operate with price systems quite as free as those of many long-established and successful market economies.

While price reform has been broadly successful, it was neither an instantaneous nor a smooth process. In transforming the system of economic allocation, governments faced two dilemmas. The first related to the impact of price reform on those segments of the economy ill-adapted to respond to the new system. The potential political and social costs of collapse of large-scale enterprises are obvious. Moreover, it does not make economic sense to force the premature collapse of enterprises which might, if allowed time to adjust, have a reasonable chance of viability. Another set of problems related to the impact of reform on the consumer price level, both the risks of open inflation as price controls are removed and the consequences for consumers of the sharp changes in relative prices resulting from price reform.

In Vietnam, the almost complete abolition of price controls had been achieved by 1989. During a transitional period transactions at free prices progressively increased their share of total activity. During the deep crisis of the late 1970s open inflation developed and for a decade high open inflation was combined with the persistence of symptoms of repressed inflation, such as rationing and shortages of inputs and consumer goods at official prices. There was a partial breakdown in the allocation of subsidized inputs, and of state procurement of consumer goods to service the rationing system. Enterprises, agricultural co-operatives, and individuals were thus forced to try to obtain the goods from non-official sources. State companies began to trade commodities, inputs, and spare parts with each other outside the official allocation system, in an informal, spontaneous reform process.

Political leaders responded to spontaneous change by a series of concessions, while trying to regain control of the process. In the industrial sector in 1981 state enterprises were given the right to do business with each other and to sell their production freely after they had fulfilled their obligations to the state. The 1979–81 reforms within agriculture and industry, simultaneous liberalization of retail trade, a cautious price reform, and a certain decentralization of foreign trade represented important movements towards a market system, but, prior to the price reform in early 1989, the economy remained segmented between production within and outside the central plan. In general, free market prices tended to be several times higher than official prices. The strong open inflation of the late 1980s facilitated the shift from official to market prices, as official prices became increasingly irrelevant even before they were formally abolished. A fundamental change took place in the entire economic environment, with profound effects on the behaviour of economic agents. The former sellers' market was replaced, with the shift towards market-clearing prices.

Early attempts to reduce the differences between free-market prices and official prices were made in 1987 following the official announcement of *doi moi*. In 1987, the ration system was abolished for many commodities, and official prices of non-essential goods were raised to a level close to free-market prices. Administered prices of most consumer goods and many inputs were increased sharply in 1987 and 1988. However, differences between official and free-market prices continued to be large in the markets for key agricultural products, such as rice, and for foreign exchange (and, as a consequence, in the markets for all imported goods).

In 1989, price reform was accelerated and virtually all prices deregulated. With the exception of a few social benefit items (such as electricity, house rent, medicines), consumer goods sold through the state outlets were now sold at prices very close to the free-market level, and were frequently adjusted to keep pace with free-market prices. The price reform was accompanied by a drastic devaluation (which brought the official rate of exchange close to the free-market rate), by improved producer prices for rice, and (during 1989) by positive real interest rates. With the 1989 price reform and increased autonomy for state enterprises, the state allocation of resources almost vanished, together with physical planning targets. The traditional model of central planning was, for all practical purposes, liquidated.

In the Lao PDR, price reform has also been quite comprehensive. In 1988, a one-price market-oriented price policy was put into effect. Aside from electricity, water, fuel, post and telecommunications, and air fares, official retail prices were to be set on a parity with parallel market prices, while wholesale prices were to be freely negotiated between buyer and seller. This meant that salaries of government personnel had to be adjusted.

3.3. Enterprise Reforms

Enterprise reform is at the very core of the debate over institutional reform. For reform to be successful, effective responses to decentralized market stimuli are needed, which requires a profound change in enterprise behaviour, by altering the behaviour of publicly owned enterprises by changing the rules of the game under which they operate, by opening the economy to private initiatives, or by privatizing publicly owned enterprises. Thus any programme of enterprise reform must strike a balance between three elements: (i) changing the system of state enterprise control and management; (ii) liberalization, to allow non-state entrants into areas of economic activity previously monopolized by state firms; and (iii) privatizing the ownership of state enterprises.

There have been deep changes in the legal and regulatory framework within which state enterprise operates and, more importantly, changes in behaviour by many public enterprises, often ahead of the changes in official rules. However, a process of transition is still in progress, and an appropriate and stable legal and administrative framework within which the state sector can operate efficiently in the emerging mixed economies is far from fully developed.

Overt privatization has not yet been a major theme in the reform programmes. However, the autonomy of many state enterprises has been carried to the point that they now have the attributes of private business in virtually all respects other than legal form, and joint ventures between state enterprise and foreign business have been widespread. The apparent success of this process has been somewhat at variance with the view which has gained ascendancy in discussions of reform in Eastern Europe, where it is argued that there is no half-way house—it is not possible to transform enterprise management under public ownership and that therefore a decisive shift to private ownership is needed. Apart from any ideological considerations, the pragmatic basis for this view has been the apparent difficulty in changing the behaviour of state-owned enterprises without a transformation in ownership, as state-owned firms can too readily avoid the harsher realities of the market by recourse to state subsidy and to credit from state financial institutions (although the 'soft budget constraint' is not unique to state enterprise, as governments prop up private enterprises even in thoroughgoing market economies when politically advantageous).

Experience in Asia offers contrary evidence, as early successes of the reform period have been in part based on lively responses to new market opportunities from publicly owned enterprises, particularly at the provincial and local levels, suggesting that pragmatic open-mindedness might be appropriate before concluding that any particular model of enterprise ownership will emerge as the dominant form. Nevertheless, the contribution of the private sector in the rural economy and liberalized commerce is consistent with the view that a vigorous private sector is a necessary component of market reform. The necessary balance between public and private ownership for the adequate functioning of a market economy is, however, still an open question. Enterprise reform should not be judged by the degree of transition to some abstract model of a market economy, which can be as much a utopia based on ideology as previous visions of communism, but should be based on how enterprises, public and private, respond to market stimuli in practice.

The strength of the Asian transition has been that, precisely because change has not been preceded by a sharp ideological break, the reform process has had a strong pragmatic content. A working set of institutions is likely to result from pragmatic responses to experience and to political realities, much as they emerged historically in established market economies, rather than from the application of any *a priori* model. The strength of the experience of enterprise reform so far is that it has emerged more as a pragmatic response to the needs of economic development than as the product of an ideological cataclysm.

Although weaknesses in state enterprise performance continue to impose costs, systems of state enterprise management have changed and a gradual change in the balance between public and private ownership achieved. The key elements in the process of change have not only included legislative and administrative reforms (i.e. changing the formal 'rules of the game') but also include a strong spontaneous component whereby behaviour has changed in response to new opportunities ahead of changes in, or even in conflict with, official rules. In describing he reform process, however, it is much easier to chronicle legal initiatives than it is to record more subtle changes in behaviour at the enterprise level, identifiable mainly on the basis of anecdotal evidence. The distinctive elements of the Asian experience have not been so much at the readily observable level of legal and administrative strategies as at the more relevant, but less readily observable level of enterprise response.

Even if major programmes of privatization are not adopted, steps will be required to clarify ownership rights and responsibilities, to put *de facto* changes onto a more satisfactory and explicit legal footing. The behaviour of significant segments of the state enterprise sector has changed enough for them to have played a positive role in developing the market, exhibiting initiative and independence from central control in pursuing market opportunities and disposing of the returns from market success. However, that very success has resulted in an increasing ambiguity regarding the real ownership status of parts of the 'public' sector, as control is somewhat obscurely located between management and decentralized political interests.

The relative success of state enterprise reform is to be explained partly by the importance of light industry under provincial and local control, which was responsive to the opportunities provided by the loosening of systems of plan control and decentralization of economic decision-making. The difference between the problems of state enterprise management in the larger-scale, heavier industries and the smaller-scale, lighter industries is illustrated by the case of Vietnam. The larger-scale public enterprise sector, largely controlled by the central government, has suffered great difficulties in the face of the move towards market prices and the collapse of Soviet aid which supported that sector. Too swift and ruthless an exposure to the effects of the market would have had dire consequences in terms of employment and output, so that steps had to be taken soften the transition. After central planning was abandoned in 1989, the pressure of market competition upon many enterprises became intolerable. Denied access to cheap inputs, many became exposed to the full implications of market-determined prices, and without support would have rapidly gone to the wall in 1990 and 1991. In the event, the authorities chose to slow this process through *ad hoc* tax concessions and recourse to the credit system, undermining the macroeconomic stability attained in 1989 and leading to a resurgence of inflation.

By contrast, many light industrial enterprises and some service-sector activities, mainly under the control of provincial authorities but also controlled by national level institutions (including the military), were successful in seizing market opportunities, including in foreign markets (e.g. sea-food processing and clothing). The autonomy enjoyed by enterprises which are ostensibly publicly owned poses issues related to the allocation of the rewards from market success when 'ownership' is ill-defined in practice even more than in law. By 1990–1 the authorities were attempting to confront the issue of state property through measures to enhance the flow of resources to the budget (including direct attachment of state enterprises' accounts, interest penalties, and possible penalties to be imposed upon the unit's bank for non-payment, a ceiling of 50 per cent of the wage fund on workers' bonuses, and a ceiling on managers' salaries of three times average wage levels) and alternative models for enterprise reform, introduced to help the emergence of a more efficient property-rights system. Enterprise reforms initiated in 1991 included creation of management boards, transformation of firms into share companies, leasing or contracting out production units, and defining more clearly the responsibility of management to preserve the capital value of the enterprises under their control.

The search for an effective system of control over and management of the state enterprise sector in Vietnam continues. It brings into play a diversity of interests, of the various ministries and bodies of the central government, the provincial authorities, and the management and employees of the state enterprises, with the locus of control over enterprises depending not only on the emerging legal framework but also upon the realities of power in the Vietnamese political and administrative system.

Some of the problems which can arise during the reform process, when state enterprise operates halfway between a tightly controlled planned system and a privately owned market system are also exemplified by the Lao experience. The Lao PDR has faced considerable difficulties in trying to ensure that state enterprises are run in a profit-oriented way while retaining state ownership. This is one reason why the government adopted a new policy of disengagement from the state enterprise sector in mid-1989. However, since a number of 'strategic' enterprises will remain state-owned and it will be some time before divestment of the majority of state enterprises and the new company law is in operation, the problems of accountability and control of state enterprises are of continuing importance.

The freeing of wages and the ability of managers and workers to vote themselves bonuses led to a pay explosion. From rough parity with pay in the civil service in early 1988, pay levels within state enterprises were reported in 1992 to be as much as five times those in government service. While this provided incentives to increase productivity, the appropriation of much of the potential surplus as extra income for the work-force had implications for the long-term viability of the enterprises, in particular in relation to its capital base and its financing requirements.

With operational autonomy in the face of the threat of privatization, state enterprises have little incentive to conserve their capital. Under continuing state ownership, while the state retained ultimate ownership, enterprise management and workers have effective usufruct rights over company assets, the state receiving a fixed principal repayment towards reimbursement of the capital invested in the enterprise by the state. Given the diversion of surplus to bonus payments, the ability of state enterprises to fund investment from their own resources has been severely limited, although managers do have an incentive to borrow to invest so that employees can increase their incomes, as long as investments contribute to net profits. Coupled with pressure on the profit margins of state enterprises, due to the effects of liberalization, the net effects of the changes has been under-saving by state enterprises and a rapid rise in recourse to loan finance through the banks. The management reforms had a negative effect on the operations of the country's banking system; the rapid growth in lending to state enterprises, in the absence of measures to safeguard the asset base of these enterprises, led to a deterioration in bank portfolios.

In 1991 the Lao PDR made a further effort to reform state enterprises, through the State Enterprise Decree (1991) which reaffirmed the state's ownership and ultimate right to the benefits from the use of state assets, but invested the responsibility for management of state enterprises with a Board of Directors. At the same time, the reimbursement of government capital through the payment of depreciation, which has contributed to the decapitalization of state enterprises, was replaced by dividend payments to the owner. The decree also provided for the conversion of capital into shares and for the sale of shares to the employees of the enterprise and/or the general public. The right to dispose of after-tax profits has been transferred from the managers and workers to the directors. To safeguard their rights, an elected representative of the work-force has to be a member of the board of directors. A decentralized system of management was still recognized as essential for the efficient operation of state enterprises and managers retain significant autonomy, subject, however, to the board of directors. How effective this system will be has still to be seen.

In general, efforts of the Asian reforming economies to increase the role of private non-agricultural enterprise have been more through liberalizing measures to open up areas of activity for private initiative than through privatization of state-owned enterprise. The response of nationals was initially predominantly through small-scale activity, particularly in trading, services, crafts, and light industry, while foreign investors have been involved in larger-scale ventures, typically in joint ventures with state enterprises. However, given the success of private business, larger private concerns can be expected to quickly emerge, while something close to private business may emerge from the spontaneous evolution of public enterprises.

In Vietnam, the high private-sector potential resulted in part from the quite short experience of socialist planning, particularly in the south, which meant that private business skills and experience were not lost. It is true that the private sector in Vietnam suffered greatly during the period of 'hard' socialization, when assets were confiscated and businessmen condemned as anti-social. Throughout most of the 1980s, economic liberalization did not include encouragement of the non-state sectors. But when, around 1988, formal policy shifted, there was a significant population of businessmen either with direct experience of business before the unification of Vietnam or with exposure to a strong family tradition. Moreover, many overseas Vietnamese were ready to take advantage of the business opportunities provided by *doi moi*. It is in the area of trade that the growth of the private sector has been most rapid. The share of the private sector in reported trade has grown to dominance, while the 'penetration' of the state sector by commercialization means that the extent of 'private' trade is higher than the data indicates.

Credit and tax breaks are still used to support the state sector and there is still political support for maintaining the leading role of the state sector. Given continuing ambiguity in official attitudes, much private sector activity remained concealed from view, making analysis uncertain. The private sector involvement in production activity remained very small, according to official data, but almost certainly its size was underestimated.

Since the 1990 revisions to the Foreign Investment Law, private companies have been permitted to enter into joint ventures with foreign partners. From 1991, foreign investment grew very fast, not only in the oil sector but also in a wide range of other activities, particularly involving investors from East Asia.

In the Lao PDR, there is no doubt that the private sector already dominates economic activity, in the sense that agricultural production, which is almost entirely in private hands, is the dominant source of economic output. However, the non-agricultural private sector had been seriously depleted with the departure after 1975 of a large number of managers, artisans, merchants, and shopkeepers, many of the latter groups being of Chinese and Vietnamese origin. By 1978, much of the country's Chinese community, numbering an estimated 30,000, had left.

An initial change in the government's attitude towards the private sector came as early as the economic reforms of December 1979, which acknowledged the role of the capitalist as well as socialist sectors in the country's economic growth and stressed the need to promote all sectors of the economy. The new policy towards the private sector, and the role it was to play in the 'transition to socialism' was reaffirmed in April 1982. None the less, considerable uncertainty over the role of the private sector remained until after the Fourth Party Congress in November 1986, when the party came out strongly in support of the private sector. Much private sector activity through the early 1980s was technically illegal, although tolerated.

Following the Congress, there was a further relaxation of controls on internal trade, including the removal of road checkpoints, and reforms introduced in March 1988 further improved the policy environment for the private sector. While liberalization was principally aimed at the domestic private sector, the liberal, draft Foreign Investment Code in August 1988 (Decree 44 1988) extended a welcome to foreign investors. The private sector also benefited from the more general moves to a market economic environment, through exchange rates reform, decontrol of prices, and the end of state trading monopolies.

3.4. Reforms in Foreign Trade and Payments

Transformation in foreign trade regimes is perhaps the most potent force for change in the economic structures of the reforming economies. Opening up to imports from world markets, encouraging national enterprises to take full advantage of export opportunities, and exposing the local economy to the opportunities and challenges of technology available internationally can have profound effects on the commodity composition of production and on the choice of technology in economies which were previously cut off from open trade with convertible currency economies.

Planned economies which had been integrated into the CMEA could develop a structure of production with little reference to relative prices prevailing in world markets. Given the total separation between domestic and international prices effected through the foreign trade system, prices in centrally planned economies were largely insulated from international influences. Exposure to world markets and to the price system prevailing in those markets has powerful effects, both on activities which are no longer sustainable when faced with international competition and on those activities which benefit from the stimulus of international export opportunities. Trade policy reform has involved a movement away from a system of highly centralized control, in which changing institutional arrangements through which trade is conducted have been the key factor. The end of the CMEA trading bloc and the collapse of Soviet aid have lent a great deal of urgency to the need for trade reform.

The limited extent of government control over trade in reality has meant that trade liberalization has moved faster and deeper in practice than was intended by governments. Import liberalization was important in supplying a flow of commodities to the domestic market, providing the material basis for the rapid development of commodity markets and the ready availability of incentive goods, which was a striking feature of the economies towards the end of the 1980s.

The central authorities in Vietnam practised what could almost be described as involuntary liberalism. Analysis of Vietnamese foreign trade is complicated by the prevalence of unrecorded trade, which is believed to have been of a similar size as official trade in some recent years. In this as in other aspects of the reform process, spontaneous initiatives in contravention of prevailing regulations have led government policy changes.

A critical determinant of the performance of reforming economies is the degree of adaptability and resilience of the underlying real economy in the face of new trading opportunities. It is in this respect that the performances of Vietnam has been in striking positive contrast to those of the Eastern European economies and the successor states to the Soviet Union. The swift reorientation and expansion of Vietnamese exports enabled the Vietnamese to withstand the shock of the sudden collapse in Soviet support in 1990, in the face of a continuing US trade boycott and in the absence of a compensating increase in non-Soviet assistance. This was the result of Vietnamese oil coming on stream, the fast expansion in paddy production following agrarian reform, and a rapid increase in exports of light industrial and marine exports to convertible currency markets. Opening up has had particularly dynamic effects partly because of the regional context; with high growth rates in international trade and with neighbours which are themselves going through structural transitions, with rising labour costs and a progression under way in the product cycle, the potential for expanding trade and investment is enormous. In the face of the drastic decline in Soviet finance since 1989, and the resulting collapse in imports previously received from the CMEA bloc, Vietnam has succeeded in both expanding its exports and shifting their direction decisively towards the convertible currency area.

The high level of informal activity which characterizes the foreign trade sector has been organized by, among others, various actors within the state sector. Thus a good deal of foreign trade takes place outside effective central state control, although many state organizations are actively involved. In a sector in which the central government seems to have had little success in imposing its authority, it is perhaps not surprising that the direction of policy was unclear. The government made feeble attempts to implement a system of quotas and licences. In 1989, it was officially recognized that informal trade had led to a great increase in goods supply—especially consumer goods—on domestic markets, but it was also argued that unregulated trade had resulted in the circulation of counterfeit goods, tax evasion, and severe competition with domestic production. The government, however, concluded that mainly administrative measures in support of domestic industry could reduce the deemed harmful effects of foreign competition. In this, the government showed wisdom, as the ready supply of low-priced imported goods throughout the country made a strategic contribution to expansion of the market and to decentralized growth in economic activity.

However, state trading agencies remain powerful. They control large financial resources and their 'owners' (either a line ministry or a local authority) could retain control of foreign currency, depending on their negotiating position *vis-à-vis* central government. Within the 'post-1989' Vietnamese economy, state trading agencies play an influential role in determining how commercial profits are utilized. It is widely believed that they pay amongst the highest salaries (after foreign companies) and distribute profits to their effective owners. They are controlled by agencies at important levels of the state administrative system (line ministries and local authorities) which also control other economic units as well as regulation and supervision of commercial activity. They are therefore a key part of a system of interlocking structures, which, combined with their access to cheap credit through the state banking system, gives them opportunities to reap economic rents in various ways.

As the trading system and domestic price system are liberalized, the exchange rate takes on much greater importance. If the prevailing exchange rate does not realistically reflect the relationship between the domestic price of tradables and border prices, then rents will be available to be reaped. Governments can adopt a range of exchange rate regimes between strict controls and full convertibility, such as multiple exchange rate systems and selective export earning retention, in the attempt to influence the pattern of trade. In practice, the modification of exchange regimes involved a period in which parallel and official foreign exchange markets have operated alongside each other, with large gaps between the parallel and official rates. However, during the reform process, there has been a readiness to move quite decisively to bring the rates together. In contrast to widespread efforts to defend official exchange rates at unrealistic levels and maintain exchange controls in many developing mixed economies in the past decades, the speed and degree of the movement towards uniform exchange rates and convertibility was remarkable.

The evolution of foreign exchange policy in Vietnam was both unorthodox and successful. In 1989, a dual foreign exchange system, with an official and unofficial rate, replaced a complicated system of multiple exchange rates. The formal system was based upon obligatory delivery, in principle, of a variable proportion of hard currency earnings to central authorities, whilst the large informal system involved direct quasi-legal transactions between businesses, most of which are part of the state sector. After a period of great laxity, in 1991 the central authorities attempted to enforce centralization of control, but without much success. In principle, the dong remained unconvertible and enterprises that earned foreign currency were supposed to deposit it with the officially approved banks, retaining a right to use part. The system of control, however, was weak. The official foreign payments system was subject to a degree of risk, as banks were not trusted to honour obligations in hard currency. This encouraged those in receipt of hard currency to retain control over it, inhibiting development of an effective official exchange market.

Foreign-exchange regulations have been persistently and widely violated, with currency not being deposited in banks, interest-bearing accounts being kept overseas, and foreign exchange being used at the discretion of the institutions which earned it. For some years, the dollar has circulated freely in the main urban centres and is used as an alternative, if not precisely legal, medium of exchange. It has been quite typical for state enterprises to retain foreign exchange for lending, to finance joint ventures, and even deposit abroad. Numerous attempts to tighten control over foreign exchange have had little effect. Efforts to reduce the use of foreign currency within Vietnam and to pressure Vietnamese to deposit foreign-currency holdings in bank accounts were frustrated by the lack of trust in the banking system and the continuing gap between the state rate and the free market rate. Although for a time in the late 1980s Vietnamese citizens were free to hold dollars, now they are not supposed to, although in practice they do so quite openly. Many domestic transactions are denominated in gold, which can be bought and sold freely in a well-developed free market. Many of the dealers in foreign currency are state units, and their owners—ministries and local authorities—are responsible for violations. There is a substantial informal foreign exchange market which operates openly. Rates on the free market are reported in the official media.

Since 1989 the margin between the official and free-market rates has not been high by the standards of many developing countries, although it continues to subsidize those who gain access to foreign exchange at the official rate. During 1989 the margin averaged 12.2 per cent and in 1990 9.4 per cent.

In the Lao PDR official exchange rates were unified early in 1988, and multiple rate practices were done away with. The unified rate dropped to half its value within the space of six months in 1989, but later staged a remarkable recovery to a rate stable at around 700 kip to the dollar. The almost two thousand kilometres of riverain border with Thailand and the existence of kerb markets in urban areas have led to a flourishing parallel market in foreign exchange. As in Vietnam, for many years the government tolerated the parallel market and there were daily quotations for the US dollar, the Thai baht, and gold and silver bullion. The informal market for foreign exchange provided a basis for comparison for the periodic adjustment of the official exchange rate. In recent years, the official and parallel rates have moved closely together, with deviations of less than 5 per cent at year end since 1989. Some technical restrictions still exist on currency convertibility, especially in connection with the import of goods, but the existence of informal markets and the difficulty of policing the long borders with five neighbouring countries makes enforcement difficult.

In the case of the Lao PDR a substantial increase in aid accommodated the rise in the deficit in the balance of trade with the convertible area, which rose from $47 million in 1987 to $108 million in 1991, with imports rising to more than three times exports, in spite of the increase in the two largest exports: timber and wood products (despite a logging ban), and electricity sales to Thailand.

4. IN PURSUIT OF FISCAL AND MONETARY STABILITY

4.1. The Objectives of Fiscal and Monetary Reform

The monetarist view that inflation is associated with excessive growth in the money supply can be taken as a useful starting-point for a discussion of fiscal and monetary stability. However, it is only a starting-point, as it is then necessary to explore why money supply gets out of control. This can happen because governments lose control over their own budget; however, even if the state budget is balanced, the borrowing requirements of state enterprises might also need to be accommodated by expansions in money supply. 'Cost-push' inflation can also occur, when money supply is expanded to accommodate increases in wage and cost levels, both in the public and private sectors. In all these cases, the reasons for instability can be seen as either resulting from the *inability* of government to take the necessary action to control the source of the imbalance (e.g. the lack of policy instruments needed to balance the state budget) or the *unwillingness* of the authorities to take action because of the undesirable consequences (e.g. bankruptcy of state enterprises; increases in unemployment).

The experience of Vietnam in 1989 suggests that the key problem was the inability, or lack of means, to achieve the necessary stability. In 1989 the Vietnamese authorities demonstrated the political will to implement a rigorous IMF policy package (without IMF assistance to sweeten the bitter medicine), including positive real interest rates, drastic exchange rate adjustment, and efforts to contain the state budget. While the programme had very positive short-term results, particularly in sharply reducing inflation, the results could not be sustained because of the weakness of the policy instruments available to the government, conforming to wider experience that, although governments in centrally planned economies had the means of direct control over economic activity, they had neither the need nor the means for powerful fiscal or monetary interventions in the economy. The paradox of the transition to the market economy is that, while it involves loosening direct government control over economic decisions, the success-ful management of the market economy requires *strong instruments of fiscal and monetary policy* to be put into place.

Under central planning, government is able to transfer resources from the enterprise and households sectors through direct control over resource allocation, incomes, and prices. Inter-sectoral financial transfers can be extracted from the state enterprise sector through direct claims on profits (the level of which in turn can be manipulated through price controls) and through quite crude tax mechanisms, such as turnover taxes. Efficiency and incentive effects are not too important, as state controls are intended to act as the binding constraint on actors in the economy. The prevalence of direct controls also means that the impact of macroeconomic financial imbalances can be repressed.

Despite starting from an initial position of pervasive controls over actors in the economy, reforming governments have found it difficult to put into place the instruments of fiscal and monetary policy which are a routine feature of most mixed economies. One source of difficulty is the interde-pendence between macroeconomic reform and changes in the system at the enterprise level. Effective macroeconomic policy is needed to provide an appropriate environment for decentralized decision-making at the enter-prise level, but successful reform of the state enterprise sector is, in turn, a necessary ingredient for successful stabilization.

Inefficient and undisciplined state enterprises can be a drag on the fiscal and monetary system in a number of ways. The objective of market reforms is to develop an enterprise sector which is not dependent on state subsidy and is faced with a 'hard budget' constraint, but it is very difficult for governments to stand on the side if, in the reform process, there is wide-spread enterprise failure, resulting in collapse of output and spiralling unemployment. It is difficult to introduce financial discipline and limit the demand for public subsidy unless there is a reasonable chance that re-formed enterprises can generate positive real economic results. Obviously, when state enterprises are subsidized they are a direct drain on the govern-ment budget. However, even where subsidies are not paid, poor perform-ance detracts from the public revenue base, both in terms of tax revenues and profit remittances.

Another barrier to the achievement of fiscal stability is the difficulty of creating a working tax system. At first sight, it should be relatively easy to move from the tight state disciplines of central planning to the less onerous burdens of tax payment. However, an effective tax system needs to be built on a foundation of reliable accounting, experienced tax administration, and a reasonable degree of voluntary compliance—none of which exist in the reforming economies.

The gains from tightening the state budget can be undermined by a weak credit system. As government tightens access to budgetary resources, laxity in the provision of credit to state enterprises has become an increasing source of inflationary pressure. Enterprises denied direct government subsidy seek to continue the 'soft budget' constraint by borrowing. However, the concept of the 'hard budget' constraint is more ambiguous than rhetoric might suggest. In market economies, it is typical for firms to have access to credit and for creditors (including banks) to tide over firms with temporary losses and cash-flow problems. A system which worked without credit would be woefully inefficient. Enterprises require access to a credit market, and for the economic system to be efficient that market should provide access to funds on the basis of the application of reasonable financial criteria. A 'soft budget' constraint implies that state enterprises (or, for that matter, private firms) have access to funds in excess of amounts justified by the application of sound financial judgements— which *ex ante* necessarily involves a strong element of judgement, exercised for example by competing commercial banks and other financial intermediaries. Efficient financial discipline is thus dependent on the existence of a financial system capable of applying good judgement to the provision of credit.

However, an effective two-tier banking system cannot be created overnight, and the reforming economies do not yet have a fully operative system of competitive, autonomous commercial banks. The difficulties faced by financial institutions in many fully developed market economies (e.g. in the USA) in managing their portfolios in recent years suggests some of the complexities of creating an efficient credit market. Weakness in the banking systems in the reforming economies is likely to result in inefficient resource allocation and, in so far as the mechanisms for controlling total credit supply prove weak, accommodation of the financial needs of state enterprises can become the driving force for inflationary credit expansion.

4.2. Reforming the Fiscal System

4.2.1. Tax Reform

The process of systemic reforms tends to fuel macroeconomic instability, bringing the risk of severe inflation, suggesting that it would be advantageous for macroeconomic stabilization to come early in the reform process. However, reform in the price system and enterprise reform initially weakens the old fiscal base, and creating a modern, market-style tax system takes great effort and time. With the shift from a centrally planned, state-owned economy it becomes both less feasible and less desirable to fund the state budget from transfers of surpluses from state enterprises. It is less feasible, as prices and outputs can no longer be so readily manipulated to generate the required surplus. And it is less desirable, as the essence of a decentralized market system is that enterprises should control after-tax profits (and profit taxes should be uniform and not be too high) as a key incentive to performance and as a device to channel investment funds into profitable lines of activity.

The decline of revenue at the first stages of the reform process is illustrated by the Lao experience, where total domestic revenue declined from 15 per cent of GDP in 1986 to a low of 8 per cent in 1989, before climbing back to 11 per cent of GDP by 1991, leaving the Lao government with a quite weak revenue base. As in other centrally planned economies, revenue used to depend heavily on contributions from state enterprises, which transferred all their revenues to the government and financed all their expenditures from the government, accounting for as much as 90 per cent of total domestic revenue as recently as 1986 and 1987.

With the advent of the New Economic Mechanism, transfers and turnover taxes from state enterprises were replaced by profits taxes and external trade taxes as the main revenue sources. In 1988, the Lao PDR introduced a comprehensive tax policy revision. Taxes on profits, turnover, and agriculture were introduced, which were uniform regardless of the sector and the nature of the enterprise, whether state or private, and a personal income tax was introduced for the first time. Following further revision in 1989, Lao PDR has five main types of taxes: (1) agricultural commodity taxes, (2) land taxes, (3) natural resource taxes on mineral resources, land concessions, and agro-forestry products, (4) taxes on imports, and (5) internal taxes, composed of turnover and income taxes respectively. In 1987 turnover taxes provided 47 per cent, import and export duties 19 per cent, and profits taxes 11 per cent of tax collections; by 1990, the share of foreign trade taxes had increased to 48 per cent and profits taxes to 21 per cent, while turnover taxes declined to 19 per cent.

The Vietnamese authorities have been struggling with similar problems. As a result of reforms already implemented, the tax base is being broadened. However, with persistent problems in collection, receipts remain low—thus in the 1991 budget the forecast revenues from foreign trade taxes were put at 900 billion dong (perhaps $100 million), which compared with a hard currency foreign trade turnover of probably over US$4 billion, if 'informal' trade and smuggling are included.

As part of the overall fiscal reform, towards the end of 1990 Vietnam introduced new profit and turnover taxes, based on a relatively simple system, which did not formally discriminate on the basis of ownership, and steps were taken to introduce an orthodox system of personal income tax. However, the effects of this new tax system upon incentives are still hard to judge. One serious problem is a lack of transparency in the system. The state still required enterprises to pay depreciation charges to the state as some sort of 'capital charge', and taxes actually paid continued to be subject to negotiation, so that managers found it difficult to have a sense of the tax obligations of the enterprise.

4.2.2. Tax Administration

The fashioning of an efficient and equitable tax system is not merely a matter of an appropriate tax code. The Vietnamese authorities designed a tax system that is in many ways admirably neutral in its treatment of public and non-state sectors. However, to increase fiscal effectiveness, tax collection needs to be stabilized and the predictability of assessment increased. Tax officials need to be paid adequately and effective discipline imposed. *Ad hoc* tax breaks for the state sector and 'special taxes' imposed by local authorities need to be reduced.

For effective fiscal discipline, local government autonomy in revenue and spending matters may need to be curbed. The case for fiscal control of local government is illustrated by the Lao experience. In 1986, the Lao central government turned over much of the tax collection to provincial and district governments, to promote greater decentralization and self-reliance among the government units. Surplus revenues were to be transferred from the five or so more affluent surplus provinces to poorer provinces. As a defensive response, the provinces in surplus increased expenditures to reduce surpluses, and the central government's revenue base was eroded. Following budget difficulties of 1988 and 1989, the government recentralized both revenue collections and expenditures.

The sort of administrative steps required to create a new tax collection system can be illustrated by recent efforts made in Vietnam, where significant steps have been taken to strengthen central fiscal institutions since 1989—for example, through creation of the National Treasury system and the National Tax Collection Office. Key unresolved issues related to the relationship between central and local government, the relationship between the government and business interests, and the extent to which central policy-making was informed by analysis of the economic impact of policy. The establishment of the National Tax Collection Office under the Ministry of Finance was designed to improve the level of tax collection from the non-state sector. However, corruption, aggravated by the effects of low official wages and the need for officials to take second jobs, usually in the private sector, continued to weaken the system.

Similar reforms in tax administration were initiated in the Lao PDR. In 1990, the responsibility for the collection of all taxes was vested in the Ministry of Economy, Planning, and Finance, with all tax collectors and customs officers becoming employees of the central government and reporting to the ministry. In August 1991, a separate Treasury was created and control over all revenue and expenditures concentrated in the MEPF. A unit was created in MEPF to monitor and make projections on tax collections, and three national organizations were created to administer customs duties, domestic taxes, and major user fees and charges. Budget execution was assigned to an expanded national Treasury.

4.2.3. Controlling Government Expenditure

If it has proved difficult to achieve revenue buoyancy in the reforming economies, the alternative route to fiscal stability through reductions in government expenditure has also proved no easier to achieve. Vietnam, for example, has faced a difficult task in seeking to control public expenditure. In the face of the considerable need for infrastructural investment, rural development programmes, and social spending, exisiting levels of spending are woefully inadequate. For example, levels of spending upon infrastructure were roughly equal to around US$150–200 million (US$2 per head of population).

The Lao PDR had some success in reducing the burden of government expenditure. From 1988 onwards the government undertook massive reorganization, which included an initial retrenchment of about one-fifth of the government work-force, followed recently by further retrenchment, and the amalgamation of previously separate ministries into one Ministry of Economy, Planning, and Finance, with responsibility for revenues, budgeting, and planning, and with a personnel complement of about half the previous level. Total government expenditures (including provincial governments, but excluding state enterprises) declined from a high of 33 per cent of GDP in 1988 to 20 per cent by 1991 and overall budget deficits reduced from as high as 13 per cent of GDP in 1989 to as low as 5 per cent by 1991.

However, changes in the composition of expenditures should give cause for concern. Despite retrenchment there was a sharp increase in the proportion of the budget going to salaries. Prior to the implementation of the NEM in 1986 salaries accounted for about 16–19 per cent of current expenditures, but claimed as much as 51 per cent of the budget by 1990, materials and supplies declining from 80 per cent of current expenditures in 1984 to a low of about 37 per cent by 1990, and the capital expenditure budget declining from 20 per cent of GDP in 1988 to only 9 per cent by 1991. This suggests that the government continued to maintain expenditures on public employees while sharply reducing the real supply of government services.

4.3. Reforming the Financial System

4.3.1. The Changing Role of the Banking System

Under central planning systems, the main function of the banking system was to facilitate transactions and act as a component of the state accounting system; the banking system was not typically used as an active instrument of economic policy. Control over macroeconomic aggregates was through the direct controls of the planning system, any potential inflationary press-

ures resulting in excess monetary balances in principle being repressed by
planning constraints on the use of money; and the allocative functions of
credit were minimized, resources being directly allocated through the plan,
the function of credit being merely to accommodate the physical allocations
made by the planning system. Credit was allocated administratively, the
interest rate being viewed neither as an allocative device nor as an incentive
to savings. Given the limited functions allotted to monetary institutions, a
banking system based on one tier of banking institutions (essentially one
bank), combining the functions of central and commercial banks, was
sufficient.

As the economies moved towards greater market orientation, it became
apparent that existing financial institutions were woefully inadequate.
There was no institutional distinction reflecting the differing functions of a
central bank, responsible for managing monetary aggregates and overseeing
key national policy instruments, such as the exchange rate and interest
rates, as distinct from the functions of commercial banks, operating to
allocate credit to enterprises and to provide a range of options for households and enterprises to hold liquid assets. Needless to say, there was a
virtual absence of any other form of formal financial intermediation or of
equity markets.

The first steps in financial sector reform therefore consist of the development of a two-tier banking system, with a clear distinction between the
central bank and commercial banks, the development of financial markets
and the creation, by the central bank, of effective monetary policies. The
importance of the development of effective commercial banking to the
reform process relates to the need for a proper financial context for enterprise reform mentioned above. As enterprises are given greater autonomy,
the umbilical cord providing access to automatic state subsidies is cut with
the dual intention of submitting the enterprise to the rigours of the market
and laying the foundations for enhanced macroeconomic stability. The
attempt to introduce a 'hard budget constraint' will be easily thwarted if
enterprises have the option of unrestrained access to bank credits, while the
absence of adequate credit facilities could drive the enterprise system into
an unjustified collapse. Effective banking is therefore needed both to confront enterprises with the realities of market operation subject to budget
constraints and to provide them with access to financial markets capable of
operating according to reasonably market-orientated principles.

The creation of a two-tier banking system is one step in the process of
creating a mature, decentralized system of financial intermediation, in
which decentralized financial institutions operate autonomously and com-
mercially, subject only to general banking regulations and directives, which
set limits within which they conduct day-to-day business, and the learnt
principles of prudent banking practice which provide a guide to business
survival. There are dangers in the transition. Newly created commercial

banks may be subject to pressures to provide credit imprudently and attracted to the potential returns from reckless lending. It may be difficult for a neophyte central bank to strike the right balance between encouraging autonomy and the need for prudent supervision of the new commercial banks. Failure to control the process can have both inflationary consequences and undermine the effort to expose enterprises to a market environment.

4.3.2. The Development of Commercial Banks

It is not possible to create a commercial banking system with a sound portfolio of assets and reasonable profitability at a stroke, and certainly not under the pressures rising from more general reform measures. The practical and political contraints on the smooth development of a more commercial banking system are demonstrated by Vietnamese experience. Formally, the basic structure of a market-based financial system has already emerged in Vietnam. Following reforms in the banking system, the four state-owned commercial banks are, in principle, required to operate on a profit-making basis. There are also a number of small 'share' banks, some of which are in turn owned mainly by other state enterprises. There are also a number of credit co-operatives and housing banks, and some branches of foreign banks are now opening.

However, the Vietnamese banking system is limited in its technical capacity to handle many basic banking functions, such as fund transfer, clearing, and so on. These inadequacies result both from technical weaknesses (absence of modern equipment, etc.) and limitations in personnel and basic management skills, aggravated by low wages. The weakness of the banks can be seen as part of a more general phenomenon. Despite a number of the key institutions appropriate to a market economy being put into place, making them work effectively is difficult in the face of entrenched interests, established habits of work, and the continued existence of potential rents in the system. The continued lack of clarity regarding the status of the state sector, especially the rights of banks to foreclose, means that there is a lack of financial discipline, bank balance sheets are in a questionable state, banks are unable to play an effective role in the adjustment process, and financial intermediation is ineffective.

State banks in principle received subventions from the state budget intended to cover the large negative spread between deposit rates and lending rates, but in practice they were not paid. Most state bank lending is still to the state sector, despite its low share of output and government statements asserting the need to treat all sectors equally, although some selected private-sector businesses are now gaining access to credit. After 1989, action to prevent an immediate collapse of a large number of state enterprises, suddenly deprived of access to subsidized inputs from the Soviet aid programme, was an immediate practical necessity.

4.3.3. First Steps in Monetary Policy

One purpose of the creation of a two-tier banking system is to develop and use the instruments of monetary policy as key components of the indirect means available to governments to achieve macroeconomic stability. In particular, central banking needs to be developed, so that money supply and interest rates can be adjusted as required to achieve desired levels of real economic activity and reasonably stable price levels.

In Vietnam, central banking is in its infancy. Vietnam has experienced high rates of inflation during the reform period. In 1989 an attempt was made to check inflation through a draconian stabilization programme, which had some success but then foundered because of the inability of the government to control money supply growth given the weakness of the government's fiscal base and the need to avert a collapse in the real economy in the face of the collapse of Soviet aid. In principle, since May 1990 the State Bank of Vietnam has been endowed with the normal powers and obligations of a central bank in a market economy. The key question is to what extent these powers are exercised. Given its earlier role, which combined the functions of a central and commercial bank, the State Bank had a branch network at province level, with a high degree of formal branch autonomy, which left the potential for political pressures for granting of credit to be brought to bear at the provincial level. The State Bank also continued to have a close relationship with the state commercial banks, which placed in question the degree to which the central banking and commercial banking roles had been separated. Despite such questions about the degree to which an effective central banking system was yet operating in Vietnam, in 1992 considerable progress was made in stabilizing the value of the dong.

In March 1988, one of a series of decrees issued to provide impetus to the New Economic Mechanism converted the Laos State Bank into a 'socialist business system', including the separation of commercial banking from the central banking activities of the State Bank and the encouragement of competitive banking. In June 1990, the central banking law was enacted creating the Bank of Lao PDR out of the State Bank. The swift transition of the monetary and banking system with the establishment of a central bank separate from the commercial banks is one of the more impressive accomplishments of the Lao PDR. This was accompanied by the increasing autonomy of the central bank from the government. The introduction of private commercial banking provided competition for the commercial banks created from the regional branches of the former monolithic bank.

Confidence in the banking system by households has grown slowly, with bank services for simple deposits and withdrawals long considered unsatisfactory, payment by cheque not acceptable for the great majority of household transactions, and households having the alternative of holding and making payments in foreign currencies. For all intents and purposes, there are no formal financial institutions dealing with the general public other than the commercial banks, although non-bank foreign exchange dealers have been allowed to operate since November 1990. There is a thriving informal credit system in the major population centres, usually centred in the public markets, handling short-term transactions at high interest rates. Moneylenders usually deal in currency exchange and precious metal sales as well as credit.

Most available credit continued to be channelled to the government and to the state enterprises, amounting to 80 per cent of domestic credit in 1990. In terms of the commercial banking system alone, loans to state enterprises accounted for 90 per cent of total loans made (the combined government and state enterprise sectors accounted for all of such credit as late as 1987). However, with the advent of commercial banks and state enterprise financial autonomy, the automatic availability of credit from the government banking system to state enterprises has come to an end. The banks are learning to refuse such accommodation, and to make credit judgements based on financial evaluation.

The management of interest rates has been the most politically sensitive aspect of the reform of the monetary and banking system, so much so that until fairly recently changes in interest rate policy were enforced through decrees issued by the Prime Minister's Office or the Cabinet. While the intention has been for interest rates to reflect market conditions more closely, the country has had a long history of very favourable costs of funds. Interest rates prior to 1988 resulted in negative spreads with respect to deposit and loan rates. Rates were adjusted in October 1988 to allow banks to undertake profitable deposit and loan operations, but some negative spreads were still permitted. In August 1989, at the height of inflation, new interest rate policies were explicitly adopted, seeking to introduce positive real interest rates and positive spreads, and since then commercial bank spreads have been broadly positive. With the inflation rate dropping to 18 per cent in August 1990 and declining further in 1991, positive real rates have been achieved and stated principles broadly met. However, in June 1991, the central bank reduced the maximum short-term rate for agricultural loans to 15 per cent and the long-term rate to 7 per cent; with the minimum savings deposit rate set at 16 per cent, this resulted in negative spreads for one of the more important forms of bank credit.

Experience has demonstrated that it is not possible to transform fiscal and monetary institutions at a stroke and that whether the rhetoric of 'big bang' stabilization or gradualism is adopted, in practice an unsatisfactory degree of financial instability and inflation is likely to be experienced during the transition. This suggests the need to consider second-best macroeconomic strategies, to find means of living with financial instability and inflation and limiting the damage done to the growth of market institutions.

One second-best solution, implicitly accepted in these economies, was the acceptance of a dual currency system.

The free *de facto* circulation of dollars and gold were important not only in facilitating foreign trade during the reform period but also in providing a stable basis for transactions during periods of inflation, and by so doing increasing the effciency of domestic economic transactions. By their tolerance in allowing a remarkably free foreign exchange market in practice, the Vietnamese authorities hit upon an unorthodox but effective mechanism for the facilitation of the growth of market transactions in a period in which it was not possible to stabilize the domestic currency supply and price level.

A willingness to move official exchange rates close to parallel market parity, combined with a remarkable permissiveness in allowing the holding and circulation of foreign currencies, provided a good monetary basis for the development of market transactions even in the context of a high degree of instability in the domestic monetary situation. This experience suggests that it is possible for reforming economies to sustain high levels of domestic instability without undermining real growth, providing foreign exchange policy is such that trade with the outside world is at realistic prices.

INDEX